Education and social change
in nineteenth-century Massachusetts

Education and social change
in nineteenth-century Massachusetts

CARL F. KAESTLE
University of Wisconsin

MARIS A. VINOVSKIS
University of Michigan

CAMBRIDGE UNIVERSITY PRESS

Cambridge
London · New York · New Rochelle
Melbourne · Sydney

CAMBRIDGE UNIVERSITY PRESS
Cambridge, New York, Melbourne, Madrid, Cape Town, Singapore, São Paulo, Delhi

Cambridge University Press
The Edinburgh Building, Cambridge CB2 8RU, UK

Published in the United States of America by Cambridge University Press, New York

www.cambridge.org
Information on this title: www.cambridge.org/9780521102353

First published 1980
This digitally printed version 2009

A catalogue record for this publication is available from the British Library

Library of Congress Cataloguing in Publication data
Kaestle, Carl F
Education and social change in
nineteenth-century Massachusetts.
1. Education – Massachusetts – History.
2. Massachusetts – Social conditions – History.
I. Vinovskis, Maris, joint author.   II.   Title.
LA304.K24   370′.9744   78–32130

ISBN 978-0-521-22191-7 hardback
ISBN 978-0-521-10235-3 paperback

For Liz and Mary,
and for Rika, Christine, and Andy

CONTENTS

List of tables and figures   *page* ix
Preface   xvii

1   Education and social change: Massachusetts as a case study   1
2   Trends in school attendance in nineteenth-century
    Massachusetts   9
3   From apron strings to ABCs: school entry in nineteenth-
    century Massachusetts   46
4   The prospects of youth: school leaving in eight Essex County
    towns   72
5   From one room to one system: the importance of rural–urban
    differences in nineteenth-century Massachusetts schooling   100
6   Education and social change in two nineteenth-century
    Massachusetts communities
    BY MARTHA COONS, JOHN W. JENKINS, AND CARL KAESTLE   139
7   Trends in educational funding and expenditures   186
8   The politics of educational reform in mid-nineteenth-century
    Massachusetts   208
9   Conclusion: the triumph of a state school system   233

    Appendix A: Statistical tables   237
    Appendix B: Definition of the variables contained in Tables
        A2.1 through A2.5, Appendix A   288
    Appendix C: Discussion of adjustments, estimates, and
        extrapolations made in calculating Tables A2.1 through
        A2.5, Appendix A   292

    Notes   303
    Bibliography   336
    Index   345

TABLES AND FIGURES

Tables

2.1	Annual school enrollment rates for Massachusetts and New York, 1830 and 1840	*page*	12
2.2	Annual public school enrollment rates for New York State, 1798–1850		15
2.3	Annual school enrollment rates for New York City		18
2.4	Occupations of New York City schoolchildren's parents, 1796		19
2.5	School enrollments in Salem, Massachusetts, 1820–75		19
2.6	School enrollments for New York State by town size, 1798		20
2.7	School enrollments for Massachusetts by town size, 1826		21
2.8	Enrollment rates for Glenville, New York, 1823–41		23
2.9	Length of Massachusetts public school session by town size, 1826		25
4.1	Public school attendance in eight Essex County towns, 1860 and 1880		81
4.2	School attendance of children ages 13–19 in eight Essex County towns, 1860 and 1880: eta², beta, and R² values		87
4.3	School attendance of children ages 13–19 in eight Essex County towns, 1860 and 1880: class means, adjusted means, and net deviations		88
4.4	School attendance of children ages 13–19 in eight Essex County towns, 1860 and 1880: eta², beta, and R² values		95
4.5	School attendance of children ages 13–19 in eight Essex County towns, 1860 and 1880: class means, adjusted means, and net deviations		96
6.1	Foreign-born population of Boxford, 1855–1905		141
6.2	Population of Boxford, 1765–1905		142

6.3   Feminization of Boxford's public schoolteaching force, 1840–80   156

6.4   Property valuation and per pupil expenditures (in dollars) in Boxford and Essex County, 1845–80   157

8.1   Vote in the Massachusetts House of Representatives in 1840 to abolish the state board of education: class means, adjusted means, and net deviations (in percentages)   222

8.2   Vote in the Massachusetts House of Representatives in 1840 to abolish the state board of education: eta², beta, and R² values   224

A2.1 Total enrollment and average daily attendance, Massachusetts public schools, 1840–80   238

A2.2 Length of Massachusetts public school sessions and estimated annual attendance and enrollment, 1840–80   240

A2.3 Attendance at Massachusetts incorporated academies, 1840–80   242

A2.4 Attendance at Massachusetts unincorporated academies, private schools, and schools kept to prolong the common schools, 1840–80   244

A2.5 Annual enrollment and attendance, all Massachusetts schools, 1840–80   246

A3.1 Massachusetts school attendance of young children, 1840–1900   248

A3.2 Percentage, by town size, of young children enrolled in Massachusetts schools, 1840, 1860, and 1875   249

A4.1 Average length (in days) of Massachusetts public school sessions, 1840–80   250

A4.2 Percentage of persons under 20 years of age enrolled in Massachusetts schools, 1840–80   250

A4.3 Annual number of days in Massachusetts schools per person under 20 years of age, 1840–80   251

A4.4 Percentage of children ages birth to 19 attending school in eight Essex County towns, 1860   252

A4.5 Percentage of children ages birth to 19 attending school in eight Essex County towns, 1880   253

A4.6 Comparison of the percentages of children attending school in eight Essex County towns, 1860, in the various samples   254

A4.7 Comparison of the percentages of children attending school in eight Essex County towns, 1880, in the various samples 255

A4.8 School and remunerative work patterns of females ages 13–19 in eight Essex County towns, 1860 and 1880 (percentage of each age group) 256

A4.9 School and remunerative work patterns of males ages 13–19 in eight Essex County towns, 1860 and 1880 (percentage of each age group) 257

A5.1 The urbanization of Massachusetts, 1800–1900 258

A5.2 Number of Massachusetts towns and aggregate population in the subgroups, 1840, 1860, and 1875 258

A5.3 Percentage, by town size, of children ages birth to 19 enrolled in Massachusetts public schools, 1840, 1860, and 1875 259

A5.4 Percentage, by town size, of children ages birth to 19 attending Massachusetts public schools (average daily attendance), 1840, 1860, and 1875 259

A5.5 Percentage, by town size, of young children enrolled in Massachusetts public schools, 1840, 1860, and 1875 260

A5.6 Percentage, by town size, of older children enrolled in Massachusetts public schools, 1840, 1860, and 1875 260

A5.7 Percentage, by town size, of children ages birth to 19 enrolled in Massachusetts public and private schools, 1840, 1860, and 1875 261

A5.8 Average length (in days) of Massachusetts public school sessions, by town size, 1840, 1860, and 1875 261

A5.9 Average number of public school days attended per child ages birth to 19, by town size, in Massachusetts, 1840, 1860, and 1875 262

A5.10 Average number of public and private school days attended per child ages birth to 19, by town size, in Massachusetts, 1840, 1860, and 1875 262

A5.11 Average monthly male teacher wage rates (in dollars), including board, in Massachusetts public schools, 1840, 1860, and 1875 263

A5.12 Average monthly female teacher wage rates (in dollars), including board, in Massachusetts public schools, 1840, 1860, and 1875 263

A5.13 Percentage, by town size, of female public schoolteachers in Massachusetts, 1840, 1860, and 1875 264

A5.14 Female teacher wages as a percentage of male teacher wages, by town size, in Massachusetts public schools, 1860 and 1875   264

A5.15 Average number of pupils per teacher, by town size, in Massachusetts public schools, 1840, 1860, and 1875   265

A5.16 Average number of pupils per Massachusetts public school, by town size, 1840, 1860, and 1875   265

A5.17 Massachusetts public school expenditures (in dollars) per student, by town size, 1840, 1860, and 1875   266

A5.18 Massachusetts public school expenditures (in dollars) per capita, by town size, 1840, 1860, and 1875   266

A5.19 Massachusetts public school expenditure as a percentage of assessed valuation, by town size, 1860 and 1875   267

A5.20 Variables used in the 1860 regression analysis   267

A5.21 1860 regression analysis: means and standard deviations   268

A5.22 1860 regression analysis: correlation matrix   269

A5.23 Results of the regression analysis predicting the percentage of persons under 20 years of age enrolled in Massachusetts public or private schools, 1860 (Y_1)   270

A5.24 Results of the regression analysis predicting the average length (in days) of the Massachusetts public school year, 1860 (Y_2)   270

A5.25 Results of the regression analysis predicting the average number of Massachusetts public and private school days per person under 20 years of age, 1860 (Y_3)   271

A7.1   Amount of money spent for Massachusetts public schools, 1837–80, in dollars adjusted for cost of living (1860 = 100)   272

A7.2   Tuition paid for Massachusetts incorporated and unincorporated academies, private schools, and schools kept to prolong common schools, 1837–80, in dollars adjusted for cost of living (1860 = 100)   273

A7.3   Cost per hundred days of school attended in Massachusetts, 1837–80, in dollars adjusted for cost of living (1860 = 100)   274

A7.4   Massachusetts school expenditures in dollars per
       $1,000 of state valuation, 1837–80   275
A7.5   Income sources for Massachusetts public schools,
       1837–80, in dollars adjusted for cost of living (1860
       = 100)   276
A7.6   School expenditures as a percentage of overall
       town budgets, excluding state and county taxes, in
       eight Essex County communities and Boston, 1860
       and 1880   278
A7.7   Per capita school expenditures in budgets of eight
       Essex County communities and Boston, 1860 and
       1880, in dollars adjusted for cost of living (1860 =
       100)   278
A7.8   Public school, institutional, and police expendi-
       tures as percentages of the overall Boston city bud-
       get, including state and county taxes, 1820–80   279
A7.9   Boston's per capita expenditures for public
       schools, institutions, and police, 1820–80, in dollars
       adjusted for cost of living (1860 = 100)   281
A7.10 Trends in inequality among Massachusetts towns
       in public school expenditures per school-age child,
       1841–80   283
A7.11 Massachusetts public schoolteachers' monthly
       wages, including board, 1837–80, in dollars ad-
       justed for cost of living (1860 = 100)   284
A7.12 Number of individuals who taught in Massachu-
       setts public and private schools, 1834–80   285
A7.13 Individuals who taught as percentages of the Mas-
       sachusetts white population ages 15–59, 1834–80   286
A7.14 Percentage of the Massachusetts white population
       ages 15–29 who have ever been teachers, 1834–80   287
C.1   Attendance figures for eight Essex County towns,
       1860, comparing U.S. census population figures
       and town population figures   293
C.2   State average length of Massachusetts public
       school sessions, 1841–42, calculated with weighted
       and nonweighted county averages   295
C.3   State average length of Massachusetts public
       school sessions, 1840–80, comparing weighted and
       nonweighted county averages   296
C.4   Calculation of estimated long-term and short-term
       students, 1848–9 and 1849–50   300

Tables and figures

C.5   Estimated division of Massachusetts unincorporated private schools into short-term and long-term schools, 1840–50   301

Figures

2.1   Percentage of persons under 20 years of age enrolled in Massachusetts schools, 1840–80   34

2.2   Total number of students enrolled in Massachusetts schools, 1840–80   35

2.3   Average daily public and private attendance as a percentage of all children ages birth to 19, 1840–80   38

2.4   Length of Massachusetts public school sessions, 1840–80   39

2.5   Average number of days of public or private school attended per person under 20 years of age in Massachusetts, 1840–80   40

3.1   Estimated percentages of literacy from signatures on New England wills, 1650–70, 1705–15, 1758–63, and 1787–95   48

3.2   Percentage of young children enrolled in Massachusetts public schools, 1840–1900   63

3.3   Percentage, by town size, of young children in Massachusetts public schools, 1840, 1860, and 1875   67

4.1   Percentage of children ages birth to 19 attending school in eight Essex County towns, 1880   73

4.2   School and remunerative work patterns of females ages 13–19 in eight Essex County towns, 1860 and 1880   78

4.3   School and remunerative work patterns of males ages 13–19 in eight Essex County towns, 1860 and 1880   79

5.1   Percentage of the Massachusetts population living in urban areas, 1800–1900   112

5.2   Percentage, by town size, of children ages birth to 19 enrolled in Massachusetts public and private schools, 1840, 1860, and 1875   118

5.3   Average length of Massachusetts public school sessions, by town size, 1840, 1860, and 1875   119

5.4   Average number of school days attended per child ages birth to 19, by town size, in Massachusetts, 1840, 1860, and 1875   120

5.5 Percentage, by town size, of female teachers in Massachusetts, 1840, 1860, and 1875   123

5.6 Massachusetts public school expenditures per student, by town size, 1840, 1860, and 1875   124

6.1 Population of Lynn, 1790–1900   165

7.1 Amount of money spent for Massachusetts schools, 1837–80, in dollars adjusted for cost of living (1860 = 100)   189

7.2 Cost per hundred days of school attended in Massachusetts, 1837–80, in dollars adjusted for cost of living (1860 = 100)   190

7.3 Massachusetts school expenditures in dollars per $1,000 of state valuation, 1837–80   191

7.4 Distribution of income sources for Massachusetts public schools, 1837–80   192

7.5 School expenditures as a percentage of overall town budgets, excluding state and county taxes, in eight Essex County communities and Boston, 1860 and 1880   193

7.6 Per capita school expenditures in budgets of eight Essex County communities and Boston, 1860 and 1880, in dollars adjusted for cost of living (1860 = 100)   194

7.7 Public school, institutional, and police expenditures as percentages of the overall Boston city budget, including state and county taxes, 1820–80   195

7.8 Boston's per capita expenditures for public schools, institutions, and police, 1820–80, in dollars adjusted for cost of living (1860 = 100)   197

7.9 Trends in inequality among Massachusetts towns in public school expenditures per school-age child, 1841–80   199

7.10 Massachusetts public schoolteachers' monthly wages, including board, 1837–80, in dollars adjusted for cost of living (1860 = 100)   200

7.11 Annual number of individuals who taught in Massachusetts public and private schools, 1834–80   201

7.12 Individuals who taught as percentages of the Massachusetts white population ages 15–59, 1834–80   204

7.13 Percentage of the Massachusetts white population ages 15–29 who have ever been teachers, 1834–80   205

Tables and figures

8.1   Occupational distribution of Massachusetts legisla-
      tors, 1840   212
8.2   Distribution of Massachusetts legislators according
      to town population, 1840   213
8.3   Distribution of Massachusetts legislators according
      to the economic development of their towns, 1840   214

PREFACE

The laudatory tradition of educational history that prevailed in the United States until the 1950s emphasized democracy, opportunity, humanitarianism, enlightenment, and the development of an American consensus as motives for public schooling. Historians of education, often committed to the schools of their day by virtue of their positions as school administrators or education professors, saw public schools as the engines of American democracy, as the bulwark of free institutions, and as the "balance wheel of the social machinery," in Horace Mann's famous phrase. This tradition emphasized the relationship of schooling to the political system and to the development of a common American culture. It was an idealist tradition, which was, and still is, widely shared by the American public.[1]

The past fifteen years, however, have seen a pendulum swing among some historians on questions about the initial and continuing purposes of public schooling. A new critical view has emerged, emphasizing socioeconomic realities rather than political ideals. Revisionist historians have emphasized class and cultural conflict, bureaucracy, and the schools' role in inculcating submissive attitudes. Their work constitutes a reaction against the old history of education, and also against the consensus view of American history of the 1950s. Although their normative perspective is often much more negative, the revisionists share a basic assumption of their predecessors: They assume that the structure and content of public schooling have been largely determined by the political and economic system in America.[2]

Most of these recent studies, critical of the purposes of nineteenth-century public schools, have relied upon the study of urban sites that experienced severe social stress. Few have given attention to the functions and development of education in small-town and rural America. Therefore, these works, even taken collectively, do not constitute a satisfactory revision of the older national synthesis, quite apart from the authors' normative stance. Furthermore, neither the revisionists nor their predecessors have given sufficient attention to the available detailed behavioral information concerning schooling in individual lives and in town development, both across space and across time.

The current historiographical situation in the history of American education, then, leaves a number of important questions unanswered. How did schooling patterns differ in rural and urban areas? Are there important distinctions among urban communities in the extent and type of educational development? What was the age structure of school attendance in different kinds of communities and among different social groups? Our study addresses these questions and is centered around a broad historical problem: How did the changing extent, structure, and control of schooling relate to the social, economic, and cultural features of different nineteenth-century communities, and how did these relationships change over time? Much of the effort is of necessity descriptive. We cannot evaluate assertions about the causal relationship between factory production and increasing public school enrollments until we have carefully traced the sequence and magnitude of those developments. We cannot assess the importance of class and ethnicity in determining school attendance until we have attempted to weigh their relative association with attendance patterns. That the task is largely descriptive does not make it easy; indeed, the effort is bedeviled constantly by conflicting testimony, ambiguous terminology, and incomplete quantitative evidence. To the extent that we have successfully reconstructed the numerical record, we hope that this study may serve as a primer on the methodological problems, as well as on the substantive trends, in nineteenth-century quantitative educational history. But of course there is more to history, and to this book, than mere description. The facts do not speak for themselves. We must select them, arrange them, and discuss the connections among them. The several discrete probes we made into the history of nineteenth-century Massachusetts schooling added up to a general interpretation of the development of public education in an urbanizing, industrializing society.

This book is based on research carried out with the generous assistance of the National Institute of Education. Carl F. Kaestle of the University of Wisconsin was the Project Director, and Maris A. Vinovskis of the University of Michigan was initially designated the Statistical Consultant. Soon, however, the full collaboration indicated by our coauthorship emerged. Both authors participated in the research, statistical work, and writing of each chapter, with the exception of the case studies in Chapter 6, which were researched and written by graduate assistants Martha Coons and John Jenkins, under Kaestle's guidance, and were then revised by Kaestle.

During the past five years we have incurred many debts to those who have provided financial assistance and helpful criticism; many others rendered archival, programming, and research assistance. The following specific acknowledgments do not exhaust the list; our apologies and gratitude go to any whom we may have omitted. The National Institute of Education, Department of Health, Education and Welfare, made this study possible by providing funds for most of the travel, coding, computing, and research assistance, as well as substantial salary support for Kaestle. However, the opinions expressed in this book do not necessarily reflect the position of the National Institute of Education, and no official endorsement by the Institute should be inferred. The Charles Warren Center for Studies in American History appointed Kaestle a Visiting Fellow in 1974–75, providing him superb facilities, interested colleagues, and financial support for an academic year of study in Massachusetts, a year also supported in part by the Research Committee of the Graduate School, University of Wisconsin at Madison. To the Director of the Charles Warren Center, Professor Donald Fleming, and to the Center's staff and seminar members for 1974–75, Kaestle registers his special gratitude for a year of busy research and challenging ideas. Thanks are also due the Spencer Foundation; funds accompanying a Spencer Fellowship with the National Academy of Education aided Kaestle in his research. Funds for some of the time required for revision of the manuscript were provided by a John Simon Guggenheim Memorial Fellowship awarded to Kaestle for 1977–78, with a supplement from the University of Wisconsin Research Committee, for both of which he here records his gratitude.

To Professor Bernard Bailyn of Harvard University, who served us both as mentor in graduate school, we express our thanks again. He would, no doubt, have preferred to see us spend less time in the Computer Center than we have; yet he has continued to provide encouragement for, and insights into, all aspects of our work.

Many other scholars have read and commented helpfully on some part of the research. These include Samuel Bowles, Lawrence Cremin, Alexander Field, Jurgen Herbst, Deborah Hood, Michael Katz, Michael Olneck, John Rury, Fred Salzillo, and Steven Schlossman. We are especially grateful to David B. Tyack, who made many suggestions for improving the study. Two archivists who were particularly accommodating are James Parla of the Massachusetts State Library Annex and Irene Norton, formerly of the Essex Institute in Salem.

An early version of Chapter 3 was prepared for a conference on the history of the family sponsored jointly by the Russell Sage Foundation and the *American Journal of Sociology,* held in New York City in

Preface

April 1975. We owe thanks to Professor Sarane Boocock of the Russell Sage Foundation and Professor John Demos of Brandeis University, who co-chaired the conference, and to Professor Charles Bidwell, editor of the *American Journal of Sociology*. Helpful criticism of that chapter also came from the other conference participants: Anne Foner, Frank Furstenberg, Tamara Hareven, Rosabeth Kanter, Michael Katz, Joseph Kett, John Modell, Matilda Riley, Richard Sennett, Neil Smelser, and Carroll Smith-Rosenberg. Chapter 3 is an abridged version of our article "From Apron Strings to ABC's: Parents, Children, and Schooling in Nineteenth-Century Massachusetts," which appeared with the other conference papers in Sarane Boocock and John Demos, eds., *Turning Points: Historical and Sociological Essays on the Family* (Chicago: *American Journal of Sociology* 84, supplement, 1978–79), reprinted here with the kind permission of the editors and the *American Journal of Sociology*.

Chapter 4 draws upon material prepared for the Conference on the Family Life Course in Historical Perspective sponsored by the Mathematics Social Science Board of the National Science Foundation, chaired by Professor Tamara Hareven and held at Williams College in July 1975. In addition to Professor Hareven, we wish to thank the participants for criticism: Bengt Ankarloo, Howard Chudacoff, Glen Elder, Karen Mason, John Modell, and Peter Uhlenberg, as well as Ruben Hill and Stanley Engerman, who joined us for a follow-up conference at Airlee, Virginia, in December 1975. The papers prepared for this conference appeared in Tamara Hareven, ed., *Transitions: The Family and the Life Course in Historical Perspective* (New York: Academic Press, 1978). Portions of our article in that volume, "From Fireside to Factory: School Entry and School Leaving in Nineteenth-Century Massachusetts," are reprinted here in revised and abbreviated form with the kind permission of the editor and of Academic Press. The 1880 Essex County family census data file used in Chapter 4 was prepared by Professors Hareven and Vinovskis with the assistance of a grant from the Rockefeller Foundation.

The large volume of statistical work reported here required countless hours of assistance in coding, keypunching, programming, and running statistics, as well as much research assistance for surveying and assessing the qualitative historical evidence that helped us make some sense of the statistics. Kaestle directed the student assistants, who included, at various times: Nancy Manor, Joseph Reed, Donna Rittelsprigger, and Susan Titus, University of Wisconsin undergraduates; Barbara DeWolfe, Diane Melish, and Michelle Wasserman, graduate students in Cambridge; Dexter Arnold, John Bjerke, Jacqueline Jones,

Susan Kuyper, Henry Maier, William Reese, Barry Teicher, Mark Van Pelt, and Susan Wegner, graduate students at Wisconsin; and especially Martha Coons and John Jenkins, the graduate assistants at Wisconsin who carried out the case studies of Boxford and Lynn. Some of these students worked with us only briefly, others for as long as a year; some did routine coding, others did research requiring historical training. All brought to their tasks intelligence and care.

Steve Shedd of the University of Rhode Island programmed the compressed file used in the Essex County family-level study; Mary Vinovskis programmed the multiple classification analysis (an OSIRIS program at the Institute for Social Research, University of Michigan) for both Chapter 4 and Chapter 8, and gave unstintingly of her time and talent to the project. Most of the remaining computing was done at Harvard, using the statistical package called Data-Text, programmed variously by Kaestle and Vinovskis. Lois Corcoran typed the manuscript with speed and accuracy; the staffs of the Department of Educational Policy Studies and the Department of History, University of Wisconsin, have given cheerful and indispensable aid throughout the project. While we acknowledge here our debt to these and others, we exempt all but ourselves from responsibility for any failings or inaccuracies in this book. The research and writing of this book has involved us in much traveling and weekend work. For their forbearance and cooperation, we thank our wives, and we gratefully dedicate this book to them and to our children.

C.F.K. and M.A.V.

1

Education and social change:
Massachusetts as a case study

We do not present a theory of educational development in this volume. Indeed, we have been impressed by the inadequacy of various one-to-one models that have characterized some recent works relating education to social change in nineteenth-century America, works that argue, implicitly or explicitly, that factory production caused educational reform, that urbanization caused school bureaucracy, that capitalism caused increased enrollments, or that modernization caused increased literacy. When these propositions have been sufficiently specific to test, as in the case of factory production and educational reform, they have at worst proved incorrect and at best provided only a partial picture of educational development.[1] When the explanatory concept is more comprehensive, as with the notion of modernization, the danger lies in reifying the umbrella term into a cause independent of its parts. Furthermore, even among its most talented practitioners, modernization theories are plagued by the equation of modernity with progress and desirable change.[2]

We seek in this volume to describe in detail a complex set of educational developments and to discuss some of their more important cultural, political, and socioeconomic concomitants. Systematic state schooling did not develop in a vacuum. It was not just the gradual evolution of some universally desirable idea. It developed in relationship to the evolving social structure, economic system, and cultural relationships of community, region, and nation. Because schooling had a cultural content more compatible with some groups than with others, and because schooling cost money, both to communities and to individuals, there were predisposing characteristics associated with school participation and educational reform. An ecological model of research, including many cultural and economic variables, suits the complexity of the subject. Ecological studies should not be one-dimensional. Various recent studies have shown the salience of conflict and diversity across rural–urban, middle-class–working-class, industrial–nonindustrial, Protestant–Catholic, and native–immigrant lines, but as soon as

1

we focus solely or emphatically on one of these, we risk reducing the complexity of educational history and overestimating the importance of dichotomous categories.

We have therefore attempted to keep a broad range of variables before us, in both our quantitative and our qualitative investigation of Massachusetts's educational development. On some matters we discovered that intellectual developments were important, as in the case of the theological and medical ideas discussed in Chapter 3. In other cases, as in Chapter 8, political ideology loomed important, substantially transcending community variables. Through multivariate analysis we have explored the social, economic, cultural, and political factors associated with rates of school participation and with enthusiasm about or resistance to the emerging state educational system of mid-nineteenth-century Massachusetts.

The creation of a state system of schools in nineteenth-century Massachusetts

Much has been written about antebellum school reform, particularly in Massachusetts. The broad program of educational expansion and consolidation advocated by reformers and school officials in that state succeeded to a remarkable extent. "Reform" consisted of many different desired changes in the quantitative, qualitative, and organizational dimensions of public schooling. Various of these reforms occurred at different times, and some were more important to some people than to others, or to some communities than to others. Despite this diversity, the following list summarizes the major systematic changes in Massachusetts schooling during the nineteenth century, changes that eventually applied to almost all communities and groups:

increased enrollment;
increased average daily attendance;
increased length of school year;
increased consolidation of control at the town and state levels;
increased expenditures per student, leading both to improved physical facilities and to increased teacher salaries;
increased standardization – for example, of textbooks and subjects included in the curriculum;
increased classification of students, through graded schools, leading to a clearly articulated curriculum sequence;
increased differentiation of programs for particular groups who were considered problematic – for example, nongraded intermediate schools for working children;

2

increased professional training for teachers;
increased supervisory personnel over teachers;
increased authority over children for teachers; and
increased formal equality of access for females and blacks.

Our study is only incidentally about the motives and activities of the reformers who sought these changes. It is, rather, about the contours of the changes themselves: where they occurred, in what magnitude, and how various types of communities responded to demands for educational changes. By breaking down the vague notion of "educational reform" into a number of distinct educational variables, we were able to investigate how different levels of educational activity related to indicators of social and economic status.

The choice of Massachusetts as a case study

There are several reasons why we chose Massachusetts as a case study. First, Massachusetts was a leader in the first half of the nineteenth century, both in economic development and in education, and it was so regarded by contemporaries. The state was untypical, in the sense that it systematized its schools, industrialized, and urbanized early and thoroughly. Yet, by the same token, it is a laboratory for studying the interrelationships between schooling and social change.

Second, the quantitative record is better for Massachusetts than for any other state. The statistics gathered there were better and earlier than in most states; equally important, very substantial files of this data had already been collected in machine-readable form before our study began. Thus we had access not only to our large files, newly coded and keypunched with the assistance of the National Institute of Education grant, but also to large files created by Maris Vinovskis in his work on Massachusetts fertility, and to the 1880 Essex County family data file created by Professors Tamara Hareven and Maris Vinovskis with Rockefeller Foundation support. If these quite elaborate sources of quantitative information did not give us more grasp, they at least gave us a great deal of reach.

Third, several recent studies of social change and education have centered upon Massachusetts, such as the works of Michael Katz, Alexander Field, and Samuel Bowles and Herbert Gintis. One cannot assess the validity of their many conclusions unless one examines the same historical record. This requirement, of course, can lead to too many books about Massachusetts, and we certainly support the need for similar studies of other states and other areas. However, scholars are still a long way from understanding even the most basic trends and social correlates in nineteenth-century Massachusetts education, and we believe that the lively debates about this important state are still fruitful.

The need for quantitative educational history

Historians who investigate literary sources in the attempt to relate various aspects of social change rely upon the perceptions of historical observers. For example, a public school advocate might link poverty and the need for education in a public speech or in private correspondence. If the association occurs frequently and represents a widespread contemporary perception, a plausible case can be made that schooling efforts were generated to some extent by poverty. A quantitative approach allows a different perspective and, to some degree, provides a check on the more impressionistic links. In this approach, used by historians long before the invention of computers, the historian asks: Was the incidence of poverty associated in any measurable way with levels or types of schooling in various communities or at different time periods? Both methods have drawbacks and advantages. One of the important contributions of numerical correlations is negative; that is, in the absence of a correlation, causal links are rendered implausible. Beyond this negative function, correlation and more sophisticated multivariate analysis can be suggestive about causal relationships. If statistical analysis uncovers persistent strong links among different social phenomena, historians should pursue the possible reasons for those links with all of their skills, evidence, and insight. Quantitative study also sometimes allows us to investigate the relationships that prevailed in the past between perceptions and behavior and between elite initiatives and popular response, as we hope to show in Chapter 3, which focuses on the age at which children first entered school.

This study is about aggregate trends, about towns and their educational characteristics, and about groups of families and their children's enrollment patterns. It is not, to any great extent, about the experiences children had within the schoolroom, although our case studies in Chapter 6 touch upon this subject. We believe that a sound social history of American education should begin with questions of who went to school, where, and for how long; how those patterns relate to other measurable community or family characteristics; and how the relationships changed over time. Other scholars can add much further meaning to the subject by studying curriculum, classroom practices, the significance of schooling in individual children's lives, and the non-school settings in which children learn.

Values and themes

Neither our use of quantitative techniques nor the fact that we eschew overarching theories about social change should be taken as a claim that we are any freer from value judgments about history and American society than other scholars. Nor do they mean that this book is without themes and conclusions. It may be helpful therefore to state at the outset some of our beliefs about history and some of our major conclusions.

We believe that intellectual discourse, religion, ethnic traditions, and other spheres of social experience play determining roles in human events and are in some regards independent of the productive system and the social relations it generates; yet we believe that social structure and economic conditions provide a bedrock that heavily influences the shape and direction of human activities. We believe that both the fundamental importance of economic conditions and the independent importance of other factors are demonstrable through the use of quantitative and qualitative kinds of evidence. We believe that individual human beings' intelligence, will, avarice, courage, and other qualities account for much in history, but that the cultural milieu, social system, and economy provide the parameters for the actions and ideas that are favored, promoted, and generalized. We therefore focus on the latter in order to understand long-range trends. Finally, we do not argue that the development of public schooling in Massachusetts was fundamentally unjust, or that it was fundamentally just. Education is a complex process, its consequences as diverse and elusive as its social roots. There are nonetheless some winners and some losers in our story. Although nineteenth-century Massachusetts witnessed an impressive expansion of educational participation and expenditure across the entire society, various inequities and tensions play an important part in our analysis. Our central intention has been to determine trends in nineteenth-century Massachusetts schooling, the social context of these trends, and the nature of resistance to the developing state school system.

Three major trends may be distinguished. The first, an expansion of annual enrollments, preceded substantial state intervention in schooling. Defined as an increase in the percentage of children receiving some sort of schooling each year, educational expansion did not depend upon the creation of a state school system. Its origins were not only local but rural, and the big surge probably occurred between 1750 and 1830. Although its magnitude and its causes are murky, the religious and political as well as the economic purposes of schools played

5

a role. Chapter 2 explores the evidence on this problem. In the period of increasing state involvement after about 1840, enrollment rates in Massachusetts stabilized at a high level. A second trend in school participation then looms more important, an intensification rather than an expansion of schooling. As annual school sessions lengthened and average daily attendance increased, the amount of education received by the average child increased. The details of this process, and some of its possible ramifications, are also presented in Chapter 2.

The third major trend in Massachusetts schooling concerned organization, not participation. From the mid-nineteenth century on, schooling became more centralized. At the local level this meant the development of more tightly organized urban systems and pressure to consolidate independent rural districts into town units (as we detail for Lynn and Boxford in Chapter 6). At the state level the existence of a school fund, a board of education, and a growing body of educational legislation did not constitute anything approaching the extensive state regulation of education to which we have become accustomed in the late twentieth century; however, the new influence of the state was clearly evident, and it appeared sufficiently potent to contemporaries to rouse considerable opposition, as our analysis of politics in Chapter 8 illustrates.

The first trend, expansion of enrollments prior to 1840, is only tentatively supported by the limited evidence; if it actually took place, however, it is important, and the occurrence of such a trend is supported not only by our work but by the ongoing research of others as well. The second trend, the intensification of schooling per child after 1840, is indisputable and should be seen as the most substantial quantitative impact of educational reform in mid-nineteenth-century Massachusetts. The third trend, toward centralization and bureaucracy, has been strongly emphasized by recent historians of education. It was against this trend that most resistance was directed.

In the course of the analysis we discuss many further educational trends, such as the shift from private to public schooling, and we treat some special aspects of school attendance in depth. Chapter 3 explores age of school entry as a way of understanding changing definitions of educational responsibility between the school and the family. Chapter 4 investigates the age of school leaving as a way of measuring the differential use of schools by different social groups.

Whereas Chapter 4 analyzes schooling differences among groups within communities, Chapter 5 investigates differences among communities by analyzing the characteristics of towns associated with high levels of educational activity. On questions of social context, our negative findings are as important as our more complex positive findings. When controlling for a variety of other factors, we found that neither a town's size nor its extent of manufacturing activity was a key predictor of educational activity, contrary to what one might expect from recent works emphasizing urbanization and industrialization as causes of educational activity. Of course, such associations are not wholly mistaken, but multivariate analysis reveals some of the complexity of the process of education on the one hand and of indicators of social change on the other. In the case of urbanization, the problem is partly one of definition, which we explore in detail. Some measures of educational participation are indeed ranged along a rough rural–urban continuum, best measured by an index of the population density and agricultural land in a community, rather than by simple population size. But other cultural and economic factors were also relevant, and population size itself appears to have played an important role in the organization and bureaucratization of schooling, a process difficult to quantify but evident in our analysis of Lynn and in other scholars' recent studies of urban education. The finding that, among Massachusetts towns, manufacturing was not strongly associated with measures of educational participation or measures of supply, such as the length of the school year, raises doubts about the relationship of educational reform and factory labor.

It is difficult to state a summary conclusion about the complex social context of educational change, but the following generalizations held true in our various analyses and capture part of the ecological picture. On the one hand, high annual enrollments were associated with rural communities, rural life-style, and Protestant churchgoing. The social context of our first trend, then, was rural, and it built upon traditional schooling practices. On the other hand, the intensification of education and the support for centralization were associated with those dense urban places that were highly developed economically. For example, commercial activity was strongly associated with high average days of schooling per child (see Chapter 5), and both commercial and manufacturing towns displayed legislative support for the state board of education (see Chapter 8).

During the period 1840 to 1880, on which our statistics concentrate, there was a tendency for the educational practices of Massachusetts towns to converge in terms of enrollment, age of students, expenditures, use of female teachers, and other matters, although some of the characteristic differences still persisted. Furthermore, the homogenization and escalation of schooling across different groups and different communities should not be allowed to obscure resistance to the kind of educational system that was being created, resistance voiced throughout the nineteenth century and lingering to some degree at its close. Although there was virtually no opposition to school going as such, many Democrats opposed the creation of state power over education and voted accordingly, many Catholics resented the Protestant bias of public schools and created their own schools instead, many rural communities resisted consolidation and clung to district control, and many urban employers flouted early compulsory school laws and hired youngsters anxious to augment family income. None of these were simple battles, however, as we hope to show in Chapter 8 in the case of the board of education. No single characteristic is sufficient to predict how a person or community would stand on the many educational issues of the day. Furthermore, opposition to state involvement in schooling was somewhat compromised by the almost universal support for formal education; and opposition to increased expenditure was eventually overcome, not only by this traditional support for education, but by the expansive economy of Massachusetts, which, as we show in Chapter 7, helped to support a simultaneous transfer from private to public education and an increase in per capita expenditure for schooling. At the same time, the absolute scale of things was increasing rapidly, both in cities of Massachusetts and in the state as a whole. Systematization was to some extent a response to population growth.

But none of this seemed simple or inevitable at the time. Nor would it have seemed very likely to a Massachusetts resident in 1800. We return, then, to the beginning of the story, and to the beginning of our analysis of education and social change in nineteenth-century Massachusetts.

2

Trends in school attendance in nineteenth-century Massachusetts

The "sleepy" period: enrollment levels in the American Northeast, 1800–1840

Leading political theorists of the Revolutionary generation considered an educated citizenry essential to the survival of the American republic. Some, like Thomas Jefferson and Benjamin Rush, devised plans for systems of common schooling.[1] But these plans generally came to naught, and the discussion of them has too long dominated the educational historiography of this period. If the fragile American nation could be saved only by an educated citizenry, and if an educated citizenry could be maintained only by a state system of common schools, why were two generations of town officials and state legislators so lackadaisical about providing systematic, universal education? Why was there a lag of forty years between the creation of the republic and the creation of a state board of education in Massachusetts?

Perhaps the public did not share the anxieties of the Founding Fathers about the American polity. Perhaps they shared their anxieties but did not share their faith that schooling would preserve republican institutions. Perhaps, on the contrary, they agreed with both propositions but believed that schooling in their society was ample and that most children received the kind of rudimentary intellectual and moral training the political theorists had in mind, even though much schooling was neither publicly controlled nor free. We believe that this third explanation best fits the evidence, and we believe that research into the educational history of the early United States should, for its central focus, turn from the unfulfilled plans of political elites to local patterns of schooling and other forms of education, that is, from the intellectual to the social history of education. Economic historians, like historians of the family and childhood, wish to know more about actual patterns of mass education than about the impressions of reformers, and although we have long known that the two are not synonymous, it has been difficult to get at the educational behavior of ordinary children in a prestatistical age.

Education and social change in nineteenth-century Massachusetts

Americans' apparent indifference to the educational schemes of republican theorists in the early days of nationhood led to the myth of the "sleepy" period in our educational history. The illusion that there was little schooling prior to 1840 in the American Northeast can be traced to school reformers like Horace Mann and Henry Barnard, who were hostile to private schools, such as academies, as well as to the small district schools that prevailed in rural areas. They preferred the model of the mid-seventeenth-century New England town, where schools served the whole town and were required by colony-wide laws. As population dispersed, however, the district system developed in rural areas; and in the eighteenth century urban development fostered private educational alternatives.[2] Mann revered the early Puritan system and considered both of the later developments part of a "deep sleep" interrupting New England's commitment to schooling.[3] This story was adopted by later educational historians who shared Mann's commitment to centralized public schooling. The evolution of American public schooling was checked by the Revolutionary War, wrote Ellwood Cubberley, and "something like half a century of our national life passed before we note again the rise of a distinctively American educational consciousness and the development of distinctively American schools once more begins."[4] The study of educational legislation has led historians to similar conclusions; Elsie Hobson labeled the period 1795 to 1810 "a period of educational decadence in Massachusetts and Connecticut."[5] Historians have criticized the 1789 Massachusetts law for formalizing the district system, blasted Connecticut's 1795 law for vitiating local initiative, and lamented the expiration in 1800 of New York's 1795 law, which had provided matching funds on a voluntary basis.[6]

The notion of "decline" in schooling during the early years of the nation, then, is supported by a venerable historical tradition. Yet even if we wipe away these preconceptions and set out *tabula rasa* to assess the extent of schooling in the early republic, difficulties loom. Precisely because schooling was unregulated and voluntary in the early national period, records are scarce. It is not accidental that the appearance of the first systematic school statistics coincides with the educational reforms of the late 1830s and 1840s. The data were a crucial tool of the reformers in their public relations efforts. To get comparable data for the "sleepy" period from the 1790s to 1840 requires some hard digging and some cautious extrapolations, but it can be done.

A key criterion for the extent of schooling is the percentage of school-age children enrolled, so we shall concentrate on enrollment as

10

the starting point in assessing assertions about the rise or decline of common schooling. If we wished to assess the "impact" or "influence" of schooling, we would need to know more about daily attendance rates, the length of the school year, the average number of years attended per child, the distribution of schooling patterns by social groups, the quality of instruction, the organization of the schools, and the curriculum. Even with all this information it would be difficult to infer what children actually learned in schools. But the first task is to determine how many people were going to school. If total enrollment is accepted as a crude index of the extent of schooling, the thesis of a rise in common schooling during the 1830s or 1840s in the Northeast is open to challenge. Albert Fishlow, writing in 1965, questioned the assumption that the efforts of Horace Mann and his fellow reformers had increased the amount of education received in New England. Fishlow's regional figures for total annual enrollments between 1840 and 1860 showed a slight decline in New England, a slight rise in the Middle Atlantic states, and more substantial gains in the South and West.[7] He concluded that the "common school revival" of the 1840s consisted principally of a shift from private to public schooling and the diffusion of higher school-going rates to the less-developed regions of the country, not a rise in the quantity of education in New England. Maris Vinovskis has refined the data for Massachusetts by controlling for age and has somewhat qualified Fishlow's denial that Horace Mann greatly affected enrollment in his home state; but the main outline of Fishlow's argument about the period 1840 to 1860 remains valid.[8]

More important for our purposes in this section, Fishlow also attempted to assess levels of education before 1840. Using scattered reports, and extrapolating for missing data, he produced a state-level comparison of annual enrollment in 1830 and 1840, concluding that "little change occurred between the two dates." Table 2.1 reproduces Fishlow's figures for the two largest northeastern states, New York and Massachusetts, both leaders in school reform, in both of which there was even a decline in enrollment. Fishlow concluded that "what scattered reports are available suggest a more optimistic evaluation of the state of educational facilities prior to the reform efforts of the 1830s and 1840s."[9] This finding leads to the question whether a substantial rise in enrollment occurred in these two states *before* 1830. Fishlow thought not. Though admitting that estimates for the years before 1830 are "more hazardous," he nonetheless concluded tentatively that "education was being prosecuted with comparable vigor over the whole period" from 1800 to 1830.[10]

Table 2.1. Annual school enrollment rates for Massachusetts and New York, 1830 and 1840

	1830		1840	
	% of white children 5–19 enrolled	% of white children 0–19 enrolled	% of white children 5–19 enrolled	% of white children 0–19 enrolled
Massachusetts	72.9[a]	54.7[a]	68.9	51.7
New York	73.8	55.4	69.4	52.1

[a]1832

Source: Albert Fishlow, "The American Common School Revival: Fact or Fancy?" in Henry Rosovsky, ed., Industrialization in Two Systems (New York: Wiley, 1966), Table 1, p. 43. We have converted his rates to percentages of the estimated population aged birth to nineteen for comparability with later tables.

This generalization is not only very speculative but very important, and it deserves to be pursued. It has ramifications for the administrative and political history of education as well as for the economic history of the new nation. Some recent historians, influenced by the reform failures of the 1960s, have questioned the efficacy or the desirability of state intervention in such activities as schooling. Because the enrollments of the early nineteenth century were the product of a mixed private–public, nonregulated mode of education, accurate estimates of school participation for different social groups and different regions prior to state systematization could be helpful in providing perspective on the necessity and the effects of intervention.[11] Economic historians are also interested in the magnitude and timing of shifts in school participation. Fishlow, for example, argued that estimates of increased schooling per capita between 1800 and 1840 were greatly exaggerated and that therefore we should be skeptical about any alleged contribution of education to rising productivity during this early period of industrialization.[12] E. G. West, on the contrary, has dated England's enrollment rise earlier than is traditional among English historians, thus resurrecting for England the very possibility Fishlow denied for America.[13] In short, if it proves true that enrollment levels were high in 1800 and did not rise substantially between 1800 and 1830, one might argue, first, that state intervention in education was not necessary to maintain an educated citizenry or to disseminate basic intellectual skills, and, second, that a connection between educational enrollment and rising productivity is doubtful.

Our purpose in this section is to assess Fishlow's basic hypothesis about annual enrollment rates, leaving aside until later two additional important factors in measuring the quantity of education – length of school year and average daily attendance – which he dealt with only incidentally. Because Fishlow relied primarily on data from New York for his conclusion of little increased enrollment from 1800 to 1830, and because interesting enrollment data exist for New York State at the turn of the century, we shall analyze the existing scattered evidence for both New York and Massachusetts, evidence that partially corroborates and partially refutes Fishlow's assertions about this period. Each enrollment ratio presented should be taken with a grain of salt. Not only are attendance figures collected in different ways from place to place and time to time, but even the estimates of the relevant school-age population differ, depending upon whether the figures are from state and federal censuses or from school officials. All one can do is to assemble as many examples as possible, standardize as nearly as possible, and hope to discern long-term trends that transcend the biases of the evidence.

We have achieved nominal comparability of our enrollment rates by stating each as a percentage of all children aged birth to nineteen. This involved converting rates like Fishlow's, which were stated as a percentage of children aged five to nineteen, and those from school reports that tabulated eligible children variously at ages four to sixteen, four to fifteen, or five to fifteen. In each case we converted on a simple arithmetic basis, assuming an equal number of children at each age. This procedure has the virtue of consistency and results in estimates that are usually close to the truth (when detailed figures by age are available). Unless stated otherwise, blacks are included in our population and enrollment figures.

One further caveat is required because the enrollment rates are artificial in yet another way: the numerator and the denominator are not comparable. Enrollment figures (the numerators) capture all persons taught at schools during a year, including all who leave the area during the period as well as those who move in. Population figures (the denominators) in contrast, are not longitudinal. They catch the number of persons living in an area on a given day. Expressing one as a percentage of the other, therefore – though commonly done by nineteenth-century educators and twentieth-century historians – is mixing apples and oranges and, obviously, overstates the percentage of the school-age population enrolled in school on a given day. We discuss this and related issues in detail later in this chapter. That the enrollment rates are artificial creations should be recognized, but that recognition need not devastate our analysis, for we are seeking relative comparisons and shifts over time, not absolute levels of enrollment. If we wished to test an assertion that political stability depended upon a certain amount of education, or that a certain level of enrollment would herald a takeoff in productivity, we would have difficulty assembling the required statistics. But we are interested in different questions: When, if ever, were there substantial increases in school enrollment during the period 1800 to 1840, and, in general, how does the "sleepy" period compare to the "revival" period in the northeastern United States?

First, although our central interest is in Massachusetts, we must examine the New York State enrollment data that Fishlow cited to support his contention of little or no increase in enrollments in the Northeast from 1800 to 1830. After arguing briefly that the legislative history of the northeastern states does not demonstrate a decline of commitment to schooling in the early national period, he stated:

For the state of New York, fortunately, it is possible to be more precise. Its schools do show an increase in enrollment rates of some 25 per cent from 1815 to 1830 . . . Note, however, that by 1823 the 1830 level had already been reached and that as early as 1798 a partial enumeration of school attendance suggests no great difference from the 1815 level.[14]

This is the entire extent of Fishlow's evidence for enrollments before 1830, and it is not quite clear what he was trying to argue from it. To argue, as he seems to, that there was no change from 1798 to 1815 and then a tremendous rise between 1815 and 1823, after which there was no change up through the 1830s, not only contradicts his contention that 1800 rates were about the same as those of 1830 but is also incorrect. The 1798 data he mentions vaguely appeared in the New York State Assembly's *Journal,* by town, and we have calculated the school-age population for the towns that returned enrollment reports, to give us a base-line figure to compare with Randall's statewide figures for the period 1815 to 1850.[15] This 1798 rate, 37.1 percent, is substantial, but not high enough to support Fishlow's contention that there was little rise from 1800 to 1830. Indeed, using the same data Fishlow cited, plus our 1798 data, we can chart a steady increase from 1798 to 1830, by which date, if the figures are valid, school enrollment in New York State leveled off (see Table 2.2).

Table 2.2. Annual public school enrollment rates for New York
State, 1798-1850

Year	Number of scholars	Number of children 0-19 (est.)	% of children 0-19 enrolled
1798	58,475	157,756[a]	37.1
1815	140,106	294,670	47.5
1820	304,559	530,447	57.4
1825	425,566	660,629	64.4
1830	499,424	830,830	60.1
1835	541,401	902,276	60.0
1840	572,995	989,582	57.9
1845	736,045	1,153,242	63.8
1850	742,423	1,174,676	59.9

[a]Whites only, sixteen of twenty-three counties reporting. New
York City is among the missing counties.

Source: For 1798 enrollment figures, New York Assembly Journal
(1798-1800), pp. 282-5; for population, Second United States
Census (Washington, D.C., 1800), pp. 32-3. For 1815-50 attendance and population figures, S. S. Randall, The Common School
System of the State of New York (Troy, N.Y., 1851), p. 91.

Must we, then, discard Fishlow's conclusion that enrollment rates
from 1800 onward were so similar that education could not have contributed to increasing productivity? Must we conclude that during the
"sleepy" period of our educational history enrollments were steadily
rising in New York? Not necessarily, for Fishlow's discussion of education before 1840 confused publicly assisted schooling with schooling
in general; that is, it entirely overlooked the private sector. This is
strange, because the oversight biased his data against the point he was
attempting to make. Also, it was he who emphasized that the major
development of the later period, 1840-60, was a shift from private to
public schooling, not an increase in enrollment.

Fishlow looked at Randall's New York State figures, treated them
as if they represented all schooling in the state, and then glossed over
a very substantial rising trend in enrollment. The question is not
whether these data illustrate rising enrollment; they clearly do. The
question, rather, is whether these rising *public* enrollment rates reflect

a rise in *total* school enrollment or a shift from unreported private to reported public enrollment, a distinction Fishlow made clear for the 1840 to 1860 period but left hanging for the crucial early national period.

To answer this question we must get beyond aggregate state reports of publicly assisted schools in two ways. First, we must find some way to assess private schooling before 1840; such data are rare and fragmentary but are better than none. Second, we must recognize rural–urban differences in schooling in the early national period. The informal mode of education inherited from the eighteenth century operated very differently in large commercial towns and in small rural communities. Although dichotomies run the risk of oversimplification, it may help us to understand school enrollment in the early national period if we think of two different institutional solutions to schooling needs in rural towns and large cities: institutional arrangements that resulted in characteristically different enrollment rates and that were affected differently by state intervention and assistance, which increased throughout the first half of the nineteenth century.

In both kinds of communities schooling resulted from a combination of governmental and parental initiative. In small towns and rural villages there was relatively little independent entrepreneurial schooling and usually only one kind of town or district school. The combination of governmental and parental efforts concerned funding. Although New York State had a common school fund and a state superintendent of common schools beginning in 1812, local schooling was still financed largely by client fees called rate bills. In little Glenville, New York, for example, bills paid by parents in the 1830s equaled from one to three times the amount of public monies for schooling.[16] Statewide, the amount of rate bills exceeded all public monies until 1840, when the receipts from the U.S. Deposit Fund boosted state aid to local schools.[17] In Massachusetts there were no rate bills, but communities typically lengthened short school sessions by assessing parental fees "to prolong the common schools," and those who did not pay could not send their children. This practice was still widespread in the 1840s.[18] Entirely free and "public" education for all children came to most rural communities only after the middle of the nineteenth century.

In larger towns the mixture of governmental and parental initiative was different. It was characterized not by varying contributions to a single set of common schools, but by the creation of diverse, separate institutions, more accurately labeled charity schools and pay schools than public and private schools, because charity schools were variously under the control of churches, town councils, and voluntary benevolent societies. We shall nonetheless use the word "private" here (as the word is so engrained in discussions of economic history) to refer only to the pay schools (whether incorporated or not) supported entirely by tuition payments by clients. In Schenectady and Albany as well as in New York City, in Salem and Newburyport as well as in Boston, charity schools, Lancasterian free schools, infant schools, and Sunday schools supplemented dame schools, academies, female seminaries, and other independent day schools. Early state statistics either underestimate or entirely omit schooling in such areas (New York City and Boston, significantly, are missing from the earliest state reports of New York and Massachusetts).

A glimpse of the extent of enrollment under this diverse mode of schooling is possible for at least one city. Figures for New York City in 1796 were generated by New York's 1795 law providing matching funds to schools offering a common education. The common council members eventually decided to distribute the monies only to religiously affiliated or incorporated charity schools, but in the process of making that decision they made a survey of the city's independent schoolmasters as well. Carl Kaestle analyzed the extant enrollment lists and by extrapolation estimated that 52 percent of all children over five and under fifteen years of age were enrolled in New York's private and public schools in the 1795–6 school session.[19] Converted according to our assumptions about population, these data yield an enrollment rate of 24.7 percent of all children from birth to nineteen. This falls far short of the 37.1 percent rate for the state just four years later and is much lower than the typical 50 to 60 percent statewide rates of the period after 1830. More striking, however, are comparisons with later rates available for the city itself, which in the succeeding fifty years exceeded the 1796 rate by only about 7 percent (see Table 2.3). These figures were the basis for Kaestle's conclusion, similar to Fishlow's, that the major change in New York City schooling between 1800 and 1850 was not in the rate of enrollment but in the numbers of students and the organization of schooling. In response to population growth, immigration, and other social changes, schooling became predominantly public and standardized. Moreover, the segregation of schoolchildren by social class that one might have expected of a mixed voluntary private–public school situation may have been no greater in 1796 than in 1850, when many wealthy parents still supported private alternatives and some children of poor parents still attended no school. Indeed, there may have been less segregation then than there is today, when – despite universal compulsory attendance – class and racial

Education and social change in nineteenth-century Massachusetts

Table 2.3. Annual school enrollment rates for New York City

Year	% of children 0-19 enrolled	% of school-children in private schools
1796	24.7	89.7
1829	32.0	62.2
1840	21.9	--
1850	26.3	18.3

Source: For 1796, Carl F. Kaestle, The Evolution of an Urban
School System: New York City, 1750-1850 (Cambridge: Harvard
University Press, 1973), Table 10, p. 52; for 1829 and 1850,
Kaestle, Evolution of an Urban School System, Table 12, p. 89;
for 1840, Sixth Census of the United States (Washington, D.C.:
Blair and Reives, 1841), p. 115.

segregation are reinforced by residential segregation as well as by private schooling. Kaestle analyzed the extant 1796 enrollment lists and found considerable overlap and considerable range in the occupational and wealth status of charity school students' parents when compared to the parents of students at the common pay schools of the city. The occupational status of parents sending their children to school (both types combined) roughly approximated the occupational structure of the city as a whole, although we may surmise that the least well-off *within* each category were least likely to send their children to school (see Table 2.4). The New York City data suggest, then, that the mixture of charity and entrepreneurial schooling characteristic of cities in the late eighteenth and early nineteenth centuries resulted in enrollment rates similar to or slightly lower than rates in the mid-nineteenth century.

Scattered enrollment figures for private and public students in Salem, Massachusetts, reinforce the impression that the shift from private to public, and the development of a state-assisted public school system, had little effect upon the proportion of children enrolled in northeastern commercial cities. Salem in 1820, like New York in 1796, had a well-developed dual network of independent pay schools and free schools, although its free schools, accommodating about half of the school goers, were operated by the town, a practice inherited from the colonial period. As this public sector grew in Salem schooling, the total enrollment remained remarkably stable (see Table 2.5). Enrollment records for Boston tell the same story. In 1826, when 44.5 percent

18

Table 2.4. Occupations of New York City schoolchildren's parents, 1796

Occupational category	Number of parents	% of school parents	% of all workers in directory
Laborer	4	2.4	5.5
Mariner	8	4.8	3.7
Cartman	21	12.6	9.5
Skilled craftsman	66	39.5	43.1
Clerical worker	10	6.0	2.0
Proprietor	31	18.6	14.3
Professional	0	0	4.0
Merchant	13	7.8	13.0
Other	14	8.4	5.4
Total	167	100	100

Source: Kaestle, Evolution of an Urban School System, Table 11, p. 54.

Table 2.5. School enrollments in Salem, Massachusetts, 1820-75

Year	% of children 0-19 enrolled	% of schoolchildren in private schools
1820	41.3	50.0[a]
1827	46.6	57.8
1834	41.4	49.6
1837	44.7	56.3
1875	41.8	17.9

[a]Estimate.

Source: Attendance figures for 1820, public schools from Board of Education Minutes, MS, Salem Public Schools, Superintendant's Office, August 28, 1820, private attendance estimated assuming a minimum of 50 percent private, on the basis of later known figures; for 1827, Salem Register, May 21, 1827; for 1834, Board of Education Minutes, November 25, 1834; for 1837, Salem City Directory for 1837. Population figures from the federal census and the Massachusetts census of 1875, extrapolated arithmetically for 1827, 1834, and 1837.

Table 2.6. School enrollments for New York State by town size, 1798

Town size	Number of towns in the state	Number of towns reporting	Mean enrollment	Standard deviation
0-999	101	12	33.1	13.3
1,000-2,499	115	52	38.7	16.5
2,500-4,999	70	43	36.7	13.9
5,000-9,999	5	3	27.5	3.3
New York City[a]	1	1	24.7	--
Total (excluding New York City)	281	110	37.1	

[a]Data for public and private schools in 1796. New York City population (est.) = 46,397.

Source: For New York City, Kaestle, Evolution of an Urban School System, p. 52; for New York State, New York Assembly Journal (1798-1800), pp. 282-5, and Second United States Census (Washington, D.C., 1800), pp. 32-3.

of all children aged birth to nineteen were in some school, 32.6 percent of all schoolchildren were in private schools. The 1840 enrollment rate was 39.2 percent, and by 1850, when the percentage in private schools had dropped to 12.2, the overall enrollment rate remained at 45.4 percent.[20]

These data for large commercial towns do not support the notion of a substantial school enrollment increase in the period before 1840. But most people did not live in cities; they lived in smaller towns and rural villages. It remains, then, to assess whether in these towns, which in large part accounted for the statewide public school enrollment figures, increasing enrollments can be attributed to a shift from private to public schooling prior to 1840. To do this we shall dissect the earliest surviving state returns for both New York (1798) and Massachusetts (1826).

When the New York State school returns of 1798 are calculated by town size (Table 2.6), they demonstrate a durable generalization for schooling in the Northeast that applies until well after the middle of the nineteenth century: annual school enrollment rates are negatively associated with community size. Except for the smallest category of towns (population under one thousand), where long distances from

Table 2.7. School enrollments for Massachusetts by town size, 1826

Town size	Number of towns reporting	% 0-19 in public schools		% 0-19 in private and public schools	
		Mean	Standard deviation	Mean	Standard deviation
0-1,249	50	75.9	15.2	81.7	17.9
1,250-2,499	48	71.7	12.9	82.1	21.5
2,500-4,999	13	56.1	24.1	74.1	31.7
5,000-9,999	7	37.9	22.9	54.7	22.1
Salem (pop = 12,875)	1	20.9	--	49.5	--
Boston (pop = 54,154)	1	30.0	--	44.5	--

Source: Massachusetts, Secretary of the Commonwealth, School Returns for 1826, MS, Massachusetts State Library, Annex, Vault.

farm to school may have inhibited enrollment, smaller towns exhibited higher school enrollment rates than larger towns and cities. This may surprise students of other societies, particularly traditional societies, but not those familiar with the early American district school, which served a social as well as an educational function, and whose relatively brief summer and winter sessions accommodated the seasonal nature of children's agricultural work.

The earliest school returns for Massachusetts confirm the pattern and reinforce our conviction that the shift from private to public schooling cannot account for more than a small portion of the enrollment increases outside commercial cities. Table 2.7 reveals the systematic relationship between town size and school enrollment in Massachusetts in 1826. The public school enrollment rates display a regular negative association with town size, except that Salem's public school attendance rate is lower than Boston's. This variation is explained by Salem's far greater proportion of students in private school. The column for enrollment rates at public and private schools combined reverses the rank order of Boston and Salem and otherwise displays a regular progression from high-enrollment rural communities to low-enrollment urban communities, except for the smallest towns, which had very little private schooling to augment the town schools. Also, the gap between the highest rate and the lowest rate is smaller when private schooling is added in. The private sector, more extensive in the cities, had a somewhat leveling effect on total enrollment rates, although the rural–urban contrast is still striking. Most important, the proportion of private schooling is very small in Massachusetts towns with fewer than two thousand five hundred inhabitants, where a large proportion of the population lived. If New York was similar to Massachusetts in this regard, it seems unlikely that the shift from private to public could account for the large public enrollment gains we discovered in New York State.

Extant records for school attendance in small upstate New York towns begin too late to chart a rise in school attendance during the period 1790 to 1820, but they do conform to Randall's figures and to our assertion that rural rates, unaffected by entrepreneurial schooling, were high and stable from the 1820s forward. Table 2.8 gives enrollment rates for Glenville, a small village across the Mohawk River from Schenectady. Established as a town in 1820, when its population was 2,514, Glenville operated district schools (eight in 1820, sixteen by 1840). Despite annual fluctuations, Glenville's high and level rates from 1823 to 1841 portray a town unaffected by the decline of private education (there is no record of any private schooling in Glenville) or increasing state aid (which failed to alter Glenville's already high enrollments).

Our conclusions about enrollment rates may be stated as a rural–urban contrast. The shift from private to public schooling was gradual but decisive in commercial cities of New York and Massachusetts between 1800 and 1850. Moreover, it accounts almost entirely for the rising public enrollment rates in those cities. The combined public–private rates were stable and considerably lower than in smaller communities. The shift from private to public schooling, our data suggest, was not nearly as important in small towns as it was in the cities. Some small towns had private academies, and their decline was much applauded by antebellum reformers; but the shift could account for only a part of the steady rise in official enrollment figures. The increasing substitution of governmental financing for parental financing may have had some effect, yet the influence of government intervention on total enrollment rates may still be doubted because the most important state developments – for example, the dramatic increase in state aid in New York after 1839 and the activities of the state board of education in Massachusetts after 1837 – occurred after statewide enrollment rates had leveled off.

Table 2.8. Enrollment rates for Glenville, New York, 1823-41

Year	Amount of tax money received ($, half state, half local)	Number of children enrolled	% of children 0-19 (est.)
1823	293	660	41.7
1824	293	--	--
1825	293	697	45.1
1826	293	774	50.4
1827	289	709	42.2
1828	289	684	41.9
1829	288	785	47.9
1830	294	747[a]	47.0
1831	294	682	44.9
1832	260	736	48.5
1833	260	726	48.4
1834	261	640	44.0
1835	260	778	48.4
1836	263	--	--
1837	306	--	--
1838	506	691	48.5
1839	806	715	47.4
1840	768	753	50.8
1841	764	688	47.1

[a] One partial district not reporting (excluded also from school-age population estimate).

Source: Reports of the Commissioners of Common Schools in Glenville, 1821-41, MS in the possession of Mr. Donald Kieffer, historian of Glenville. We are grateful to Mr. Kieffer for providing us with a copy of these reports.

Thus far we have discussed only enrollment rates; but reformers like Horace Mann were as concerned to promote regular attendance and longer school sessions as they were to enroll the small percentage of nonattenders. Similarly, economic historians interested in human capital formation want to know the average number of days of schooling attended annually per child, not just the number of children enrolled each year. Relying partly on inferences from expenditure data, Fishlow argued that "neither average daily attendance rates nor length of school year is likely to have shown rapid change" before 1840.[21] Accurate estimates for this period await further research on these variables. In the meantime, we believe that substantial increases may have occurred in school length and average attendance, as they did in total enrollment, during the period 1800 to 1830. The 1826 Massachusetts returns show a clear association between length of school year and town size (Table 2.9). If this cross-sectional association persisted over time, the statewide average length of school must have increased as the state urbanized. Data from the period 1840 to 1880, which we present in the next section, support this inference. The statewide average length of public schools in Massachusetts rose from 150 days in 1840 to 192 days in 1880. Our estimate of the number of school days attended per person aged birth to nineteen in Massachusetts, combining public and private schooling, shows an increase from 60 in 1840 to 72 in 1880. We see no reason presently to assume that such trends did not also characterize the preceding forty years.

Our study of enrollment rates does not suggest that the old derogatory characterization of the "sleepy" period should be replaced by nostalgia for the good old days when widespread schooling resulted from parental, local, and entrepreneurial initiative. We do not wish to make a normative judgment here about whether more schooling for more people is a Good Thing, or whether more state intervention was desirable in American educational history. But our examination of the evidence reestablishes the capacity of the educational institutions of the late eighteenth and early nineteenth century to increase the extent of schooling in the decades before the common school "revival."

Two quite different unregulated modes of schooling, characteristic of commercial cities and rural communities, had by 1800 resulted in enrollment rates high compared to other nations but still capable of expansion in the period 1800 to 1830. Per capita consumption of schooling in the American Northeast was probably increasing substantially before the reforms that began in the late 1830s, although the exact dimensions are as yet unknown. If enrollment is our index, 1800 to 1830 was more a "sneaky" than a "sleepy" period. Quietly, and with little regard for later historians, parents in New York and Massachusetts sent their children to school in increasingly greater numbers. The magnitude of the increase is undetermined, but it was substantial, even when private schooling is accounted for, and it took place not in the cities but in the towns and villages of the hinterland.

The causes of increasing school enrollment rates are as difficult to discern as the figures. The argument that the country was becoming more urbanized and commercialized will hardly do, for as we have seen, local enrollment rates were negatively correlated with population size during this period. Although it seems that the availability and

Table 2.9. Length of Massachusetts public school session by town
size, 1826

| Town size | Number of towns reporting | Average length of school per district (in days) | |
		Mean	Standard deviation
0–1,249	50	127	36
1,250–2,499	48	143	80
2,500–4,999	13	172	104
5,000–9,999	7	204	34

Source: Massachusetts, Secretary of the Commonwealth, School
  Returns for 1826, MS, Massachusetts State Library, Annex,
  Vault. Length of school session not reported for Salem or
  Boston.

diversity of schools was increasing in America's commercial centers in
the Revolutionary era, our figures indicate that New York City by 1800
and Salem by 1820 had reached the gross enrollment rates they would
have in the mid-nineteenth century, and moreover that their enrollment
rates were lower than the smaller towns in their states.

Less hard information, but more plausible arguments, can be ad-
duced for three factors that influenced the hinterland. First, the political literature of the Revolutionary period, and the excitement of nation
building, added secular political reinforcement to traditional motives
for widespread education. Of course, the colonies had been substantially self-governing before Independence, and the American Revolution did not generate any immediate steps toward state intervention in
schooling. Still, the question of rebellion, and then the anxieties of the
constitutional years about chaos or overweening central government,
had some local impact, emphasizing the conventional wisdom that the
survival of the nation, like its creation, depended upon the intelligence
and the good behavior of the yeomanry.[22]

A second, related, and more certain cause of higher enrollment rates
was the increasing provision of schooling for girls in the period from
the Revolution to 1830. Unfortunately, state statistics were not sex
segregated until the late 1830s, but research in local records indicates
that the Founding Fathers' exhortations to educate the mothers of
future citizens were not just rhetorical flourishes. Female literacy appears to have increased dramatically between 1790 and 1850, and Kath-

ryn Sklar's current research on Massachusetts suggests that starting in the 1780s and 1790s more and more towns established summer schools for girls or admitted girls to the regular writing schools previously limited to boys.[23] David Fischer's ongoing research also supports a decided surge in school provision in Massachusetts in the late eighteenth and early nineteenth centuries, attributable largely to increased female education in small and medium-sized towns.[24] This was not an innovation that spread from the commercial centers. In 1790 the Reverend William Bentley noted in a diary entry about his work on the Salem School Committee, "all the girls unprovided for, as upon the Boston establishment."[25] Although Salem had private schools for girls, it did not establish town-supported "woman" schools (schools taught by women, for young children of both sexes) until 1801, and it did not admit girls to its public writing schools until 1827. By this time, a newspaper correspondent lamented, Salem was behind everyone:

There is probably no town in the state where female education is more neglected. In our villages the public schools are open alike to males and females . . . The importance of female education is now so unanimously acknowledged . . . that it is not to be supposed that the inhabitants will be backward in yielding their assent to the proposition of the School Committee.[26]

The third factor that increased Massachusetts school enrollment in the late eighteenth and early nineteenth centuries was the decentralization of the location and control of schools. As the population of Massachusetts towns dispersed in the eighteenth century, residents of outlying areas began to resist taxation for central town schools too distant for their children's use. The first innovation in response to this problem was the moving school, taught in rotation in the various districts by a single teacher. Although individual towns varied widely in the organization of schools, the historian of the moving school dates this trend roughly from 1725. The next step, toward separate teachers, longer sessions, and the construction of separate schoolhouses, began in many towns by 1750 and increased thereafter. By the time the district system gained legislative sanction in the Massachusetts education law of 1789, the General Court was only institutionalizing widespread local practice. Then, from 1789 until 1827, according to Updegraff, "the period of the perfection of the school district" occurred. Much maligned by later reformers, the district system no doubt increased the availability of common schooling during the "sleepy" period.[27]

The spread of the district system increased the demand for teachers. This demand, coupled with changing ideas about women's intellectual abilities, led to the hiring of many women as teachers for summer schools or "woman's" schools. This trend, in turn, enhanced the provision of schools and thus the expansion of enrollment, because women were paid lower wages than male teachers. Finally, the incorporated academy, a new institution, appeared in Massachusetts in the 1760s. There were fifteen such academies by 1800 and many more thereafter (seventy-five by 1840). Although the impact of these schools on total enrollments was not great, they did supplement the existing grammar schools and generally offered a broader curriculum. More important, they provided secondary education to girls, who were excluded from most grammar schools.[28]

The expansion of popular education went unrecognized by the educational leaders of the 1830s and 1840s. Although there had long been common school advocates urging state assistance, and although some loosely structured state education funds had been allocated before 1840, the economic, cultural, and political conditions of the last two antebellum decades were conducive to more extensive and systematic intervention in education. We shall explore these contextual matters in subsequent chapters. First, however, we present the basic trends in school attendance during the formative years of educational systematization in Massachusetts.

School attendance in Massachusetts, 1840–1880

By 1840 the "sleepy period" had ended, and educational reform was in full swing. School attendance became a constant preoccupation of public school advocates. Horace Mann sounded the main theme in 1846:

Is it not a fearful thing to contemplate that so large a portion of our children passed through the last year, without the advantages of any school, public or private? . . . What would be said, if we saw a large portion of our fellow citizens treasonably engaged in subverting the foundations of the republic, and bringing in anarchy or despotism?[29]

Expressing the same concern, the Lawrence School Committee complained in 1854 that truant children received their education in the streets, "where the violation of every moral precept and duty form the morning and the evening lesson." Schoolmen were concerned not merely with annual enrollment but with regular attendance and an ample school year. "Show me a member of a common school who adheres to an unflinching purpose of punctuality and constancy," declared the chairman of the Chicopee School Committee, "and I will show you one who lays a strong hold on the highest success in life."

Topping Chicopee's honor role in 1861 was champion school attender Phebe Howard, who had attended 107 weeks without an absence.[30] State and local school reports in Massachusetts abound with concern about who was attending school, at what age, how regularly, for what period of the year, and whether that attendance was at public or at private schools. However, even for the period after 1840, when most states were collecting detailed education statistics, there are numerous obstacles to constructing valid long-range time series on school attendance.[31]

Complexities and confusions in school attendance rates

The difficulties may be summarized under four general headings: (1) confusion of different types of attendance figures, (2) noncomparability of annual school enrollment figures with cross-sectional census figures, (3) shifts in required reporting categories over time, and (4) the unreliability of private school data.

Types of attendance figures. School participation figures are of two basic types: enrollment data, which express the number of children participating in a system at some time during a given period, and attendance data proper, which tell us the regularity of participation, that is, the average daily attendance, or the number of children who attended a certain number of days of school. Average daily attendance figures, combined with the length of school sessions in days, yield the average number of school days consumed per year per school-age child (or per capita), a statistic of some interest in comparing levels of education at different places or times.

It is not sufficient simply to say that nineteenth-century schoolmen were preoccupied with attendance. Demographically different towns developed different attendance problems. Concern for regularity of attendance was widely shared in rural and urban towns, but anxiety about nonenrolled children – those completely untouched by schooling – was characteristically an urban phenomenon. Also, the different aspects of attendance changed at different rates over the century. As we have seen, a rise in total enrollment rates probably occurred between 1800 and 1830; after 1840 total enrollment leveled off and then actually declined. During the middle of the nineteenth century average daily attendance was stable and the length of school year rose substantially. In this section we examine these aggregate statewide trends over time, as a first step toward assessing the impact of educational systematization on enrollment, attendance, and the amount of schooling consumed in Massachusetts during the middle decades of the nineteenth century.

Because there are many different types of enrollment and attendance figures, we must be careful not to combine or compare the different types. For example, recent scholars have added the average enrollment, given for Massachusetts private schools, and total annual enrollment, given for public schools, to arrive at the total number of children attending school.[32] But, we have discovered, they are not the same statistic; therefore we have devised a ratio to convert average enrollment into estimated total enrollment; the rationale for this and other estimation procedures is given in Appendix C. The following list displays and distinguishes between the four chief types of nineteenth-century attendance figures available to historians. Real values for these statistics, when available, would occur in descending order, that is, the highest number would be all children enrolled during the year, and the lowest number would be the average daily attendance.

Statistic	*Meaning*	*Usual source*
1. Total annual enrollment	All children enrolling during the entire period	Local and state school reports
2. Percentage of population who attended school during the year	Of those present at the time of the census, the number who had attended any school in the previous twelve months	State and federal family census returns
3. Average enrollment	The average number of children enrolled on a single day	Local and state school reports (for Massachusetts private schools in early nineteenth century, for public schools in later nineteenth century)
4. Average daily attendance	The average number of children going to school on a single day	Local and state school reports

Noncomparability of annual enrollment figures with school-age census figures. The most common attendance ratio, used by both nineteenth-century educators and recent historians, is the total annual enrollment divided by the number of children of school age. As we noted in the first part of this chapter, the numerator (annual enrollment) includes all children moving in and out of schools – often including those promoted as well as those entering and leaving the community – whereas the denominator (the number of children of school age in the community) is from a census, one point in time, which does not account for transience. Thus the ratios are artificially inflated, resulting commonly in so-called enrollment rates of over 100 percent, routinely included in nineteenth-century reports but usually attributed to the double counting of individual children moving within the system, rather than to the basic problem, the noncomparability of the longitudinal enrollment figure and the snapshot population figure.[33]

Average enrollment figures (which would be comparable to census figures) are rarely available until late in the century, and conversely, census figures for the number of children who lived in an area over a year's time (which would be comparable to annual enrollment rates) do not exist. Thus it is necessary to live with the artificial statistic. It is not a measure of any absolute level of school participation but may be used to compare relative levels across space or time, assuming that mobility rates do not differ substantially in the communities being compared.[34]

A second problem arises from the *daily* mobility of school goers. Children can cross district lines, or board, to attend schools in areas where they will not be counted among the population. Children from small towns without high schools frequently walked or rode to neighboring cities to school. For example, the Newbury, Massachusetts, School Committee reported in 1850 that "34 students from this town are on the catalogue of the Putnam Free School," in Newburyport. Ten others attended Dummer Academy, and about fifteen attended other private schools in Newburyport. In the same year, Dracut reported, "The proximity of Dracut to Lowell affords the youth in Dracut good opportunity for attending the high schools in that city." School attendance by the teenagers of these small towns would thus be underestimated in the official figures because school committees were expressly instructed not to count them. Conversely, figures for the towns with academies and high schools were inflated by out-of-town scholars. South Hadley, for example, a town with only 381 public school students at all levels, hosted an additional 225 girls at the Mt. Holyoke Female Seminary.[35]

There is no way to correct systematically for the distortions in school attendance rates caused by mobility. We can only hope that out-of-district students were usually a small part of total attendance. The problem, obviously, is of greater impact for teenagers than for young children. Also, the smaller the unit of analysis, the greater the problem. There is less distortion at the state level than at the town level, and at the intracity level (for example, in comparing wards) it is impossible to estimate accurately the relevant school-age population. In sum, enrollment ratios are beset by problems stemming from the noncomparability of schooling figures and population figures, problems that should be recognized but that, for the most part, cannot be resolved.

Shifts in required reporting categories over time. As state school officials came and went, and as their policy interests shifted, they changed the educational items on which towns were required to report. Age categories and other definitions shifted, creating discontinuities in long-range series of school statistics. For some states, such as Wisconsin, numerous inconsistencies in reported categories over time have made the creation of long-range time series on matters like expenditures and teachers virtually impossible. For Massachusetts, the problem has necessitated the kind of statistical estimates and extrapolations discussed in Appendix C.

The major discontinuity in the available Massachusetts data occurred when Barnas Sears succeeded Horace Mann as secretary of the state's board of education. For his second annual report (1849–50), Sears redefined school-age children as those between four and sixteen, rather than those between five and fifteen; he also ceased asking for the length of session of private schools; and he switched from the private to the public category those public schools kept open by subscription beyond the agreed session, the so-called schools kept to prolong the common schools. The latter change is an example of an arbitrary reporting change that could be misinterpreted as a historical change, for it created the illusion of a dramatic decline in enrollment in private unincorporated schools in a single year. In 1848–49 the average enrollment reported for all such schools was 27,583; in 1849–50, after Sears changed the instructions, the average enrollment dropped to 19,534. Actually, Mann and Sears both opposed the long-standing practice of prolonging the common school session by subscription, which accounted for a large share of the so-called private education in Massachusetts before 1850, and the practice did decline as increasing public funds for education allowed increasingly longer regular public school sessions, but the decline was not as dramatic as is suggested by the official enrollment figures, which first aggregated the prolonged common schools with other unincorporated private schools and then, after 1850, lumped them with the tax-supported public schools. Because the shift from private to public schooling is one of the most important trends in nineteenth-century education, we have developed a detailed hypothetical picture of the real trends in private and public education from 1840 to 1850, controlling for Sears's artificial shift of the "prolonged" common schools.

The unreliability of private school data. Private schools were not required to report to the Massachusetts Board of Education. Figures on private schools were collected or estimated by local school committees. In his first annual report, Barnas Sears warned that "the number of children who receive their education in private schools, or at home, is not accurately ascertained. Those who know the summary manner in which committees often arrived at their conclusions in respect to this particular, will use some degree of caution in reasoning from such data."[36]

The paucity and unreliability of private school attendance data is particularly unfortunate in view of two important present concerns about the history of American education: the effect of government intervention either in increasing total school attendance or in shifting control from private to public schools (two distinct processes difficult to separate without adequate private school data), and the growth of the Roman Catholic parochial school system as an alternative to the Protestant-biased public school system.

One cannot create statistics where none exist, though one can sometimes tease enough scattered figures from local sources on private and parochial schools to construct time series where no systematic information has previously been collected. Short of making more such expeditions to unearth the facts of private attendance, we should keep two generalizations in mind: First, school attendance and public school attendance are quite different matters, so we must take care to avoid making generalizations about the former on the basis of data for the latter alone.[37] Second, because figures for private schooling are probably better for later decades than for earlier, we must acknowledge that recorded trends in total enrollment may be biased, underestimating schooling in the early nineteenth century.

Taking all these complications together, we conclude that alleged trends in school attendance may sometimes depend more upon the choice and interpretation of extant data than upon the realities of schooling in the nineteenth century. The margin of error caused by the ambiguities and incompleteness of the data may be greater than the magnitude of some of the trends we are talking about. Thus, to study attendance rates without dealing as explicitly and as sensitively as possible with these problems is not valid and may lead to generalizations no better founded than impressions about attendance based on traditional literary sources. On the other hand, to go into the details of these data problems not only involves us deeper and deeper in a morass of uncertainty but risks the loss of all readers save the most ardent specialists, owing to acute boredom.

Our solution to this dilemma is as follows. We have constructed new time series of trends in Massachusetts school attendance during the formative decades of educational systematization, 1840 to 1880. In doing so we have explored many of the problems cited above. We reserve to the appendixes all the definitions, extrapolations, and explanations of procedure. There the interested reader will find documentation of the trends discussed in the following section. The appendixes also illustrate some of the pitfalls possible in taking official nineteenth-century statistics at face value. Those who wish to forego the task of reading the appendixes should take stern warning that there are discontinuities in the data on school attendance presented in the next section. Although portions of our graphs are based on reported data, for other years the values are hypothetical projections of what we believe happened, based on study of the literary evidence, the instructions to towns for filing school returns, and the detailed manuscript town returns that were used to tabulate the state reports.

The principal trends

State and local school officials wished to see more children in public schools more days each year. Their reasons, if we take them at their word, were to impart to children the intellectual skills necessary for daily life in their society; to produce both intelligent and orderly citizens; to inculcate in children the values and discipline they would need to become productive and moral adults; and to keep children occupied, away from other, less desirable, activities. Our purpose here is not to assess their motives but to assess how well they succeeded in attaining their attendance goals, looking first at the state as a whole during the decades when social changes were diverse and rapid and when state intervention in education increased substantially.

The shift from private to public schooling. Mann and other reformers presented the defeat of private schooling as a major objective. Claiming that "perhaps a majority of the wealthier persons in the state" patronized private schools, Mann argued in his first report that this practice drew off from the public schools some of the best scholars and the support of their influential parents. He believed that it had led to depressed conditions in the public schools and had fostered a divisive

Figure 2.1. Percentage of persons under 20 years of age enrolled in Massachusetts schools, 1840–80 (from Tables A2.2–A2.5)

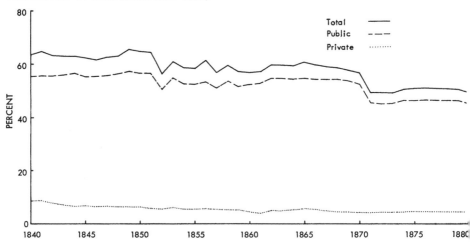

system of sectarian education. "Of such disastrous consequences, there is but one remedy and one preventive. It is the elevation of the common schools."[38] Figures 2.1 and 2.2 show that public school reformers succeeded in their campaign to decrease the proportion of schoolchildren in private schools. In 1840, 13.8 percent of all those enrolled were in private schools; by 1880 the percentage was 8.4. However, the graphs also underscore Mann's basic argument, that the problem was not the *quantity* of students in private schools, which even by 1840 was quite a small proportion of the whole. The problem was rather, *who* those students were, namely, the children of wealthy and influential parents, whose support was needed to develop a truly common school system. Seen in this light, the campaign against private schooling was only partially successful; socially elite parents (as well as others) continue to withdraw their children from the public schools even today. During our period, as Figure 2.2 shows, private schools held their own in absolute numbers; at the same time, the social composition of their clients almost certainly became more elitist.[39] What occurred was not, then, a victory over separate elite schooling, as Mann would have liked, but a conversion of low-priced pay schools, local academies, and subscription schools (kept to prolong the common schools) into town-controlled, tax-supported schools.

Total enrollment. Figure 2.1 shows a slight but steady decline in total

Figure 2.2. Total number of students enrolled in Massachusetts schools, 1840–80 (from Tables A2.3–A2.5)

enrollment levels during these decades. This finding would be surprising to anyone who thought of the common school "revival" as an effort to herd unschooled children into schools. Of course, although the percentage of children in school was declining, the public school system was expanding rapidly, just to keep up with the absolute increase in the number of school-age children and to absorb the relative enrollment shift from private to public schools. In Salem, which had a vigorous private school network in the early nineteenth century, the mayor attributed increasing school expenditures in 1843 to the increasing population and to the shift to public schooling. He predicted that the school budget would continue to be a larger part of the city budget "until the result which seems inevitable should be reached, and all or by far the largest part of the children of the City shall be included within the Public Schools."[40]

Expansion of the public schools, then, was not the result of an increasing percentage of children enrolled. This was disquieting to some. Public anxieties are often based upon percentages (crime rates, employment rates, enrollment rates), not absolute numbers. Thus, despite the much-vaunted expansion of public schooling during this period, the relative decline in annual enrollment rates made some impact on the public mind. We may briefly summarize its probable causes and possible effects as follows.

Why did enrollment levels fail to rise, in a state that was rapidly urbanizing and industrializing, a state that was modernizing its school

35

system and was increasingly willing to legislate on school attendance? First, enrollment was already very high by 1840. Although the rates are biased upward by students migrating through towns, they are nonetheless stated in a way that looks misleadingly low, because they are stated as a percentage of children in the whole age range from birth to nineteen. Obviously we would not expect that a child would go to school from birth until the age of twenty, nor was that a goal of Horace Mann. Enrollment rates were very age-specific and were very high in the middle school-age range of eight to thirteen years old. Thus, for example, although the Essex County total public and private enrollment rate for 1860 was 56 percent, school enrollment among the eight-to thirteen-year-old children (as reported by families in the U.S. census) was over 90 percent, among both urban and rural towns and across all ethnic and occupational groups.[41] To increase total enrollment, then, public policy would have had to be directed mainly at the younger or the older children.

This observation leads us to the second reason that enrollment did not increase. With regard to young children, public policy was aimed in the opposite direction. As we shall see in the next chapter, from the 1840s onward, state officials, medical spokesmen, and others discouraged the attendance of very young children at school, because of the growing belief that school was physically, intellectually, and psychologically harmful to children younger than five or six years of age.

Third, at the upper age range, child labor in mid-nineteenth-century industry increased the opportunity costs of schooling for working-class teenagers, and in many cases teenagers may have preferred work to school quite apart from economic constraints. We can only guess how widely shared in our period were the sentiments of the fourteen-year-old immigrant girl in early twentieth-century Chicago who declared, "Schools is de fiercest t'ing youse kin come up against. Factories ain't no cinch, but school is worst."[42] Even school reformers and town school committees sometimes complained that corporal punishment, dull recitations, and decrepit facilities blunted children's enthusiasm.

The cultural diversity introduced by massive European immigration created a fourth factor. On religious grounds and on general cultural grounds, some immigrants resisted public schooling and, lacking sufficient alternatives, did without. The value placed on schooling in their native countries also probably played a role in the decision of recent immigrants whether to enroll children in schools. This cultural dimension may have reinforced, but was not synonymous with, economic constraints and possible ideological class conflict that reduced the enrollment of working-class teenagers. Although the relative importance of the specific motives is difficult to assess, it may be stated broadly that immigration and industrialization led in the short run to a slight downtrend in annual school enrollments, and that in addition to the strictly economic reasons for individual decisions, there was definitely a cultural and possibly an ideological dimension to nonenrollment.[43]

Finally, although various social reformers of the 1870s and later decades advocated stiffer compulsory school laws and more effective enforcement of those that existed, school officials themselves were ambivalent, and they were sometimes blamed for being lukewarm in their support for universal attendance.[44] Local school administrators bent on perfecting their schemes for classifying students and organizing their schools in the most efficient manner were not at all sure they wanted or could handle the resistant minority of nonattenders, whom they considered the least academically talented and cooperative.

The effects of the slight overall decline in annual enrollment are more difficult to discern. The literature on school reform after the Civil War suggests that public anxiety centered not on the young children at home, who were considered better off with their mothers, nor on working teenagers, whom the state ignored after age fourteen, but rather on the complete truants – the idlers and delinquents neither at home nor at work. Thus, although our time series may provide some quantitative backbone to the urban jeremiads of the 1870s and 1880s, it was probably those irregular attenders and street urchins who prompted public pressure for compulsory attendance legislation, rather than the toddlers at home and teenagers at work, who together constituted the largest share of nonenrolled children.

A more specific effect of the effort to attract nonenrolled students into public schools was the differentiation of curricula and of types of schools. As a way to resolve their ambivalence between an all-encompassing system and a well-ordered system, urban school administrators created special nongraded, segregated alternatives for irregular students, schools designed to keep them enrolled but at the same time to keep them from interrupting and confusing the efficient progress through the system of regular school attenders. Examples include evening schools and half-day schools for working teenagers, as well as intermediate schools to bridge the elementary and grammar levels for irregular attenders. The clients of these schools were often explicitly labeled children from poor families or the children of immigrants. Thus the differentiation process had a decided social as well as bureaucratic effect. School organization, in this as in many other ways, reflected and reinforced social stratification.

Whereas total statewide enrollment was slightly declining during the

Figure 2.3. Average daily public and private attendance as a percentage of all children ages birth to 19, 1840–80 (from Table A2.5)

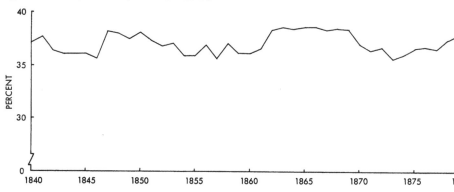

period 1840 to 1880, the average number of school days attended per child in the state, a second key index of the level of education in a society, was increasing. We now turn to a discussion of the two components of that statistic, average daily attendance and length of school session per year.

Average daily attendance. As Figure 2.3 shows, average daily attendance was almost level from 1840 to 1880. The average daily attendance was stable even though total enrollment was declining; average daily attendance as a percentage of total enrollment (rather than of all school-age children) rose from 62.4 at the beginning of the period to 76.4 at the end. Also, average daily attendance held its own despite substantial increases in the school year. We may therefore conclude that the campaign for regularity of attendance, bolstered by the rhetoric of efficiency and morality and encouraged by prizes and honor rolls, had a substantial effect during the period of educational modernization in Massachusetts. Quantitatively, in conjunction with the increasing length of the school year, the stable level of average daily attendance meant that the average Massachusetts child was getting more days of schooling each year.

Length of school year. Our recalculated estimates of the length of the public school year, displayed in Figure 2.4, demonstrate substantial increases in this aspect of school attendance, from 150 days per year in 1840 to 192 days per year in 1880. These estimates do not include private school; the length of session is reported only for public schools

Figure 2.4. Length of Massachusetts public school sessions, 1840–80 (from Table A2.2)

after 1850. However, because private students were a small part of the whole throughout, and private school sessions were much longer than public sessions in the 1840s, when the figures are known, the rise in length of public session is the crucial determinant of increasing average days of school per child during the period. The goal of longer sessions was argued continually as a reason for increased taxes, and it was fostered by the increasing urbanization of the state. Longer school sessions seem to have been more compatible with the lives of urban children than with those of rural children, because of the seasonal nature of agricultural work.

Annual days of schooling per child. The average number of days of school per child is the product of the average daily attendance and the length of the school session. Figure 2.5 demonstrates the rise in this index from 60.6 days in 1840 to 71.6 days in 1879. The immediate reasons have been outlined above: a stable percentage of children in school daily, plus a substantially longer school year – both aspects of the successful school reform program of state officials and of town school committees. Thus, although the total enrollment index went down, the days per capita index rose. Massachusetts could in this

Figure 2.5. Average number of days of public or private school attended per person under 20 years of age in Massachusetts, 1840–80 (from Table A2.5)

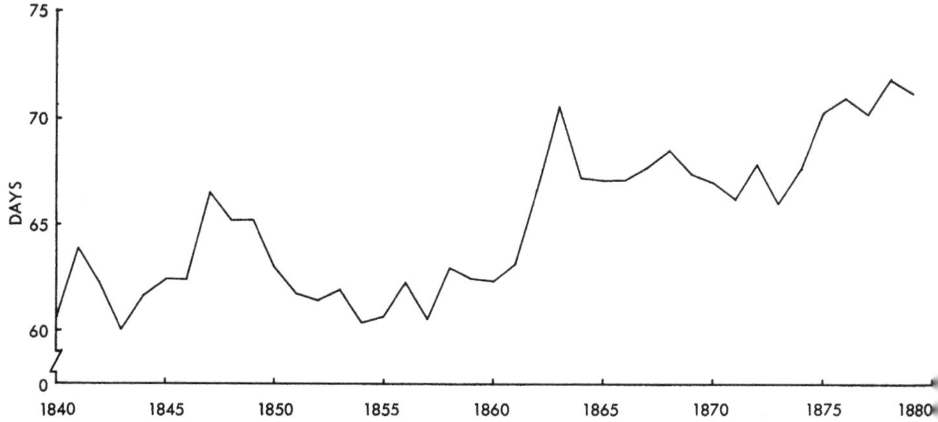

important sense, then, be termed a more "educated" society in 1880 than in 1840.

Some consequences of educational expansion and intensification

We have assessed a wide variety of data about schooling attendance in Massachusetts from the late eighteenth century to 1880. We have concluded that total enrollment rates (and probably the amount of schooling as well) were rising from the late eighteenth century until the 1830s, after which the percentage of children aged birth to nineteen attending school leveled off and even declined slightly. In the period 1840 to 1880, for which better information is available, increasing length of annual school sessions and increasing regularity of attendance resulted in a more intensive schooling experience for those enrolled, and thus a higher per capita consumption of schooling averaged across the whole population from birth to nineteen. We have suggested briefly some of the causes for the expansion of schooling, and we shall pursue these in detail in subsequent chapters.

But education does not merely react to social change; it may also be an agent of change. We may ask not only the causes of educational expansion and intensification but their effects. Unfortunately, neither educational historians nor economic historians have developed very persuasive methods for assessing the effects of rising educational levels, nor does our research contribute directly to this problem. Nonetheless, the trends we have documented have some implications for existing arguments about the contribution of education to economic development and for current work on the evolution of the family. These may serve as a useful prelude to discussions in later chapters about the intentions of educators and the stated purposes of increased schooling.

Leaving aside questions of both the quality and the content of education, economic historians have generally assumed that a quantitative rise in schooling levels *could* have contributed to rising economic productivity, and they have therefore devoted their attention to the magnitude and timing of trends in the two sectors of activity. In his pioneering article, Fishlow took issue with the then scant literature on the role of education in the nineteenth-century American economy. He doubted that antebellum school reform contributed as much to economic activity as some scholars believed twentieth-century schooling had contributed, simply because he found relatively little increase in educational attainment in the Northeast during the so-called revival. Indeed, he found no evidence of expansion in enrollments during the preceding decades, 1800–40. On the other hand, for the nation as a whole, over the whole course of the nineteenth century, Fishlow asserted that educational consumption increased substantially, and he concluded that "education will have to be figured as a considerable factor in nineteenth-century economic development."[45] Subsequent accounts of nineteenth-century American economic growth have reiterated the importance of human capital, even for the early decades, but have left the trends and the specific mechanisms vague.[46] Different economic historians have suggested different ways in which education may have affected productivity: by spreading literacy, increasing the circulation of information, inculcating problem-solving attitudes, creating a meritocratic screening process for talent, fostering innovation, accustoming people to mobility and change, or, quite in contrast, imposing a new, regimented discipline upon workers.[47]

Some of these alleged intentions, for example, work discipline and problem-solving flexibility, are contradictory if aimed at the same group of students. Others, such as the meritocratic selection of talent, display an idealized version of early school systems that is at best imperfectly supported by evidence about how schools actually worked in the early nineteenth century. Granting that schools can perform these diverse functions, if we wish to sharpen our assessment of the relationship between education and the economy, we still need to specify what kinds of education would be salient to economic development in a given period and why. The organization and content of state schooling would necessarily vary to achieve different goals. If widespread rudimentary literacy would enhance economic growth, the most functional educational system would be as inclusive as possible at the lower levels and would emphasize intellectual skills. To the extent that the training of talent is the greatest aggregate economic need, a responsive educational system would be intensive rather than extensive, characterized by meritocratic mobility to secondary education and technical training. If work discipline is the essential requisite to economic growth in a given period, a functional school system would maximize working-class enrollment in the years just before employment and would stress regular attendance and attitudes deemed appropriate by those who control the workplace.

We should delineate the scope and content of schooling in a given period and then ask whether apparent human capital needs of the evolving economy can be linked plausibly to them. When we discover an ostensibly functional relationship between the schools and the evolving economy, we may further ask whether the relationship is accidental, is incidental to other educational purposes, or is the central and deliberate result of policy by economic decision makers. Combining our revised education data with a modicum of knowledge about the economy, we can suggest some partial and tentative answers to these questions for Massachusetts in the nineteenth century.

From the late eighteenth century to the 1830s the major trend in Massachusetts schooling was an increasing rate of total enrollment. The system was becoming more inclusive. On the one hand, then, we have rescued from Fishlow's skepticism the capacity of the local schooling arrangements of this period to expand enrollments just at the right time to educate the generations who participated in the surges of economic growth prior to 1840.[48] On the other hand, when we compare the details of expanded schooling in this period with the needs of the economy, we must confess to some skepticism ourselves.

Because the major trend was toward expanded common school enrollments, not more intensive secondary education, and because the different levels of education were not well coordinated or regulated, little meritocratic selection and training of talent was going on, quite apart from discriminatory attitudes that have always compromised the "sorting" process. Besides, early industrial development did not require upgraded skills; on the contrary, skill requirements were reduced by factory production.[49] As for education spurring inventiveness, such creativity needed to involve only a small elite and hardly needed popular education at all; additionally, America was importing not only ideas but workmen, who brought English innovations with them in this period: Technical innovation was largely derivative in the early

nineteenth century.[50] Further, much of the expanded school enrollment consisted of females. This makes the human capital argument
more complex and indirect. Despite the prominence Lowell mill girls
have played in the historiography of early industrialization, women
constituted a small share of the wage-earning work force before mid-
century. For nonsalaried females the contribution of education to productivity would have to lie in home management, training of children,
or shaping family attitudes about mobility, work, or new procedures.
All of these contributions may have taken place, but they seem to lie
irretrievably in the area of speculation. Finally, whatever difference
education made to economic growth before the 1830s, it was not the
result of deliberate economic policy, because state involvement was
minimal, and few explicit connections between schooling and productivity can be found in the literary evidence prior to the 1830s.[51]

Although our periodization by a watershed in the 1830s runs some
risk of telescoping gradual trends, the intensification and centralization
of education after 1840 were quite different and may have had a different relationship to economic growth. In the period 1840 to 1880, Massachusetts school attendance was characterized by high, roughly stable
annual enrollment rates and by increasing per capita consumption of
schooling. Schools became increasingly bureaucratic and hierarchically structured, rural–urban differences converged, and increasing
attention was devoted to discipline and moral education.[52] These features of the developing school system would seem to lend themselves
to the work-discipline theory, which, briefly stated, asserts that increased general education did not cause the initial shift to wage labor
and factory production but rather the reverse; that is, the evolving
capitalist economy demanded new work attitudes that schools could,
and did, help inculcate. This theory has been stated forcefully in two
recent works dealing with nineteenth-century Massachusetts, Samuel
Bowles and Herbert Gintis's *Schooling in Capitalist America* and
Alexander Field's dissertation, "Educational Reform and Manufacturing Development in Mid-Nineteenth Century Massachusetts."[53]

In our judgment, this previously ignored theme has now been exaggerated. Although there is an element of truth to it, there are a number
of specific problems with the work-discipline thesis as applied to the
educational data of Massachusetts. If one attaches central importance
to expansion of enrollments, as do Bowles and Gintis, one cannot then
claim a surge of schooling in the 1840s and 1850s, coincident with a
critical shift to wage labor. Our data suggest an earlier and more gradual rise of enrollments. As in Vinovskis's earlier compilation of the
data, Field argues that enrollments *were* increasing in the 1840s if we

43

control for age, discounting the drop in schoolchildren under five years of age. Controlling for these children is defensible in assessing the schools' role in work discipline, and it does restore a somewhat positive trend for this decade; however, it does not differentiate the 1840s from the early decades of the century, when, if our analysis is correct, a much more substantial expansion took place. An alternative reformulation would be to suggest that it is not large-scale manufacturing but capitalism – broadly conceived, emphasizing rising productivity and the spread of wage labor – that required new work attitudes, and development of this sort of capitalism did occur gradually over the very period when school enrollments increased substantially in the Northeast. This argument is much more diffuse, however. There is little explicit evidence that contemporary policy makers were aware of the connection, and there is little state intervention in schooling. More important, an emphatic interest in discipline, including industriousness, punctuality, and other virtues associated with work in the industrial world, accompanied the invigorated state interest in schooling after 1830.

A third alternative, then, would be to return to the 1840s and 1850s as a focal point and attribute to economic development not enrollments but the increasing attention educators gave to character formation, regularity, and punctuality. Here indeed is where the work-discipline thesis best matches specific and deliberate developments in schooling with the apparent human capital needs of the economy. Then, we must ask, was the connection incidental, or was it a crucial intention of educational policy? The question cannot be answered with precision, but a central causal relationship between changing work roles and the content of schooling is suspect. First, the surge of interest in moral discipline is attributable to several factors, such as urban disorder, Jacksonian malaise, immigration, pedagogical theories, and the bureaucratic nature of schools, and these are more prominent in discussions of schooling than is behavior in the workplace.[54] Second, the best place to learn productive behavior for a factory is in a factory, even according to the latest modernization studies.[55] Third, although Horace Mann's work was supported by an industrialist patron, Edmund Dwight, manufacturers in general were not very active in promoting school reform in Massachusetts.[56] School discipline was consonant with time–work discipline in the mid-nineteenth century, but with or without the schools' contribution, manufacturers probably would have attained similar behavior through the training and sanctions of the workplace itself.

Despite the importance of the socioeconomic context for the history of education, therefore, we must not overestimate the tightness of the links between economy and education. The connections were multiple and to a large extent indirect. Schools and school spokesmen responded to needs articulated by social elites and widely supported in nineteenth-century Massachusetts: the need for restraint, cohesion, and communication in a society ever more demographically expansive, technically complex, ethnically diverse, and economically stratified. In return, education may have had some general role in economic development, by expanding literacy and shaping attitudes, throughout our period. Perhaps the increasing per capita level of schooling by 1880 helped lay the human-capital groundwork for later stages of industrialization, which – unlike the initial industrialization of the antebellum period – did increase skill requirements for many workers and expanded the white-collar service sector of the occupational structure. Even for the late nineteenth century, however, we must agree with Richard Easterlin that "knowledge concerning the effect of education on economic growth is still far from adequate."[57]

Turning from the relationships between schooling and the economy, we shall inquire in the next two chapters about the relationships between schooling and the family. Here, at least, one change is clear: the increased time spent in school signified a custodial shift from family to school, an increasing shift of authority and responsibility from parent to teacher, a widespread and seemingly irreversible increase in the extent of state intervention in the rearing of children.

As with the economy, however, the relationship is more complex. It is not a mere aggrandizement of the school at the expense of familial responsibility. In some respects school officials and other commentators urged families to give more attention to education, especially in the case of young children. In our next chapter we analyze the gradual redefinition of parental and school roles in the lives of children from age two to age six.

3

From apron strings to ABCs: school entry in nineteenth-century Massachusetts

Despite periodic enthusiasm for infant schools, kindergartens, and Head Start programs, progressive educational thought in America has not always endorsed early schooling. In the period from 1830 to 1880, educational spokesmen and medical authorities counseled against the school education of children between the ages of two and four or even five, and they waged a slow but successful battle with parents to keep children of those ages at home. Although in the early nineteenth century it was normal for very young children to attend dame schools, infant schools, or district schools, by the mid-nineteenth century educators counseled against sending three- or four-year-olds to any school. Furthermore, whereas in the late eighteenth and early nineteenth centuries children were encouraged to learn to read at an early age, by the mid-nineteenth century educators argued that children should not engage in such disciplined intellectual activities too early.

Children, parents, and the schools in colonial Massachusetts

Education had been one of the cornerstones of Puritan society. Because the Puritans believed that reading and understanding the Bible were essential to the religious development of their children, they considered it important to insure opportunities for rudimentary education. Early leaders in Massachusetts assumed that parents would instruct their children in reading and writing, as well as in religion. They expected parents to catechize their children at home as a normal part of their initial religious training. Although the primary locus of education for the Puritans was the family, the state was willing to intervene when families failed to educate their children.[1]

The Puritans' earliest organized educational efforts were directed at Harvard and the town grammar schools, which prepared children for the university. A few towns, such as Salem, did maintain petty or dame schools to teach children reading and writing, but most towns simply assumed that the parents rather than the school would instruct children in the rudiments of literacy. By the mid-1640s, it was evident that many Massachusetts towns needed schools to supplement familial training. As a result, the Massachusetts General Court in 1647 enacted a law that required the establishment of schools for reading and writing in towns with fifty or more households, and grammar schools in towns with a hundred or more households.[2] Parents were not, however, required to send their children to school if the children were being trained at home. The law of 1647 is a good indication of the attitude of the Puritan leadership toward schools, but it was never vigorously enforced. In a comprehensive survey of seventeenth-century education in the Massachusetts Bay Colony, Geraldine Murphy found that all of the eight towns required to maintain grammar schools did so, whereas only a third of the towns required to establish reading and writing schools complied with the law.[3] Colonial Massachusetts had taken a step toward the creation of a school system, but the amount and type of formal education available in the towns varied widely.

No systematic records exist to measure the impact and extent of children's education at home or in school in colonial Massachusetts. However, we can assess the state of elementary education indirectly by looking at estimates of literacy. In the most recent analysis, Kenneth Lockridge uses signatures on wills as a crude index of literacy in colonial New England. His study demonstrates that there was a significant difference between the signature literacy of men and of women in colonial New England (see Figure 3.1). In samples of the early settlers, about 60 percent of the men and 30 percent of the women could sign their wills. There was a steady increase in both male and female literacy during the colonial period; by 1789 about 90 percent of the males and almost 50 percent of the females in New England could sign their wills.[4] If Lockridge's estimates do approximate the actual levels of literacy in colonial New England, they demonstrate that not everyone in early Massachusetts received a rudimentary education. A significant proportion of the population, especially among females, could not even sign their own names. This was particularly true of the rural population; the literacy rate in Boston was higher for both males and females than in the countryside.

We must bear in mind, however, that the Puritans stressed the importance of reading, not writing. For example, when Watertown officials admonished parents for not educating their children, they focused only on the ability to read: "William Priest, John Fisk, and George Lawrence, being warned to a meeting of the Selectmen . . . were admonished for not learning their children to read the English tongue: were convinced, did acknowledge their neglects, and did promise

Figure 3.1. Estimated percentages of literacy from signatures on New England wills, 1650–70, 1705–15, 1758–63, and 1787–95 (from Kenneth A. Lockridge, *Literacy in Colonial New England: An Enquiry into the Social Context of Literacy in the Early Modern West* [New York: W. W. Norton, 1974], pp. 17–19, 38–39.

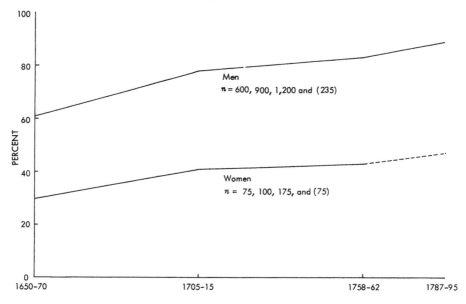

amendment.''[5] Consequently, we may speculate that some of the colonial New Englanders who could not write may have had an elementary ability to read. Some scholars have argued that the writing skill of a population is usually below its reading ability.[6] It is therefore possible that estimates of New England signature literacy underestimate the minimal ability to read. On the other hand, the attainment rate for the level of functional literacy necessary to read and understand the Bible might be considerably lower than the signature rate. The problem, obviously, is that although illiteracy is absolute, literacy is a matter of degree. As elusive as the numerical levels are, it seems reasonable to assume that trends in reading skills paralleled trends in signature literacy.[7]

Unfortunately, there is even less evidence about the means of acquiring literacy than there is about its extent. In general, it seems that children were taught initial reading skills at home, though some went to private dame schools or were taught by the local minister. Most of the towns that provided schools for reading and writing expected entering children to have already acquired the rudiments of reading. The relative role of fathers and mothers in educating the child within the home is unclear. Nineteenth-century Americans stressed the mother's role in childhood education, but the larger share of educating children in colonial New England probably fell to the father. For example, according to a 1648 law, the master of the house was expected to catechize the children and servants each week.[8] Whether the father was also expected to teach the children the rudiments of reading and writing is not clear, but because males were more often literate than females in colonial New England, there was little choice in many households about which parent would instruct the young child.

Colonial New Englanders did not devote much attention to the age at which their children should learn to read and write. Apparently they assumed that children should learn to read as soon as possible in order to prepare themselves for salvation in the next world. As Cotton Mather put it, "The *Children* should *learn to read* the *Holy Scriptures;* and this, as *Early* as may be . . ."[9] In Puritan doctrine children were innately stubborn and evil; they therefore needed to be strictly disciplined and controlled at a very early age. Though sinful, children were also treated as more mature individuals than in modern society. John Demos has aptly summarized the nature of childhood in colonial America:

Colonial society barely recognized childhood as we know and understand it today. Consider, for example, the matter of dress; in virtually all seventeenth-century portraiture, children appear in the same sort of clothing that was normal for adults. In fact, this accords nicely with what we know of other aspects of the child's life. His work, much of his recreation, and his closest personal contacts were encompassed within the world of adults . . . In short, from his earliest years he was expected to be – or try to be – a miniature adult.[10]

This does not mean that the New England colonists did not see childhood as separate from adulthood. In fact, they treated children below the age of six or seven differently from older children. Very young children were not expected to be as diligent in their studies and work as older ones. Nevertheless, they believed that young children were capable of more extensive intellectual development than did mid-nineteenth-century educators. As a result, children often learned to read at ages three and four and some even received training in Latin at ages five and six. Parents encouraged their children to learn at such ages and proudly gloated over their early accomplishments.[11] John Locke had a more positive conception of childhood than the Puritans, but his essay on education was widely read and quoted in colonial New England, and it too counseled early literacy:

When he can talk, 'tis time he should begin to learn to read. But as to this, give me leave here to inculcate again what is apt to be forgotten, viz., that great care is to be taken that it be never made as a business to him nor he look on it as a task . . . children may be cozened into a knowledge of the letters, be taught to read without perceiving it to be anything but a sport, and play themselves into that which others are whipped for.[12]

To summarize, although the relationship between family and school was quite flexible in colonial Massachusetts, there was a general agreement on the importance of education. Puritans assumed that parents should educate their own children, but the state was willing to intervene to force negligent parents either to teach their children at home or to send them to a local school. In addition, the Massachusetts colonists were agreed on the importance of learning to read early, because the ability to read the Bible was an essential prerequisite for the salvation of their children and for the survival of their "errand in the wilderness."

Education in early nineteenth-century Massachusetts

The relationships among children, parents, and schools in the early nineteenth century were the result of the colonial heritage as well as new social conditions. Although some fundamental assumptions about education remained unchanged, others were gradually altered. For example, education in seventeenth-century Massachusetts had been justified explicitly and centrally by religious purposes. Although Puritan orthodoxy also served the earthly purposes of political and social stability, nonetheless education was vitally preoccupied with the process of salvation. By the early nineteenth century, the Calvinist hegemony had ended, and the relationship between the church and education had changed. Massachusetts society was still deeply religious, but the new conditions of denominationalism encouraged an increasing secularization of public life and public policy. The rationale for public schools by then included direct attention to the preservation of political and social order. The justification for the state commitment to education in the Massachusetts Constitution of 1780 stressed the political rather than the religious benefits of an educated public.[13]

Although the diverse churches of nineteenth-century Massachusetts agreed on the value of education, they could not agree on its content. The only way that the public schools could avoid endless and bitter sectarian battles was to eliminate all teaching that favored the distinctive views of any religious group. Thus, although early public school advocates acknowledged the connection between religion and moral training, they urged teachers to avoid detailed religious instruction within the classroom.[14] The development of a pan-Protestant morality, free from doctrinal dispute, was a prerequisite to the development of the extensive state school system of the mid-nineteenth century.

There was also a significant change in religious thought about the nature of young children. Infant depravity came under strong attack by Unitarians such as William Ellery Channing, and New England's population became leavened with non-Calvinists who did not share the tradition. Increasingly, those who wrote about children viewed them as innocent beings who had to be protected and nurtured rather than subdued and disciplined. Although the doctrine of infant depravity lingered, most writers gradually deemphasized the innate wickedness of young children. Significantly, both the proponents and the opponents of infant damnation began to view childhood as a distinct phase of human development that required special attention and training. Child-rearing techniques grounded in an Enlightenment view of innocent childhood gained currency even among those who did not share the presupposition.[15]

Another key change was the great expansion in the number of schools in the commonwealth. The Puritans' seventeenth-century laws had provided the skeleton of a statewide school system, but the effort was largely unsuccessful. Then, as we saw in Chapter 2, a combination of demographic, economic, and intellectual factors in the late eighteenth and early nineteenth centuries spawned an extensive, decentralized network of public and private district schools in Massachusetts.

Parents increasingly relied on schools to teach their children, both boys and girls, to read and write. In most towns there were no rigid rules about the age at which children could or should attend school, and many attended as early as age three or four. The Massachusetts state law of 1789 did insist, however, that children enrolling in grammar school should already be able to read and write. This latter requirement posed a problem in Boston, where the town initially financed the grammar schools but not the primary schools. The ensuing debate illustrates attitudes toward urban schooling in the early years of the nineteenth century. Critics alleged that many poor children never received an adequate education because their parents could not afford to send them to a private school to learn to read and write in order to qualify for admission to the grammar schools. However, a subcommittee appointed by the Boston School Committee in 1817 to investigate this matter concluded that public primary schools were not necessary.

For children under the ages of seven years, it is true, no schools are main-tained at the public expense. But experience has proved in past times, and it has been demonstrated by the present inquiry to the satisfaction of the sub-committee, that this class of children with us is not neglected. Perhaps as large a proportion of them enjoy the advantages of instruction as would avail them-selves of it if schools were maintained in sufficient number by the public treasury. The system of small private schools for pupils of this description, supported by the parents, operates upon them as a tax, which, however, is not very unequal or burdensome . . . The sub-committee believe that most parents have some leisure, and that with us few are unequal to the task of teaching the elements of letters. It ought never to be forgotten that the office of instruction belongs to parents, and that to the schoolmaster is delegated a portion only of the parental character and rights. In the retirement of domestic life, parents have opportunities to impart instruction, and to gain an influence over their children which the public teacher does not possess.[16]

Although opponents of public primary schools in Boston argued that parents could educate their own children at home, they assumed that in fact most parents would send their children to a private school. Indeed, the subcommittee conducted a survey of young children which confirmed that most Boston children ages four to six were already attending such schools.[17] Although the colonial notion that parents should teach their own children had not disappeared, few parents any longer fully educated their own children in the rudiments of literacy. The debate in Boston was really over who should finance the schools rather than over the usefulness or desirability of primary schools for young children. The argument that private schooling charges were an unfair burden on the poor finally prevailed, and in 1818 the city agreed to provide free primary schools for children four to six years of age.

The creation of primary schools in Boston accounted for part of the shift from private to public education. Whereas 61.8 percent of all children in school in 1817 attended a private institution, that figure had dropped to 32.5 percent by 1826. Nevertheless, private schools were still an important factor in educating young children in the metropolis. Of the children ages four to six in school, 22.4 percent of the males and 31.4 percent of the females were still in private schools.[18] Further-more, the private schools continued to enroll children younger than four, whom the public primary schools excluded. In 1826 about 5 per-cent of the city's children under four (or approximately 20 percent of the three-year-olds) were enrolled in private schools.[19] Because most other Massachusetts towns did not bar children under four years of age from entering their public schools, it is likely that a sizable proportion of three-year-olds were enrolled. The idea that children could and should be educated at very young ages persisted in early nineteenth-century Massachusetts; increasingly, our evidence suggests that education took place in schools.

The idea of educating very young children in school received a great boost in the late 1820s with the introduction and spread of infant schools in America. Infant schools had been first developed in Europe to educate poor children, and the idea quickly attracted notice in the United States. The first infant schools in Massachusetts were opened in Boston in 1828 and were intended to educate poor children between eighteen months of age and the time they could legally enter the public schools. Although some expressed skepticism about the value of these new institutions, many parents and educators warmly greeted them.[20] As one Boston newspaper responded, after a visit to a local infant school in 1829:

> Infants, taken from the most unfavorable situation in which they are ever placed, from the abodes of poverty and vice, are capable of learning at least a hundred times as much, a hundred times as well, and of being a hundred times as happy, by the system adopted in infant schools, as by that which prevails in the common schools throughout the country.[21]

The amazing thing about the infant school movement in America is how rapidly communities adopted the innovation. In contrast to the hostility that greets many new ideas in education, infant schools were welcomed not only in Massachusetts's cities, but also in rural communities like Concord. There are several possible explanations for the rapid spread of these institutions. First, infant schools were strongly endorsed and actively promoted by such educational reformers as William Russell, editor of the influential *Journal of American Education.* In addition, a number of popular journals, such as the *Ladies' Magazine,* and many local newspapers endorsed the movement. Another reason for the rapid spread of infant schools is that their establishment required very little money or expertise. An enthusiast could purchase one of the many published infant school manuals and set up a school with no training and little expenditure. As the *Boston Recorder* said, "In any school district where there is interest and liberality enough to raise Ten Dollars to procure apparatus, a beginning can be made the present season."[22]

The infant school movement also benefited from the general climate favoring reform and institution building in Massachusetts at this time. It was a period of great optimism that society could eliminate problems like crime and poverty through reform efforts. Some supporters of infant education were able to draw upon their experiences in the Sunday school movement, another educational venture aimed at the poor.

Furthermore, they were helped in all these efforts by the willingness of the churches to support new attempts to alleviate poverty.

It is a familiar fact today that if programs designed to give disadvantaged children a head start appear to be successful, they are often adopted by middle- and upper-class parents for their own children. Similarly, although infant schools in Boston were originally opened to assist the children of the poor, the enthusiasm rapidly spread to the rest of the population. The *Ladies' Magazine* reported in February 1829:

The interesting subject of Infant schools is becoming more and more fashionable . . . We have been told that it is now in contemplation, to open a school for the infants of others besides the poor. If such course be not soon adopted, at the age for entering primary schools those *poor* children will assuredly be the *richest* of scholars. And why should a plan which promises so many advantages, independent of merely relieving the mother from her charge, be confined to children of the indigent?[23]

Thus, in addition to the philanthropically supported infant schools provided for the poor, there were soon many independent, private-venture infant schools. Because they were not regulated or licensed, private schools in general were easy to create in the early nineteenth century. A person simply declared himself a teacher, acquired some students, and established a "school" either in his home or in rented space in a nearby building.

One might expect that the existing public schoolteachers would have been hostile to a new idea like infant education. But few teachers had taught very long or planned to make teaching their career. Therefore, there was relatively little entrenched opposition to the idea of infant education among them.[24] Furthermore, most schools were operated very casually with few procedures and little bureaucracy. Only in Boston was there a very elaborate school system under the control of a central school committee. It is interesting to note that the Boston Primary School Committee did oppose the introduction of infant education in the public schools – mainly because the manner in which children were being taught in many infant schools directly challenged the more traditional methods employed in the Boston schools. The Boston primary schools taught young children only reading and writing, and the school committee constantly resisted efforts to expand their basic curriculum beyond these intellectual rudiments. Furthermore, the committee was reluctant to adopt a new program that might increase the overall tax burden of the city by attracting more students to its classrooms. Thus infant schools could be seen as clashing with the recently established Boston primary school system. But in most Massachusetts towns, the curriculum as well as the control of schools was much more casual and open to innovations.

A final reason for the quick adoption of infant schools in Massachusetts was that most parents already accepted the idea of educating very young children in school. We have seen that some three-year-olds and many four-year-olds were attending school long before the infant education movement reached America. Therefore, it is not surprising that parents were willing to send their children to the new infant schools.

It is impossible to gauge the precise impact of the infant school movement on the enrollment of young children in school in Massachusetts. Much depends upon our estimate of the number of children under four in schools in the first two decades of the nineteenth century, before the arrival of the infant school movement. Unfortunately, little systematic information on the age structure of school attendance in these decades has been preserved. Our tentative conclusion is that children under four were commonly sent to school in early nineteenth-century Massachusetts, but that the infant school movement significantly increased the popularity of the practice, not just in special infant schools, but in other schools as well. Our detailed analysis of school registers for Concord and Worcester public schools in the 1830s shows many children ages two and three enrolled.[25] Furthermore, though the infant school movement in Massachusetts was in rapid decline by 1840, in that year at least 10 percent of the state's children under four years of age were still enrolled in the public schools.[26]

Although infant education followed in a tradition of educating very young children, many of its supporters advocated new methods of instruction. They saw early childhood as a distinct stage of development. Because young children were not fully developed intellectually, emotionally, or physically, it was important that they not be taught in the same way as older children. The proper education of young children demanded that as much attention be devoted to their physical and moral development as to their intellectual growth. The European advocates of infant schools were split on the issue of how much intellectual activity young children should experience. Some leaders of the movement, like Samuel Wilderspin, encouraged the schools to teach very young children how to read. Others, such as Robert Owen, felt that books should be entirely excluded from infant schools. However, even Owen was forced to compromise his position on reading because of the pressure from parents. His son noted in 1823:

It has been deemed necessary, in order to meet the wishes of the parents, to commence teaching the children the elements of reading at a very early age, but it is intended that this mode should ultimately be superseded, at least until the age of seven or eight, by a regular course of Natural History, Geography, Ancient and Modern History, Chemistry, Astronomy, etc., on the principle that it is following the plan prescribed by Nature to give a child such particulars as he can easily be made to understand concerning the *nature and properties* of the different objects around him before we proceed to teach him the *artificial signs* which have been adopted to represent these objects.[27]

Despite this theoretical underpinning for a new pedagogy, and despite the perception of the Boston Primary School Committee that infant schools were a threatening innovation, the manner in which most infant schools demonstrated their achievements to the general public in Massachusetts emphasized the children's intellectual skills and encouraged parents to interpret infant schools simply as an improved form of intellectual education. Ironically, the view that infant schools were mainly an effort to teach children to read and write at very early ages contributed to their demise, for educational writers soon turned against the instruction of young children in reading and writing.

Reactions against the enrollment of young children in school

The sources of the opposition to early intellectual training were quite varied, but at least three major considerations were involved: first, the growing emphasis on childhood education at home, reinforced by increasing stress on the role of mothers in the home; second, the stress on the need for gradual and balanced child development, including the fear that excessive intellectual activity at a very young age might cause insanity; and third, the emerging bureaucratic structure of public schooling.

In colonial Massachusetts, as we have seen, the role of parents in the education of their children had been stressed. By the early nineteenth century, however, most parents in fact had relegated to schools the education of their children at early ages. In the late 1820s and 1830s, there was a strong revival of the idea that young children should be educated at home. The revival was based both on an emerging view of early childhood as innocent and pliant and on an emerging definition of women's function in the nineteenth century. Building upon the views of such Founding Fathers as Benjamin Rush about women's role in the education of future citizens, the domestic literature that poured from American presses in the 1830s encouraged mothers to devote themselves to the training of their children. Child-rearing manuals provided mothers with extensive advice on how to raise their children in an increasingly complex society where traditional values and practices were being eroded by urban and industrial growth. The domestic literature argued that more effective child-rearing efforts in the home could help prevent the further moral and spiritual deterioration of American society.[28]

Although neither the family nor society as a whole was "disintegrating" in Jacksonian America, some important shifts of function were occurring. The increasing separation of home and workplace removed husbands from the family and reduced wives' role in material production. The domestic literature can be seen as an attempt to redress this functional imbalance by defining an enhanced affective and educational role for the mothers of young children. The writers of domestic tracts were seldom explicit about such a connection between increasingly larger, remote workplaces for employed workers and new domestic roles for wives and mothers. Yet the notion that the "cult of domesticity" acted as an ideological rationalization for the new, differentiated gender roles encouraged by industrialization is plausible. The changing structure of the workplace is not a sufficient explanation of the changing theological, medical, and pedagogical ideas embodied in domestic education literature, but it does place the literature in a socioeconomic context, a context that predisposed people to accept some ideas more readily and enthusiastically than others. It also helps explain the sense of urgency in social commentators' discussions of domestic roles for women during this period. However, we should not assume that the decline of household manufactures actually left many women so idle that they needed their domestic roles redefined. We must not underestimate the amount of work required of most working-class and even middle-class wives, to raise children, shop, cook, and wash, with less help from older children or other relatives, who were increasingly in school longer or employed for wages outside the home.[29] The impact of domesticity literature on such stubborn realities remains unknown. Nonetheless, we do know that books and periodicals elaborating the ideal were in wide circulation, and we know that they had an effect on an institution other than the family: the school.

The renewed interest in home education placed the supporters of infant schools in an ambiguous and uncomfortable position. At first, they had argued that their schools were mainly intended as a substitute family for poor children from unsatisfactory families. As the number of infant schools expanded and middle-class parents began to send their own children to these new institutions, their supporters stressed their similarity to the home and the ways in which they complemented the efforts of the mother. Yet the reformers were not clear about the exact relationship among parents, young children, and infant schools, and when hostility developed against early childhood schooling in the 1830s, many middle-class parents abandoned infant schools in favor of more extensive education of children within the home.

The second major factor that contributed to the growing reluctance of educators to have very young children in school was the growing emphasis on the necessity for the gradual and balanced development of children. One of the foremost educational theorists of the early nineteenth century was Johann Heinrich Pestalozzi. Knowledge of his writings spread rapidly throughout Europe and to the United States. Pestalozzi argued that a child's development must not be unnaturally hurried by either parents or schools. "All instruction of man," he wrote, "is only the Art of helping Nature to develop in her own way; and this Art rests essentially on the relation and harmony between the impressions received by the child and the exact degree of his developed powers."[30] Pestalozzi stressed the importance of the physical development of children; a child's intellect should not be overextended before his mind and body had been sufficiently developed physically. This viewpoint was quickly popularized in America in the 1830s by William Woodbridge, who succeeded Russell as the editor of the *American Journal of Education*. Woodbridge felt that the training of young children should begin early but that their education should reflect their stages of physical and intellectual development. Efforts to produce child prodigies would only result in an unnatural, asymmetrical development of the child that might produce permanent damage.[31] Thus, whereas colonial Americans had praised the intellectual achievements of very young children, by 1830 many writers began to emphasize the importance of more gradual, balanced development. As early as 1827 the *American Journal of Education* was advising "misguided" parents not to teach infants their letters, lest they suffer that "fatal languor arising from premature application." In 1831 the *American Annals of Education* ran a series on Fellenberg, in which it was emphasized that "physical education occupies a most important place in the system of Hofwyl . . . It is justly regarded as the base of success in other branches of education." In 1834, Dr. J. V. C. Smith cited other European examples to the same effect. New England schools that drilled children of two, three, and four years of age were doing something "diametrically opposed to the clearest indications of nature." He continued:

Do not urge on the mind for the present. Take care of the body . . . Adopt the plan of the Infant Asylum of Geneva and some others in Europe, which aim chiefly at the physical health and enjoyment of the pupils, and give them only as much intellectual occupation as their feeble minds and immature bodies can endure.[32]

Some theorists even believed that premature intellectual development might cause insanity. This concept was most clearly and forcefully stated by a physician, Amariah Brigham, in his popular book *Remarks on the Influence of Mental Excitement upon Health* (1832):

Many physicians of great experience are of the opinion, that efforts to develope the minds of young children are very frequently injurious; and from instances of disease in children which I have witnessed, I am forced to believe that the danger is indeed great, and that very often in attempting to call forth and cultivate the intellectual faculties of children before they are six or seven years of age, serious and lasting injury has been done both to the body and the mind . . .

I beseech parents, therefore, to pause before they attempt to make prodigies of their own children. Though they may not destroy them by the measures they adopt to effect this purpose, yet they will surely enfeeble their bodies, and greatly dispose them to nervous affections. Early mental excitement will serve only to bring forth beautiful, but premature flowers, which are destined soon to wither away, without producing fruit.[33]

Brigham's book had a large impact on attitudes toward early childhood education in America. It was reviewed very favorably in popular journals such as the *American Annals of Education,* the *Christian Examiner and General Reviewer,* and the *Ladies' Magazine.* Many shared Brigham's fears. An article reprinted from the *London Christian Observer* labeled intellectual precocity "a disease," which could lead to "future imbecility or premature old age." Samuel Woodward, warning of the dangers of confining children under the age of eight in school for more than one hour at a time, argued that "intensity" might lead to precocity, which was a "morbid condition" of the brain that might lead to "epilepsy, insanity or imbecility."[34] Despite the protests of the supporters of infant schools that their institutions did not really overemphasize the intellectual development of the young child, there was increased public suspicion and hostility toward the infant schools. Many of the middle-class reformers who had financed the infant schools withdrew their support. As a result, infant schools in Massachusetts found it more and more difficult to survive financially.[35]

The hostility toward early education also became increasingly evident in the domestic literature of the 1830s and 1840s. Previous advocates of early childhood education, such as Lydia Sigourney, now reversed themselves: "I once admired precosity [*sic*], and viewed it as the breath of Deity, quickening to ripe and rare excellence. But I have since learned to fear it."[36] Similarly, Heman Humphrey in his popular advice book in 1840 observed that

it is obvious how difficult a task it must be, to persuade parents to let their sprightly little darling alone, till the rain and the sunshine have opened the bud and prepared the way for mental culture . . . the common idea, that if you can teach an infant to read with considerable ease . . . in its third or four year, it is . . . so much clear gain, is extremely fallacious.[37]

Humphrey formalized the new concept of early childhood by positing three stages prior to adulthood: infancy (from birth to age four or five), childhood (to age ten or eleven), and youth (to age seventeen, eighteen, or nineteen). During infancy, he argued, intellectual training is unsafe; infants should play while parents guard against "hurtful extraneous influences."[38]

Educators increasingly began to warn parents of the harmful physical as well as mental effects of sending their children to school too early. The local school committee in Weymouth protested in 1840 against attendance of sixty-six children under the age of four. Their teachers were not nurses, they said, and parents who sent such young children to school should understand that it was "generally injurious to the child's mental and physical frame."[39] Similarly, the local school committee in Sandisfield that same year objected to the practice of sending children to school when they were only two or three years old:

In such cases, an injury is inflicted upon both the child and the school. The child is injured by being confined for several hours, upon the hard benches and the impure air of the house, – and the school is injured, by having a considerable portion of the instructor's time occupied in endeavoring to teach, and especially to govern, such children . . . The proper order is, to begin with the education of the body, and then proceed to that of the *mind*. The practice of sending children, two or three years old, to school, to "get them out of the way," cannot be too much deprecated. Every teacher, it should be remembered, is employed to *give instruction, not to act the part of a nurse.*[40]

At first, school officials concentrated only on excluding children under four from the public schools, but by the 1850s educators did not want even four- or five-year-olds to attend school. Barnas Sears, secretary of the Massachusetts Board of Education, wrote in his annual report for 1851–2 that "education in its widest sense commences as soon as one is born. From that time till the school-going age, which with most children does not properly begin till after they are six years old, the freedom and activity natural to childhood may better be accorded to it than denied."[41]

Thus we have witnessed a major change during the first half of the nineteenth century in the age at which educators, physicians, and authors of child-care manuals thought children should be engaged in such intellectual activities as reading, as well as in the age at which they should enter schools. Because the third major reason for the exclusion of young children from schools – the increasingly bureaucratic structure of schools – became more evident after mid-century, we postpone discussion of this factor until after we have assessed parents' reactions to the educators' initial shift of opinion.

Patterns of enrollment of young children, 1840–1900

During the 1830s and 1840s educators strongly urged parents not to allow their children to engage in strenuous intellectual activities at an early age and not to send them to school until they were five or six. But did parents actually heed the warnings of these authorities? One of the major limitations of using such historical materials as child-care manuals or reports of school superintendents is that they provide information only on the recommendations of specialists, not on the actual practices of parents. Because there are no extensive historical surveys of the manner in which parents raised their children in nineteenth-century America, historians have not been able to determine how closely parents conformed to the advice literature on child care. In the case of school attendance, however, we are fortunate to have behavioral evidence to compare with our literary sources. We investigated the extent of school attendance by young children in Massachusetts from 1840 to 1900 to see whether the dire warnings against sending young children to school were effective. This provided us an opportunity to see if changes in the pattern of school attendance of young children coincided with the growing opposition among child-care specialists against the education of very young children. Parents were probably the major factor in deciding when their youngsters should be sent to school. Although Boston officials did not permit children under five to enroll in its primary schools, most public schools in the 1830s and 1840s did not systematically regulate age of entry. In 1839, Horace Mann, the secretary to the board of education, summarized the situation thus:

> Exclusive regulations, founded on age, exist in but very few towns – probably in not more than fifteen or twenty – in the State. And although the great majority of the children in the schools are between the ages of four and sixteen, yet in almost all the towns, they are allowed to attend both earlier and later, and they are found from three, and sometimes from two years of age up to twenty-one, very frequently, and sometimes to twenty-four or twenty-five.[42]

We conclude, therefore, that school attendance rates for young children principally reflect parental attitudes and needs.

The Massachusetts Board of Education required towns to submit annual statistics on the number of children under four years of age attending public schools; after 1848–9 the school returns were revised to ascertain the number of children under five years of age in public schools, reflecting the rising expected age of entry. The answers to this question somewhat underestimate the extent of schooling for young children because information was not obtained from the private schools on this matter. However, because the percentage of children in private schools was small by 1840 (see Chapter 2), the returns for the public schools provide a valid approximation of the statewide trend in the school enrollment of very young children during these years. Using population estimates based on the federal and state censuses, we estimated the percentage of children under four (or five) years of age in public schools from 1840 to 1900 (see Figure 3.2).

There is a steady decline in the percentage of children under four years of age in public school between 1839–40 and 1848–9, the last year for which information on the number of children under four was obtained. The percentage of children under five in public school declined from 15.6 in 1849–50 to .6 in 1888–9. Then there was a gradual rise in the percentage of children under five in public school to 3.5 in 1899–1900 – in large part because of the development of kindergartens for young children in Massachusetts after the Civil War.

The percentage of young children attending school was declining during the period of opposition to the education of very young children. This suggests that parents might have been responding to the warnings of educators, physicians, and other theorists. Yet it is also important to observe how gradual was the shift in the pattern of school attendance during these years and how high were the absolute levels of attendance among young children. Even though Amariah Brigham and others condemned in the early 1830s the practice of sending young children to school, almost 40 percent of three-year-old children were still enrolled in public schools in 1839–40. In other words, although some parents were influenced by the warnings against early childhood education, most parents were very slow to remove their young children from the public schools.

Using this town-level information, we can infer with somewhat greater certainty that the gradual decline occurring in the 1840s resulted from parental decisions, not from local school committees that actually prevented young children from enrolling in the public schools. We calculated the percentage of towns that had no children under four

Figure 3.2. Percentage of young children enrolled in Massachusetts public schools, 1840–1900 (from Table A3.1)

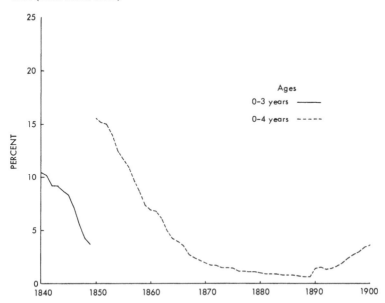

in their public schools, in order to establish the maximum percentage of towns that effectively regulated minimum entry age. In 1840–1, only 6.8 percent of Massachusetts towns did not have any children under four in public school, whereas in 1847–8 that figure had risen to 13.4 percent. To see how much of the decline in the percentage of children under four in public schools might have been the result of changes in the number of towns that prohibited very young children from attending school, we calculated the decrease in the absolute number of children under four in public schools from 1840–1 to 1847–8. Approximately 80 percent of that decline occurred in towns that still permitted children under four to be in public schools in 1847–8. Thus it appears that at mid-century most Massachusetts parents still decided when they should start sending their children to the public schools.

Despite the consensus among educators that early childhood education was harmful, local school committees were reluctant to compel parents to keep their children at home. Similarly, although Barnas Sears strongly condemned sending children to school at an early age, he did not try to have the state pass a law to halt this practice. When localities did pass rules about minimum entry age, many parents ignored them. The 1841 school report for Palmer mentions that the town meeting had voted the previous year to exclude children under four from school, yet the usual number attended, "thus," said the school committee, "confirming our opinion at that time expressed, that the vote was wholly inexpedient."[43] It appears that expert opinion against early childhood schooling was never sufficiently strong to warrant action more forceful than simply warning the parents of the potential dangers. Although physicians warned parents about the danger of overeducating their young children, it was not the major focus of discussions of mental health. In fact, very few actual cases of insanity in antebellum Massachusetts were attributed to this factor.[44]

When school officials condemned early childhood education, they focused almost as much on the disruption and inconvenience it caused to the teachers as on the potential injury to the children. Throughout the local school reports one finds complaints about the irregular attendance of young children, as well as their inability to sit still for long periods of time. This brings us to the third major cause of the ultimate rise in school-entry age: the increasing bureaucratization of schools and their increasing functional and structural differentiation from the family. It was this factor that finally prompted widespread passage and enforcement of rules about age of entry to school, rules ensuring that parental behavior would conform to the views of educators.

By mid-century, schools in the larger towns had adopted the features of age grading and standardization that reformers deemed best suited both to character formation and to efficient cognitive instruction, and these practices were being urged on the smaller towns. Children under five or six, who in the past had toddled along to school with older siblings, simply did not "fit" this rationalized structure. The frustration of local committees over the persistent attendance of young children is exemplified by the Chelmsford town report of 1858:

So far as our knowledge extends, physicians and practical educators who have expressed an opinion, have united in condemning the practice of confining very young children to the school-room . . . Sending children to the public schools under five years of age is pernicious, especially in places where schools are continued through a large portion of the year. Besides the injury to the young child, a very serious evil results to the schools from admitting children who are sent at an age so tender that no motive can exist for it on the part of the parent, except the desire to be relieved from a little care at home.

Complaining that one of their district primary schools had been "particularly annoyed by infantile pupils," the committee decreed that a five-year-old entry age would be strictly enforced in that district the following year.[45] The same year, George Boutwell, Sears's successor as secretary of the state board of education, discussed age of entry in his annual report, recommending age seven or eight as appropriate for children from "proper" homes and age five for those "not blessed with suitable training at home." The Stoneham School Committee complained in 1858 that parents "cast off their children" by sending them to school before the age of five. Similarly, the Springfield School Committee reported that forty children under five had been admitted despite a rule to the contrary. Claiming that parents merely wanted the schools to take care of their children, the committee urged that the town raise the limit to age six or seven. Such local rules became more common in the 1870s. In Salem the minimum age of entry was five, and in 1873, Marblehead increased its minimum age of entry from five to six, a rule approvingly cited in the state board of education report for that year.[46]

Very young children were inconvenient and unmanageable in the eyes of public school officials devoted to age grading, efficiency, and the inculcation of habits of silence, industry, and deference. These goals reinforced earlier theories about the appropriate role of mothers in early domestic education and the dangers to health and sanity from early school training. By 1880 these factors had led most towns to prevent by regulation the attendance of young children at school. The persistent tension between the custodial concerns of parents and the bureaucratic concerns of the schools, however, is apparent in a discussion about the appropriate length of the school day in the Lynn School report of 1880. The report quotes Dr. D. F. Lincoln, who had argued in the previous year's state education report that two or three hours of school each day should be the maximum for children under seven years old:

The arrangement by which these young people are kept in school the same number of hours as those of seventeen, is absurd from every point of view except one. That one is, however, the one taken by a majority of parents, who consider that they pay to have their children *taken out of their way* for a given number of hours, and are annoyed by their presence at home.[47]

The Lynn school officials would have liked to send their primary schoolchildren home after part of the day, but they agreed with Dr. Lincoln that "it would not suit the purpose of parents who wish to have their children cared for through the greater portion of the day."

The differentiation of the family and the school had not solved the problem of divergent aims of the schools' governors and the schools' clients. After a fifty-year campaign by educators against early entrance, many parents acquiesced only reluctantly. They were interested, presumably, in their young children's intellectual education, but also, apparently, in getting them out of the home, which for many weighed more heavily than educators' arguments about the dire effects of early schooling and the mother's crucial role in early childhood education. When persuasion did not work, educational officials turned to regulation. While they moved toward compulsory attendance for children of the appropriate ages, they also implemented compulsory nonattendance for those deemed unsuitable.

We have concentrated thus far on the statewide trends in the percentage of children under four or five years of age in Massachusetts public schools from 1840 to 1900. Now we shall consider whether there were significant variations in the patterns of early school enrollment among towns of different sizes. For 1840, 1860, and 1875 we computed the percentage of young children attending public schools for each town. (There is nothing in the time series presented in Chapter 2 to suggest that any of these sample years was untypical.) We subdivided the towns into six groups according to their population size in those years and averaged for each of those subdivisions the rates of school attendance of young children (see Figure 3.3). Generally, the smaller communities in all three years had a higher percentage of young children in public schools. Children under four or five years of age who were living in towns with less than 1,250 inhabitants were more likely to go to public school in 1840, 1860, and 1875 than their counterparts in the larger communities. This may reflect the fact that school committees and teachers in urban areas were more likely to exert pressure on parents to keep their young children at home. Perhaps both parents and school officials in the larger towns were more apt than their rural counterparts to be aware of and respond to the recommendations of experts against early childhood education. Furthermore, it may simply indicate that it was easier and more reasonable to send young children to the relatively informal one-room country schools. Whatever the reasons, rural parents were slower to give up the traditional practice of sending young children to school.

One might suspect that early schooling would have been encouraged in urban areas, where there were more opportunities for mothers to work outside the home. However, because very few married women in nineteenth-century Massachusetts were gainfully employed outside the home, this factor was not very important.[48] In this regard, the situation in the United States may have been very different from that of Europe, where one of the explicit functions of infant schools was to provide a place for young children while their mothers were working. Finally, whatever social control motives may have earlier operated in

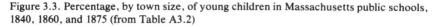

Figure 3.3. Percentage, by town size, of young children in Massachusetts public schools, 1840, 1860, and 1875 (from Table A3.2)

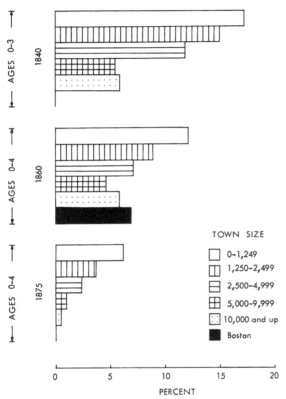

the infant school movement – that is, the impulse to give moral training to the young children of poor or otherwise untrusted parents – seem to have been negated by the reaction against early schooling and by the bureaucratic development of schools, both of which were more extensive in urban areas.

Theories of childhood and the organization of schools both made four-year-olds poor candidates for character training in the schools of mid-nineteenth-century Massachusetts, and both the theories and the organization eventually diffused to the hinterland. If we compare the rates of public school attendance of children under five years of age in 1860 and 1875, we discover significant decreases in towns of all sizes. Thus, although there are systematic variations among these groups of towns in the pattern of early school attendance, they all contributed to the general decline in the percentage of children under four or five in Massachusetts public schools from 1840 to 1875. In research reported elsewhere we also assessed the family characteristics of individual children as predictors of the age of school entry in eight sample towns. By 1880, the ethnic and occupational status of parents played little part in the decision to enroll little children in school for at least some portion of the year.[49] The patterns of school entry had substantially converged across communities and across social groups.

The kindergarten movement in Massachusetts

Despite the adverse publicity given to the education of young children in the nineteenth century, kindergartens were established for children ages three to six in several Massachusetts communities after the Civil War. We must briefly consider why these institutions, which catered to very young children, began to flourish in the late nineteenth century in spite of educators' long-standing hostility toward early schooling. The originator of the idea of kindergartens was Friedrich Froebel, a German educator who had spent several years working with Pestalozzi at his school in Yverdon, Switzerland, in the early nineteenth century. Froebel tried to create a system of education for very young children that emphasized the gradual development of the child, the importance of female teachers, and the use of games and objects rather than letters and books. Froebel's efforts failed at home when the Prussian government suddenly banned all kindergartens in 1851, but his ideas were quickly disseminated throughout western Europe and America in his writings as well as by people who had worked with him.[50] Several German-speaking kindergartens were established in America before the Civil War, although they did not have much impact.[51] It was not until Elizabeth Peabody, the sister-in-law of Horace Mann, started the first English-speaking kindergarten in Boston in 1860 that these schools began to attract notice from American educators. In large part through her tireless efforts to spread the idea of these new institutions, the kindergarten movement gradually gained momentum in the late nineteenth century in America.[52]

Peabody had been acquainted with infant schools in Massachusetts during the 1820s and 1830s and had taught in Bronson Alcott's famous Temple School in Boston. Yet when she advocated the establishment of kindergartens some forty years later, she rejected the older infant schools as being too narrowly focused on discipline and rote memorization. Furthermore, she felt that intellectual activities, such as reading, should not be thrust upon children at an early age: "This art [of reading] should be taught simultaneously with writing, or, more properly printing; and I should certainly advise that it do not come till children are hard upon seven years old.''[53]

Elizabeth Peabody and most other advocates of kindergartens wanted young children ages three to six to be educated in a social setting with other children under the supervision of a trained kindergarten teacher. But they also strenuously protested against any efforts in the kindergartens to teach these young children how to read. Thus, although kindergartens were an innovation in education in late nineteenth-century America, they did not clash with the well-established notion that excessive intellectual activity by very young children was undesirable. Furthermore, the stress in kindergartens on games and physical activities minimized the earlier complaints from educators and parents that young children in school were being forced to sit quietly at their desks for long periods of time. The relatively slow rate of growth of kindergartens in late nineteenth-century Massachusetts was the result more of their high cost than of the fear that sending young children to these kindergartens might be harmful for them. Also, despite the movement's early effort to respond to the special needs of the three- to six-year-old child, educators soon accommodated kindergartens to the age-grading, efficiency principle, and they became a year-long introduction to public schooling for five-year-olds.[54]

Conclusion

In this chapter we have traced a change in the way families and educators dealt with children between the ages of three and six in Massachusetts history. In the colonial period, it was assumed that children were capable of such intellectual activities as reading at very early ages. The New England Puritans saw children as innately sinful; salvation required literacy as well as discipline, the sooner the better. Furthermore, although children were encouraged to attend schools, rudimentary education was a parental responsibility, and many young children learned to read at home. In the early nineteenth century, educators and parents still assumed that children should be taught the alphabet and reading at a very early age. However, there was a shift in the relative role of parents and schools in the training of the young. Increasingly, private and public schools in Massachusetts replaced the family as the agency that taught young children how to read and write. The idea of sending children to school at very early ages was reinforced by the infant education movement in the late 1820s and early 1830s. Furthermore, the early nineteenth century witnessed the growing belief in America that experiences during early childhood were very important in the ultimate development of the adult. Gradually, writers on childhood came to view the young child as an innocent being, in need of protection and gentle guidance.

By the third decade of the nineteenth century, when a large portion of children under four years of age were enrolled in school, there was a reaction against sending young children to school. This hostility to early schooling was based on at least three considerations: the growing emphasis on child rearing at home; the stress on the need for gradual and balanced child development along with the fear that early intellectual activity would cause insanity; and the bureaucratic development of age-graded and standardized schools. By the middle of the nineteenth century, there was a consensus among educators, physicians, and child-care specialists that young children should not be enrolled in school or taught to read at an early age. Yet parents were very slow in responding to these warnings. Parents showed a persistent desire to have schools share their custodial and educational responsibilities for young children. Although school officials were initially reluctant to enforce minimum ages for entering public schools, by the late nineteenth century most schools prohibited attendance earlier than age five.

The waning of the harsh Calvinist view of infants, along with the dissemination of Lockean and Pestalozzian notions of the unique emotional, physical, and intellectual needs of pliant but frail young children, fostered the delineation of a distinctive stage of childhood – the preschooler. In the period 1830 to 1880 the boundary between family and school became more sharply demarcated; schools became more age graded, standardized, and regimented, and the early childhood years became more protected, through both the postponement of intellectual training and the later entry into school. This new relationship between school and family was initiated by school spokesmen and child-rearing theorists; parents, it seems, adjusted to it only gradually and reluctantly.

Whether parents liked it or not, school officials succeeded not only in delineating but also in standardizing this clearer and more abrupt transition from family to school. As the nineteenth century progressed, differences in age of school entry faded between urban and rural communities, between rich and poor families, and between natives and immigrants. Given the widespread demand for schooling, the educators' prescription and enforcement of minimum entry ages had, by 1880, made initial school entrance at age five or six a nearly universal aspect of childhood in Massachusetts.

Of course, once enrolled in school, children from different backgrounds and in different communities had highly varied educational experiences. For some, cultural shock must have begun the first moment, and for all, the socioeconomic and cultural compatibility of family and school must increasingly have joined with brains, pluck, and luck to determine the fruitfulness and the length of a child's school career. In the next chapter, on the prospects of youth, we examine the association of family characteristics with the age of school leaving in eight Massachusetts towns.

4

The prospects of youth: school leaving in eight Essex County towns

Introduction

In Chapter 3 we analyzed a situation in which educators quite unanimously wanted young children out of school, while many parents demonstrated a persistent desire to have them in school. After 1860 this conflict was gradually settled at the local level by rules prescribing the minimum age of entry to schools. Because most parents, it seems, still wanted schooling as early as possible, the minimum age requirements tended to result in most children entering school at about the same age, five or six. In other words, the initial transition from family to school was postponed but became nearly universal and was accomplished within a narrow age range.

To illustrate, we may arbitrarily define the duration of this life-course transition for a whole population as the number of years between the age at which 20 percent of the children were enrolled and the age at which 80 percent of the children were enrolled.[1] Using a large sample of children who resided in eight diverse Massachusetts communities in 1880, we calculated the transition time as about three years in 1880.[2]

In this chapter we shall use the same files of census information to analyze school leaving in the teen years, a transition that was more spread out than school entry. The transition from 80 percent enrolled down to 20 percent enrolled took between four and five years in 1880 and, as we shall see, was clearly associated with individual family and community characteristics. (The shape of these transitions is represented in Figure 4.1.)

The dependent variable in this analysis is the U.S. census item indicating whether the subject attended any school in the previous year. It is possible, of course, that some children left for a year or more and then returned, but in a large sample like ours, the census information on nonattenders in a given year should reflect the characteristics of those who had left school permanently. As for the truthfulness of the

Figure 4.1. Percentage of children ages birth to 19 attending school in eight Essex County towns, 1880 (from Table A4.7)

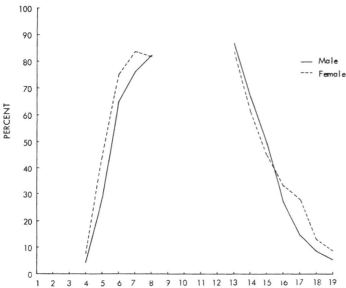

responses, there would seem to have been little pressure for false claims of school attendance in our sample of thirteen- to nineteen-year-olds. The only children covered by attendance legislation in this age group were the thirteen- and fourteen-year-olds, and the enforcement of attendance laws was very imperfect. Secondly, even if some parents claimed school attendance for nonattenders, the converse seems unlikely. Because our data reveal substantial numbers of parents reporting nonenrollment, which we have no reason to disbelieve, our multivariate analysis should reveal the relationships between the independent variables and school leaving.

If we seek to discover the relative statistical association of possible causal factors upon school attendance, multivariate analysis is required. Also, if we wish to study the influence not only of individual and family characteristics but also of the type of community in which the child lived, a multicommunity sample is essential.[3] The research we report in this chapter meets these two requirements. It is a study of five rural and three urban towns in Essex County, Massachusetts, in 1860 and 1880, using multiple classification analysis to investigate the determinants of school attendance. Our file consists of all persons in

73

five rural Essex County towns (Boxford, Hamilton, Lynnfield, Tops-field, and Wenham) and a sample of persons in three cities in that county (Lawrence, Lynn, and Salem) from the manuscript federal censuses of 1860 and 1880. In order to make our urban samples roughly comparable in absolute number of individuals, we selected persons in every sixth urban household for 1860 and in every tenth for 1880.[4] From these large samples – over fourteen thousand persons for each of our years – we created for 1860 and 1880 compressed files of all people ages birth to nineteen. In each compressed file information was added concerning siblings, parents, and household. The analysis in this chapter deals with the people in the compressed files who were thirteen to nineteen years of age. Before discussing our results, however, we must describe some aspects of youth in Essex County and in Massachusetts that influenced the decision to stay in school.

Schooling and success

Nineteenth-century American success literature paid almost no attention to school going. One looks in vain through youth periodicals and success tracts for exhortations to stay in school in order to get a good job. There was a vast literature for male youths on how to get ahead, and it did advocate education; but beyond some early years of common schooling, which were assumed, the emphasis was on *self*-improvement.[5] Whether aspiring to become a tinkerer–inventor or an Algeresque office-boy-made-good, young men were urged to work hard, live virtuously, and improve their minds through observation, reading, and lectures.

By 1860 there was an industrial working class in Massachusetts for whom this advice was increasingly irrelevant. For them, cleverness had little outlet in the workplace; hard work meant holding one's own; and success, as portrayed in Stephan Thernstrom's well-known Newburyport study, meant putting away some money or acquiring better housing, through stringent underconsumption and utilization of all the family's wage earners.[6] The opportunity costs for extended schooling were steep in such circumstances. Even for youth in more advantageous circumstances, schooling at the intermediate and secondary levels was not directly related to job skills, although more years in school may have improved general abilities and, more important, may have reinforced middle-class status despite its loose connection with employment. Still, the large numbers of middle-status and professional families whose children left school at young ages cast some doubt on the importance of this function.

In sum, the value of extended schooling in the teen years was compromised by the availability of teenage employment, the lack of career-related education in the schools, and the nonacademic themes of middle-class success literature. Nor was there a substantial change between 1860 and 1880 in the relationship of teenage schooling to work opportunities. There was more emphasis on increased school attendance for traditional purposes – social cohesion, keeping youths busy, and creating good citizens – but schools had not by 1880 very substantially adopted differentiated, utilitarian curricula geared to a specialized, industrial society.[7] It is not surprising, therefore, that overall school enrollments were not climbing in Massachusetts in this period, when the enrollment of preteen children was already nearly universal and industry still provided many jobs for teenagers. Still, as we shall see, extended schooling did correlate with various family characteristics; secondary education had some significance.

Further ambiguity is added to the picture when we consider that both school officials and industrial employers were uncertain about the desirability of compulsory schooling for all children into the early teens. Nonetheless, legislation on this matter had begun as early as 1836 in Massachusetts, and before we speculate further about the school enrollment decisions of parents and children, we must determine to what extent schooling was coerced by the state.

Massachusetts laws affecting education and child labor

The legislative history of child labor and compulsory school attendance laws in Massachusetts is complicated; we shall summarize those statutes that affected our two sample years, 1860 and 1880. As of 1860, no child under ten years of age was to be employed more than ten hours a day (1842); children under fifteen years of age working in manufacturing establishments were to have attended school for three months during the preceding year and to have obtained a certificate proving this attendance (1836, 1838); and school committees were instructed to enforce the law (1842). Towns were permitted to make further provisions to enforce the laws (1850); truants could be incarcerated (1850); and all children, whether employed or not, were to attend school for twelve weeks each year, unless they already knew the rudiments, were physically or mentally defective, or were impoverished (1852).[8] Evidence abounds to show that these laws were neither widely nor strictly enforced.[9]

During the late 1860s and the 1870s there was a flurry of legislation on these subjects, spurred in part by the studies of the newly created

Massachusetts Bureau of the Statistics of Labor. As of 1880, then, the towns of Essex County were charged with implementing the following regulations: No child under ten was to be employed in a manufacturing, mechanical, or mercantile establishment (1876); children between the ages of ten and fourteen thus employed must have attended school for twenty weeks in the preceding year (1876) and were not to work more than sixty hours per week (1867); a deputy constable of the commonwealth was assigned to enforce child labor laws (1867); towns were required to provide truant officers (1873); all children aged eight to fourteen, with the same exceptions as in 1860, were to attend school for twenty weeks a year (1874); no child under fourteen was to be employed during public school session if unable to read and write (1878); and employers were required to keep proof of their employees' birth and school attendance on file for truant officers' inspection (1878).[10]

That these laws were still controversial is suggested by the constant seesaw revision of age limits and length of schooling requirements. Despite steadily stiffening provisions for reports by truant officers and school committees, and despite requirements that employers prove both age and school attendance for employees under the age of fourteen, the laws were still very imperfectly enforced. In the late 1860s and early 1870s the Bureau of Statistics of Labor collected and published voluminous evidence of abuse. Children under ten worked in factories, children aged ten to fifteen had not been to school for years, and factory officials falsified records.[11] General Henry Oliver, appointed deputy constable of the commonwealth to enforce the child labor and truancy laws, wrote in 1870:

Nobody looks after it – neither town authorities, nor school committees, nor local police – and the large cities and many of the towns of the state are full of unschooled children . . . and nobody thinks of obeying the school laws. In fact, most persons are ignorant that there is any such law.

George McNeil, Oliver's successor, stated flatly in 1875, ''Immediately after accepting my commission, I commenced my investigations and found the laws inoperative.''[12] He estimated that 60,000 children in the state between the ages of five and fifteen had not attended school the past year, many in violation of the law, including 1,363 in Lawrence, 1,986 in Lynn, and 1,589 in Salem.[13]

Despite widespread complaints of noncompliance with child labor and school attendance laws, it would not be accurate to assume that there were no differences in enforcement between 1860 and 1880. In rural towns the laws were cited by school officials to reinforce their traditional pleas to parents, and sometimes officials used the statutes as a stick to persuade uncooperative parents.[14] In the large towns, including Lawrence, Lynn, and Salem, truant officers could harass and cajole, and sometimes actually compel, truants to go back to school. The Lawrence school superintendent boasted that Lawrence's truant officer had nearly eliminated truancy, and a report of the Bureau of the Statistics of Labor claimed in 1882 that Lawrence's working class was better educated than that of other factory towns and that the factory laws regarding children were generally in force.[15] Meanwhile, Lynn's school superintendent complained in 1880 that truancy seemed "to be a growing and, at present, an irrepressible evil."[16] Obviously, enforcement of child labor and truancy laws varied from town to town. It is important to note, however, that no school laws affected children aged fifteen or older, who constituted a large part of our teenage sample. Whatever effect the factory laws had on our thirteen- and fourteen-year-olds, their older contemporaries were free from legal constraints in making school enrollment decisions.

The employment of children

Swimming, berry picking, and loitering around the wharves presented alluring alternatives to recitations and hard benches. But our statistics do not catch the occasional truants, any more than the truant officer did. Our analysis in this chapter considers whether children attended school at any time in the previous twelve months, and the most common cause of sustained nonattendance among teenagers was employment. This was not the only alternative, of course. Many teenagers in our file were neither enrolled in school nor employed for remuneration. In 1860 this category of youth amounted to 17.2 percent of the males and 28.6 percent of the females. In 1880 it included 7.7 percent of the males and 21.9 percent of the females (see Figures 4.2 and 4.3). We cannot assume that these teenagers were idle. For boys, labor on family farms often went unrecorded, and for girls, who constituted most of this category, unremunerated housework went unreported. Still, the great majority of youths not in school had a recorded occupation.

There was a greater percentage of teenagers of both sexes employed in 1880 than in 1860, with a corresponding reduction in those at school or at home. This change is the result partly of underreporting of employment in 1860, and partly of the fact that our 1880 sample is more urban than our 1860 sample because of rural-to-urban migration in the intervening years. To the extent that the increase in the percentage of youths employed is the result of these factors, the differential is some-

Figure 4.2. School and remunerative work patterns of females ages 13–19 in eight Essex County towns, 1860 and 1880 (from Table A4.8)

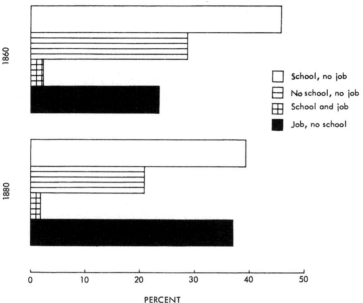

what artificial. Also, however, the 1880s were the heyday of teenage employment in cities like Lawrence. The economy was recovering from the depression of the mid-1870s, and neither automation nor labor unionization had yet squeezed teenagers out of industry. These work opportunities can be judged from different angles. In economic terms, it may have been the height of the exploitation of youthful labor; it also made the opportunity costs for extended schooling high. In terms of life-course analysis, the availability of jobs for teens increased their ability to migrate and support themselves.[17]

Employment opportunities differed substantially between urban and rural towns. Most labor for children in the rural towns was agricultural, which meant that it was more seasonal than urban work and, to the extent that children were working on their parents' farms, the work was often nonremunerative. Of course, such work contributed to the family income, just as factory wages did for urban children's families. Urban youth employment, which in good times was year-round, was not only recorded in the census more accurately but was also more often in conflict with school attendance. Thus, whereas older boys in rural areas commonly attended winter school, perhaps for the lack of

Figure 4.3. School and remunerative work patterns of males ages 13–19 in eight Essex County towns, 1860 and 1880 (from Table A4.9)

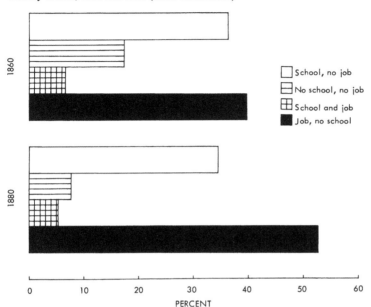

anything better to do, urban employers complained of the disruption of having to replace children who had to take time off to complete their requisite schooling. This problem generated some new forms of schooling, such as half-time and evening schools for factory youths, which – however educationally meager – were more compatible with teenage work.

Aggregate census data provide information about youth employment in the eight towns. The 1880 federal census gives separate figures for employees ages ten to fifteen but includes those over fifteen with all adults. More interesting for our purposes are the Massachusetts census aggregate employment figures for 1885, because most youth workers were over fifteen. The wider variety of employment opportunities for children in the large towns, combined with the nonseasonal nature of urban work, helps account for the lower rate of total school enrollment among urban youths. In the rural towns very few youths were employed except in farm work for boys and in housework for girls. In the cities girls worked not only in housework and as servants, but also as bookkeepers and clerks and as operatives in the mills. For example, women were more than half the work force in Lawrence's cotton mills, and 27 percent of the women operatives were between the ages of fourteen and nineteen. Boys of these ages also made up a substantial portion of the labor force in manufacturing.[18]

The structure of school systems in urban and rural towns

Although the availability of youth employment in cities probably inhibited school attendance, the availability of the more developed and differentiated urban school systems probably enhanced it. Larger population centers had since colonial times been able to sustain schools above the primary level, and in the nineteenth century the levels of schooling in urban systems became further differentiated. By 1880 our three Essex County urban towns had not only the standard three-tiered system of primary, grammar, and high schools, but also various bureaucratic innovations such as intermediate, middle, mixed, evening, or ungraded schools – designed largely to deal with working-class and immigrant children. Rural systems, in contrast, were much simpler. Each district had its multigraded district school, and sometimes there was a grammar department in the center district. Rural children who wished to attend high school had to board in one of the larger towns or commute a long distance.

Private and parochial schooling was also more available in urban areas, although data on private schooling is much less reliable than on public schools. For example, Boxford had an academy throughout this period but reported none for 1860. Lawrence school officials reported 1,200 private students in 1880. These children were all in St. Mary's parochial schools, of which the public school officials approved. The figure does not include children in French Canadian parochial schools, of which the school board did not approve, nor did the board collect any figures on nonparochial private schooling. Salem's figures for 1880, on the other hand, seemed to be more thorough. In the returns to the state for 1879–80, the Salem board reported thirteen private schools and academies, enrolling 950 students during the year. In the board's own local school report for the following year, the figure given is higher but not drastically so, and the report enumerates the categories of students: Of 1,210 children of all ages then in private institutions, 67 were in college, 884 in Catholic schools, 183 under private tuition, 45 in asylums, and 31 in reformatories.[19]

Leaving aside for the moment the problem of private school estimates, Table 4.1 presents some basic data on the public systems in our communities for 1860 and 1880. With some anomalies (notably, the marked decline in attendance in Hamilton and Boxford), the following

Table 4.1 Public school attendance in eight Essex County towns, 1860 and 1880

	Law-rence	Lynn	Salem	Tops-field	Ham-ilton	Wen-ham	Box-ford	Lynn-field
Population								
1860	16,114	15,713	20,934	1,250	896	1,073	1,034	883
1880	39,178	38,284	27,598	1,165	935	889	824	686
No. children								
1860	7,420	8,124	9,107	521	282	462	437	335
1880	15,638	13,605	10,266	371	305	299	289	218
Length of school year (in days)								
1860	228	232	253	133	113	165	143	183
1880	220	224	224	184	183	184	201	185
Average daily attendance								
1860								
Number[a]	1,662	2,971	2,575	141	107	168	181	127
% 0–19	22.4	36.6	28.3	27.1	37.9	36.4	41.4	37.9
1880								
Number	4,232	4,667	2,807	116	80	138	89	81
% 0–19	27.1	34.4	27.3	31.3	26.2	46.2	30.8	37.2
Total attendance (enrollment)								
1860								
Number[b]	2,873	4,045	4,031	231	182	275	294	188
% 0–19	38.7	49.8	44.3	44.3	64.5	59.5	67.2	56.1
1880								
Number	5,866	6,183	3,858	202	134	183	135	124
% 0–19	37.5	45.4	37.6	66.2	43.9	61.2	46.7	56.9

[a] Average summer attendance plus average winter attendance, divided by 2.

[b] Estimated: winter attendance plus .25 times the summer attendance.

Source: Calculated from Massachusetts Board of Education, Annual Reports for 1859–60 and 1879–80.

generalizations may be made: Rural attendance levels, both average and total, are higher than in urban towns, and the difference persists in 1880, even though for the state as a whole there is a tendency for urban rates to catch up with rural rates during this period. Second, the school year was much longer in the cities, so that those children who did attend regularly were receiving more education. By 1880 the rural towns had increased their public school length substantially but had not caught up with the large towns. This phenomenon makes sense in view of the seasonal nature of family work in agricultural towns; schools were kept longer in the urban communities because reformers and school officials desired longer school sessions for a variety of reasons, and families wanted schools, at least in part, to share the custodial functions of child rearing, because more adult work was out of the home in the cities.

As we saw in Chapter 2, there was a substantial rise in Massachusetts in the number of days in school per person ages birth to nineteen from 60.6 in 1840 to 72.2 in 1879 – largely because of the increasing length of public schools in the smaller towns. The trend in Essex County was very similar – the average number of days in school was 63.7 in 1840 and 75.1 in 1880. Our particular sample of towns in Essex County, however, did not follow the pattern of either the state or Essex County as a whole. Instead, the number of school days per person under twenty declined from 92.8 in 1840 to 74.8 in 1880 in our three urban communities and declined from 61.7 in 1840 to 60.1 in the five rural towns. We believe that the chief reason for the decline in the cities was increasing teenage labor, with the nonschool teenage population swelled by youths who migrated in order to work. The slight decline in days of schooling per capita in the rural towns probably resulted from declining resources of those towns that were economically marginal, resulting in a lack of demand for increased school expenditures. The case of Boxford, presented in Chapter 5, will strikingly illustrate a declining town in the midst of the expansive economy and schools of Essex County.

Multiple classification analysis of school leaving in 1860–1880

Introduction

The foregoing descriptive introduction has emphasized rural–urban differences in schooling and youth employment in order to provide an ecological context for studying the individual choices made by (or for) children in these varied communities. In urban towns the school system was more bureaucratically differentiated; high schools and special schools were available. Truant officers attempted to insure school attendance. On the other hand, the cities offered youth more diversions and more alternatives; also, to the extent that the urban population was more heterogeneous, there was more alienation and less consensus on the values promoted in schools. Most important, youth made up a substantial portion of the labor force. In the country towns schooling was more compatible with family and work and also probably had entertainment value for children of all ages, as they had fewer places to congregate with their peers than their urban counterparts.

These generalizations speak to the community environment as a whole, however, not to individual and group differences within eight communities. To examine the effect of ethnicity, occupation, and family characteristics on the activities of youth, we now turn to our analysis of the manuscript census returns for 1860 and 1880. In this section we seek to explain the pattern of school attendance of children on the basis of their personal characteristics, their family backgrounds, and the communities in which they lived. Unfortunately, family information is not available for all the children in our sample. We do not have family background information on children who had migrated without their parents to these towns in order to seek employment or on children whose parents had died or had abandoned them. We decided to restrict our multiple classification analysis (MCA) of school attendance to those children who were living with at least one parent so that we could study the relationship between family characteristics and the likelihood of a child's attending school.[20] Naturally, the omission of children who were not living with their parents introduced some biases in our study. Therefore, we compared the school attendance pattern of the teenagers in our MCA analysis with that of those who were omitted (see Tables A4.6 and A4.7 in Appendix A). Of the overall sample of children ages thirteen to nineteen, our MCA sample included only 72.7 percent in 1860 and 82.1 percent in 1880. The large difference between our overall sample and our MCA sample for children ages thirteen to nineteen is the result of the extensive immigration of young people seeking work in Lawrence, Lynn, and Salem. As a result, it is not surprising that school enrollment rates were considerably lower for the older children not in our MCA sample than for those who were living with their parents.

Explanation of multiple classification analysis

Multiple classification analysis (MCA) is a form of multiple regression analysis with dummy variables that expresses results in terms of adjusted deviations from the grand mean of the dependent variable associated with the various classes of the predictor variables.[21] For example, MCA answers the question: Controlling for such other variables as age of parents, ethnicity, and community, how much decrease in average school attendance is associated with being the child of an unskilled laborer? Similarly, it provides an approximate answer to the question: *Ceteris paribus,* what is the effect of parents' age on youths' school attendance? MCA "controls" for other variables by assuming, while it looks at one class of a predictor variable, that the distribution of all other predictor variables will be the same in that class as in the total population, thus "holding constant" their effects. Although this is also true of traditional multiple regression programs (described in Chapter 5), MCA has three advantages: It does not require variables to be interval variables; it does not require or assume linearity and thus can capture discontinuities in the direction of association; and, finally, it is useful descriptively because it presents the reader with the gross effects of a predictor class, that is, the actual mean of each class, as well as the mean after adjusting for the influence of other variables.

Although MCA does not assume linearity, it does, like other forms of regression analysis, assume that the effects of the various predictors are additive, that is, independent of one another. In fact, of course, for most variables this assumption is not valid. In our sample, for example, children's sex is not correlated with father's occupational status, but ethnicity and occupational status are correlated substantially. However, the problem of the interaction effects of variables can be corrected by creating a new variable that combines two variables, as we shall do with occupational and ethnic status.[22]

The statistics generated by MCA analysis provide information to answer a variety of related issues. If one asks how "important" an independent variable (X) is in determining the variation in a dependent variable (Y), the question can mean several things. Most studies that have used MCA have focused primarily or exclusively on the magnitude and direction of the adjusted means within the classes of a given predictor variable X; that is, they have emphasized the question: How much of the difference in Y is attributable to membership in a particular class of X? The statistics that are the most useful in analyzing this issue are the class mean, the adjusted mean, and the net deviation of the independent variables. The class mean (often called the gross mean) is simply the value of the dependent variable for that class or category of that independent variable. The adjusted mean indicates what the mean would have been for that class or category if that group had been exactly like the total population with respect to its distribution over all the other predictor classifications. And the net deviation of a class or category of a predictor variable is simply the adjusted mean minus the grand mean of the dependent variable.

Another question, however, is: How important is the whole predictor variable X_1 compared to predictor variable X_2 or X_n in explaining variation in dependent variable Y? Here we ask, not how much higher is the attendance rate for professionals' children as opposed to unskilled workers' children, when controlling for other variables, but rather, how much of the variation in attendance rates is explained by father's occupational status, in comparison with the amount of variation explained by a child's ethnicity? To attempt to answer this question we must turn to the predictor summary statistics, which provide expressions of each predictor's unadjusted and adjusted contribution to explaining the variance in the dependent variable. A word of caution is in order, however. These statistics are heavily dependent upon the particular distribution of the sample and are not simply comparable across samples. We present them as indicators of the relative importance of our variables in explaining school attendance in each year. The eta^2 statistics are an unadjusted measure of variance explained; that is, they express the zero-order relationship between the predictor variable and the dependent variable. They are thus analogous to the square of Pearson correlation coefficients for interval variables. Our adjusted measure is β, the partial beta coefficient. The rank order of these betas indicates the relative importance of each variable in explaining variance in the dependent variable while controlling for all other included variables. However, beta^2 does not express percentage of variance explained.

Finally, we may want to know how much of the total variance of the dependent variable can be accounted for by our whole series of predictor variables. To measure this, we use R^2 adjusted, which indicates the proportion of the variance of the dependent variable explained by all the predictor variables together after adjusting for the number of cases, categories, and predictors (i.e., adjusting for the degrees of freedom) that have been used in the analysis.

In order to present the reader with adequate statistical information on our MCA analyses, we will present two tables for each of our major runs. The first table will contain the eta^2 and beta coefficient for each of the predictor variables, as well as the overall adjusted R^2. The second table will present the class mean, the adjusted mean, the net deviation, and the number of cases for each class or category of each of the predictor variables, as well as the grand mean and the total number of cases for that particular MCA.

Discussion of results

Youths in late nineteenth-century Essex County had to weigh several factors in trying to decide whether they would remain in school. They could stay in school in the hope of improving their job opportunities in the future – but there was no consensus in that society that continued education would lead to economic success in later life. Their entry into the labor force was affected not only by the number and type of job openings in their communities, but also by the economic needs of their families. These youths were beginning to face a world of economic exigencies in which their career opportunities were often constrained by their membership in particular subgroups of the population. At the same time, they were entering a phase of their lives of greater personal freedom and choice – growing independence from their parents as well as independence from the state regulation of their schooling and work. Our data capture only a small part of this interplay between choice and constraint, but they suggest patterns of influence that may have pervaded this crucial transitional period in the life course.

To investigate the determinants of school attendance of older children, we ran multiple classification analyses for 1860 and 1880 for children ages thirteen to nineteen with at least one parent present in the household. As our predictor variables we used the type of community, the literacy of the parents, the sex of the child, the ratio of workers to consumers in the family, the child's ethnic status, the occupation of the head of the family, and the age of the parent. The results of these MCA runs are displayed in Tables 4.2 and 4.3.

Age is the single best predictor of the school attendance of older children (see the beta coefficients in Table 4.3). Whereas most thirteen-year-old children were still in school, by the age of nineteen the overwhelming majority of children had left the classroom. The decline in school attendance by age is very similar in both 1860 and 1880 and is only slightly affected by adjusting the results for the effects of other predictor variables. The finding that school leaving is largely a function of age is hardly surprising. We are interested, obviously, in how other factors influenced whether a youth of a given age attended school during the previous year.

The effect of community on teenage attendance shows a strong, rural bias toward school going. Both young children and youths went to school at greater rates in the countryside in Essex County, demonstrating the greater communal role of the school in rural children's lives, as well as the compatibility of schooling and agricultural labor. Comparing 1860 and 1880 figures, we note a rough and imperfect convergence

Table 4.2. School attendance of children ages 13–19 in eight Essex County towns, 1860 and 1880: eta^2, beta, and R^2 values

	Eta^2		Beta	
	1860	1880	1860	1880
Age of child	.3479	.2881	.5786	.5502
Community	.0627	.0338	.1982	.1010
Literacy of parent	.0087	.0187	.0233	.0194
Sex of child	.0500	0	.0226	.0205
Work/consumption index	.0089	.0136	.0507	.0960
Ethnicity of child	.0393	.0606	.1198	.1860
Occupation of parent	.0450	.0466	.1011	.1181
Age of parent	.0227	.0037	.0812	.0540

R^2 for 1860 = .4329
R^2 for 1880 = .3802

of rural and urban school experiences. One of the effects of urbanization and state intervention in education was the partial homogenization of school experiences of rural and urban children, a phenomenon we analyze in Chapter 5. Our MCA analysis of eight Essex County towns demonstrates, however, that substantial differences in enrollment patterns still lingered in 1880.

We anticipated that illiterate parents would be less likely to keep their teenage children in schools – either because they valued education less or because they were more likely than literate parents to be financially disadvantaged and therefore more likely to be dependent upon the supplementary income their children could provide. Although it is true that children of illiterate parents were less apt to continue their education in both 1860 and 1880, we note again that this variable is not very important in comparison to the other predictor variables in those years – in part owing to the small number of illiterate parents in our samples.

Many of our hypotheses are concerned with the effects of the economic circumstances of the family on the school attendance of its children. We will first focus on the occupation of the parent. The classes under this predictor variable do not form one simple hierarchy. Farming was so common to the small towns and so unusual in the cities that this designation relates to community as well as to status and will be discussed separately. The father-absent categories are not an occupational status but rather summarize the experience of subjects with-

Table 4.3. School attendance of children ages 13-19 in eight Essex County towns, 1860 and 1880: class means, adjusted means, and net deviations

	Class mean 1860	Class mean 1880	Adjusted mean 1860	Adjusted mean 1880	Net deviation 1860	Net deviation 1880	Number of cases 1860	Number of cases 1880
Age of child								
13	87.0	87.4	84.7	86.5	+39.1	+46.2	208	198
14	75.8	65.7	75.8	68.4	+30.2	+28.1	244	236
15	60.8	50.0	60.8	49.6	+15.2	+9.3	217	212
16	36.7	31.8	38.0	32.2	-7.6	-8.1	196	223
17	20.9	23.4	21.1	23.8	-24.5	-16.5	201	184
18	11.4	13.8	13.4	12.5	-32.2	-27.8	176	218
19	7.0	9.1	6.0	7.9	-39.6	-32.4	171	209
Community								
Salem	35.3	40.8	36.3	42.7	-9.3	+2.4	317	292
Lawrence	39.6	30.0	46.2	36.9	+.6	-3.4	280	434
Lynn	34.1	37.5	34.8	35.2	-10.8	-5.1	311	373
Rural	62.4	54.6	57.7	47.5	+12.1	+7.2	505	381
Literacy of parent								
Illiterate	23.4	19.0	40.2	37.4	-5.4	-2.9	64	137
Literate	46.6	42.5	45.8	40.6	+.2	+.3	1,349	1,343
Sex of child								
Male	43.1	39.6	44.4	39.3	-1.2	-1.0	699	750
Female	48.0	41.1	46.7	41.3	+1.1	+1.0	714	730
Work/consumption index								
·0-19	47.2	41.5	47.4	42.5	+1.8	+2.2	271	234
20-24	51.2	43.4	47.0	42.0	+1.4	+1.7	217	205
25-29	48.2	51.1	47.3	48.2	+1.7	+7.9	226	237
30-34	36.2	31.0	46.0	34.5	+.4	-5.8	174	203
35-39	56.1	45.0	48.5	32.0	+2.9	-8.3	114	131
40-49	43.3	40.0	41.8	39.2	-3.8	-1.1	120	120
50 & up	40.2	34.3	41.7	39.6	-3.9	-.7	291	350

Table 4.3 (cont.)

	Class mean		Adjusted mean		Net deviation		Number of cases	
	1860	1880	1860	1880	1860	1880	1860	1880
Ethnicity of child								
1st generation	22.0	17.8	31.8	24.5	-13.8	-15.8	218	258
2nd generation Irish	45.3	35.7	45.9	36.3	+.3	-4.0	86	339
2nd generation other	50.0	38.2	44.4	36.9	-1.2	-3.4	48	170
3rd generation & up	50.2	51.2	48.4	48.8	+2.8	+8.5	1,061	713
Occupation of parent								
Prof. & semiprof.	56.8	56.4	55.3	51.8	+9.7	+11.5	213	156
Farmer	63.7	56.0	49.7	41.0	+4.1	+.7	179	150
White collar & skilled	46.2	48.9	44.1	46.1	-1.5	+5.8	541	325
Semiskilled & unskilled	30.0	32.9	39.3	36.8	-6.3	-3.5	273	607
Father absent, Mother working	33.0	32.2	43.1	35.7	-2.5	-4.6	97	59
Father absent, Mother not working	40.9	25.7	45.2	33.0	-.4	-7.3	110	183
Age of parent								
0–34	75.0	43.8	58.7	35.8	+13.1	-4.5	32	32
35–39	60.0	47.0	46.3	35.6	+.7	-4.7	150	164
40–44	48.1	42.0	44.0	38.4	-1.6	-1.9	339	334
45–49	45.6	42.4	48.6	43.0	+3.0	+2.7	349	340
50–54	39.4	39.7	44.6	42.2	-1.0	+1.9	310	310
55–59	40.1	35.0	36.7	42.7	-8.9	+2.4	137	160
60 & up	32.3	30.7	50.5	38.4	+4.9	-1.9	96	140
Total	45.6	40.3					1,413	1,480

out a father to bring home any income. Our three hierarchically ranked occupational categories, then, are professional and semiprofessional, white collar and skilled, and semiskilled and unskilled.[23]

The three ranked categories of father's occupation display a consistent relationship to school attendance. Youths aged thirteen to nineteen whose fathers were professionals or semiprofessionals attended school at the highest rates, whereas those whose fathers were in the semiskilled or unskilled occupations were least likely to enroll. The causes of these levels of school attendance by occupational status are multiple, plausible, and somewhat obvious. Higher-status families enjoyed more income on the average and could therefore afford the luxury of extended education for their children. A related possibility is that families in higher-status occupations placed a greater value on extended education. This attitudinal factor may be associated with occupational groups but may operate independently from income per se. Thus one might speculate, for example, that an ill-paid struggling doctor might press harder for extended education for his children than a relatively affluent factory foreman, simply because extended education played a larger role in the expected career pattern of the former's children than of the latter's. Different constructions may be put upon this attitudinal influence. Michael Katz, for example, argues that middle- and upper-status parents were increasingly looking to secondary education in the nineteenth century as a means of transferring their status to their children in a world where such status was increasingly difficult to transfer merely by ascription.[24] It may have been, however, more than just an arbitrary credentialing process. Secondary education may have actually transmitted some general skills that were more useful for children who aspired to middle- and upper-status jobs. The clearest example is preparation for teaching as a career goal for girls, as Katz points out. For boys, advanced writing and reading skills might have been prerequisites to professional and white-collar occupations. For some or all of these reasons, and despite the lack of emphasis on schooling in the success literature of the day, children of fathers in upper-status occupations stayed in school longer as teenagers, though not at nearly the rates they would achieve by the early twentieth century.

The school attendance of farm children was influenced not only by their fathers' occupations but also by the fact that they lived in rural communities, where children remained longer in school than did their urban counterparts. The overall rate of school enrollment of farm children is substantially higher than that of any other occupational group in 1860 and is only slightly lower than that of children of professionals and semiprofessionals in 1880. When we control for the effects of the other variables, including community type, the school attendance of farm children is still very high but is significantly less than that of children of professionals and semiprofessionals in 1860 and 1880 and is also lower than that of children of white-collar and skilled workers in 1880.

In fatherless families, the mother's work status had a strong negative association with teenage school attendance in 1880. The net deviation for fatherless families with the mother working was −4.6 percent in that year, whereas the net deviation for fatherless families with the mother not working was −7.3 percent. The effect was less pronounced in 1860 but went in the same direction. We infer from these findings that families without fathers were more likely to send their children to work and that if the mother in those families was not working, the teenage children would be even more likely to have left school for work.

In addition to the occupations of the parent, we used a work/consumption ratio as another measure of the economic situation of the family. Ideally, we would measure the actual income and consumption needs of the family, as several contemporary studies have done. Unfortunately, such data do not exist for the past. We can go beyond just the occupation of the head of household, however, by taking into consideration the number of persons in the family who were employed, as well as the number of consumers within that family. Because the earning and consuming ability of individuals varies by age and sex, we adjusted our data by a set of weights to take these factors into consideration. Our work/consumption index is therefore a crude measure of the number of working units in each family (excluding the subject) divided by the number of consuming units (including the subject). Though this index does not fully capture the individual family variations in income and consumption needs, it does provide at least a first step in measuring a family's economic situation, rather than just relying on information on the head of the household. The work/consumption ratio is a measure of family members working over consumer units within the family. It is an attempt to define the income strategy of a family unit, without reference to the father's occupational group, which is accounted for elsewhere in the multiple classification analysis.[25]

We hypothesized that the higher (i.e., more advantageous) the work/consumption ratio of the family, the greater the likelihood that the child would remain in school rather than enter the labor force to supplement the family's income. The results of our analysis indicate just the opposite – the higher the work/consumption ratio, the less likely a child is to attend school – though the overall importance of the work/consumption variable in our MCA runs is not very strong. This is a surprising result, because it implies that those families which most needed income from their teenage children allowed them to remain in school.

Because our attempt to construct a crude family work/consumption ratio is an innovation and because that ratio did not predict school attendance as we had anticipated, we devoted considerable effort to further checking our results. We reran the MCAs without the children whose fathers were absent in order to eliminate the possibility that our results had been distorted by the presence of fatherless families, which were concentrated in the lowest categories of the work/consumption ratio. In addition, we reran our MCAs by occupational groups, such as the white-collar and skilled workers, and semiskilled and unskilled workers, to see if the pattern of the work/consumption ratio varied by these occupational groupings. None of these tests explained satisfactorily the inverse relationship between the work/consumption ratio and teenage school attendance in our basic MCA runs for 1860 and 1880.

There are several possible explanations for our results using the work/consumption ratio. Despite the crudeness of the data, we do not believe that the measure is hopelessly invalid, because the same work/consumption ratio, used in a study by Hareven, Mason, and Vinovskis that analyzed the same population, did operate in the anticipated direction in predicting the probability of women working. Our results with school attendance as the dependent variable may suggest that families did not expect their teenage children to leave school early simply because the family was encountering economic difficulties. Or perhaps, because not all children who left school went directly into the labor force, school leaving was not as dependent on family economic considerations as was teenagers' entry into the labor force. Another plausible explanation is that the father's occupational status does not control adequately for the actual economic situation of the family. Therefore, if any of the other members of the family besides the father had to work, it might be an indication of the extent of the economic distress within that family, even though the family's work/consumption ratio would seem favorable. A fourth possibility is that families which sent other members besides the father into the labor force (and thereby improved their work/consumption ratio) may not have valued education very highly and therefore were willing to have their other children also drop out of school to work. We hope that other students of past family behavior will continue to develop indexes like our work/consumption ratio that try to measure the economic situation of the entire family, rather than relying only on the occupation of the head of household or on the size of the family. In the meantime, our results do not support the notion that older siblings worked *in order* that younger siblings could remain in school longer; rather, they suggest that school going was less likely when more members of the family were working.

In addition to the influence of the economic circumstances of the family on the school attendance of their older children, we anticipated that the children of foreign-born parents would be less likely to attend school than those of native parents – either because foreign-born parents valued education less or because they found the schools objectionable or unappealing on cultural grounds. Our MCA runs indicate that even when other factors are controlled, ethnic status had a clear linear relationship to school attendance: The longer a child and his parents had been in America, the greater the likelihood that the child would attend school as a teenager.[26] The results for 1860 and 1880 are consistent, and the net deviations strongly differentiate the subgroups on attendance. In both 1860 and 1880 the ethnicity of the child was a stronger predictor of school attendance than was the occupation of the parent. Because of the importance of these two independent variables, and because occupation and ethnic status are substantially correlated, we explored the problem of interaction, which we discuss in the next section.

We included the age of the parent in our MCA runs in an attempt to approximate the life-course situation of the family. We anticipated a curvilinear relationship between the age of the parent and the school enrollment of the teenage children, with low attendance rates in the early and late stages of the family when family income might have been the most strained. However, the results of our analysis for 1860 and 1880 did not reveal any consistent pattern. We then speculated that this lack of consistent pattern in the impact of parents' age on school attendance may have been the result of the fact that the income profiles of wage earners differ by occupation. Therefore we ran separate MCAs for the group including white-collar and skilled workers, and for the semiskilled group. The results partly confirmed our hypothesis. The adjusted school attendance in 1880 of thirteen- to nineteen-year-olds whose fathers were lower-level white-collar or skilled workers was directly related to the age of the parent – a relationship that probably paralleled the earning profile of those families. However, there was no single consistent age pattern for the white-collar and skilled workers in 1860. Similarly, the 1860 adjusted school attendance of children ages thirteen to nineteen whose fathers were semiskilled or unskilled workers varied inversely with the age of the parent. In 1880 the pattern of school attendance of older children whose parents were semiskilled or unskilled workers was not consistent. As a result, we cannot conclude that our crude measure of the life course of these families was a good predictor of the school attendance of their older children. It is hoped that future studies will be able to improve our estimate of the life-course situation of the family by obtaining more detailed information on the actual conditions and past experiences of those families than can be approximated from the age of the parent.

Interaction: ethnicity and occupation

Multiple classification analysis, like other forms of multiple regression, does not analyze well the impact upon a dependent variable of two or more highly correlated variables. The most serious interaction problem involved in the present study is the overlap between ethnicity of the child and the occupation of the parent, because of both the degree of overlap and the importance of the question. The problem is not only statistical but conceptual and historical as well.

The conceptual problem is to define the relationships between the ideas of culture and class. It will not do to think of culture as an isolated sphere in a person's identity and motivation, independent of the social structure and the distribution of goods. Obviously, culture is related to and interacts with social structure, partly arising from it, partly acting upon and shaping it. But culture is neither the same as social structure nor merely a phenomenon determined by it, because there can be (and constantly are) lags, discontinuities, and diversity in the interaction of culture and social structure. The language, the imagery, the prejudices, the aspirations, and the daily customs that fall under the rubric of culture – whatever their relationship to the social structure in which they arise – may stubbornly persist when transported to a new social structure, or when technology, politics, and other developments transform social structure. One of the failings of functionalist, equilibrium approaches to history is that they underestimate tensions and distinctions between culture and the social system.

In what sense, then, is economic motivation more fundamental than cultural baggage in the actions of ordinary people, who are the stuff of the "new" social history? Because life requires sustenance, the closer a person gets to rudimentary subsistence – a threshold toward which vast numbers of people in human history have been pressed – the more salient will become straightforward economic strategies, and the more potently will these overrule such competing inclinations as an abstract

Table 4.4. School attendance of children ages 13–19 in eight Essex County towns, 1860 and 1880: eta^2 , beta, and R^2 values

	Eta^2		Beta	
	1860	1880	1860	1880
Age of child	.3479	.2881	.5817	.5541
Community	.0627	.0338	.2016	.1077
Literacy of parent	.0087	.0187	.0303	.0459
Sex of child	.0018	0	.0237	.0185
Work/consumption index	.0089	.0136	.0514	.0920
Ethnicity & occupation combined	.0529	.0739	.1607	.2259
Age of parent	.0227	.0037	.0816	.0543

R^2 for 1860 = .4303
R^2 for 1880 = .3806

value on education or sanctions against women's work. Obviously, the formula is not predictive. Given the range of human diversity and the complexity of motivation, some people will approximate the calculative economic man, whereas others in the same position will doggedly pursue courses opposed to their economic self-interest, or even their survival, because they are imbued with cultural commitments. Choices are constrained, of course. Many plain folk of the past did not have the latitude to pursue either their economic well-being or their cultural preferences. The constraints imposed by others, once again, are themselves both economic and cultural.

In addition to this conceptual problem, ethnicity and class are related in the minds of the historical actors, and they are often mutually reinforcing. If we could go back in a time machine to interview an Irish laborer in Lawrence in 1880, inquiring why his thirteen-year-old son had not attended school during the previous year, he might tell us that the public schools are insulting, that they turn kids away from the church, that parochial schools cost too much, that the family needs his son's mill wages, that his son doesn't need extended education, and that anyway the boy prefers the factory to the school. The father might be baffled about which reason is the most salient, or about whether he and his son are motivated more by "class" or by "ethnicity," because all the factors reinforce the same behavior. This is analogous on the individual level to the statisticians' advice for the aggregate level: "If two correlated predictors each explain a portion of the variance in a

Table 4.5. School attendance of children ages 13–19 in eight Essex County towns, 1860 and 1880: class means, adjusted means, and net deviations

	Class Mean		Adjusted Mean		Net deviation		Number of cases	
	1860	1880	1860	1880	1860	1880	1860	1880
Age of child								
13	87.0	87.4	85.1	87.1	+39.5	+46.8	208	198
14	75.8	65.7	76.0	68.6	+30.4	+28.3	244	236
15	60.8	50.0	60.6	49.2	+15.0	+8.9	217	212
16	36.7	31.8	37.9	31.8	−7.7	−8.5	196	223
17	20.9	23.4	21.1	23.3	−24.5	−17.0	201	184
18	11.4	13.8	13.0	12.5	−32.6	−27.8	176	218
19	7.0	9.1	6.0	8.2	−39.6	−32.1	171	209
Community								
Salem	35.3	40.8	37.1	42.4	−8.5	+2.1	317	292
Lawrence	39.6	30.0	44.2	35.3	−1.4	−5.0	280	434
Lynn	34.1	37.5	34.7	36.6	−10.9	−3.7	311	373
Rural	62.4	54.6	58.3	48.2	+12.7	+7.9	505	381
Literacy of parent								
Illiterate	23.4	19.0	38.6	33.3	−7.0	−7.0	64	137
Literate	46.6	42.5	45.9	41.1	+.3	+.8	1,349	1,343
Sex of child								
Male	43.1	39.6	44.4	39.4	−1.2	−.9	699	750
Female	48.0	41.1	46.7	41.3	+1.1	+1.0	714	730
Work/consumption index								
0–19	47.2	41.5	47.0	42.8	+1.4	+2.5	271	234
20–24	51.2	43.4	47.5	42.5	+1.9	+2.2	217	205
25–29	48.2	51.1	46.8	47.6	+1.2	+7.3	226	237
30–34	36.2	31.0	45.9	34.9	+.3	−5.4	174	203
35–39	56.1	45.0	49.2	32.4	+3.6	−7.9	114	131
40–49	43.3	40.0	42.2	38.4	−3.4	−1.9	120	120
50 & up	40.2	34.3	41.6	39.3	−4.0	−1.0	291	350

Table 4.5 (cont.)

	Class mean		Adjusted mean		Net deviation		Number of cases	
	1860	1880	1860	1880	1860	1880	1860	1880
Ethnicity & occupation combined								
Prof. & semiprof.	56.8	56.4	57.0	56.1	+11.4	+15.8	213	156
Farmers	63.7	56.0	51.6	46.5	+6.0	+6.2	179	150
White collar & skilled (foreign-born)	32.7	35.5	36.3	33.6	-9.3	-6.7	98	169
White collar & skilled (native-born)	49.2	63.5	46.9	60.8	+1.3	+20.5	443	156
Semiskilled & unskilled (foreign-born)	25.0	27.0	29.2	29.1	-16.4	-11.2	164	407
Semiskilled & unskilled (native-born)	37.6	45.0	44.8	43.8	-.8	+3.5	109	200
Father absent, mother working	33.0	32.2	39.8	37.0	-5.8	-3.3	97	59
Father absent, mother not working	40.9	25.7	46.7	32.9	+1.1	-7.4	110	183
Age of parent								
0–34	75.0	43.8	58.8	35.2	+13.2	-5.1	32	32
35–39	60.0	47.0	46.3	35.8	+.7	-4.5	150	164
40–44	48.1	41.9	43.8	38.6	-1.8	-1.7	339	334
45–49	45.6	42.4	48.9	43.3	+3.3	+3.0	349	340
50–54	39.4	39.7	44.4	41.7	-1.2	+1.4	310	310
55–59	40.1	35.0	37.0	42.8	-8.6	+2.5	137	160
60 & up	32.3	30.7	50.4	38.1	+4.8	-2.2	96	140
Total	45.6	40.3					1,413	1,480

dependent variable . . . either predictor can do equally well for this part of the variance."[27]

This returns us to the statistical problem. One approach to assessing the independent impact of ethnicity (defined here by country of birth) and class (defined here by occupational group) is to explore the cases or groups where the two factors do not combine in the same way. An analysis of the distribution of occupations among ethnic categories for our samples shows that there is substantial but not complete overlap. Farmers and professionals are overwhelmingly native, and immigrants are disproportionately laboring class. Is our ethnicity variable, then, simply reflecting an economic phenomenon? One technique for sorting out the interaction in MCA analysis is to combine the related variables, as we have done in the MCA analyses presented in Tables 4.4 and 4.5.

Except for the combined ethnicity–occupation variable, the analysis is the same as that presented earlier in Tables 4.2 and 4.3. By dividing our middle and lower occupational groups into native-born and for-eign-born fathers, we can demonstrate the independent effect of eth-nicity. For example, the net deviations on teenage school attendance in 1880, in rank order, are as follows: native white collar and skilled, +20.5 percent; native semiskilled and unskilled, +3.5 percent; foreign white collar and skilled, −6.7 percent; foreign semiskilled and un-skilled, −11.2 percent. It may be that within each broad category for-eign-born children's fathers were concentrated nearer the bottom; nevertheless, foreign-born children of white-collar and skilled workers attended school at substantially lower rates than did native-born chil-dren of semiskilled and unskilled workers. The same pattern prevailed in 1860. Clearly, something is operating here besides occupational sta-tus. Several factors may explain the association of immigrant status with lower attendance. For example, the level and role of schooling in the nations from which some immigrants came probably made them less oriented toward extended formal education than the American-born population. In addition, the public schools were biased against foreigners and Catholics. To the extent that there was alienation from schooling among the working-class Americans in the nineteenth cen-tury, it was probably greater among the foreign-born than the native population. Whatever the reasons, some aspects of ethnic status oper-ated independently of occupational status in schooling decisions.

Conclusion

Rudimentary schooling was an established, uniform feature of Ameri-can childhood by 1860 and probably long before. Beyond elementary education, however, from about the age of thirteen, youth began experiencing choices, sometimes forced choices, between work and school. Even teenagers from native and middling ranks, although they had higher attendance rates than their immigrant and working-class contemporaries, were not attending school nearly as long as their counterparts did forty years later, when the high school had become a mass institution. Despite the lack of compulsory legislation, length of schooling was not as widely varied in late nineteenth-century Massachusetts as one might have predicted. Yet a small difference could mean a great deal, not because education was so precious, but because the marginal choices were shaped by cultural differences and economic exigencies. Whatever was learned in school, school leaving taught Essex County youth something about how their world was ordered.

5

From one room to one system: the importance of rural–urban differences in nineteenth-century Massachusetts schooling

Introduction

The Essex County teenagers discussed in Chapter 4 were influenced in their school enrollment decisions not only by their family situations but by the communities in which they lived. We also noted, in Chapter 2, that enrollment rates varied by town size in early nineteenth-century Massachusetts. Indeed, one of the strong motivations for undertaking our study of Massachusetts education was our interest in the rural–urban dimension of educational history. In this chapter we broaden our scope again, from the eight Essex County towns to all of the towns in the state, and we move from the individual to the town as a unit of analysis. Using a file of town-level data from censuses and state school reports, we shall investigate the relationship between various educational trends and several types of community characteristics. We also hope to clarify some of the conceptual problems involved in using urbanization as an explanation of educational change.

American laymen have long perceived important differences between rural and urban schools. The little red schoolhouse of the countryside has a hallowed place in popular educational lore. Despite this rosy, nostalgic view, however, educators have generally taken a negative view of rural education, beginning as early as the mid-nineteenth century, when the process of schooling became professionalized. Their criticism stemmed partly from their impulse to centralize and standardize education, which rural districts resisted, and partly from their admiration for the apparent efficiency and elegance of large, differentiated institutions, which rural schools lacked. In Horace Mann's view the crisis in Massachusetts education in the 1840s was largely attributable to the district system of local control; he and his successors fought long and hard to impose town-level control throughout Massachusetts while they bemoaned the inadequate facilities and poorly trained teachers of small rural schools.

During the early years of the twentieth century, reformers lauded the urban school for its size, bureaucratic organization, and rich educational programs. Despite determined and persistent local defense of community control, Progressive reformers pulled rural schools into a more centralized network by consolidating rural districts and by increasing state regulation over education in the towns. This effort to "urbanize" rural schools was not new to the Progressive era, nor did it end in this period. The fact that the rural school "problem" persisted so long suggests that significant differences between urban and rural schools also persisted. Rural areas differed in population density, educational resources, and educational needs; there was no way to homogenize rural and urban education completely – not even with such devices as school buses, standardized teacher training, state aid, and television. Although twentieth-century reformers sought to bring rural education into a centralized framework, they recognized the particular needs of rural communities and endeavored to develop rural curricula appropriate for rural children. Nonetheless, rural–urban differences remained a recurring theme in educational monographs of government bureaus and schools of education, and despite the attention to revitalizing education for country life, the major thrust of this literature was to demonstrate the deficiencies of rural schools and the disadvantages of rural youth.

The ebullience of this worship of urbanism was perhaps best expressed by Commissioner of Education William Torrey Harris in 1900, when he wrote that the appointment of Horace Mann as secretary of the Massachusetts Board of Education had been "the beginning of the great urban epoch in America," explaining that "the city school is a stronger moral force than the rural school because of its superior training in the social habits named – regularity, practicality, orderly concerted action and self-restraint."[1]

In the 1960s, however, the focus and the normative tone changed. The crisis was in urban education, and problems were bigness, impersonal bureaucracy, racism, ineffective teaching, and heartless socialization for failure. The tables had turned. Whereas the enthusiastic Progressives had seen the urban school as a remedy for urban problems, latter-day reformers saw it as a symptom. A revived nostalgia for the small, nongraded school found its practical expression in various urban free-school experiments, and community control advocates tried to undo the highly centralized urban systems that Progressives had fostered. The nation had become more and more urbanized, but urbanism had proved no panacea. Gradually the upper-middle-class suburban school had become the ideal and the center of innovation. A crisis in urban education replaced the old rural school problem.

The categories "rural" and "urban," then, have been prominent in educational thought, both at the popular level and as analytical categories among students of education. They have remained loosely defined, however; the concepts of urbanization and of a rural–urban continuum have yet to receive from students of American educational history the kind of scrutiny given them by sociologists. What size defines an urban community? Is it valid to speak of a rural–urban dichotomy, or a continuum, or a set of demographic types, like rural, suburban, and urban? What qualitative as well as quantitative differences are there in schooling in demographically different communities? Most important, what *is* it about urban places that most influences their educational development? Is it size per se, or density, or is it that urban areas just happen also to be the sites of greatest cultural heterogeneity, industrialization, and class differentiation?

Here we treat this complex subject in three ways: first, we review briefly some recent studies by educational historians that focus implicitly or explicitly on the process of urbanization; second, we discuss some relevant definitions and conceptual caveats made by sociologists in their long-standing debate over the merits of the rural–urban dichotomy; and finally, we describe some actual rural–urban differences in nineteenth-century Massachusetts schooling and speculate on their causes.

Recent studies dealing with urbanization and American education

The critical view of urban education of the late 1960s found its counterpart in educational history. This is not to say, necessarily, that contemporary policy studies dictated the focus or the conclusions of historians, but journalistic and popular disillusionment with urban schools provided a congenial backdrop for reassessments of their nineteenth-century evolution. Looking to large cities, where social stress had been greatest and where public school bureaucracies first arose, several historians discovered anxiety about social stability at the heart of educational efforts, both in the antebellum period and since the Civil War. They also underscored the enthusiastically technocratic mentality of schoolmen and pointed out the close relationship between bureaucracy and conformism in the schools. These histories have been loosely labeled "revisionist," and although they differ in their conclusions, they have indeed helped to revise the older laudatory tradition in American educational history.[2]

One of the first scholars to direct attention to the development of urban education was Michael Katz. He must be credited with first emphasizing "social control" and "reform by imposition" in urban school reform from the early nineteenth century to the present. In an analysis that depended largely upon developments in Beverly, Lawrence, and other Massachusetts towns, Katz concluded,

> We must face the painful fact that this country has never, on any large scale, known vital urban schools, ones which embrace and are embraced by the mass of the community, which formulate their goals in terms of the joy of the individual instead of the fear of social dynamite or the imperatives of economic growth.[3]

Subsequently, two scholars produced detailed accounts of educational developments in eastern seaboard cities, Stanley Schultz on Boston and Carl Kaestle on New York City. They found the roots of the American public school system in the antebellum city and its problems. Despite differences in scope and conclusions, Schultz and Kaestle agreed that the development of the urban school system was a response to social problems perceived by urban elites and that among the central functions of nineteenth-century urban education were the acculturation of immigrants and the inculcation in the lower classes of values deemed appropriate for urban–industrial society. According to Schultz:

> The public school movement in the United States matured in response to what contemporaries viewed as an urban crisis . . . Between 1800 and 1860 those seeking a new urban discipline created as one of their most useful tools a system of public education. City leaders championed education to secure social order in a disorderly age.[4]

Their implicit causal argument, then, is that urbanization led to the peculiar bureaucratic structure and normative content of schools in these cities. By urbanization, however, these authors meant the economic and cultural concomitants of American urbanization as well as the growth and concentration of population. Their effort was not to weigh among them as causal factors, but rather to show how the myriad problems of cities combined to produce highly regimented urban school systems. As Kaestle concluded:

> The roots of educational systematization . . . are in the economic system, in ethnic problems, and in the very demography to which urban school systems must respond . . . Social disruption, caused by inequitable distribution of income and housing, and by ethnic and racial diversity, has intensified the demographic pressure in cities. These forces have shaped the urban school system from its earliest stages to the present.[5]

103

In the most recent attempt to synthesize urban educational history, David Tyack's *The One Best System,* the causal argument is also diffuse. Whereas Schultz and Kaestle each studied the development of education within a particular city, Tyack ranges over several cities and ultimately depicts the development of education in the whole urbanized society. By urbanization, Tyack means "the highly complex changes in ways of thinking and behaving that accompanied revolutions in technology, increasing concentrations of people in cities, and restructuring of economic and political institutions into large bureaucracies."[6] Tyack's study provides a superb analysis of the administrative mentality of school people from the late nineteenth century to the present, highlighting their quest for technique – thus the title, *The One Best System.* Extending one of Schultz's themes into the twentieth century, Tyack concludes that "increasingly the school developed a curriculum, overt and implicit, that served as a bridge between the family and the organizational world beyond – that is, helped to create an urban discipline."[7]

These studies and others have contained important new insights about education in American cities, but they have left hanging some questions about the relative importance of different processes of change that have been gathered under the rubric of urbanization. We designed our research to address these questions. We have included all the towns of Massachusetts in our sample, in order to permit comparisons of educational levels and practices in towns of differing size, and we have quantified various economic and cultural characteristics of the towns and then attempted to assess their independent relationship to educational variables. We have defined urban status narrowly, as measured only by size and density of population. We wish to discover whether these two demographic variables were characteristically associated with indexes of educational activity, or whether other economic and social characteristics, such as type of economic activity, ethnic composition, or wealth, were better predictors of school attendance, teacher characteristics, and educational expenditure patterns. If the latter is true, we should be cautious in using the concept of urbanization as a "cause" and should rather talk of urban or rural "settings." The other variables, though they may have characteristic associations with our urban variables, may be historically or geographically specific, and they are therefore not necessary concomitants of the process of population growth and concentration. Caution on this problem of definition is reinforced by the sociological literature on rural–urban differences, which we now briefly review.

Rural places, urban places, and sociologists

Dichotomies and continua

The rural–urban dichotomy, suggesting polar opposites or ideal types, is related to various other time-honored polarities in sociology intended to describe social evolution: traditional versus rational (Weber), *gemeinschaft* versus *gesellschaft* (Tönnies), folk versus urban (Redfield), traditional versus modern (Lerner, for example), and others.[8] The Tönnies formulation, perhaps the most cosmic watershed concept, has had much influence on the writing of American history, and its seemingly inexhaustible appeal continues. The notion of a transition from a stable, small, personal community to a larger, transient, impersonal society seems to summarize aptly an endless number of social developments in various time periods. The rural–urban dichotomy is also alive and well and has its practical embodiment in the long-standing U.S. census categorization of places with populations of more than twenty-five hundred as "urban" and of those smaller than twenty-five hundred as "rural." That it has been thus perpetuated, however, does not necessarily make it a useful distinction.

The idea of crude dichotomies has come in for much criticism from sociologists. Even Wirth, himself responsible for one of the most influential statements of the urban ideal type, emphasized that such constructs were only hypotheses without much empirical verification. Others, such as Sorokin, stressed the idea of a gradual transition from rural to urban rather than a dichotomy of types. In 1957, Duncan stated that "no competent sociologist, for at least a generation, has maintained that the distinction between urban and rural is a sharp one"; he recommended inductive classification of communities along more than one dimension. Recent critics have grown more strident. Hauser labeled such global dichotomies as the rural–urban continuum "catchy neologisms which often get confused with knowledge" and said that they obscured "complex systems of variables which have yet to be unscrambled." R. E. Pahl's review of the problem in 1966 began with the declaration, "In a sociological context the terms rural and urban are more remarkable for their ability to confuse than for their power to illumine." Nor can the idea of continuum completely rescue the dichotomy, Pahl argued, for there are several different and non-overlapping continua, as well as some important discontinuities, like the interaction between state and local systems, whether urban or rural.[9] Hauser, reinforcing Pahl's criticism of the continuum concept,

pointed out that 1950 census data "not only indicate that the urban–
rural dichotomy might better have been stated as a continuum, but also
that the continuum itself does not hold when reality is examined."
Some characteristics of populations ranked by size revealed nonlinear
relationships.[10] In sum, not only should we approach the question of
rural–urban differences with a continuum rather than a simple dichotomous framework, but we should recognize that there are several continua, that they do not always overlap, and that it remains in every
case to establish, rather than assume, a linear trend along any rural–
urban continuum.

Ecology and culture

Recognizing that there are several different variables that might serve
as a basis for a rural–urban continuum does not solve the problem of
defining urbanization. Older ideal types dealt not only with the size
and density of a community but with many presumed consequences of
population concentration, ranging from family structure to an individual's sense of well-being. The breadth of the construct is best summed
up by Wirth's phrase "urbanism as a way of life." Because many of
these variables seem to differ considerably in different historical and
geographical settings, urban sociologists a generation beyond the Chicago School of Wirth have recommended reducing the definition of
urbanization to a few clearly measurable demographic variables, the
practice we have adopted. Cultural and psychological variables, the
sociologists have decided, are especially bound to particular times and
places and should therefore be excluded from definitions of urbanization. Even if we limit the definition to Wirth's three central defining
elements – size, density, and heterogeneity – one can raise questions
about the latter because of historically specific ethnic patterns not
consistent with size.[11] Ethnic heterogeneity plays a particularly important role in American urban development because of the unprece-
dented volume and diversity of American nineteenth-century immigration. But to see immigration as part and parcel of urbanization would
be to ignore the history of rural immigrants and muddle the definition
of urbanism. Richard Dewey also argues against cultural elements in
the definition of urbanism: "There is no such thing as urban culture or
rural culture but only various culture contents somewhere on the rural–
urban continuum."[12]

The best advice on this problem has indeed been around since 1942.
Hope Tisdale Eldridge, defining urbanization simply as an increase in
the number and size of cities in an area, advised: "The criterion must

be in terms of population. Then we can study traits, relationships and characteristics to our heart's content.''[13] The second recommendation to be drawn from the literature on the rural–urban continuum, therefore, is clear: Do not include cultural variables in the definition of urbanization, and do not assume, prior to investigation, that cultural changes are necessary concomitants of demographic change.

Most sociologists now seem to agree on the desirability of a multi-dimensional notion of rural–urban continuum rather than a one-track transition, and on the undesirability of cultural content in definitions of urbanism. Having restricted the basic definition of urbanization to size and density of population, however, scholars show less consensus about whether any observable concomitants of urbanization are inevitable, for example, in the area of social and economic organization. This issue is, of course, crucial to understanding the relationship of urbanization to the systematization of schooling. Dewey argues that despite "the mistaken assignment to urbanism of a welter of cultural items," there are five universal concomitants of increases in size and density: (1) anonymity, (2) division of labor, (3) heterogeneity, (4) formally prescribed relationships, and (5) impersonal status symbols. One could quibble about whether these are distinct ([4] and [5] seem to be aspects of [1]) or about how strongly correlated size and heterogeneity are, but no matter – Dewey is modest about the sociological importance of these traits, labeling them "real but relatively unimportant."[14]

Other scholars, however, focusing on this very process of differentiation, assert a wide variety of consequences that have had immense impact on the structure of society. Although Hauser points out that many of Wirth's hypotheses about urban behavior are unproved and questions their applicability to less-developed countries, he subscribes to the view, essentially following Durkheim, that increased population size and density lead inevitably to increased complexity and differentiation in social structure and material production, and that these lead inevitably to more formally regulated social interaction: "As an inevitable consequence of the increased division of labor and specialization, an ever more interdependent society has necessarily evolved new forms of coordination and integration, including increasing government intervention." Bureaucracy, Hauser asserts, is also the inevitable urban form of "rational–formal–legal" organization. Reflecting an ideal-typical view of the subject, he continues, "bureaucracy is necessarily impersonal and requires the subordination of the individual to the organization."[15] Although these urban developments in organization and human relations may not be "cultural" by some definitions, they certainly have an impact on culture. Thus it seems that some of

107

what was excluded under the rubric of culture has come back as social structure. Excluding nondemographic variables from the *definition* of urbanization does not end the debate on its *consequences*. As later chapters will reveal, we find merit in the notion of bureaucratic concomitants of population growth per se; evidence for this notion in the sphere of educational development consists of increasingly bureaucratized, standardized systems, such as those depicted by Tyack in *The One Best System* and in our case study of Lynn, presented in Chapter 6 of this study.

Anomalies and exceptions

Lest we fall back into the "urbanism as a way of life" quagmire, however, we should briefly reiterate a third point made in the literature on the rural–urban continuum, that there are many anomalies and exceptions to the generalizations that accompanied the older ideal-typical polarity. Family historians have found that urbanization has not spelled a transition from extended to nuclear families; students of real bureaucracies have found that they are not consistently efficient, impersonal, or rule governed; and sociologists have provided numerous examples of village mentality and behavior in metropolises. Lenski has written about surviving communalism in Detroit, Hoselitz about traditional behavior in dense Bombay, and Gans about Boston's "urban villagers."[16] An empirical study by Fischer questions Wirth's equation of urbanism with alienation and powerlessness, and another by Reiss challenges the notion of impersonality of city life in terms of time spent with relatives and intimate friends.[17] Some stereotypical differences derived from the Wirth and Redfield traditions, it seems, are not as universal as urbanists had supposed. Conversely, small and sparse populations cannot predict with much certainty the attitudes and behavior of rural residents; thus our case study of Boxford in the next chapter cannot be taken as typical of all or even most rural communities in nineteenth-century Massachusetts. All these qualifications and revisions underscore the advice summarized in the preceding section: Do not define urbanization with cultural and psychological constructs.

Urbanization and technological stages

A fourth generalization that may be drawn from the literature on rural–urban differences is that their nature depends upon historical stages of technological development. As Oscar Lewis has argued, urbanization is not a single, universal process. It "assumes different forms and meanings, depending upon the prevailing historic, economic, social and cultural conditions."[18] Sjoberg has designated three stages, the preindustrial, transitional, and industrial, and he has described the different character of the rural–urban relationship in each. In a transitional society, for example, the ties between urban and rural places are increased by increased migration and by the emerging structure of state administration in which both urban and rural communities are subsystems. The interchange between urban and rural places is greater, and therefore the similarities are greater than in preindustrial societies, where urban dominance is maintained by market towns and government officials, but not as great as in fully industrialized societies, where mass communication, national markets, and widely accessible transportation greatly reduce rural–urban differences.[19] The consolidation of school districts and the increasing imposition of state regulation in education are also forces that dissolve rural–urban differences.[20]

Thus studies of contemporary developing nations that discover strong rural–urban differences in "modern" attitudes are not very pertinent to the history of the United States.[21] In developing nations, urban residence, more clearly than in early America, may offer unique access to media, education, politics, and other modernizing influences. Eighteenth- and early nineteenth-century rural society in America was not a peasant or folk society. High levels of mobility, land ownership, and education, as well as emerging markets and developing technology, mark it as transitional; and even among "transitional" societies there may be important differences in the impact of urbanization, depending upon patterns of city size, educational access, colonial status, and other historically specific factors. Despite the assertions of urbanists like Hauser and Schnore about the universal concomitants of urbanization, the qualifications of commentators like Sjoberg and Lewis suggest again that we define urbanization demographically and then investigate the impact in specific historical and geographic settings.

Urbanization defined

We have followed the sociologists' injunction to use a bare-bones definition of urbanization, in order to see what insights it may yield into educational patterns in nineteenth-century Massachusetts. The most straightforward and precise definition of the urban status of a given community is its population size and density. Data on population size are readily and systematically available beginning in 1790 for the United States; for this reason population size is the most frequently used index. Data on population density are very difficult to assemble, without systematic figures on the area of towns, but because of the theoretical importance of density, we have used an approximation of density in our multivariate analysis.

In the long run, density is quite highly correlated with population size, despite some persistent anomalies like the density of present-day Los Angeles compared to New York City. Duncan argues for classification by size on the grounds that this procedure will yield ordering by density as well.[22] This may not be true in the short run, however; and moreover, town size and population density are quite different phenomena. Size depends not only on demographic growth but also on the formal organization of an agglomeration of people – the governmental boundaries. Size can thus change quite dramatically through consolidation or partition without changing density or other characteristics. Conversely, a city can grow in real terms without changing its outmoded boundaries. The problems of urban sprawl and suburbs have led recent demographers to replace official population definitions with such concepts as the Standard Metropolitan Area.

Considering the arbitrariness of town size, one might predict that density would be a more central or meaningful index of changes in human interaction. However, there is one important effect attributable to size per se. To the extent that government services such as police, schools, and welfare are provided by the town, the size of the population will determine the scale of the service organizations, which in turn affects their bureaucratic structure and modes of operation. Population size alters the character of the civil reference group to which each inhabitant relates. Getting schooling from the town of Boxford is not the same as getting schooling from the city of Boston; law enforcement is not the same in units of eight hundred people as it is in units of eighty-thousand. Population size alone, then, may affect the level of efficiency, variety, anonymity, and formality of organizational life.

Density complements or reinforces such tendencies but has additional effects. Density is a demographic, not an arbitrary, variable and thus should affect informal relationships as well as formal organizations. At lower levels density may affect the frequency and diversity of human contact; at higher levels density may adversely affect the material quality of life by creating crowded living conditions or congested transportation facilities. Of course, high density may be a proxy in specific situations for other variables we are unable to measure, such as high migration, which have important social effects and are also part of the process of American urbanization.

In sum, both population size and density contribute to the universal concomitants of urbanization proposed by Durkheim and reiterated by Hauser and by Schnore, because those consequences flow from role differentiation, which is a function both of scale and of density.

Urbanization in nineteenth-century Massachusetts

One reason recent scholars have associated nineteenth-century school reform with urbanization is that they coincided. The major system-building decade for New England educators was the 1840s, when the rate of urbanization peaked in Massachusetts.[23] But correlations are not causes, and the details of both urbanization and school reform are complicated. To put our Massachusetts data in context, we present some of the basic facts about urbanization from 1800 to 1900.

Urban growth was not, of course, new in the nineteenth century. Taylor has emphasized that urbanization was proceeding at a rapid rate before the American Revolution, with the number of people in towns of more than eight thousand inhabitants rising 33 percent from 1750 to 1760 and 50 percent from 1760 to 1770. This rate of growth was sharply curtailed by the war, and the urban population made a slow recovery from 1780 until 1810. The decade 1810 to 1820, which Taylor calls "the great turnabout" in American economic development, is the only decade during which the percentage of the population in towns of more than twenty-five hundred persons declined. Thereafter the urban population in the United States increased steadily from 7.2 percent of the total population in 1820 to 39.7 percent in 1900.[24]

Massachusetts was more urbanized than the rest of the nation throughout the nineteenth century.[25] The proportion of urban dwellers in Massachusetts rose from 32.0 percent in 1800 to 91.5 percent in 1900 (see Figure 5.1). The rate of increase in the percentage of the population urbanized in Massachusetts is particularly significant in the two decades between 1830 and 1850. The surge of urban growth in the 1830s and 1840s coincided with a shift from commercial seaport dominance to the rise of numerous manufacturing cities in Massachusetts. The state saw a substantial rank-order shift in medium-sized cities, from commercial seaports like Salem, Nantucket, and Gloucester to inland manufacturing centers like Lowell, Lawrence, and Worcester. As we would expect, the proportion of the population engaged in manufacturing increased with urbanization, making its biggest gains in the 1840s. After mid-century, increases in the proportion of manufacturing workers slackened, not because industrialization had slowed but because the developing tertiary sector of the maturing economy absorbed some of the shift from agriculture.[26] However, even in the first half of

Figure 5.1. Percentage of the Massachusetts population living in urban areas, 1800–1900 (from Table A5.1)

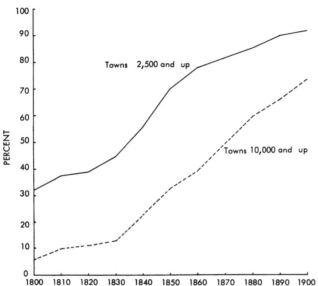

the century there were discrepancies in the timing and magnitude of increases in urban population and manufacturing workers. Lampard properly cautions us against any "easy identification of the urbanization and industrialization processes."[27] There is a considerable degree of independence between urbanization and industrialization in Massachusetts during the nineteenth century. Multivariate analysis will help to untangle these processes and to assess their relative relationship to educational development.

The urban crisis: real or imagined?

The gross trends in nineteenth-century urbanization are not in doubt. Their meaning for social history is less clear. The rough coincidence of industrial development and heavy immigration with the period of increased urbanization in the 1840s and 1850s, with all the attendant human problems of these developments, has contributed to the notion of an "urban crisis" in the nineteenth century, a notion resoundingly affirmed by reformers of the period. The urban crisis often accompanies the *gemeinschaft–gesellschaft* transformation; historians discover the crisis in different decades, depending on the city and the period they have chosen.[28] But an increasing rate of urbanization is not inevitably accompanied by the deterioration of living conditions on all fronts, and there is an important distinction between reformers' perceptions of urban crisis, which are ubiquitous, and the objective indexes of change.

Three further distinctions should be made. First, American cities, for all their similarities, may have been substantially different in quality of life. New York City, much studied by urban historians, surely experienced the greatest growth and the worst problems of all American cities; if there was an urban crisis in the nineteenth century, it was there. But we should not assume that Boston was the same, or as bad, as New York; and there doubtless were differences in degree between the problems of the medium-sized cities like Springfield and the great metropolises. Impressionistic evidence suggests differences among Massachusetts mill towns; living conditions and attendent urban ills were allegedly worse in Fall River than in Lawrence, for example. Urban history has been characterized by studies of single sites; in the future we need more comparative studies to determine which urban developments were idiosyncratic and which were systematic.

The second distinction is that a decline in one aspect of living conditions does not necessarily imply a decline in other aspects. For example, despite increasing population density and the invention of the tenement, urban life expectancy in Massachusetts was not declining in the mid-nineteenth century – perhaps because average per capita income was rising and public health efforts were increasing in the cities.[29]

The third distinction is between averages, extremes, and distributions among the population of a city. Averages can be misleading and can be used to mask serious injustices in the history of common people. On the other hand, there has been a tendency in urban history to highlight the most abject and exploited city dwellers, reflecting the focus of reformers in the past. For New York City's historians, for example, the infamous Five Points area has become a symbol of urban squalor, as it was in Victorian America. Yet it was also an extreme. Similarly, the Shattuck Report of 1850 on sanitary conditions in Boston is widely cited; but before we make it an emblem of Boston filth at mid-century, we should recall that it, too, focused on the worst areas of the city and that it followed on the heels of a terrible cholera epidemic.[30] In fleeing from elite history we must avoid a tendency to concentrate only on the poor and the downtrodden so vividly portrayed by contemporaries; nineteenth-century cities were also populated by various middle groups who were neither the instigators nor the objects of reform. Looking at average levels of wealth, status, and services for various groups within a city, we discover the pockets of middling affluence and the pockets of persistent inequality, as well as the extremes of poverty and luxury.

Do the fragments of known trends add up to an urban crisis? Some conditions, obviously, were changing dramatically and created strain. Population size per se required some organizational changes, as in the systematization of Lynn's schools or the professionalization of Boston's police. Heavily increased immigration rates were changing the composition of urban populations and causing cultural conflict.[31] One of the most dramatic examples was Holyoke, which grew from farmland to milltown virtually overnight, and was inundated by Irish laborers.[32] Elite Yankees perceived the assimilation problem as a crisis and mustered schools, religious tracts, and police for the task. But again, we must not rely solely upon elite Yankees' perceptions of our history. Recently, scholars have challenged the earlier cultural shock theme in immigrant history, emphasizing instead the integrity and viability of the immigrant family, neighborhood, and cultural organizations. David Ward, arguing against the pathological view of immigrant residential districts, says they "were often erroneously identified with high rates of infant mortality, crime, prostitution, drunkenness, and various other symptoms of social ills."[33]

The reformers' litany about the disorder of working-class lives must be tested against fragmentary and imperfect statistical evidence about living conditions, and we must be sensitive to extremes, averages, and patterns of distribution. Income provides a complex example. Available evidence suggests that in the period 1800 to 1860 poverty was increasing while per capita income was also increasing for many groups, because of the growing inequality of wealth distribution as well as the rise in productivity.[34] Similarly, a decline in the rate of infant mortality did not help the unemployed immigrant who could not afford food for his own dying child. Nonetheless, among most groups life expectancy was not decreasing in nineteenth-century Massachusetts, and such trends are also part of the history of ordinary people.

Deviance, so much talked about at the time, is even more resistant to quantification than health and wealth. Was crime increasing with urbanization? Perhaps, but Lane, arguing that Boston police were organized largely for mob control, asserts that "those mad or desperate offenses which accounted for most serious crime were not proportionately on the increase during the nineteenth century," and that "it is impossible to assess accurately the changing incidence of the disorderly behavior of which drunkenness was the center and symbol." In

Waltham much of the increase in arrests between 1872 and 1890 was the result of native Protestant crusades to stop the Irish from drinking.[35] It is not clear whether drunkenness or intolerance of drinking was increasing.

Clearly, nineteenth-century urbanization, with accompanying immigration and industrialization, put strains on human relations and demanded new forms of organization. To take reformers at face value and posit a constant urban crisis as a causal factor in institutional development, however, oversimplifies. Were particular problems getting objectively worse, or had more people in mid-nineteenth-century America come to believe that they could intervene to solve social tensions through institutions?[36] Obviously, both were happening to some degree, but "urban crisis" is not a sufficiently elegant concept to sort out the problem.

The rural crisis

Another problem with an emphasis on an antebellum urban crisis as a way of explaining the development of public schooling is that it overlooks a simultaneous rural crisis that also had an important impact on schooling development. The intense western competition for agricultural markets allowed by improved transportation spurred technological improvements and created widespread anxiety among New England farmers during the forty years preceding the Civil War.[37] Horses replaced oxen as iron ploughs replaced wooden ploughs. Self-sufficient production and household industries declined as farmers felt the influence of national markets and factory production. "This transition from mother-and-daughter-power to water-and-steam-power," wrote Horace Bushnell in 1851, will "carry with it a complete revolution of domestic life and social manners."[38]

But the revolution – in agriculture and in rural manners – was not entirely welcome. Progress was often accompanied by discouragement, decline, and defection to the cities. This rural crisis affected education in at least two ways. First, competition and declining relative productivity led to efforts by agricultural journals and societies to disseminate scientific farming methods, efforts that met with mixed success. Second, the straightened resources of the many antebellum farmers inclined them against increased expenditures for public schools. Both of these developments have lent credence to the image of the farmer as a conservative opponent of common education. Agricultural journalists bemoaned the ordinary farmers' resistance to innovation while educational reformers criticized their poor school facilities and lack of commitment to common education. The complaint that ordinary farmers did not read agricultural journals seems borne out by estimates of their limited circulation.[39] But the assertion that "the rural population as a whole contributed little to the contemporary rise of the public common school" should be treated with caution.[40] Although farmers may have opposed school reform, they favored schooling. As we saw in Chapter 2, rural parents enrolled their children of all ages in school at higher rates than did their urban neighbors. Reform or no reform, the school played an important role in rural children's lives. But in the eyes of school reformers, high enrollments were not enough. The rural school crisis was a matter rather of poor physical facilities, poor equipment, untrained teachers, short sessions, and other deficiencies resulting from scant resources. These should be seen in the context of a general rural transformation before the Civil War. Before we attribute too much of the motivation for school reform to urban problems, we should acknowledge their rural counterparts in early nineteenth-century New England: depopulation, declining relative productivity, and a perceived crisis of rural values.

The rationale for common schooling was similar in rural and urban communities: Schools should be supported because they teach morals, deference, citizenship, and the rudimentary skills children will need. However, in rural areas, where enrollment was high and resources low, reform discussions centered more on expenditures and organization, whereas in urban areas reformers focused more on the clients of the schools and anxieties about social disorder. Because the patterns and problems of schooling differed in demographically different towns, we now turn to a discussion of educational patterns in Massachusetts towns of different sizes.

Rural–urban differences in Massachusetts schooling

We have computed educational statistics for towns grouped into six size categories, including Boston as a separate category (see Table A5.2, Appendix A, for the number of towns and the population in each category for 1840, 1860, and 1875). There are three obvious problems with this mode of presentation. First, the rural–urban distinction had been blurred somewhat by 1840 and considerably by 1875. The "rural" towns of Massachusetts were in close proximity to large towns, and farming was widely accompanied by household industries such as shoemaking or straw weaving. The countryside was also dotted with small-scale factories that produced such items as matches. The farming communities of mid-nineteenth-century Massachusetts, then, were transitional. They were tied in various ways to the emerging industrial order. Conversely, the cities of this period were semirural. Thus, Robert Frost, who grew up in Lawrence in the 1880s, remembered fondly his frequent walks in the surrounding countryside. After graduating from high school, he taught in Methuen, to which he simply walked from the big city each day.[41]

Second, as discussed at the beginning of this chapter, the rural–urban continuum is not unidimensional; population size captures only one dimension of social change. Nevertheless, it can provide us with a starting point for analysis, and the figures and tables that accompany this chapter do display substantial and systematic differences in schooling associated with population size.

Third, the analysis throughout this chapter is for the town level; the averages and other statistics given are for town rates, not for individuals within the towns. When we speak, for example, of average male teacher wage rates, we refer to the wages paid to male teachers in the average *town* in Massachusetts. The town rates are not weighted for the number of teachers in the town. This procedure is appropriate to our interest in the statistical determinants of towns' educational development, but the reader is cautioned against confusing the two kinds of averages.

The first clear pattern we note is the higher participation rate in rural schools (see Tables A5.3, Appendix A). As in the early period discussed in Chapter 2, the percentage of children ages birth to nineteen enrolled in school is consistently and negatively related to town size. Given the traditional negative view of the commitment of rural areas to learning, as well as modern research on other societies that show lower education, literacy, or intelligence in rural areas, one might have expected lower school enrollment in nineteenth-century rural Massachusetts.[42] But this is not the case. Total participation as well as average daily attendance is higher at all age levels in the rural public schools; the picture does not change when private schooling is added (see Figure 5.2). The overall percentage of children ages birth to nineteen in public and private school was steadily declining from 69.4 in 1840 to 58.1 in 1860 and 55.0 in 1875. Whereas the percentage of older children in school remained relatively constant, there was a sizable drop in the percentage of very young children attending school – a reflection of the growing conviction among educators that early education was harmful to children. Finally, there was a convergence in the rates of school attendance among communities of varying sizes.

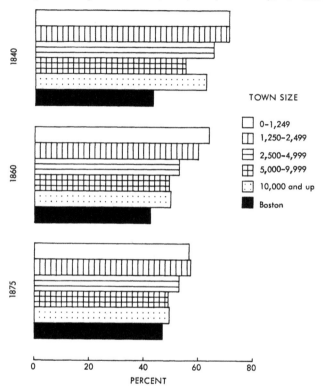

Figure 5.2. Percentage, by town size, of children ages birth to 19 enrolled in Massachusetts public and private schools, 1840, 1860, and 1875 (from Table A5.7)

There were also significant differences in the length of the school session among Massachusetts towns. Detailed information on the length of the school year is available only for the public schools; as a result, our analysis of variations by town size for this factor will be restricted to the public schools (see Figure 5.3). Whereas there was an inverse relationship between town size and school attendance, exactly the opposite is the case for the length of the school year: the larger the town, the longer the school session. Overall, there is a statewide increase in the length of the school year from 145.8 days in 1840 to 158.8 days in 1860 and to 176.5 days in 1875. Similar to the pattern of school attendance, there is a convergence among Massachusetts towns in the length of the school year from 1840 to 1875.

The length of the school year and the average daily attendance com-

Figure 5.3. Average length of Massachusetts public school sessions, by town size, 1840, 1860, and 1875 (from Table A5.8)

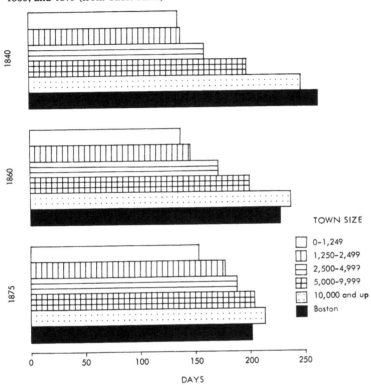

bine to determine the days of school attended per school-age child in a given year:

$$\frac{\text{Length of school} \times \text{average attendance}}{\text{Children ages } 0-19} = \frac{\text{Days of school attended}}{\text{per child ages } 0-19}$$

Figure 5.4 demonstrates the effect of the longer school year in larger towns. The length of the school year more than offsets the lower average daily attendance rates to produce higher per capita consumption of public and private education. In other words, fewer children went to school in the larger towns, but those who did went much longer each year and thus consumed more schooling. The number of days of schooling per child in Massachusetts rose from 60.3 in 1840 to 63.1 in

119

Figure 5.4. Average number of school days attended per child ages birth to 19, by town size, in Massachusetts, 1840, 1860, and 1875 (from Table A5.10)

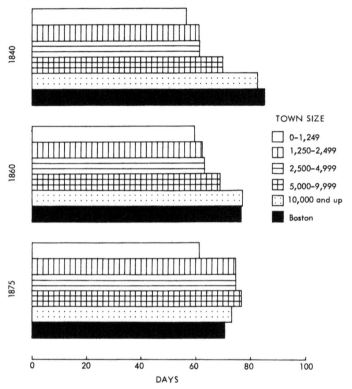

1860 and to 70.1 in 1875. Again, there was a convergence in the number of days in school per child among Massachusetts towns throughout this period.

We can only begin to suggest the meaning of these interesting and remarkably systematic rural–urban differences and the tendency to convergence. As of 1840 – the earliest date for which fairly complete figures are available, and one prior to the major impact of the state's board of education, founded in 1837 – Massachusetts public school data reveal great differences between the largest and the smallest towns in total enrollment (32.4 percent vs. 62.4 percent), in average daily attendance (24.3 percent vs. 37.5 percent), and in length of school session (264.0 days vs. 136.0 days). In predominantly agricultural towns, short sessions accommodated the seasonal nature of farm work, and the relative lack of alternative activities in winter boosted

120

total enrollment at all ages. In cities, child labor, though perhaps sporadic, was not seasonal, and long school sessions helped accommodate the recruitment of as many children as possible into the schools. Nonetheless, participation rates were lower because of work opportunities and (we hypothesize) other diversions, as well as the cultural and religious diversity that made the public schools alien or threatening to more people.

For the educational reformer – who believed that more education for more people was certainly a good thing – the rural attendance problem and the urban attendance problem were quite different. The reformers' task in the countryside, where most school-age children already attended, was to increase the length of the school year; in the larger cities, some children did not set foot in school all year and therefore, in the eyes of the reformers, needed recruiting. Rural reports are preoccupied with regularity of attendance; urban reports, while sharing this concern, increasingly reflect attention to nonattenders as the nineteenth century progressed. This latter concern seems characteristically urban. The bare figures thus suggest important differences in the relationship of school to community in small towns and in cities. Rural figures suggest cohesion and the limited but firmly established role of school attendance for children in the community. It was the quality and amount of rural schooling that worried educational reformers. In cities, with more mobile and more diverse residents, school going did not reflect cohesion. Schooling was looked upon as an instrument for *creating* cohesion, but the clients were not always readily at hand.

These commonsense reflections suggest the importance, not of town size, but of heterogeneity, in the urbanization process. Other recent scholarship, in contrast, has emphasized the central role of industrialization and has portrayed the public schools as the molders of a disciplined industrial work force. Of course, the issue is relative emphasis; no one denies outright the influence of cultural conflict or economic development in the history of common schooling. Nor is there anything incompatible in the schools' efforts to create harmony, social stability, and an industrious, compliant work force. Nonetheless, emphasis is of the essence in trying to sort out the social context of school-attendance trends. Multivariate statistical analysis can contribute to that sorting process.

First, however, we briefly present statistics by our six town groups for education variables other than attendance, in order to see how rural–urban differences pervaded several aspects of the schooling process. In teacher salaries, there were great differences between males and females, as well as between rural and urban systems (see Tables A5.11 to A5.14, Appendix A). Female teachers always received less than male teachers. At the state level, the average female monthly rate was only 50.6 percent of the male rate in 1860; it rose gradually to 56.9 percent of the male rate in 1875. The discrimination in wages against women was the greatest in the largest towns and the least in the rural communities. Furthermore, for both male and female teachers, salaries were higher in the larger communities. Although some portion of the differential wage rates might be accounted for by differences between the average educational credentials or experience of males and females, there is no systematic data on these matters, and the simply sexual basis of the discrimination was widely acknowledged at the time.

Throughout the period, rural schools paid lower wages to teachers of both sexes, paid women teachers more nearly at the rate for men, but hired a lower proportion of women (see Figure 5.5). Many rural school committees deemed female teachers inappropriate for their non-graded district schools, especially in winter, when the older boys attended. In urban graded schools headed by male principals, subordinate roles for female teachers were being developed. Also, because rural pay rates for both sexes were very much lower and closer to each other than urban rates, the budgetary advantage of female teachers was not as great. Thus innovation on this matter emanated from larger towns. Nonetheless, fiscal pressures were great on rural areas with straightened resources. As we shall see in Chapter 7, feminization was one way to meet demands for longer school sessions and other improvements. By 1875 rural school boards had conformed to the urban norm and substantially feminized teaching.

The average number of pupils per public school teacher and the average number of pupils per public school in Massachusetts declined from 1840 to 1875 (see Tables A5.15 and A5.16, Appendix A). There was a positive relationship between town size and the average number of pupils per public schoolteacher or the average number of students per public school in 1840, 1860, and 1875. In the smallest towns a teacher was virtually synonymous with a school; in the cities, larger buildings with several teachers permitted grading while fostering the impersonality of larger classes and a developing bureaucracy.

The expenditures on pupils also varied by town size (see Figure 5.6). The school expenditures per pupil increased dramatically from 1840 to 1875 – reflecting in part the increasing cost of education, as well as the inflation of money during that period.

Figure 5.5. Percentage, by town size, of female teachers in Massachusetts, 1840, 1860, and 1875 (from Table A5.13)

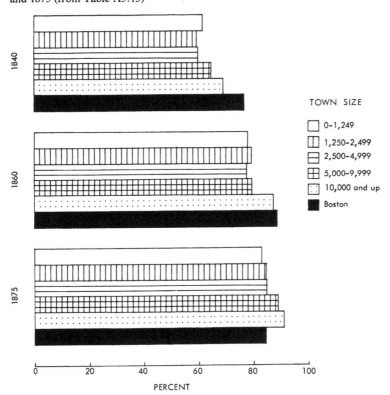

The resources dilemma for small towns is illustrated by the fact that, even though they achieved lower per pupil expenditures, smaller towns had to tax proportions of their rated property wealth similar to those of the larger towns; Boston had the highest per pupil expenditures in the state, though its school budget required the lowest percentage of property wealth (see Table A5.17, Appendix A). To some extent, higher urban expenditures may reflect differences in costs of living for teachers and not necessarily differences in quality of education. Still, the differences in expenditures were considerable between the smallest towns ($3.09 per student in 1840) and the towns with populations greater than ten thousand ($5.35 per student in 1840). One of Horace Mann's favorite devices for upgrading local expenditures was to publish annually a ranked list of per pupil expenditures in the public

Figure 5.6. Massachusetts public school expenditures per student, by town size, 1840, 1860. and 1875 (from Table A5.17)

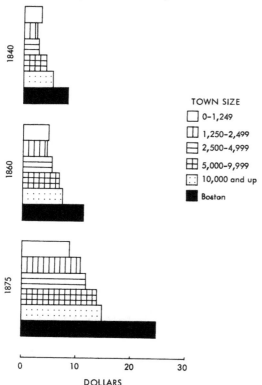

schools for all the towns in the state. Local school committees responded in their annual reports with dutiful statements of pride or shame concerning their high or low rating. Our figures for 1840, 1860, and 1875 suggest that such tactics worked to some degree. Chapter 7 returns to the question of local school finance in detail.

In summary, statistics on education in towns of different population sizes reveal persistent and systematic rural–urban differences, with some tendency to convergence by 1875. There were, nonetheless, clear differences between demographically different communities regarding measurable aspects of schooling. We have suggested a few common-sense reasons, gleaned from quantitative and literary sources, for these differences. But how do we sort out the relative importance of economic, cultural, demographic, political, or religious changes in shaping the process of schooling? No statistical method can identify causes in the instrumental sense, that is, how something made something else happen. But let us ask the question at a simpler level. Many processes were going on in the growing towns of nineteenth-century Massachusetts – commercial development, increasing manufacturing, class stratification, immigration, and others. Which of these processes correlates best with the characteristics of urban school structures and attendance? Answers to this question will help elucidate some possible causes and eliminate others. It is for such answers that we designed our multivariate analysis of the ecology of schooling in these towns.

Multiple regression results for 1860

In the preceding section of this analysis, we subdivided our data for 1840, 1860, and 1875 into six categories based on town size in order to test for rural–urban differences in the school attendance characteristics of these towns. We discovered a pronounced and regular relationship between the categories of town size and educational variables for each of those years. It is possible, however, that the strengths of the relationships between town size and school attendance or length of session are exaggerated by the presence of intervening variables, such as industrialization or the percentage of foreign-born persons in the population, which may be correlated with both town size and educational characteristics. In addition, although subdividing town size into six categories permits a clear presentation of the material, it does not make full use of the data from a statistical point of view because distinctions in town size within each of those groups are lost.

We therefore investigated in more detail the relationship for 1860 between attendance variables and the socioeconomic and cultural characteristics of towns, using a multivariate technique for analysis called multiple regression. Multiple regression analysis attempts to determine how much change in each of a series of independent variables (for example, population size, immigration level, percentage of workers in manufacturing) is associated with a given unit of change in a dependent variable (such as the rate of school enrollment). The mathematical concept behind determining these simultaneous linear relationships is called the sum of least squares method. The resulting regression coefficients tell us how much change occurs in each independent variable when the dependent variable changes one unit, assuming that the other independent variables are constant. The regression coefficients are not comparable to one another because the units used to measure the various independent variables differ; for example, we measure expenditures in dollars, population in people, and immigration levels in percentages. Through a process of rescaling, the computer also provides us with a standardized regression coefficient, often called a beta weight; unlike regression coefficients, beta weights are comparable. Multiple regression thus allows us to estimate the relative strength of association of an independent variable with a dependent variable while controlling for other independent variables. Multiple regression is an additive model and assumes that the independent variables are not strongly correlated with one another; thus when two potential independent variables are highly correlated, one must be omitted from the equation.

We developed, tested, and considered over fifty different independent variables for the 316 towns but limited our final analysis to nine that included, in our judgment, the most statistically important or conceptually interesting available indexes of community development. For a list of our final dependent and independent variables, see Table A5.20 in Appendix A.[43]

As indicated in our earlier discussion of urbanization, we included two different rural–urban variables – the total population of the community and the number of acres of farmland per capita. Total population is a measure of the scale effect of population size within a local governmental unit, whereas the number of acres of farmland is a rough approximation of density. We could have used an estimate of the total number of acres in each town, which is available for 1860, rather than the number of acres of farmland, as the latter is a reflection of agricultural development as well as density. However, we preferred to use farm acres because data on total acres per town are not available for 1840 and 1875, our other cross-sectional data sets, and we wanted to keep the variables as comparable as possible.[44] Because these two measures of density are highly correlated (.82), the substitution of one for the other does not introduce significant differences in our 1860 regression analysis. Our two measures of urban development, population size and the number of farm acres per capita, are inversely related, of course, but not very strongly ($-.16$). Therefore we may include both of them in our analysis in order to weigh their relative importance as predictors of educational development.

As we have seen, school attendance patterns varied quite systematically by town size when grouped in six categories. In our multiple regression analysis we introduce not only a second urban variable, density, but several other variables: each town's commercial and industrial status, per capita wealth, pauper expenses, proportion of immigrants, and two crude measures of religious participation. In this way we reintroduce some of the aspects of urban development excluded from our definition of urbanization. These variables may have characteristic associations with urbanization but are not synonymous with it. The regression analysis will help sort out these economic and cultural indexes and indicate the strength of their relationship to schooling patterns.

The 1860 U.S. census did not provide town-by-town summaries of occupational data. Therefore, we calculated from other sources the percentage of the population ages fifteen and more in each town who were merchants (as an index of commercial development) and the percentage of the population ages fifteen and more who were engaged in manufacturing (as an index of industrial development).[45] The distinction between commercial and industrial development is important analytically because these two variables were not highly correlated in antebellum Massachusetts (.06, using our 1860 measures). Manufacturing developed throughout the state, whereas extensive commercial activity tended to be restricted to such larger, older urban centers as Salem and Boston.

Even among the large population centers, there was not much overlap between those with the highest number of merchants and those with the greatest number of workers in manufacturing. In many towns, commercial and industrial development were successive phases of development, the former declining in importance as the latter increased.[46] Most cities rated high on both indexes only at the time of the transition. Other cities, such as newly created factory towns like Lowell, never had a commercial phase. Also, especially in the early nineteenth century, geographical features influenced the location of predominantly commercial towns (largely coastal) and industrial cities (near water power) at any given time. As a result, lists of the top quintile (sixty-three towns) on these two separate indexes had only twelve towns in common. Among the top commercial cities in 1860 were Boston, Salem, Nantucket, Plymouth, Cambridge, Worcester, and Pittsfield. The cities with the highest proportion of manufacturing workers included Chicopee, Holyoke, Lowell, and Danvers. In the upper quintile on both variables were the industrializing coastal towns of New Bedford, Lynn, Gloucester, Marblehead, and Fall River.

One of our tentative conclusions from the grouped educational data was that towns with fewer taxable resources would have more difficulty in providing adequate educational facilities for their children. Therefore, we used the assessed valuation per capita as an index of taxable resources in each of the communities.[47] In addition, we hypothesized that communities with a higher level of per capita wealth would be more likely to encourage their children to attend school than would the less affluent towns.

The pauper expenses per capita in each town were included as a possible measure of the extent to which different communities were burdened (and hence concerned) with providing public resources for the poor. Some nineteenth-century commentators argued that education was an effective means of reducing or even eradicating poverty. Therefore, we anticipated that areas with a high burden of public support for the poor might be more willing than others to provide resources for the schools in order to reduce the burden of pauper support in the future.[48]

Studies of school attendance in the nineteenth century have usually found that children of foreign-born parents were less likely to attend school – partly because their parents were more apt to need the additional income their older child could earn, partly because foreign-born parents may not have valued extended education as much as their native counterparts, and partly because immigrants may have found the public schools more culturally or religiously offensive. To test for this possibility, we wanted to include the percentage of the population who were foreign-born in our regression equations. Unfortunately, there are no town summaries of the percentage of the population foreign-born available in the published federal census for 1860. We therefore made an estimate on the basis of a straight-line interpolation of the percentage foreign-born listed in the Massachusetts state censuses of 1855 and 1865. Because this percentage remained relatively stable between 1855 and 1865 in the state, this procedure probably yielded reliable estimates of the relative levels of the foreign-born population in Massachusetts towns in 1860.

Because many of the studies of educational reform have stressed the importance of religion, we wanted to include some variable on the level of religious activity of the community. Systematic data on religious membership at the town level do not exist for Massachusetts in 1860. Consequently, it was necessary to use an approximation that was available – the number of church seats per capita for each denomination.[49] As there is probably a three- or five-year lag between a sizable increase in church membership and church construction, this index reflects religious affiliation three or four years earlier. In addition, this index might also reflect differences in the relative affluence and concern about church buildings among the denominations. Nonetheless, the combined number of church seats, controlled for population, is the best available index of general religious activity in the towns. Finally, because Catholic parents were disturbed by many of the ideas that were taught within the public schools, they often either sent their children to parochial schools or kept them home. As an indication of the concentration of Catholics within communities, we included the number of Catholic church seats per capita as our ninth and final independent variable.

The distribution of values of the independent variables requires some comment. Some of the variables, particularly the total population, have high standard deviations relative to the means, indicating skewed distributions. Statistically normal distributions are rare in the real world, and multiple regression can tolerate a substantial amount of skewness and still yield viable results; however, radical "outlying" cases should be examined, and sharply skewed distributions avoided when possible. In our study the skewness of the population variable is attributable partly to the inclusion of Boston, but trial runs excluding Boston resulted in no differences worthy of note, and we decided to keep Boston in the analysis. The skewness could be reduced in the multiple regression analysis by transforming the values to logarithms or square roots, but trial runs of the procedure altered little, and we decided to stay with the straightforward use of the absolute values.[50]

Boston and other large cities would be a different problem if we were focusing our analysis on individuals rather than towns; that is, if we wished to talk about the average pay of individual male teachers statewide, we would have to weight each town's pay rate by the number of male teachers employed in the town. However, throughout this chapter, we are interested in town-level developments and town-level policies. All averages are for town rates and are appropriate to our ecological analysis, not to the mean characteristics of individuals statewide.

Of course, we do not claim that such ecological analysis by multiple regression is a magic tool nor that it yields unassailable results. We do believe that it is appropriate to our data and questions and has helped us to sort out some of the complex relationships between educational development and community characteristics.

The first dependent variable we investigated was the combined public and private school enrollment of children under twenty years of age. There was considerable variation among the towns in school enrollment, with an average among the towns of 58.22 percent of children under twenty in school (see Table A5.21, Appendix A). Our overall regression equation using the nine independent variables accounted for 35.0 percent of the variation in the percentage of children under twenty in Massachusetts schools.

The total population of the town was not an important predictor of school enrollment after we controlled for the effects of the other independent variables on the dependent variable (see Table A5.23, Appendix A, for the beta weights for this particular analysis). Farmland per capita, our density measure, was a stronger predictor of school enrollment. The less densely populated an area, the more likely its children were to attend school. It may be that the further a child lived from school, the less likely he or she was to attend that school. However, our measure of density does not tell us much about this issue, because even in rural areas district schools were scattered among the population; thus the walking distance to a country school may not have been very much further than that to an urban school. Our measure of density more likely reflects the rural and agricultural nature of the communities and the fact that children in such environments were actually more likely to attend school than their urban counterparts, as we noted for the early nineteenth century in Chapter 2.[51] The higher school enrollment of children in rural areas confirms our earlier discussion about the nature of the rural school crisis: The problem in rural areas was not how to encourage children to attend school during some part of the year, but how to increase the regularity of their attendance and the length of the school year, as well as the quality of their schools and teachers.

School enrollment had a stronger association with commercial activity than with manufacturing activity. However, the commerce variable was not very influential in this equation. The negative relationship between manufacturing and school attendance may reflect the greater job opportunities for young people in industries; local children in these areas were more likely to be attracted by early employment, and teenagers from other communities would be more likely to migrate to these industrial towns to participate in the labor force than to attend the schools.

We wondered whether children from more affluent communities would be more apt to attend school, because their parents would be more anxious to have them educated and because the quality of the schools and teachers in those communities might be more attractive. The regression analysis is compatible with this interpretation, in that there is a positive relationship between the assessed valuation per capita and school attendance; but the relationship is weak, and we conclude that the wealth of the community had little impact on total school enrollment.

We were also curious whether children in areas of high public pauper expenditures would be more likely to attend school because of the greater public concern about education as an antidote for future poverty, or whether this factor was offset by the fact that the children of paupers were probably less likely to attend schools. The results indicate a positive relationship between pauper expenses per capita and the school attendance of children under twenty, both at the level of a simple correlation (.32) and when controlled for the effects of our other variables (see Table A5.23, Appendix A). This relationship suggests that where pauper expenses were higher, there was a successful effort to encourage school attendance, although whether the two were causally related – education intended to prevent poverty – we cannot say. Our caution in such speculation is reinforced not only by the crudeness of the data, but by the lack of a positive relationship between the length of the school year in the towns and their pauper expenses, which we mention later in this chapter.

The strongest predictor of school enrollment in our regression analysis was the percentage of the population who were foreign-born. There is a very strong negative relationship between foreign immigrants and school enrollment in the towns, both as a simple correlation (−.56) and in the regression equation. There are several possible explanations for this relationship, each of which we believe is true to some extent. First, the foreign-born variable may capture some of the personal economic situation of a town's inhabitants that is not reflected in the per capita assessed valuation variable. The per capita evaluation variable is simply the total property wealth of a town divided by its population and therefore does not tell us anything about the distribution of wealth or income. Immigrants, disproportionately on the lower end of the income scale, disproportionately needed the income of their children who were old enough to work. As we saw in the family-level analysis of Chapter 4, children of foreign-born parents left school at earlier ages than those of native-born parents. Second, immigrants may have been culturally alienated from the public schools, and alternatives may have been unavailable or too expensive. Third, some immigrant groups may have valued schooling less than the native-born as a group. Fourth, the immigrant variable may reflect some religious alienation, particularly among Roman Catholics, that is not measured well by our crude measure of religion, the church seats per capita variable. All of these factors probably contribute to the potency of the foreign-born variable in predicting low school enrollments. Although immigrants' children attended in large proportions in the preteen years, educators who saw the school as a crucial tool of assimilation had to face the fact that immigrant children's schooling patterns were different from – more often abbreviated or interrupted than – those of the children of native-born parents.

Finally, we hypothesized that religious participation and school attendance would be positively related, because much of the impetus and concern with education came from persons who had a strong religious orientation. Our regression analysis showed a positive relationship between school enrollment and the number of church seats per capita. The number of Catholic church seats per capita, once we controlled for the effects of other variables, had virtually no relation to total school enrollment in the towns. However, because our measures of religious participation are so crude, and because the inference is ecological, our conclusions on this issue are tentative.

This cross-sectional, town-level view of school enrollment of all children under twenty years of age does not reveal one of the basic factors involved in the decision of parents to send their children to school. The single most important factor in determining school attendance, not surprisingly, was the age of the child. In our study of school enrollment registered in the manuscript federal census for eight Essex County towns in 1860 and 1880 (see Chapter 4), we found that age was the single best predictor of enrollment. Almost all children ages nine to twelve were in school. The difference in the patterns of school enrollment among those towns substantially reflected variations in the ages of entering and leaving school. Thus it is important to realize that the variations in school enrollment in our regressions analysis of Massachusetts towns in 1860 also resulted largely from differences in the pattern of school entering and leaving, rather than from any fundamental disagreement among these communities on the importance of all children receiving at least a few years of common school training.

In 1860, prior to effective compulsory schooling enforcement, school enrollment was an alloy of supply and demand. Both the number and the type of schools supplied might influence enrollment. In very sparsely populated towns, distance from school may have influenced enrollment and daily attendance; we have found no direct evidence of this problem, but the location of rural district schools was often hotly contested. In some rapidly growing cities, supply of schools did not always keep pace with demand, and children were turned away.[52] Furthermore, the lack of parochial schools probably inhibited the enrollment of some Catholic children, despite the supply of public schools. Nonetheless, most towns successfully kept the supply of public schooling up to the level of demand, and parochial schools also responded to demand. We therefore associate school enrollment levels more with parental demand than with supply.

We now turn to a different aspect of schooling patterns, one more clearly associated with supply – the length of the public school year.

An examination of the correlates of the length of the public school year in all Massachusetts towns may provide us with some indication of the commitment of different types of communities to education. A shorter school session was one important way of reducing the high costs of providing education for children.

Whereas the regression equation for school enrollment accounted for 35.0 percent of the variation, the same set of independent variables predicts 52.1 percent of the variation in the length of the public school year among Massachusetts towns. Because the amount of variation in the length of the public school year is not much larger than the variation in school enrollment among these towns, it appears that the length of the public school year is much more highly related to the socioeconomic and cultural characteristics of these communities than is school enrollment.

Urbanization as measured by the population of the town is moderately, positively correlated with the length of the public school year (.31), but that relationship becomes unimportant after we control for the effects of the other independent variables (see Table A5.24, Appendix A for the beta coefficients for this analysis). Although population size is not an important predictor of the length of the school year, the number of farm acres per capita is strongly, negatively related to the length of the school session ($-.42$), and this relationship persists when controlling for other factors (see beta weights, Table A5.24, Appendix A). This relationship supports the complaints of nineteenth-century school reformers that rural, agricultural comunities were avoiding educational expenditures by offering shorter school sessions. The length of the public school year in Massachusetts, then, is not so much a function of population size per se as of the rural and agricultural condition of these communities, as measured by our density index.

When we leave our rural–urban measures and look at economic variables, the regression equation on length of school session again reveals a distinction between commercial and industrial development. Communities that were more commercialized had a longer school year in 1860, whereas those that were more industrialized had a shorter school year. This finding is similar to those for school enrollment: The communities that were more commercialized provided a longer school year and attracted a higher proportion of children into their schools, whereas the opposite tendencies prevailed in the more industrialized areas. Commercial status was the strongest predictor of length of school year in this 1860 analysis.

As with school enrollment, the relationship between the length of the public school year and the assessed valuation per capita is weak and insignificant. We had hypothesized that communities with more taxable resources would be willing to expend more money to maintain a longer school year. This relationship is confirmed at the level of simple correlations (.48); after we control for the effects of the other independent variables, the relationship between our index of wealth and the length of the public school year persists but becomes less important. The results show a very weak, positive relationship between pauper expenses per capita and length of the public school year.

There was a strong positive relationship between the percentage of the population foreign-born and the length of the public school year, both at the correlation level and in the regression equation. This suggests that those communities that experienced a rapid influx of foreigners in the 1840s and 1850s were anxious to provide more educational opportunities in order to encourage school going by the children of the foreign-born parents. Neither of our religious variables displayed a strong relationship to length of public school year. Our measures of religious participation and of Catholicism are very crude, and it is difficult to make inferences about subgroups of the population from ecological data. What is needed at this point are in-depth studies of the educational ideas and activities of various religious groups within the commonwealth in the antebellum period.[53]

In sum, the variation in length of public school session among Massachusetts towns in 1860 was quite sensitive to measurable town characteristics; in particular, longer school sessions were associated with commercial development, numbers of immigrants, town wealth, and high population density. Interpreting these findings is difficult. Because length of public school session was a policy matter in the hands of school committees, it may serve as a measure of commitment to education. Alexander Field has pressed the inference even further, arguing that length of school session may serve as an index of capitalist reformers' concern with disciplining an industrial work force. But this argument does not fit very well with our evidence, which suggests, other things being equal, that longer sessions were associated with a high number of merchants, not a high number of manufacturing workers.[54] Also, there is a more straightforward reason for the rural–urban differential: Rural child labor was seasonal, so that shorter school sessions were encouraged; urban child labor was less seasonal and less compatible with school attendance, so that longer school years were held, to catch as many children as possible. Third, we must beware of the dangers of moving from cross-sectional data to longitudinal inferences. At a given time, longer school sessions were associated with dense, urban places, but to attribute this fact to educational reform, a dynamic concept, requires one to look at trends over time. In fact (see Table A5.8), the reform was taking place in rural areas, where school sessions increased substantially from 1840 to 1875, not in large towns, where length of school session declined somewhat during the very years when large-scale manufacturing was increasing.

Cross-tabulations and regressions yield associations; they do not tell us the reasons for the associations. Yet we feel that the evidence supports the following interpretation. Length of public school session was influenced both by the child labor patterns of a town and by the town's willingness to pay for more public education. Both factors led to shorter sessions in sparsely populated, agricultural towns. Longer sessions were characteristic of more highly commercial towns, which, among the larger towns, seem to have had higher levels of attendance as well. Independent of these characteristics, towns with larger numbers of foreign-born inhabitants had longer school sessions, underscoring the acculturative intentions of public schooling advocates.

We now turn to our final attendance measure – the number of days of schooling per person under twenty years of age in Massachusetts in 1860. This variable is calculated by multiplying the average percentage of children under twenty in public schools daily by the length of the public school year, multiplying the percentage of children under twenty in private schools by our estimate of the length of the private school year, and adding the two products of these calculations. The variation among Massachusetts towns in the number of days in public and private school per person under twenty is slightly higher than the variation in the percentage of persons under twenty in school or the variation in the length of the public school year. The socioeconomic characteristics of these towns account for 32.8 percent of the variation in the number of days in school per person under twenty (compared to 52.1 percent of the variation in the length of the public school year and 35.0 percent of the variation in the percentage of children under twenty in school).

The number of days of schooling per person under twenty is virtually unrelated to the population of the town (see Table A5.25 for the beta weights for this analysis). The number of farm acres per capita is moderately, negatively related to the number of days in school per person under twenty. Thus, although town size itself is not a key predictor, children living in the most rural and agricultural communities obtained less education – largely because the public school year in those communities was shorter than in the state's larger towns.

The children who gained the most in overall education were those living in towns that were relatively commercialized. The combination of much longer public school sessions and slightly higher rates of school attendance resulted in a very strong, positive relationship between the number of days in school per person under twenty and the percentage of the population ages fifteen and more who were merchants. Children in the more industrialized towns, on the other hand, received less education. In those towns, the combination of a slightly shorter school year and a smaller percentage of children attending school resulted in fewer days of school per child than in the predominantly commercial towns but more days per child than in the agricultural towns, on the average. Thus the beta weight for the relationship between days of schooling and manufacturing activity had a negative sign but a value near zero. This finding is not particularly surprising in view of the fact that young people migrating to industrial areas were more apt to work than to attend school there. As a result, the overall rates of school attendance in manufacturing communities should be lower and school attendance rates elsewhere should be inflated, because teenagers who remained in their communities rather than migrating to find work would be more likely to attend the local schools.

There is a substantial and positive relationship between the assessed valuation per capita and the number of days in school per person under twenty. Children in wealthier communities received more education – because they attended schools in slightly higher percentages and because their public schools were kept open longer. The relationship between pauper expenses per capita and the number of days in school per person under twenty is positive but is less important than several other variables. There was a strong, negative relationship between the percentage of the population foreign-born and the number of days in school per person under twenty, explained, we believe, by the factors discussed previously. Finally, there were no substantial relationships between either of our two religious measures and the days of school attended per child. The signs were in the expected direction – a positive beta weight for the general measure of church capacity and a negative beta weight for the measure of Roman Catholic church capacity – but the values were very low. Again, this may reflect the inadequacy of the only systematic data available on religion in the towns.

Conclusions

In this chapter we have argued that a more precise and limited definition of urbanization should be used in studying the impact of population growth on educational development. Specifically, we have limited our definition to population size and density. We investigated the important correlates of school attendance, which varied systematically and substantially on a rural–urban, population-size basis. We included our two urban status variables in multiple regression equations that also included independent variables relating to economic and cultural characteristics of 316 Massachusetts towns in 1860.

We have, in this and earlier chapters, established school attendance trends both over time and across space. Our bare-bones definition of urbanization and our multivariate analysis, which reintroduced variables excluded from the definition of urbanization, have contributed to the following picture. Despite the common use of population-size figures to describe the rural–urban continuum, school attendance was more clearly related to the density and the agricultural nature of mid-nineteenth-century Massachusetts towns. Sparsely populated towns had a higher proportion of their children aged birth to nineteen enrolled at school, particularly at the youngest and oldest age ranges. Their school sessions were shorter, and consequently the number of school days consumed per child per year was lower. This finding seems consonant with the role of children and of education in agricultural communities, where common schooling was valued for its social as much as for its intellectual functions, but where relatively meager resources and patterns of seasonal farm labor encouraged short school sessions. The bigger, more dense communities were characterized by higher expenditures, longer school sessions, and more women teachers.

The introduction of other variables has allowed us to distinguish among aspects of social and economic development that occurred with the urbanization but are not synonymous with it. Among the denser, larger towns, then, there appear to be characteristic differences in school attendance patterns, depending upon whether a town had a large percentage of merchants, indicating commercial development, or had a large proportion of its work force engaged in manufacturing. Commercial towns displayed a greater association with long school sessions and higher school enrollment than manufacturing towns. Urbanization alone, then, even measured by density, is not a very sophisticated predictor of school attendance variables unless we know what type of economic activity was going on in a town. Commercial development led to increased schooling; manufacturing development led to short-term disruptions of educational participation, because of either child labor opportunities or other factors, such as greater indifference of the population to schooling.

Independent of these work-force characteristics, there were some associations of both religion and immigration with attendance variables. Our general index of religious participation, strongest in small-town Protestant Massachusetts, was associated with high enrollments, perhaps reflecting Protestants' commitment to the education of their own and others' children and perhaps indicating a general commitment to institutional participation: People who went to church sent their children to school. Our index of Roman Catholicism did not display any notable associations with any of the three education variables. Our measure of the foreign-born population related strongly to all three education variables. Towns with a high proportion of foreign-born residents displayed lower levels of enrollment and lower levels of education consumed, despite longer annual school sessions, suggesting the cultural and economic mismatch between immigrants and extensive schooling. At the same time, the longer sessions may reflect concern on the part of school committees with the acculturation of foreigners.

Multivariate statistical analysis does not provide an interpretation of educational change. But by separating several different independent variables and limiting the concept of urbanization to population size and density, we have come to two general conclusions. First, one can make several valid statements about how school systems developed in most cities, as David Tyack has done with great talent in *The One Best System;* nonetheless, if one is interested in more specific questions about the quantitative dimensions of schooling in different communities, one needs to know much more than their urban status. Our multiple regression analysis for 1860 (and it is supported by multiple regression analysis of 1840 and 1875 town-level data not reported here) shows that in similar-sized towns, the level and type of economic activity, and the religious and ethnic composition of population, were associated with significantly different educational practices. Our first point, then, is that quantitative analysis, particularly multivariate statistical analysis, can help us be more precise.

Second, our results on the variables examined in this chapter would not support an interpretation in which urbanization (if defined as increasing population size) or industrialization (if defined as a shift to manufacturing activity) were given the crucial role in explaining educational development. However, both of these important indexes of social change in the nineteenth century may have had effects on the purposes and organization of schooling, which we have not measured in this chapter. Because these aspects of educational change are not easily quantified, we move in the next chapter to case studies of two Massachusetts communities, one a declining rural town, the other an expanding industrial city. There, hopefully, we shall catch more of the meaning of urbanization and industrialization for the development of schools.

6

Education and social change in two nineteenth-century Massachusetts communities
MARTHA COONS, JOHN W. JENKINS, AND CARL KAESTLE

Introduction

Our analysis of some of the quantitative aspects of education in a large number of communities has afforded us the opportunity to be systematic and comparative within a particular historical setting.* But at the same time, studying all the towns of Massachusetts, or even eight selected Essex County towns, makes it difficult to capture the unique quality and meaning of educational developments in those communities. For these same reasons, the traditional case study method has maintained its appeal and its usefulness in educational history, as in social history generally.

Because we, too, wished for contact with the complexities of the local situation, we chose to complement our quantitative study of education in the towns with detailed studies of two communities. The two we chose, Boxford and Lynn, seem to have been at opposite ends of the development spectrum in the Massachusetts context. Boxford was a relatively insular, rural community, with a struggling economy and a declining population, whereas Lynn was an expanding, bustling center of the shoe industry. Of course, there is no single rural–urban continuum that links population size to other indexes of change in a predictable way for individual communities. Boxford should not be considered representative of all rural communities, nor does Lynn establish an invariant urban pattern. Many small towns in Massachusetts, unlike Boxford, were growing, were adopting innovations, and were trying to boost their way into economic prosperity. On the urban side, metropolitan centers like Boston had experiences quite different from Lynn's, as did the factory towns created overnight, like Holyoke or Lowell.

---

* The detailed case studies (in this chapter) were researched and prepared by Martha Coons for Boxford and John W. Jenkins for Lynn. Carl Kaestle revised those studies into the present form, in consultation with Coons and Jenkins, who are graduate students at the University of Wisconsin and who were members of the research staff for this project.

Education and social change in nineteenth-century Massachusetts

Rather than seek an elusive typicality, we chose Boxford and Lynn because they had relatively good records and were part of the Essex County group we had chosen for our enrollment study (Chapter 4). Stated simply, these two towns promised to illumine some of the relationships among economy, family, and schooling in starkly different communities. Lynn was a rapidly growing industrial city, with an expansive economy and articulate working-class leadership. Considering the profound changes that occurred in its work life and the character of its population during the nineteenth century, Lynn's schools could hardly have remained unchanged. Although the records of its economic and educational history are vast, they do not yield very firm answers to questions about why schooling developed the way it did or what it meant to ordinary children and adults. Lynn thus presents the same kind of interpretive challenge to educational historians that it has presented to recent historians of its working class. Boxford, almost within earshot of industrial Lynn and metropolitan Boston, was fundamentally agricultural throughout the nineteenth century. Remarkably insular considering its location, Boxford reminds us that the educational history of Massachusetts is more than the story of a functional statewide machine with a few squeaks that needed oiling as it rolled along into modernity. There were communities that persistently and sometimes belligerently resisted educational innovation, whose residents saw the legitimate scope and purposes of schooling differently than state bureaucrats and urban institution builders did. Boxford reminds us of the potent influence of tradition, inertia, and scant resources in educational history, in contention with the forces of economic development, professional innovation, and the oft-alleged logic of modernization.[1]

Boxford: on the fringe of development

"In speaking of Boxford, it is more natural to tell first of its woods, ponds, and brooks, because there are so many more of them."[2] So wrote George Herbert Palmer of the tiny, quiet farming community in central Essex County in which he grew up. Nineteenth-century Boxford, with its thick, white pine forests interspersed with ponds and marshes, and its sandy, stony open fields, could have been the birthplace of the archtypical New England yeoman. Touched only lightly by the industrial revolution, gradually declining in size and prosperity as the glitter and promise of factories and western lands lured its young people away, this rural town was slow to innovate and quick to defend its peaceful, isolated way of life.

140

Table 6.1.   Foreign-born population of Boxford, 1855-1905

	% of foreign-born population			% of foreign-born in total population
	British America	Northern and western Europe	All other	
1855	6.52	84.78	8.69	4.45
1865	12.90	83.87	3.22	3.57
1875	42.31	57.69	0	6.24
1885	44.05	52.38	3.57	10.00
1895	42.50	43.75	13.75	11.00
1905	52.31	43.08	4.61	9.77

Source: Mary J. Foley, "A Study of the Economic History of Three Marginal Farm Towns in Massachusetts" (Ph.D. diss., Massachusetts State College, 1933); Massachusetts censuses.

Throughout the nineteenth century, Boxford's people remained both ethnically homogeneous and widely scattered geographically. Almost all were either native-born Americans or immigrants from northern and western Europe. The 4.5 percent of Boxford's population that was foreign-born in 1855 grew only to 6.2 percent by 1875 and 11.0 percent by 1895; of these immigrants, between 86 and 96 percent were either British Americans or natives of the northern and western European nations (see Table 6.1). Unlike many Massachusetts towns, Boxford never developed enough industry to attract many members of other immigrant groups. The great majority of its citizens were farmers. Even when Boxford reached its peak of manufacturing development, in 1875, 48 percent of its men were listed in the census as farmers; of the 40 percent listed as employed in manufacturing and mechanical industries, most were, in fact, probably farmers who worked part-time in shoemaking or other enterprises, often in their own homes. Doctors, lawyers, and ministers, too, were part-time farmers. Somewhat over a hundred in number, Boxford's farms were spread over 13,500 acres, divided into a west and an east parish served by two small town centers located about five miles apart.[3]

Boxford's development followed a pattern of growth and improvement through the 1850s, when population decline, commercial stagnation, and agricultural retrenchment, if not actual depression, slowly set in. The contours of Boxford's population change appear in Table 6.2.

Table 6.2. Population of Boxford, 1765–1905

	Number of people	Change between census periods	% change (1765 = 100)
1765	851		100.00
1790	925	+6.92	108.69
1800	852	−8.57	100.11
1810	880	+3.18	103.41
1820	906	+2.87	106.46
1830	935	+2.25	109.87
1840	942	+.74	110.69
1850	982	+4.07	115.39
1855	1,034	+5.02	121.50
1860	1,020	−1.37	119.86
1865	868	−17.51	101.99
1870	847	−2.48	99.53
1875	834	−1.59	98.00
1880	824	−1.21	96.83
1885	840	+1.90	98.70
1890	864	+2.54	101.53
1895	727	−1.55	85.43
1900	704	−3.27	82.73
1905	665	−5.86	78.14

Source: Foley, "A Study of the Economic History of Three Marginal Farm Towns in Massachusetts"; Massachusetts censuses.

The total of 852 inhabitants in 1800 grew to 1,034 in 1855, then fell to 868 by 1865 and 704 by 1900. One cause of this decline was a drop in family size from an average of 4.85 persons in 1855 to 3.91 persons in 1895. Another was out-migration, toward the industrial centers on one hand and the wilds of Wisconsin and Oregon on the other.[4]

The years of Boxford's population growth coincided with the development of small-scale manufacturing, originally domestic crafts, later the factory system. Through the 1830s, Boxford had a thriving shoe industry carried on by farmer–artisans in backyard shoe shops, where they used hand tools to do cutting, pegging, and stitching for Haverhill and Lynn manufacturers, who provided raw materials and wages. Such rainy-day and wintertime labor produced $52,975 worth of shoes in Boxford in 1837, for instance.[5] About six small shoe factories had been erected by 1850. However, one after another of these failed during the Civil War and its aftermath; Boxford was not destined to become another Lynn. The small town's only textile mill employed about fifteen men and women for the production of cotton yarn, wicking, and batting for a time in the 1830s. Other manufacturers made use of Boxford's abundant timber; the cotton mill had been a factory for wood bowls and trays before 1830, and in 1867 it was converted into a sawmill and factory for the manufacture of sticks for the Diamond Match Company. This plant, too, had closed down by 1885, though the sawmill survived to meet local needs. Lumbering itself boomed between 1855 and 1875, providing, in 1865, 625,000 board feet of white pine and oak for Essex shipbuilders, the match factory, and local carpenters and wagonmakers.[6] Boxford wood also made fine fuel until coal furnaces became common; said one Boxfordian in 1896, "Coal killed this place." The decline of the timber industry was aided by the gradual depletion of the oak stands. The development and decline of these industries are reflected in the tax valuation of property in the town, which grew from $387,304 in 1845 to $631,940 in 1865, then fell to $569,722 in 1880.[7]

Population growth and decline were closely tied not only to manufacturing but to agriculture, which also experienced a minor boom in mid-century, leveling off after the Civil War. With the introduction of clover, crop rotation, and manuring before 1830, productivity increased; and the war brought a sudden demand for wool. When the war ended, the wool market collapsed just at a time when competition from western farms was putting additional strains on lands already experiencing soil depletion. Nevertheless, not until the last five years of the century did Boxford's total acreage of cultivated land drop, and new markets opened with the coming in 1852 of the Newburyport–Danvers railroad, joined to the Boston and Maine line seven years later. Between 1865 and 1885, milk production in gallons rose from 10,689 to 153,517 and the value of eggs sold tripled, which partially compensated for declines in other commodities, especially livestock. Because Boxford's farms were diversified and self-sufficient, they remained economically stable rather than declining sharply before the twentieth century. They could provide an adequate living for those content with moderate prosperity, but they provided little of the opportunity for financial advancement that would attract newcomers.[8]

Boxford's agricultural economy and its isolated geographical situation contributed to its citizens' parochial outlook, which shaped the development of schooling. Within the town's boundaries, self-sufficiency and the difficulty of travel between distant farms presented obstacles to social intercourse. Except for church, farm families came to the two town centers only for the relatively infrequent purposes of

143

town meetings, paying taxes, and laying in supplies. The two-parish layout further splintered the scattered population. That Boxford's isolation from other towns was as great as its lack of internal cohesion is attested by an 1846 geography text attributing Boxford's small size to her "retiring situation" and inaccessibility.[9] To some extent, the completion of the railroad closed the gap between the town and the outside world, as it made more frequent travel to cosmopolitan centers possible. Missing both town centers by over a mile, however, the railroad ensured that Boxford would never take a place among the state's thriving commercial or industrial towns. Indeed, the railroad made travel away from Boxford easier while it smothered the economic development that could have attracted travelers toward it. Furthermore, by favoring neither town center, the railroad encouraged Boxfordians to continue to define themselves as east- or west-siders.[10]

By the last quarter of the century, the central facts of life in Boxford had become economic stagnation and cultural isolation. Whether these were disadvantages was a matter of debate among Boxfordians. Some defended their town as the best possible place to produce "corn, apples and domestic virtues."[11] A visiting minister praised the town, which, "by its seclusion from many temptations, its rural scenery and its industrious habits, is peculiarly fitted for the formation of useful character."[12] Others, like the town clerk in 1893, bemoaned Boxford's lack of progress.

We are constantly reminded [of decline] by the deserted farms and gaping cellars that greet our eyes as we traverse the paths, lanes and byways of our town . . . What can be done to dispel from the minds of the rising generation the thought that nothing can be accomplished in Boxford? What can be done to stop the flight of our young people who at the age of 21 years or even before seize the valise and flee to some distant city or town to seek a fortune?[13]

Whether boon or bane, Boxford's isolation from the social changes taking place in the industrial centers of Massachusetts shaped the growth of her educational institutions.

Going to school in rural Boxford

In the eighteenth century, despite early Massachusetts laws mandating primary schools in every town, Boxford's public school system had been slow to develop. The General Court issued a warning to the recalcitrant village in 1701, as it had yet to hire any schoolmaster at that time, sixteen years after incorporation. For many years thereafter, Boxford had a moving school – one that met for only a few weeks at a time in one neighborhood before shifting to another – and in 1738 the first schoolhouse was erected. Because a 1789 Massachusetts statute required towns to establish districts and build schoolhouses, Boxford appropriated money to each of six districts, yet even this edict had limited effect. Most districts either procrastinated in building their schoolhouses or neglected the task altogether. Beginning in 1795 a school committee of between three and five men was appointed, and by 1799 five of the six districts had erected schoolhouses.

The committee's tasks were to hire teachers; to divide the money between the summer and winter, or the "woman's" and "man's," schools; to obtain fuel; to inspect classes each term; and to report to the annual town meeting. Operating on a budget of four to five hundred dollars, approved routinely along with highway repair funding and a rule requiring the restraint of hogs, the school committee supervised the schools until 1827, when the district system made inroads into the committee's central authority. That year the town took advantage of a new Massachusetts law to vote the appointment of a "prudential" committee in each district to hire the teachers. Gradually, over the next decade, the districts increased their power. By 1839 they were choosing prudential committees, dividing their appropriation into funds for a woman's and a man's school, and considering in annual district meetings the problems of schoolhouse maintenance. Thus, as Boxford grew and prospered, its common school system evolved, increasingly dependent on district control and interest.[14]

At the same time that public common schooling was expanding in Boxford, a variety of other institutions offered children educational opportunities. Next to the family, the church probably influenced the socialization of Boxford's youth most. There were two Congregational parishes in the town, one in the east and one in the west; both churches had well-established Sabbath school programs. A parish of liberal dissenters that grew out of a split in the first church, partly over doctrine and partly over personal quarrels, may also have held classes in the 1820s. Another popular source of learning in Boxford was the long-running singing schools, which aroused as much excitement for their social as for their educational functions.[15]

Private schools further supplemented the district schools. At least two were conducted during the 1830s, one a primary class held by an unmarried woman in her brother's home, another taught briefly by one Eveline Reynolds for about twenty-five young women, "to fit them for teaching." From about 1865 to 1881, Reverend Calvin E. Park of West Boxford held a private school for young men, apparently hoping to prepare them for entrance into Andover's Phillips Academy. Boxford itself had two fairly long-lived academies. Established about 1818 and incorporated in 1828 under the direction of Major Jacob Peabody, a Boston merchant and Boxford native, the first academy had about fifty pupils and survived until 1829, perhaps longer. Students came from Boxford, Boston, Salem, and other Massachusetts towns, as well as from New Hampshire and even Argentina, to study under liberal clergymen who also preached to the dissenting parish in the academy building on Sundays. Another academy, the J. Tyler Barker Free School, operated between 1883 and 1919 on a private endowment and under the auspices of the Episcopal church. Although the Barker school, like all the other nonpublic educational institutions, caused chagrin among the school committees, who feared that it "created distinctions," catered to the rich, and siphoned off support for the common schools, it thrived because it served a purpose in the community. Boxford still had no high school by the century's end; ambitious students were expected to use the Barker school. Together, the district schools, the Barker school, Sabbath schools, singing schools, and various fleeting private schools provided Boxford residents with an assortment of institutions for instructing their children and inculcating moral values.[16]

By the 1830s, in any case, the importance of common schooling, provided for every child at public expense and under local control, was widely accepted in Boxford. The "little red schoolhouse" was now firmly established as a necessary part of community life. What, then, was it like to go to one of Boxford's district schools? An examination of the experience of a typical young Boxfordian, whom we shall call Sarah, eight years old in 1860 but not dissimilar to schoolchildren throughout the century, will help illuminate the reality of education in nineteenth-century rural Massachusetts. Sarah is fictitious, but her experience is consistent with the surviving historical records of Boxford's schools.

Sarah walked about two miles each day to her District Five school, which was not little and red but little and peeling, dirty white. She sat on a hard bench with a straight back well carved with childish whimsies. In winter she sweltered near the wood stove or shivered in the drafty corners, and summer found her eager to escape into the fresh air and sunshine from the dark, airless schoolroom. Noon hours and recess periods gave her a chance to run about the road and in a nearby marshy area with classmates.

There were about thirty pupils enrolled in Sarah's one-room school, including her older brother, younger sister, and a few cousins. The students ranged in age from four to sixteen and so included a few just beginning to learn the alphabet and others ready for studies at the high school level. Sarah's daily routine included oral drill in spelling and reading, lengthy arithmetic problems worked on a slate, multiplication tables recited aloud, penmanship and grammar exercises, and work in texts in geography, history, and reading. Because her teacher was occupied much of the time drilling pupils of other ages, Sarah often found herself a class of one, responsible for her own progress. In some cases this was necessary anyway because her textbook, handed down within her family, was the only one of its kind in the classroom. In other cases the scarcity of texts among the students compelled her to share her copy with a group of two or three classmates. Sarah found the memorization of long, unfamiliar spelling words and of obscure facts about faraway places dry enough that she sometimes cared little whether she had the right textbook or not. Whispered, giggly messages from seatmates seemed more important. For part of each day, however, she escaped to the closet in the back of the schoolhouse, where some older students assisted younger pupils. Two or three of these students were themselves engaged in studying algebra, philosophy, and botany, hoping to pass the entrance examination to the high school in Danvers or North Andover.[17]

For the first several years of her schooling, Sarah had a female teacher in the summer and a male teacher in the winter. Not until 1864 did a woman teach her school for a full year, a novelty too extreme for ready adoption in District Five. The next year the procession of single-term teachers resumed in their traditional seasonal roles. For the first few weeks of each term, Sarah repeated a large portion of what she had completed the previous term, partly because she had forgotten much of it over the long vacation, and partly because her teacher had not yet determined just where Sarah stood in each of her subjects. Some teachers were more skilled at dealing with the advanced pupils, others with the younger pupils; some were flippant, others dour; some were talented, others dull-witted; some elicited affection, others warfare. All of them were young, all of their district school careers were short-lived, and all of them, without exception, told Sarah how important it was that she sit quietly and study, never squirming, whispering, or leaving her seat unnecessarily. Some enforced those edicts with free use of the rod on unruly children, whereas others maintained order by firm words and serene smiles. Still others simply lost control, and during those terms Sarah's classroom was constantly on the brink of chaos.

Through this succession of teachers and textbook, summers and winters, in the District Five school, Sarah progressed until she reached age fifteen. That year she and her parents decided that she should stay at home rather than put in more time at District Five or join those who would go on to the Barker Free School or high school in a neighboring town. Sarah helped out at home for some years, taking part in spelling bees, Sunday school, and other Boxford social events. Marriage to a young neighbor followed, and soon her own children went on to attend District Five schools and to go through an experience very similar to that of their mother.

As an adult, Sarah could read almanacs and newspapers, write legibly, and do arithmetic. She had a smattering of factual knowledge of the world beyond Boxford. She had ten years of exposure to a litany of desired character traits, to which she subscribed, more or less, and exemplified to some degree.

Goals and realities in Boxford schooling

Was Sarah's achievement what Boxford parents, school committees, and teachers hoped to accomplish by sending children to the district schools? The ideas of Boxford's parents and teachers on this matter are irretrievable, but the school committee members had the opportunity each year to set out in writing what they believed common schooling should do for a child. They described two major purposes. First, schools should teach children basic skills that would make them useful citizens in adulthood. The schools, they wrote in 1854, should insure

that the scholars in town generally should become good readers and spellers, that they attain to a thorough knowledge of mental and written arithmetic, that they be able to speak and write the English language correctly, that they possess themselves with a good general knowledge of geography and history, and that their handwriting be easy, plain and distinct.[18]

Second, teachers should discipline children, inculcating a love of order. Boxford schoolmen did not often describe the exact relationship between schoolroom order and the kind of orderly society they found desirable. Their community was homogeneous enough and sufficiently isolated from the disruptions of industrialization and urbanization that they did not see the schools as protection from threatening vice and depravity. Rather, they had a straightforward, traditional concept of school discipline, following from the Biblical injunction to "train up a child in the way he should go." The school committee elaborated in 1866:

Order in school is of the first and of the greatest importance. Here are the materials that will soon form an active and influential part of the community.

Just as the twig is bent, the tree is inclined. If the members of the schools are well-trained in good order, they will likely to be in after life the promoters, supporters and defenders of good order in the community and in the country, but if pupils in school are not trained to the observance of order there, or elsewhere, they will be likely to become disorderly members of society, and may be found very likely, if they should have the opportunity, working for the overthrow of good order and good government in the land.[19]

Moral education was the sine qua non:

The civilization of the age is owing entirely to the progress of mental and moral culture among the people . . . The former surely should not be improved at the expense of the latter. Where the mental nature is developed to excess and at the sacrifice of the moral, we may have an age of reason, but not one of vision.[20]

Whatever differences of opinion in religious matters may exist in the community, all will concur in this; that children should be taught morality . . . Moral influence is, or should be, the principal element in the government of a school.[21]

Of course, there was a more immediate and mundane reason for making children behave in the classroom. Disorder prevented students from studying.

Disorder in a school tends to prevent active and continued effort in study on the part of the pupils . . . A pupil who is engaged in school in making a noise, or in disorderly conduct, is not studying. These acts lead others to do the same. This evil work goes on through the day . . . it makes a vast difference in the work of a term. This evil may go so far as to make a school worse than useless.[22]

These aspirations – to create an environment in which students could learn practical skills and learn to behave in a socially acceptable manner – were never seriously questioned. They were so widely embraced that the means for attaining them earned unanimous endorsement among school authorities, who seemed unaware that unbending rules governing personal behavior, combined with a curriculum of rote memorization and routine progress through textbooks, might stifle a child's creativity while remaining irrelevant to most problems of adult life. Boxford educators aspired to achieve "perfect order" in the classrooms, and they believed that unhesitating obedience was a worthy objective for all concerned.

See this principle illustrated in military discipline, and especially on board ship. So, in a measure, are children under authority; they are to be trained, disciplined, fitted for citizenship – and this is best accomplished by requiring from them willing submission to rules and to authority . . . to train children to obey is to give them an education, which will be of permanent advantage to them.[23]

Children should sit still in their seats, and, above all, they should be quiet. "Among the various elements of disorder," they warned, "there is none more fraught with mischief, more generally prevalent and more difficult to suppress than the practice of whispering . . . Through this practice, every idea, impure thought originating with a single scholar, is easily propagated, till it becomes common throughout the schools."[24]

If possible, the committee wanted teachers to achieve "perfect order and stillness" through moral example rather than through corporal punishment. The teacher's "address and manners should be pleasing, and such as parents would wish to present as models to their children," they said.[25] Teachers who relied too much on "moral suasion," however, were reprimanded and encouraged to use the rod more freely. Few schoolmen took seriously the notion that schoolroom order could long be maintained without the use or at least the threat of punishment. In any case, the teachers' morals, in and out of school, were to be exemplary. In 1852 the school committee set these ideal expectations: "The teacher should be a man of correct moral habits," who can instill in his pupils "a sacred regard for truth and uprightness, and a love for whatever is of a virtuous and ennobling character." The diary of one teacher, Timothy Fuller, suggests that Boxford parents may have had some reason to worry about the propriety of his behavior out of school. Fuller attended frequent parties in nearby towns. At one, lasting until 1:00 A.M., Fuller had a "tolerably high go!" and another kept him out until 4:30 A.M.[26]

"Perfect order" through moral example was the ideal. The reality was something less, due to the human frailties of teachers and the traditional reliance on corporal punishment. "Perfect order" also remained elusive because not all Boxfordians shared the school committee's vision of the school as the bulwark of the community. Rather, parents and taxpayers were often in conflict with the schoolmen, supporting the general notion of public education, but preferring that the school play a less prominent and less assertive role in the life of the child and the community. For one thing, parents and children resisted the educators' efforts to achieve universal enrollment and regular attendance at school. Although a small number of school-age children remained unenrolled throughout the century, they were not the major concern. Summer enrollment in the public schools for children ages four to sixteen (later five to fifteen) varied between 73.6 percent and 86.3 percent between 1839 and 1869; winter enrollments were between 71.4 percent and 95.9 percent, averaging 84.1 percent. Regularity of attendance was a worse problem. Attendance ran as much as 17.6 percent lower than enrollments in winter, when families found travel across snow-covered countryside difficult, and between 14.3 percent and 23.2 percent lower in summer, when many parents encouraged pupils to stay home to work on the farm.[27] The school committee found this practice "pernicious."[28] It certainly made it difficult for a pupil to progress through his lessons:

If scholars are absent from school for two or three days they lose the recitations, and too frequently, the studies which their classes have been over during that time. This is no slight loss, as on their return they may very likely find that some important subject has been passed over during their absence with which they are not familiar, and in consequence are unable to proceed with their classes in what they are now doing.[29]

It also "caused a disturbance in class, perplexing the teacher" and destroying schoolroom order.[30] Moreover, irregular attendance wasted taxpayers' money:

It appears, then, that only 89 out of 165 scholars make the average daily attendance in all the schools. Each of these 89 costs the town more than $23. But we have provision made for the entire number and could as well receive daily 105 into school. If ⅔ of the children came to school – and why should they not? – the cost of each would then be nearly $16 – a liberal appropriation for a town like ours.[31]

As early as 1844, the town meeting directed the school committee to "inquire into and ascertain the cause of the habitual absence of children from school who are of suitable age to attend the same,"[32] but nothing formal was done. Despite local skirmishes between carping school committee members and indifferent parents, the schoolmen did not embrace state innovations to compel attendance. Truants in the sparse, isolated town were not nearly as threatening to social order as in an industrial town like Lynn or Lawrence. Also, despite the schoolmen's desire to increase the proportion of a child's time spent in school, they agreed with parents that the home, not the school, was still primarily responsible for a child's upbringing. "God places children upon their entrance into life, not in schools, but in families; he has imposed the responsibility in regard to the training they may receive, not upon teachers, but upon parents."[33] Thus when an 1864 Massachusetts law required the election of three truant officers and provided that truants be prosecuted and placed by the court in foster homes or reformatories, Boxford's truant officers went no further than to call on a truant's parents and extract from them a promise of more diligence. This method became a town bylaw in 1880, and in 1888 the school committee noted that "a town like this can hardly be expected to employ officers to be on the road every day to see that all the children were in school."[34] It was a parent's job to raise a child in proper habits, calculated to guarantee his own successful future and the peace and order of the institutions of which he was a part.

Besides friction over school attendance, Boxford parents resisted school committee attempts to improve school buildings and standardize textbooks. The 1843 school committee complained that most districts' buildings were "dark, dirty and inconvenient," with "peeling clapboard" and bad ventilation. Blaming the problem of "noisy, restless children" in part upon the hard, high-backed benches on which they were compelled to sit, the committee pleaded annually that the districts spend the money to repair their buildings and add appropriate furnishings and apparatus, or better yet, build new schoolhouses.[35] Sanitary conditions were equally bad; as late as 1883, the committee reported that "all outbuildings were found extremely filthy," the source of scarletina and diphtheria. In that year all the privies were repaired and, for the first time, limed. For the parents and taxpayers who attended district meetings, expensive facilities simply did not command a high priority. District Seven, for instance, spent three meetings in 1843 debating whether or not to add an outhouse, ultimately approving "only such a building as the [committee in charge] thinks absolutely necessary."[36]

The schoolbooks that pupils used were equally inadequate in the eyes of the school committee. Although the committee suggested in its first report to the town meeting, in 1796, that the town buy schoolbooks for everyone, the community followed the traditional practice of letting parents provide their own schoolbooks.[37] As a result, a multiplicity of texts and editions appeared in each school, and some pupils lacked any text at all in some subjects.

As in the case of schoolhouse conditions, the school committee's dire warnings were heeded begrudgingly or ignored. The districts had the power to obtain uniform books if they so chose, but they passed the responsibility on to individual parents and teachers. The school committee did make an effort to make textbooks more uniform. In 1838 they compiled a list of approved texts, probably drawn from the state board of education's recommendations, from which all texts were to be chosen, whether bought by parents, teachers, or districts. But in 1845 the committee had to plead with the town meeting to make the list mandatory, so weak was the committee's ability to enforce the recommendations, which had been largely ignored. Teachers often had their own textbook preferences, and parents found it convenient and inexpensive to pass textbooks used by older cousins or siblings down to younger children. Gradual improvement was made, but by the century's end, the committee still complained about the variety of texts used.[38]

Another barrier preventing Boxford's schools from effectively teaching skills, discipline, and morality was the shortage of teachers who met their specifications. It was clear that the success of a one-room school depended on the teacher in charge, so that the teacher had to have certain qualities suited to accomplishing the schools' purposes. As we have seen, the teacher was to be well versed in the subject matter but also "irreproachable in morals, of a genial disposition," and able to demonstrate and teach "modesty, deportment, reverence for all that is good and pure, obedience, morality and propriety." Unfortunately, it was difficult to judge which applicants for a teaching position were "apt as well as qualified," and certainly few enough actually proved blessed with all the desired qualities.[39]

Boxford's town school committee fretted about its teaching staff for a number of reasons. First, the committee mistrusted the informal means by which teachers were hired. Early in the century, the town meeting had delegated to the district prudential committees the responsibility for examining and certifying teachers, but the prudential committees were often ill educated and, in the town school committee's view, uninformed about the proper management of schools. The prudential committees commonly relied on personal acquaintance with teaching candidates, or on the recommendation of respected neighbors; a former teacher would sometimes recommend a friend or a sibling. Examinations were cursory and could not, in any case, measure a teacher's ability to govern a large class. Sometimes a teacher was hired entirely by mail, a certificate being promised upon the schoolmaster's arrival in town.[40]

These hiring practices ensured that most teachers were young and inexperienced. Not until 1850 did any teacher stay both summer and winter terms. Although some returned for consecutive summers or winters, 70 percent of all teachers hired in Boxford between 1841 and 1865 stayed only one term. The average nineteenth-century Boxford female teacher taught 2.64 consecutive terms; for men, the average was only 1.01. The average number of nonconsecutive terms taught was 3.31 for women, 1.33 for men. In 1859, Harriet Pearl and Mary Adams set records by staying to teach four and five consecutive terms, respectively. Around 1880, the first career teachers appeared, the most durable staying as long as eight to ten years.[41] Of course, many beginning teachers proved incompetent and unsuited to teaching, and such incapacity led to frequent terminations, either at the option of the prudential committee or because the teacher grew frustrated and did not reapply. Others, who were better teachers, chose to move on to larger, better-paying schools, especially as Boxford's school-age population continued to shrink at a time when other school systems were expanding. Still other teachers married or went into other occupations.

Two practices inimical to careerism persisted almost to the century's end. The first was the hiring of male college students for the winter term; theology and law students took advantage of flexible rules at Dartmouth and Harvard granting leaves or even credit for a few weeks' teaching in the country. Boxford's early schools had the benefit of such highly educated teachers as F. Eugene Clark, the founder of Christian Endeavor, a Protestant youth organization; Samuel McCall, a future governor; and Timothy Fuller, future congressman and father of the famed Margaret Fuller. Each taught for only one term.[42] The second practice that prevented teaching careers was the employment of women for summer terms only. In each of the districts, one-third to one-half of the annual school money was appropriated for a summer term of nine to fifteen weeks, for which a woman was hired. The rest of the money went for the winter terms of two to four weeks less, taught by a man.[43]

Short terms and seasonal gender requirements caused high teacher turnover, and both stemmed from the districts' desire to save money. No teacher could support a family on the low salary paid, at least not at a standard of living equal to that possible with other jobs. Talented, intelligent people were unlikely to choose teaching over more lucrative jobs; there were those, complained the town committee, who "engage in the important office of teacher for no higher motive than to get their dollars a little more easily than they can by manual labor." Some were "upstarts . . . who were a disgrace to the teacher's profession, [who] usurped the place of those who were more thoroughly qualified for their business."[44]

The fact that women could be hired much more cheaply than men, however, made the problem seem more complex, at least to the town school committee. Could qualified women not be hired year-round, and the money thus saved be used for raising salaries overall? Or were female teachers defined by their sex as the kind of second-class teachers, poorly educated and incapable of discipline, whom the town committee wished to avoid hiring? Boxford's schoolmen were aware of a shift to women teachers going on in other towns, and in 1851 they kept a woman on for the winter term for the first time. In 1857 four of the seven districts hired a women for the winter, although not always the same woman who had taught the previous summer. However, by 1860 the practice had once again fallen into disfavor. In some cases the school committee, and in others the district meetings, had instructed the prudential committee to hire a man and had accepted a prudential committee's choice of a female teacher only reluctantly. Despite scant resources, Boxfordians decided that the money saved by hiring women was not worth the loss in classroom order. The town school committee wrote of women in the winter schools that,

> however well the plan may *seem* to succeed in other towns, for us, it is not practicable . . . we believe that the *amount* of labor, both mental and physical, necessarily required to teach and govern our winter schools, unclassed as they are, is greater than is capable of being performed by them, except in very rare instances.[45]

Women seemed to lack the strength to handle the older boys, who were at work on the farms in summer, as well as the "understanding of all the detail and minutiae of the first principles, which comprise nearly all that is taught in our school."[46]

Over the next several years, however, Boxford's school committee and district committees changed their minds. Increasing numbers of women, some high school or even normal school graduates, proved willing to teach at low salaries (see Table 6.3). The financial advantage to the districts was clear and became too great a temptation to resist, in a town with declining resources. In 1845, Boxford paid its female teachers, on the average, 41 percent of the wage men received; although the town gradually lessened this inequity, it still paid women only 86 percent of the male wage in 1880.[47] At the same time, Boxford's female teachers proved themselves competent. More and more women were hired, and in 1878, for the first time, all the schools were taught year-round by women. The 1875 school committee pronounced that "the experiment of substituting female teachers in the winter has succeeded beyond our most sanguine expectations."[48] Feminization pleased the school committee, for if anyone in Boxford pressed for educational innovation, it was they, and female teachers were fast becoming the fashion elsewhere. At the same time, women candidates seem to have provided a good supply of the kind of teachers the townspeople liked: malleable to their wishes, not over-educated or "highfalutin," and cheap.

Thus, although Boxford's school committees ritually repeated their

155

Table 6.3. Feminization of Boxford's public schoolteaching force, 1840–80

	Total number of teachers	% female teachers	Average monthly wages – male	Average monthly wages – female	Female salary as % of male
1840	12	58.3	$26.66	$11.00	41.26
1845	14	50.0	24.43	10.00	40.9
1850	14	64.3	29.60	15.25	51.52
1855	15	66.7	32.11	16.67	51.91
1860	14	57.1	32.87	19.16	58.29
1865	14	71.4	38.37	20.30	52.9
1870	13	61.5	50.20	27.00	53.8
1875	9	77.8	52.00	35.00	67.3
1880	9	77.8	36.00	31.00	86.1

Source: Massachusetts State Board of Education, Annual Reports.

lofty educational ideals, they met with resistance from parents and taxpayers that perpetuated the realities of irregular attendance, minimal physical facilities, and transient, untrained teachers. In part, Boxford's marginal economic situation reinforced parental conservatism and exacerbated the school committee's problems, especially late in the century. Even during the prosperous years before the Civil War, money to buy textbooks or to hire better teachers was scarce. Boxford's farmers, barely self-sufficient, had little cash and were unwilling to spend what they had on higher school taxes. The lumber and manufacturing businesses whose higher tax assessments enriched the town in mid-century closed one by one. Meanwhile, decreases in population, especially sharp in the child-bearing age groups, caused class sizes to drop rapidly in the last three decades of the century. In 1845 the average class size in each of the seven districts was 29.0 in summer and 32.0 in winter; in 1870 it had dropped to 23.2 and 28.0, although there was one less district by then. In 1879, one school had only ten enrolled scholars.[49] The persistence of a district system, with a declining school-age population, was costly. As the years went by, each dollar spent on teachers, fuel, and repairs served fewer pupils. Classes had so few children at any single age or ability level that grading and curriculum organization were impossible; good teachers, unwilling to take on such a difficult task for so little pay, preferred jobs in larger schools.

Economic decline, however, was not the only cause of Boxford's

Table 6.4. Property valuation and per pupil expenditures (in dollars) in Boxford and Essex County, 1845-80

| | Property valuation of Boxford | Appropriation per pupil | | | |
		All Mass. towns	All Essex County towns	All Mass. towns popu- lation 0-1,000 except Boxford	Boxford
1845	387,304.00	2.99	2.54	2.14	2.72
1850	387,304.00	4.52	3.03	2.84	3.53
1855	538,288.67	5.36	4.85	3.35	4.39
1860	538,288.67	6.42	5.81	4.15	3.82
1865	631,942.00	7.37	6.07	4.40	4.86
1870	631,942.00	11.62	9.04	7.39	8.90
1875	619,045.00	15.07	12.33	9.94	10.30
1880	569,722.00	13.56	11.18	7.54	9.69

Source: Massachusetts State Board of Education, Annual Reports.

contentment with its casual, cheap school system. In fact, partly because of its declining enrollments, the town's per pupil expenditures continued to rise from 1845 to 1880, even when the property valuation was falling after 1870 (see Table 6.4). Boxford continued to compare favorably with Essex County towns of similar size, spending somewhat more than the average for these towns even during the years of economic decline. Boxford's schools remained aloof from the pedagogical and institutional innovations that the followers of Horace Mann advocated and that larger school systems were adopting, for another reason. The people of Boxford preferred a system that would closely reflect their widely scattered, localized geographical and community organization. Clinging to traditional ways, Boxfordians resisted any innovations that might transfer some of their control over their children's schooling to their neighbors on the other side of the town, let alone to the state board of education.

Localism recalcitrant

For nineteenth-century Boxford, geographical isolation was not a figment of nostalgic imagination, but a fact of life. Rarely did a farmer travel to a distant town. The railroad made trade possible, but it did not revolutionize traditional patterns of local commerce and agricultural self-sufficiency. Its out-of-the-way route had deprived either town center of the expansion that major railroad stopping points experienced, and a Boxfordian would have little reason to travel from one parish to the other. A woman who had grown up in West Boxford in the 1890s related in 1975 that she had simply never gone to the east parish and thus was no authority on what had happened there.[50]

The effect of this isolation is illustrated by the problem of schoolhouse location. Small as the school districts were in comparison to other governmental units, whenever a new building was to be built, the inhabitants invariably spent several meetings wrangling over what location would be approximately equidistant from each homestead. This intense concern that the school be equally accessible to all its constituents, along with the citizens' reluctance to sacrifice any good land for a schoolyard, accounted for the schoolhouse settings that so distressed the school committee: unsanitary swamps, rocky fields, or bare crossroads.

This localistic and jealously familial outlook helps to account for parents' indifference to other school committee appeals. Irregular attendance, for instance, reflected their unwillingness to surrender their children to the control of outsiders. Farm parents were accustomed to having their children around the farm, doing chores and caring for younger siblings when necessary. At some times, sending them to school might seriously disrupt the routine on the farm, just as the teachers and school committee complained that absence disrupted schoolroom order. Hence, too, the parents' reluctance to lengthen the terms or abandon the traditional summer and winter term schedule, which was widely losing favor in the cities. The short terms that prevailed before 1870 were compatible with farm routine; planting and harvesting were times for school recess, freeing children to help their parents.

Furthermore, parents resisted enhancement of teachers' status or authority at their expense. They wanted final responsibility for disciplining their children, and they firmly opposed attempts by the school committee and the state to professionalize the teachers, for by setting uniform certification standards and making it more difficult to hire and fire a teacher at the district's will, the schoolmen were depriving parents of their traditional, primary role in child rearing. Real distrust of the teachers caused parents to complain to the school committee and even to withdraw their child from school when they believed that a teacher had been unfair or too severe. Sarah Gould, teaching for the

158

first time in 1852, encountered "prejudice" from parents who had her called before the school committee. The committee gave her a second chance, but the class had dwindled to only a few pupils by the term's end. In 1864, District Two accepted the report of its prudential committee only after striking the last clause, in which the committee had described the last woman hired as a "model teacher." The parents also passed this resolution:

Resolved, that the expulsion of any school-child from schools is unwise and unjust, whenever they can remain with benefit to themselves and without injury to others. Resolved, that we believe the committee and teacher have exercised undue authority in exacting that which is unnecessary and uncalled for, and have thereby shown themselves unfit for the situations they hold.

In 1872 a group of parents even sued schoolmaster Henry Lewis for punishing a pupil too harshly.[51]

Of course, as the school committee regularly pointed out, parents who relied on their children for information regarding incidents of discipline in the classroom were not hearing both sides of the story. Because parents rarely visited the schools, their only impression of a teacher's abilities came from tales told by the outraged pupil. Moreover, the less support parents gave the teacher as he or she tried to discipline the unruly, the more the teacher's ability to govern deteriorated. But nineteenth-century Boxfordians, convinced that parents knew best how to raise their children, gave no teacher the benefit of that doubt.

Ill-assorted textbooks also resulted largely from the decentralization and family tradition that the townspeople valued. Attempts by the state board of education and the Boxford school committee to standardize texts failed year after year. Parents may have wanted direct control over what subject matter their children were taught, favoring familiar texts; more certainly, they appreciated the economy of giving their children old editions obtained from kin or neighbors.

The one-room schoolhouse, with its irregular scholars, miscellaneous textbooks, and inexperienced teachers, closely fit the life-style of Boxford farm families, and they resisted educational innovation. The underpinning for the one-room school was, of course, the district system, the structure most closely adapted to a widely scattered, locally oriented population. To state-level reformers and the Boxford schoolmen who read the annual state reports, however, the district system seemed inefficient, pedagogically unsound, and generally antiquated. The consolidation of district schools was an issue that provoked continuing tension between progressive schoolmen and a resis-

Education and social change in nineteenth-century Massachusetts

tant populace well into the twentieth century, providing a focus for
conflicts accompanying social change.

In 1839 the Boxford town meeting had given each district full power
to choose its own prudential committee, to hire a teacher, to divide its
appropriation for summer and winter terms, and to maintain the
schoolhouse. Just four years later, in 1843, the town school committee
first urged consolidation of the districts under town auspices. The town
could get more for its money, the committee pointed out, if it hired
three teachers with schools of forty pupils rather than six teachers for
schools of twenty. A proposition to establish a "centre" district, to
which pupils of all grades would be transported at public expense, was
defeated in 1845, defeated again later, and defeated a third time despite
a euphemistic rechristening of the "village" district.[52]

In 1864 the school committee bemoaned the citizens' recalcitrance:

We believe that a defective system exerts an injurious influence on our schools.
But so firmly are the larger part of our citizens attached to this system, so fully
are they persuaded that centralized power is dangerous – that the town ought
not to be entrusted with the entire care of the Schools (although its officers
preside in every other department), that the reserved right of choosing an agent
to have the care of the School houses, and to employ the Teachers of the
children, is a privilege of vital importance, not lightly to be relinquished – that
we do not with much hope look for better things. Yet this has been a costly
mistake, which has done more to retard the progress of an enlightened and
enlarged system of instruction, than any and all other causes combined.[53]

By reducing the number of schools to two or three, the committee
argued, the town could hire better teachers, ending high turnover, as
well as more fairly distributing funds, then shared equally by large and
small schools. Moreover, the schools could be graded, and "the
teacher could find more time to dwell on the different topics at each
recitation." Little chastened, the townspeople proceeded to defeat
proposals to abolish the districts' powers in 1866 and in March of 1869.
In April of that year, however, threatened with loss of its seventy-
five-dollar state appropriation under the new law mandating the abolition of district committees, Boxford voted in town meeting to accept
its fate. Once having made the conversion, Boxford stood by its decision, defeating 43 to 63 an 1872 motion that the town take advantage of
its newly legal option of approving by a two-thirds vote the reestablish-
ment of districts. The town even approved the lengthening of the
school year to include three terms and the consolidation of the tiny
third- and fourth-district schools.[54]

Boxford accepted less gracefully more extensive plans for consoli-

160

dation. In 1897 and 1898 respectively, Districts One and Two, and then Five and Six, were consolidated, with transportation provided for pupils in the districts inconvenienced. When parents protested that their farms would drop in value unless a school were nearby, and that transporting children so far would cause them moral and physical harm, schools in Districts Five and One were reopened in 1899. A serious challenge to traditional localism arose in 1901, when Boxford agreed to join Reading, Middleton, and Topsfield in a union district in order to afford economical schooling beyond the primary level. But in the bargain they got a progressive administrator. The new superintendent, Melville Stone of Reading, was sympathetic to the problems of widely scattered farmers; nevertheless, he was certain that Boxford would accept new ways:

The old country schools of a generation ago did good work . . . but many of those who obtained in that way, a good education and have in fair measure kept up to the times, are very well aware that the world moves, that progress is being made, in methods of education as well as in other things and are ready to endorse the modern methods.[55]

Stone opened a central grammar school in the town hall of the east parish, arguing that as soon as possible a new primary school building with a playground should be built as well. At the annual union district meeting of 1903, "much dissatisfaction" arose over these progressive ideas. Boxford and Middleton, lobbying for a new superintendent, could not agree with Reading and Topsfield and so withdrew from the union. Boxford closed its grammar school immediately and began looking for some smaller towns who might be willing to hire a less radical superintendent. In 1905, J. G. Morrell was appointed to the job.[56] Boxford was not rid of the issue of consolidation. In 1906, two of the east parish's three ungraded schools, which by this time had less than fifty pupils altogether, were again joined under one teacher for the lower and one for the upper grades. Morrell, however, was more sympathetic than Stone to the idea of local control:

I do not wish to complain about the present condition of your school system. If it is satisfactory to the committee and to the citizens and you should wish for no change, I will do the best I can to gratify your desire. But if you are willing to try a change for the purpose of getting something better, you must not complain and criticize until the changes have had time to work out the natural results.[57]

Boxford's locally oriented farmers took their firmest stance on consolidation and grading of the one-room schools, but they also resisted other innovations in the name of local control. The question of establishing a high school was an example. By the 1880s it had become evident that some pupils were now staying in school long enough to take up studies at a high school level and that Boxford's common schoolteachers had neither the expertise nor the time to handle these pupils along with a roomful of smaller children. Ambitious older pupils tried doing algebra, bookkeeping, ancient history, and Latin on their own, and one dedicated teacher held classes in French outside school hours. Other pupils entered the Barker Free School in West Boxford, which admitted children as young as age twelve but was under sectarian control. A third alternative was travel to a high school in another town. In 1884 two girls began going to the high school in Putnam, and in 1886 four more left for Newburyport, Georgetown, and Danvers. Although an 1891 Massachusetts law required that a town lacking a high school pay tuition for its young people attending high school in another town, Boxford seems not to have been doing so by 1896.[58]

Inevitably, a Boxfordian proposed at a town meeting in 1896 that a high school be erected, but geographical tensions again frustrated innovation. West Boxford was unwilling to vote support for a school that it expected would duplicate the services of the Barker Free School, located in its parish. The school committee also took this point of view, having tried for several years to convince the state that the existence of the Barker school should exempt the town from either maintaining a high school or paying out-of-town tuition. The residents of the east parish argued that the Barker school was too far away for its children and that they should build a high school. Although the larger east side could vote the west down, the resolution failed when no location could be decided upon. The only fair setting – exactly two and one-half miles from each town center – was covered with thick pine woods. In the end, it proved less divisive and cheaper to pay tuition and carfare to Danvers or North Andover for those who wished to go than to build one high school for the whole town.[59] Even at the end of the century, then, when an increasing number of young Boxford men and women were moving to the cities to seek clerical or teaching positions that called for high school training, local prejudices and geographical conflicts spelled the downfall of the project.

The high school issue represented the dilemma of education in this isolated nineteenth-century town. On one hand, Boxford's resistance to grading and consolidation, longer terms, and improved facilities had earned the rural community a bad reputation with school reformers. On the other hand, Boxford farmers had succeeded in maintaining a system fairly responsive to their needs. For a town little touched by the social changes going on in large industrial cities and commercial centers, Boxford's schools had been appropriate. They were congruent with traditionally close-knit kinship and neighborhood ties, and they fit the patterns of agricultural life. Upon graduation from District Five, our fictional student, Sarah, not only had some mastery of the crude curriculum, she had known her schoolmates in a more personal way than was possible in the increasingly bureaucratic systems of the cities. Although she had many teachers, the classes were small, and many of the teachers were local people who shared backgrounds similar to Sarah's.

The one-room schools were not divorced from the larger patterns of Boxford life. Summer and winter terms were scheduled around strawberry picking and sheep shearing; even the discriminatory practice of hiring women only for the summer terms arose from the reality of farm life, for the winter months found many more burly, unmanageable boys attending schools for lack of agricultural chores. Short school terms and noncompulsory attendance meant that children were socialized by many institutions. Boxford appears to exemplify David Tyack's characterization of rural childhood in the nineteenth century:

The child acquired his values and skills from his family and from neighbors of all ages and conditions. The major vocational curriculum was work on the farm or the craftsman's shop or the corner store; civic and moral instruction came mostly in church or home or around the village where people met to gossip or talk politics. A child growing up in such a community could see work–family–religion–recreation–school as an organically related system of human relationships.[60]

Finally, Boxford's seemingly inefficient district system continually symbolized reinforced parental control of education. District school meetings were the arena for lively battles over parochial issues. Controversies over the location of schoolhouses reflected the rivalries inherent in wide geographical dispersion, but their resolution in district and town meetings kept community control alive and lively. Moreover, the schoolhouse was the scene for all sorts of social life. The teachers presented their pupils in evening programs of declamations, dialogues, and readings in unison, and the public examinations at the end of each term entertained parents and citizens with displays of spelling, reading, and oral arithmetic. When the schoolhouse was unoccupied, the district lent it out for the use of singing schools and debating societies, public lectures and religious meetings, drawing together neighbors who had few enough occasions for fellowship.[61]

Nonetheless, as more young Boxfordians moved out to seek jobs in the city, and as those who stayed to farm were increasingly in touch with the outside world, schools that had served nineteenth-century Boxford well became anachronistic. For many students, community integrity and socialization for a slow-paced rural life-style began to lose their relevance. It was left for twentieth-century Boxford to consider how the school system might be used to revive in rising generations a love for the land and to impart the scientific skills needed to make a living from it, or to prepare those who would leave for careers in the urban environment. In 1900, Boxford had yet to face the dilemmas that social changes occurring beyond its borders had presented in the nineteenth century.

Lynn: in the midst of urban industrialism

Only fifteen miles from Boxford, Lynn had a sharply different educational history, one tied closely to its different experience with population growth, immigration, and economic life.

Lynn's shoe industry provided the material means by which a sleepy, harborless, subsistence farming community was transformed into a modern city. The shoe industry provided Lynn's means of growth; it did not, however, determine the precise nature of social and institutional relations in the city. Despite the crucial economic impact of the shoe industry, it was only one element among many that intruded into the lives of Lynn residents. As the century progressed, the scale and complexity of social life compounded; individuals increasingly stood in more diverse and fragmented relationships to one another. Thus the perceptions and attitudes of the populace were not determined by any single institution.

Almost two hundred years passed between Lynn's founding and the rise of shoemaking as its major occupation. Settled in about 1630, Lynn stagnated while neighboring towns with commercial economies, such as Salem and Boston, flourished. Lynn did not have a harbor sufficient to support commerce. Before the War for Independence, people eked out a living, primarily from farming and fishing. True, the enterprising tried many alternatives – milling, tanning, silkworm raising, printing, salt making, even shipping – but conditions were never quite right, and all attempts eventually ended in failure. War, however, brought changed conditions. With imports cut off, a market for shoes opened. From three master cordwainers in 1750, about fifty were at work in 1783. The southern United States provided a vast market, allowing rapid expansion and differentiation of the industry. By 1830, in the words of historian Paul Faler, "the contours of the organization in the shoe industry were well defined."[62]

164

Figure 6.1. Population of Lynn, 1790–1900 (from federal censuses and Lynn School Committee, *Annual Reports*)

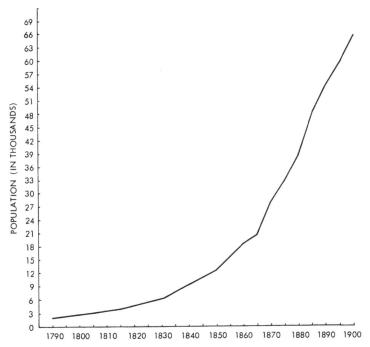

During the first third of the nineteenth century, certain changes indicated that Lynn was entering the evolving network of Massachusetts urban life. The Boston and Salem Turnpike, passing through Lynn, opened in 1803, thus providing a relatively efficient means of transportation and communication. It would serve as the main avenue of travel to Boston until 1838, when the new Eastern Railroad appropriated that function. It was also in 1803 that the Lynn Hotel began providing accommodations for a growing number of travelers. As the years passed, more people found work in Lynn. The population more than doubled between 1800 and 1830, rising from 2,837 to 6,138 (see Figure 6.1). The town's first law office opened in 1808, and the first banker went into business in 1819. Lynn still was no metropolis, but urban institutional development continued, with an almshouse, a second bank, and a newspaper all opening for business before the first *Lynn Directory* saw print in 1832.[63]

Lynn's population had reached 14,252 in 1850, when the town received a new charter and began operating under the city form of gov-

165

ernment. Besides witnessing the opening of the Eastern Railroad in 1838, the residents had built Breed's Pond in 1843 to provide water for an iron works. And finally, in 1849, another clear sign that Lynn had become a part of modern urban life appeared: The first police court went to work. Meanwhile, the shoe industry, riding the fluctuating but upward course of business, continued to expand and to support the growing complexity of urban life.[64]

During the second half of the century, Lynn took on the typical characteristics of a modern urban community. Real estate and personal valuation in 1850 of just under $5 million increased dramatically (even allowing for inflation) to almost $41 million by 1890; city expenditures rose in the same period from an annual rate of $36,704 to $1,745,229. And during the fifty-year period from 1850 to 1900, the population multiplied almost fivefold, to 68,512. Steadily, the technologies and conveniences of modern life were incorporated into the life of the city. The first use of illuminating gas began in 1853, with Lynn's gas company producing over three million feet in 1869. Electricity, too, had an early impact, as the telegraph put Lynn instantly in touch with Boston and other cities in 1858. Telephones went into operation in 1879, and the illuminating gas industry began a permanent decline with the introduction of electric lights in 1882. The city's electric works started generating the next year, making possible innumerable conveniences, including an electric street railroad system after 1888. Protection against fire finally became practicable with the introduction of an adequate city water system and an electric fire alarm network. Transportation into and out of Lynn got much easier, as the turnpike became a public highway in 1869; three years later cheap commuter trains began running to Boston. In 1862 the Lynn Public Library opened, and the Lynn Hospital was incorporated in 1881. In 1854 the Lynn business directory listed 117 occupational categories, whereas in 1901 it boasted 717. During the last half of the nineteenth century, there was much to do and many things to think about in Lynn.[65]

Throughout the second half of the nineteenth century, the shoe industry continued to serve as the growing city's economic base. It brought in large sums of money from shoe sales and reapportioned part of this money to the community through ancillary industries, taxes, and wages. Furthermore, it continued to provide enough jobs to sustain population growth throughout the century. The value of boots and shoes manufactured steadily increased throughout the period: In 1855 boot and shoe manufacturers produced over $4 million worth of goods, with the figure surpassing $22.5 million in 1895. The great economic impact of the industry is indicated by comparing the value of shoe production with that of all Lynn's industries. In 1865 the manufacture of boots and shoes equaled 83.6 percent of all goods produced. The 1880 figure was almost the same, 83.1 percent, although it dropped significantly to 65.9 percent in 1895, reflecting the diversification of industry then underway. The percentages are almost the same, too, when total town wages and wages for boot and shoemakers are compared. The shoe market determined to a great degree the amount of money circulating in Lynn at any given time. Clearly, boot and shoe manufacturing provided the city its entree into the emerging industrial order and provided its stores of machine-made wealth; shoes propelled Lynn into modern urban life.[66]

Education and the working class in Lynn

To understand the dynamics of the public school system in nine-teenth-century Lynn, we must ask what people thought the system should do and why. To anticipate the argument to follow, the answer is that the public in general consistently supported the growth of the system and expected it to train up literate and virtuous citizens who would be integrated into the work and social life of the city and nation. From all that we could learn, both the most complacent and the most disenchanted elements of the adult population agreed about the ends and means of the schools. We have found no evidence to indicate that any group, at any time during the century, actively resisted either the aims or the organizational arrangements of the public school system, except some Roman catholics, who objected on religious grounds.

Support for schools derived from a broad ideological consensus. A nineteenth-century urban ideology defined for Lynn's citizens the nature of the relationship between the individual and his society, and the means by which that society might be preserved and improved. The ideology channeled potentially dangerous dissatisfaction into harmless streams. Basic assumptions about property, production, and human relations had attained the status of self-evident truths and served as the conceptual limits for analysis of public policy and socioeconomic relations. Most reform in Lynn was therefore of the tinkering variety; the structure of property and class relations persisted without serious challenge. The history of the labor movement in Lynn illustrates this point.

The shoe industry in Lynn emerged within the context of commercial capitalism. Shoe workers labored under difficult working conditions for inadequate wages. Times of economic trouble affected the workers directly, severely, and disproportionately. Workers, not owners, paid the price of economic fluctuations. In response, labor association and eventually union agitation began in Lynn in the 1840s and continued intermittently throughout the remainder of the century. The three most severe periods of industrial strain are instructive to consider here, because by studying how the workers sought to redress their grievances, we may learn what notions of property, power, and justice were held by the largest, the most exploited, and, potentially, the most disenchanted segment of Lynn's population.

Labor association in the 1840s resulted from a growing estrangement between the owners and journeyman shoemakers. Earlier the two had worked side by side, embodying at least for a time the ideal of a satisfactory craft life. As the shoe business developed, however, the owners increasingly withdrew from the productive process.[67] Meanwhile, work life deteriorated as standards of quality gave way to pressures for increased and cheaper production. This gradually left the journeyman shoemaker in an untenable position. As owners increasingly hired cheap unskilled laborers, what little control the journeyman had exercised over the quality of workmanship – through the apprenticeship system – also slipped from his hands. The artisan class of workers, then, tended to a backward-looking, individualistic labor theory of value, and they were the first to articulate dissatisfaction with the evolving structure of business-dominated industry.[68] This dissatisfaction, however, because it looked backward to a set of conditions irrevocably gone instead of forward to new and equitable productive arrangements, did not produce fruitful criticism. Instead, in the 1840s, the artisans formed a journeymen's association and published, in historian Alan Dawley's words, a "spirited artisan newspaper," the *Awl*. It attacked "harsh bosses" and "poor quality workmen."[69] However, the emphasis was on recapturing the past, and industrial capitalism kept on its course.

Working conditions worsened. By the late 1850s, the artisans were ready to act more forcefully. They went out on strike in 1860, hoping to convince the owners of the error of their ways, so that they would change their management policies to bring quality workmanship and fair wages back into shoe manufacturing. According to Alan Dawley, because the journeymen believed the logic of their case would be acknowledged as self-evident, "they expected some support from the manufacturers in a mutual effort to raise prices and thus wages," and furthermore "felt their strike represented the best interests of the entire community, manufacturers included."[70] The owners were not persuaded, however, and the strikers were forced to capitulate after holding out for six weeks. Defeated but undaunted, they turned to the political system and elected one of their own, Hiram Breed, mayor. If justice could not be won one way, it might be won in another.

Technological advance, in the form of the sewing machine, helped to make the artisan's industrial position more untenable. With the rapid and widespread introduction of the sewing machine just after the 1860 strike, it became increasingly feasible to employ larger proportions of unskilled laborers who could produce greater quantities of boots and shoes at a reduced cost. This caused such a decline in the skilled workers' relative numbers that their ideals and interests could no longer dominate the labor movement in Lynn. The Civil War also had some influence. Diverting attention from capital–labor problems to North–South problems, the war produced a "period of silence" that allowed business to achieve almost complete consolidation of control over the shoe industry. "Moreover," states Dawley, "the War experience helped persuade members of the newly emerging working class that the state, even when controlled by the owners, functioned in the interests of the operatives."[71]

The political consensus created by the war lasted until near the end of the 1860s. In 1868, mostly as a means of achieving satisfactory wage agreements, the workers founded the Knights of St. Crispin and thereby "broke the mold of the craft-conscious, skilled brotherhood that is usually seen as the typical nineteenth century trade union."[72] For two years the Crispins were successful in achieving wage agreements to such an extent that many members believed they had reached a respectable level of "equality." After 1870, however, the owners reasserted their power. The union called a strike in 1872, but the bosses broke it easily, returning the workers to a worse position than they had occupied before 1870. Defeat was so profound that no union activity at all occurred in the two years following the strike. In 1875 the Knights reconstituted themselves, and by early 1878, they again believed that they had the power to force fair wage agreements. Unable to negotiate an agreement, they struck early in the year. The manufacturers, no longer constrained by the need for skilled workers, responded by hiring scabs to replace the strikers and by calling in the police to maintain order. The strike was soon broken, and the Knights of St. Crispin were permanently destroyed. Labor conditions then were worse than ever, and the owners were in full control.[73]

Nonetheless, the workers maintained their faith in the political system and elected another labor mayor. This time the man was George P. Sanderson, forty-two-year-old artisan and veteran of both the 1860 and 1878 strikes, who had been nominated by very large margins in each ward. Adding to the dramatic impact of the victory, Sanderson beat incumbent mayor Samuel M. Bubier for the office. Bubier, Lynn's largest shoe manufacturer, had fired Sanderson in 1861 for participating in the strike. In the years following Sanderson's election, the shoe workers retained their commitment to the political system, electing their men four out of nine times in the 1890s. Thus, throughout the second half of the nineteenth century, shoe workers in Lynn established a tradition of successful political participation, and their leaders expressed the faith that political action could ameliorate problems arising from the economic system. The Lynn Greenback Club, a worker-dominated group, argued in 1878 that the recent industrial troubles resulted from "evil legislation," which the workers could remedy by "properly exercising the privilege of the franchise and substituting honest and capable men for holding public office."[74] This faith in the political process, Dawley concludes, meant that, aside from a few socialists of little influence, the workers' "radicalism remained within the burgeois frame . . . Even at the most extreme, their leaders proposed schemes to limit the operation of capitalism, not to replace capitalism with anything else."[75] The property system would not be reconstituted; it would be ameliorated. The political system, then, functioned as a means by which workingmen's complaints were "translated" into electing labor mayors, and were moved away from strictly economic issues. "By relieving some pressure, electoral politics contained the remaining explosive energy of the factory workers."[76] More significantly, perhaps, these political successes occupied the minds of the workers to such an extent (as far as can be determined from the publicly stated positions of their leaders) that no radical analysis of the business–industrial order surfaced. Workers may or may not have adquiesced in the system, but if they did not, it seems, their resistance remained unarticulated, unfocused, and ineffectual.

Not only did the most potentially radical segment of Lynn's population acquiesce in the industrial system of power and property, it appears also to have actually shared with the manufacturers and their business associates an ideology that led to a consensus in town regarding the efficacy of municipal policies and institutional ends. From the point of view of those who were well-off, this ideology defined an ideal of social order and stability by which their interests would be justified and protected; from the point of view of the workers, it defined respectability, success, and the processes by which they could be achieved. It was this ideology's ability to appeal to both sides at once that accounts for its widespread acceptance. Of course, the benefits were not equivalent: The propertied benefited as a class, whereas the workers did so only individually and intermittently. At any rate, as Lynn urbanized in the nineteenth century, economic and social strains became apparent, and certain changes appeared necessary if stability and opportunity were to be protected.

Responses to the changing conditions were guided by the old and fundamentally Christian notion that society is constituted of separate individuals, each of whose moral value is determined by the quality of his soul. Thus the quality of society – its stability, its order, its morality – was a function of the quality of the souls of those who composed it. In New England this tradition partook of the very introspective and individualistic nature of Puritan morality. However, between the seventeenth and the nineteenth centuries, a more dynamic and environmental element was interjected into this tradition, as it became leavened by such non-Puritan ingredients as John Locke's psychology. Emphasis on soul gave way to emphasis on character. As Chapter 3 described in detail, the new interpretation denied that people were born into the world with evil souls or bad characters. Despite persistent notions about the heritability of character via class or ethnic origin, it was now increasingly to the environment, not to indications of God-given grace, that people turned to understand why someone became virtuous or evil, or to control subsequent behavior. It is this analysis that led moral reformers of the early nineteenth century to respond to the disorderly effects of urbanization, industrialization, and immigration first by establishing benevolent and ameliorative societies, and second by founding institutions such as prisons, houses of refuge, asylums, and free schools. Reformers expected these institutions to take selected individuals in hand and reform their characters. Developments in Lynn corresponded closely to this broader process that occurred throughout the western world.[77]

Paul Faler argues convincingly that in antebellum Lynn "there was a general tightening up of the moral code and a growing emphasis on self-discipline, industry, sobriety, self-denial and respect for authority. There was an equally strong condemnation of idleness and leisure, lewd and lascivious behavior, self-indulgence and prolonged celebration."[78] One of the first organized efforts to improve morality in Lynn was the manufacturer-dominated Society in Lynn for the Promotion of Industry, Frugality and Temperance, founded in 1826. Motivated by a regard for stability, the society members appealed to the workingman's concern for enhanced opportunity: "Industry, frugality, and temperance," states Faler, "if consciously followed, would necessarily result in savings that would bring a material reward to the practitioner of these habits.''[79] Faler argues that such efforts were a direct response to the growth of capitalist-dominated manufacturing in the city. Emphasis on factory production as the crucial cause, however, seems mistaken, if only because other cities with different types of economic bases developed similar ideologies. New York and Boston, for example, were primarily commercial cities at the time this same ideology developed.[80] This ideology and its institutional forms therefore should be characterized more broadly: It was an ideology that attempted to explain and govern urban, capitalist society in a culturally diverse nation. All three elements – urbanism, capitalism, and cultural diversity – are independently important, even though they occurred together historically in Lynn and tended to reinforce one another.

The institutional effects of the urban moral campaign were profound. Regarding schooling, for instance, a number of essentially autonomous district schools became organized into a school system. In the process, the scope of their control over children was greatly enlarged. The earlier schools had had as their basic purposes the imparting of elementary reading and arithmetic skills and the teaching of good morals and manners, primarily through catechetical instruction in the Bible. In the new public school system, however, character formation became more central and discussions about it more urgent.

The commitment to schooling as an effective character-forming tool and as a means of some kind of opportunity seems to have been shared throughout all segments of the city's population. To illustrate this commitment, we refer to editorials appearing in the journeymen's newspaper, the *Awl*, and to the annual addresses of working-class mayors, because there, if anywhere, labor leaders would have stated their objections to the school system and the ideology it was expected to embody, suggesting new directions for it. They did not do so, however. Instead, they embraced the modern urban ideology and education's role in it. In the March 8, 1845, issue of the *Awl* appeared an editorial advocating the establishment of a public high school in Lynn. It argued:

> There is too little attention paid to the subject of *education* by the people of this town. Our schools generally are too crowded, and we fear that there is too little care and good judgment used in seeking instructors, who have charge of the education of our children.
> We sincerely hope that our citizens will not be too parsimoneous [sic] in this matter; for we believe that there is no money so well spent as that which provides an education for the rising generation. It is to the mechanics of this town to whom we look for encouragement in this point; the rich and influential do not want a school of this kind, they can and will send their children to

private schools. So of course they will oppose the measure, unless they have got sufficient philanthropy in their souls to sacrifice a few dollars for the amelioration of the race.[81]

Michael Katz has argued that mid-century public high schools were an imposition by the middle class upon the working class.[82] In Lynn, however, according to the *Awl,* at least, a public high school would have been an imposition by the workers upon the rich. Seven days earlier, the *Awl* had carried an article describing the virtues of a proposed cordwainers' library: "It is this that will empty our poor houses of their inmates, and free our jails and prisons of the corrupt and vicious; for there is a close connection between ignorance and vice."[83] The journeymen, then, conceived of good education as having both a powerful moral influence and a literacy-imparting function. The workers expected the public school system to embody these two ends, and thus perhaps to provide the opportunity for their children to rise a bit in the world, while inculcating values that would lead to respectability and morality, which were important in their own right.

The tone for the mayoral discussion of the public school system was set in the antebellum years and never changed throughout the century. In his 1859 address, Mayor Edward S. Davis nicely stated the generally accepted purpose of the school system. He argued:

It is universally acknowledged that sound education of the heart and mind is the only sure basis of character, and is indespensible [sic] to usefulness in the world. The importance, therefore, of the public schools, in a community like ours, where they furnish to a large proportion of our youth the only means of acquiring such an education, cannot be over-estimated. What interest in any community can compare with the moral and religious education of the young?[84]

Furthermore, Davis, like other mayors before and after him, expressed pleasure with the work of the school committee, which was responsible for the actual development and direction of the school system.[85]

The labor mayors accepted the traditional view. Hiram Breed, in his 1861 address, stated: "We have long been accustomed to a high order of schools, that, like many other common blessings, we have almost ceased to appreciate the extraordinary advantage of them. We must sustain them, although much money is needed for that purpose. It is money well spent."[86] These are hardly the remarks of a man who believed that he and his fellow workers were being manipulated by a cabal of self-interested elites. George P. Sanderson, too, in his 1879 and 1880 addresses, expressed general satisfaction with the schools and the school committee, suggesting only those changes that would make it easier for working-class children to benefit from the system. In 1879 he stated:

> The educational interests of our city stand second to none in point of importance. Former City Councils have made liberal appropriations in order to furnish the best accommodations: and to-day Lynn may point with pride to her public schools . . . And now we commit this department to the very excellent Board of School Committees, who will have entire charge of it for the year, with entire confidence that whatever is for the interest of education, and consistent with the demands of economy, will receive careful and candid consideration.[87]

And in 1880, noting that most children of the working class had to leave the system before the high school years, he advocated "a change in or addition to the grammar school course as will better fit our children for the duties required of them as members of our active business community." He would leave the particulars to the school committee, because "we have every reason to expect that whatever may promise good results will meet with approval at their hands."[88] The articulate laboring element of the community, then, found little to criticize in the public school system and the ends it was intended to serve.

Conflict over educational matters was not wholly absent from Lynn. As in Boxford, disagreements with parents about school discipline and nonattendance were widespread, but they did not occur at the ideological level. It is difficult to find detailed information about incidents concerning corporal punishment, but even in the two most celebrated cases neither the school committee nor the school system were challenged. The controversies centered on the behavior of the instructor; as in the political realm, satisfaction was to be achieved by replacing the person. Parental opposition to corporal punishment did not indicate an undercurrent of opposition to the school system. Indeed, successive school committees themselves said that corporal punishment, although occasionally necessary, was generally inadvisable on both disciplinary and educational grounds. The corporal punishment controversies, then, were parent–teacher conflicts.[89]

A second form of controversy centered on the question of school attendance. It found expression in the futile efforts of every school committee to bring truants to school, and to convince others to attend more regularly. Two general factors may account for these problems. The first, and by far the most damning to the system as an educational institution, was that some children either disliked school so much or found other activities so much more attractive that they chose to stay away. The second factor was the opportunity costs of school attendance. For many, the immediate appeal of weekly wages outweighed more distant and vague opportunities in future years, and this factor helps account for the class bias in school leaving discussed in Chapter 4. It might be that nonattendance indicated an underlying opposition among parents to the school system and its goals, but no direct evidence of parental thoughts on this matter exists. Nonattendance did nothing to articulate an alternative or a coherent criticism of the school system and its guiding ideology. This form of opposition, if there was such, must be characterized as passive resistance.

To summarize, an ideology supportive of established interests in Lynn developed as the city entered into nineteenth-century urban life. That ideology promised stability for the social and economic system, security for the wealthy, and respectability for the rest, along with a modicum of opportunity. It thereby achieved wide acceptance among the adult population of the city. This ideology stressed the moral quality of each individual, and the societies and institutions aimed at shaping the characters of people received broad support. Among these was the public school system.

Evolution of the school system, 1800–1850

The pressures occasioned by a rapidly expanding population must be emphasized in any explanation of the evolution of Lynn's public school system. The sheer press of numbers meant that facilities would almost always be inadequate. School committees throughout the century raised a continuous cry for more and better facilities; they never achieved all that they wanted. Furthermore, the constraints of crowded and worn-out buildings conditioned to a great degree their organizational and pedagogical decisions regarding the best ways to educate large numbers of children of widely varying ages and achievement levels. School committees never had the luxury of making purely educational decisions. To some extent, then, Lynn's school system came into being simply as a result of rapid, substantial population growth. The particular form the system would take, however, was determined by the interaction between the existing organization and structure of the schools at any given time (for instance, the number and size of available classrooms), the ideological and pedagogical aims of school committees, and the sufficiency of available resources. In this and a following section we briefly trace how Lynn's schools evolved from 1800, when the town supported separate district schools under relatively autonomous prudential committees, to 1880, when a superintendent of schools and central school committee determined and implemented policies on a system-wide basis.

Before 1800, publicly supported schooling in Lynn reflected the town's small population and rural status. From 1696, when the town first ordered a school to be kept, until the 1790s, public education in Lynn consisted primarily of a moving school kept in the different wards.[90] During the 1790s, Lynn citizens demonstrated a willingness to organize public schooling more centrally, and in 1799 the town meeting voted to choose a "superintending committee" to consist of one citizen from each of the town's four wards. Each ward would also continue to choose a "district committee" (later known as the prudential committee), which would select and supervise its teacher, establish regulations for the school, and furnish wood and repairs for the schoolhouses. The superintending committee, on the other hand, was to establish town-wide regulations, visit the schools quarterly, settle disputes in the wards, remove incompetent teachers, and report annually to the town.[91]

Lynn's educational arrangements in the eighteenth century were not very different from those of her rural neighbor, Boxford. After 1800, however, the economic and educational histories of the two communities diverge. During the two decades between 1800 and 1820 there appeared the first signs of how Lynn's citizens would react to conditions occasioned by population growth. From 1800 to 1810, the population expanded from 2,837 to 4,087 people, and redistricting created two new wards.[92] By 1820 the pressure of numbers led the superintending committee to propose the establishment of a town-wide grammar school:

In several of the schools the number of children is so great that the instructors have only one minute and a fraction of a minute to devote to each scholar in half a day. To obviate this great hindrance to improvement the committee are decidedly of the opinion that a perpetual grammar school in town is necessary. This, under proper instruction and good regulations, would draw off a number of subjects from each Ward, and relieve them from the great burden.[93]

The proposal failed to receive adequate support, but clearly pressures associated with population growth were beginning to be felt.

In the decades between 1820 and 1850 public schooling in Lynn took on the main outlines that were to characterize it as a modern school system. It is perhaps no coincidence that within one year, 1850, the high school opened its doors to students, the town received its city charter, and the school committee was reorganized. During the same thirty years the shoe industry became firmly established, and the first tide of immigration from the hinterlands and abroad hit Lynn, raising the population to 14,257 by the end of the period. Recall, also, that it was toward the end of this time that the first stirrings of labor unrest occurred. This was the context within which succeeding school committees did their work.

These widespread social and economic changes obviously portended dangers to Lynn's social order. As we have seen, the school system came to be thought of as an important guardian of the received social order. Throughout this period school committees variously asserted that the schools, if allowed the means, could strengthen the town's "civil & religious institutions," eliminate ignorance, produce "good will to our Republic," or, in sum, assure the "progressive formation" of "the very character of the city itself. . . "[94] Even by the 1820s, however, overcrowding marred these optimistic claims. The ward schools admitted children from ages four to fourteen, making instruction and discipline ever more difficult as their enrollments swelled. The irregular attendance of many pupils further fragmented the school program. School committees exhorted parents to send their children to school every day. At the same time, they attempted to take advantage of increased numbers by creating different grades of schools that corresponded to the age and achievement levels of the children. By 1845 four grades of schools were in operation – mixed (the traditional kind remaining in low population wards), principal (for the older children), intermediate (the next step down), and primary (for the very youngest).

The first primary school seems to have been established sometime in 1827, and there were eighteen such schools by mid-century. Emphasizing character formation and rudimentary literacy skills, the first primary, having registered about one hundred children from four to nine years of age, was "not less novel than successful." Perhaps most significant was the discipline, "remarkable chiefly for its lenity and moderation, yet seeing the most perfect and cheerful obedience; and accompanied with an attachment between teacher and pupils that appears to be affectionate, sincere and mutual."[95] Other gradations of schools were established. By mid-century only a high school was needed to "meet the demands of the age":

A suitable gradation of Schools, adapted to the ages and advancement of the children, will greatly facilitate their education . . . This principle has been successfully applied in Lynn. – Here, at present, the *Primary*, the *Intermediate*, and the *Principal* Schools span over the whole School life. The *High* School only seems to be wanting.[96]

In the second term of the 1849–50 school year, just in time for Lynn's incorporation as a city, a high school opened. Crowded and poorly located, it nonetheless completed the hierarchy of graded public schools in Lynn.

Going to school in mid-century Lynn

What was it like to attend school in this urban system? Let us look at the experience of Benjamin, a fictitious but historically accurate schoolchild, a contemporary of Boxford's Sarah. Eight-year-old Benjamin was the second of shoemaker John Thompson's four children. In 1855 he was promoted to the Sheppard Grammar School, a school his older brother, Thomas, had left two years earlier at the age of fourteen. Thomas had enjoyed his studies, and had even passed the examination for entrance into the high school, but because Mr. Thompson expected this son to enter the shoemaking trade, not Harvard College, Tom took a job at one of Lynn's shoe factories. Anyway, he thought, the students at the high school, especially those whose parents owned businesses and property, would have made him feel out of place with their expensive clothes and different manners. Perhaps Benjamin would be able to benefit from the high school when his turn came.

At this time, however, Benjamin had other things on his mind. Sheppard School was so different. The year before, at Primary Number Two on Cottage Street, Miss Mary Stevenson, the schoolmistress, had spent a great deal of her time with Benjamin and the other advanced students, helping them to prepare for the grammar school entrance examination. Benjamin had waited for that year since he entered Number Two when he was five. The singing, drawing, and calisthenics were fun, but Miss Stevenson seemed never to have enough time to talk to the younger children about the pictures on the walls or to explain how to use the blocks and puzzles that gathered dust in the corner. Mostly she just assigned exercises out of the reading or arithmetic texts and tried to discover what had been learned through occasional recitations. Finally, Benjamin's third and final year had come. Miss Stevenson, who said she wanted to have more students promoted than any other primary teacher, was always there to give assignments and to hear and answer questions. It had been a good year.

Then Benjamin found himself at Sheppard School, and he was uncomfortable. It had one large room with two adjoining small ones, and over two hundred students attended daily, in contrast to the sixty or seventy who had appeared each day at Primary Number Two. Mr. Peabody, Sheppard's schoolmaster, hardly ever spoke to the younger children individually. Like Miss Stevenson, he apparently spent most of his time getting people ready for promotion. Mr. Peabody did have two nice assistants: his sister, Miss Rosanna, and Miss Lydia Tufts. Miss Lydia had charge of the new children. Occasionally she would leave part of her class under the watchful eye of Mr. Peabody while she took the rest into one of the small rooms for oral reading and discussion. Perhaps they would work in Hooker's *Book of Common Things*, which explained in words and pictures such subjects as air, fire, and water. This was Benjamin's favorite way to learn at school, but Miss Lydia had responsibility for so many children that these experiences were infrequent.

Benjamin had other reasons to feel uncomfortable. He had forgotten much of what he had learned the previous year at Primary Number Two, and at Sheppard he had to memorize even more difficult lessons. Sometimes he did not know what to do. Miss Lydia would try to explain, but she had little time for any single student, and sometimes she did not understand the lessons herself. Also, a few days earlier Miss Lydia had caught James, a new pupil from Primary Number Three, cheating during recitation. She tried to make him say he was sorry, but all he would do was to look at the floor. Mr. Peabody saw what was happening and led James to the front of the school and swatted him seven times with a switch – "as an example," he said. And so it was. The first few weeks at Sheppard made Benjamin feel alone, afraid, and inadequate, and shades of these feelings remained with him throughout his career at grammar school, though camaraderie with boys from his neighborhood helped sustain him.

Benjamin stayed at Sheppard for four more years. There was some learning, some discovery, and some joy; but mostly there was memorization. For relief, Benjamin found that he could skip school for two or three days at a time, and none of his teachers seemed to mind or notice. When the time came to join Mr. Peabody's advanced class to prepare for the high school entrance examination, Benjamin was twelve and had little enthusiasm for a further memorization marathon. Instead he followed his brother's path and took a job as a message boy at the factory. Perhaps his sister Elizabeth, soon to enter Sheppard, would be the first Thompson child to attend Lynn High School.

Perfecting the system, 1850–1880

With the opening of the Lynn High School, the school committee had said, the system of public education was complete. But this did not mean that the committee could rest on its laurels. Lynn's population continued to grow, and, after mid-century as before, overcrowding and increasing scale proved the most compelling causes of educational change.

The innovation of 1799, creating a town committee to oversee the ward committees, was now consolidated. Separate committees dealing with the same schools and teachers had created many tensions, and the new charter of 1850 eliminated the duplication. From then on the general committee was made up of representatives from each ward who assumed the duties of the ward committee. Each of these was responsible for the operation of the schools within his jurisdiction, and the high school, serving the city as a whole, was controlled by a special committee.[97]

In 1855, in the interest of further extending its control of the system, the committee arranged itself into five standing committees (school books and apparatus, finances, schoolhouses, examination of teachers, and fuel) and four visiting committees (one each for the high school, the grammars, the intermediates, and the primaries). Newly centralized and specialized, the school committee was then ready to face the educational problems of mid-century Lynn.

Lack of adequate and appropriate space for the grammar and the primary schools was a persistent difficulty throughout this period. Although five new buildings had been added between 1845 and 1850, overcrowding continued to be a real problem. Out of the fifty-six primary rooms existing in 1860, eleven averaged over eighty children in attendance (some over one hundred), at a time when educators agreed that seventy was the maximum number of children that should be allowed if good work was to be done.[98] With so many pupils per class, the problem of discipline became central, without reference to larger social issues. Not just more space, but the right kind of space, was needed. Old buildings are a constraining, conservative force in schooling, and population growth provided the occasion for Lynn school committees to innovate with designs appropriate to the developing urban school system. In 1865 the committee was still bemoaning the legacy of the district schoolhouse: "The old system of one large room, where the principal remains to have in charge one-half of all the scholars of his assistants all the time, as well as those he directly instructs, is injurious to his health, comfort and efficiency."[99] By 1870, however, the school committee reported that because of great population increases, they had erected several new grammar school buildings designed "for the accurate grading and classification which are of such vital importance to the efficiency of our schools."[100] The school committes of this era continued to spend much time and energy working on the closely related problems of the gradation of schools and the classification of children within them. In attempts to get children of similar abilities in separate classes, the committee further subdivided the primary level and experimented with various uses of the "intermediate" school, between the primaries and the grammar schools.[101]

The committees did not exhaust all their efforts, however, on matters of organization and classification. Despite the efforts of earlier committees to reduce corporal punishment, to emphasize character training by example rather than catechism, and to discourage the more mechanical approaches to learning, the 1850 committee still felt that the pedagogy of Lynn's teachers left much to be desired. "The great deficiency of our system," they lamented, is "that it is based almost entirely upon a mere knowledge of *words*, and from first to last proceeds upon this method, hardly recognizing the fact of the existence of things."[102] In 1856 they again expressed their fear of "mechanical drill superseding living assimilation; of mere external facility in the parrot-like repetition of the words of the book taking the place of a real ability to think."[103] By the 1860s they had come to advocate a pedagogical technique called object teaching, whereby learning would be meaningful instead of abstract. In 1866 the committee report described the value of object teaching for instruction in the primaries.

Object teaching is in accordance with nature and art as they exist around us and are understood by the scholars, assumes as known only what is known by the pupil, begins with *reality* and passes onward from the known to the acquisition of further knowledge, till the abstract can be understood and properly appreciated. It demands something more than mere expression of words without comprehension; it requires thought and understanding, as well as verbal expression.[104]

The report further advised that a modified version of object teaching be used in the grammar schools, although it also noted the shortcomings of the method:

Simplification, demonstration and object lessons are all proper and very beneficial, especially in the lower classes, but the learner should always bear in mind "That there is no royal road to learning." Every scholar must be taught to practice self-reliance, to labor with his intellect, to think and understand for himself.[105]

The main point, however, was that "there is too much memorizing, and not sufficient thought."[106] In 1868 the committee adopted an innovation called "oral instruction," which emphasized conversation rather than recitation and was suitable to all grade levels. "In these exercises, it is the teacher's aim to excite the curiosity of children, in order to show them how to gratify it; to lead them to form habits of enquiring, rather than to accumulate isolated facts."[107]

Object teaching and oral instruction were aimed at motivating the students and involving them actively in learning. They were designed to be less coercive and more effective means to traditional ends: basic intellectual skills, the development of moral character, and the orderly functioning of the schools. Order was still the impetus, but now the students would be enlisted on the side of the good rather than kept in check by external restraints. "The secret of good order and improvement," said the 1865 committee, "is to keep those that are not reading or reciting so interested in drawing or printing upon the slate or blackboard as not to disturb others by their restlessness or roguish pranks."[108] It was from this point of view that school committees opposed the use of corporal punishment. Thus the 1857 school report advocated moral discipline:

That is the only "discipline" worthy of the name, which makes the pupils discipline themselves; which is constantly tending towards habits of self-respect and self-government; which has no need of temporary restraints and petty punishments, because the greatest punishment of all is the consciousness of deserving it.[109]

Whatever the realities of Lynn's public school classrooms, these three pedagogical policies – object teaching, oral instruction, and discipline by moral suasion – persisted as school committee goals throughout the rest of the nineteenth century. The centralized structure of the school committee, with subcommittees for special tasks, allowed them to pursue their goals of cognitive and moral education more efficiently and professionally. Nonetheless, population growth continued unabated, and supervision of the schools became more and more difficult. Committee members increasingly had trouble finding time to make enough visits. "There is," stated the 1869 report, "a lack of uniformity in the studies of schools of the same grade, while the general exercises and oral instruction, which constitute the charm of some schools, are wholly unknown to, or receive little attention in others." The report noted that, without constant supervision, teachers tend to allow their efforts to "flag." The committee concluded that Lynn needed to hire a superintendent of schools.[110]

Before hiring a superintendent, however, Lynn school committees of the 1870s tried other techniques for achieving adequate supervision. They increased the number and length of terms of school board members in an effort to achieve better continuity of supervision. They extended the administrative authority of the grammar school principals by putting them in charge of the various departments within their own schools, and finally by placing all primaries within their respective wards under their purview. Finally, sometime in the mid-1870s, they instituted the practice of administering standardized, written examinations to all students in the high school and the grammars, at the end of each term.[111]

While tightening supervision in these ways, the committee members still talked about hiring a superintendent. As the 1877 report argued, a superintendent would be a specialist in education, a qualification that could not be expected of board members. Furthermore, with one person in charge, there could be a greater "degree of uniformity and singleness of method."[112] By 1879 the committee acknowledged that recently board members had not been able to keep up with the growth of the system and that teachers had become "discouraged by the lack of interest."[113] It was finally decided to appoint, as an experiment, a superintendent for the remainder of the school year. They voted unanimously to hire Mr. O. B. Bruce of Binghamton, New York, to fill the position. His work went well, and the school committee asked him to continue his service. The 1880 report described the new authority relationship: "The Superintendent is at the head of educational affairs, and has the assistance of a Committee who shall legislate in accordance with his suggestions, if, after intelligent survey, based on knowledge of its own, it sees fit to do so."[114] Although the school committee members continued to visit schools, within a very few years Superintendent Bruce had effective control of administration, including most policy determination. The appointment of a superintendent, then, was a decisive step in the evolution of Lynn's schools from a set of relatively separate district schools into a modern public school system. Lynn's schools had acquired a corporate structure similar in some regards to that of Lynn industry: Both were hierarchical systems that prized supervision and efficiency. This happened not by outright mimicry, but because the same logic of scale, efficiency, and division of labor seemed to apply to mass education and to the production of shoes.

Moral education was one of the chief aims of education in Lynn throughout the nineteenth century. The ideology that supported this goal had as one of its central tenets that social morality depended upon individual morality, and therein lay the main contribution of the school system in legitimizing the social and economic system. This belief was apparently widely accepted. Support for the schools drew additional sustenance from the traditional American belief in schooling, and from the openness (for white males) of a political system that formally controlled schooling as well as other Lynn institutions. Despite this consensus, even the school committees had doubts about the details and the general tone of the schools, and they periodically attempted to make classrooms more humane and education more thoughtful. Nonetheless, the heavy emphasis on discipline for life in an urban, industrial society and for order in crowded, bureaucratic schools overshadowed these pleas.

Conclusion

Although Boxford and Lynn shared the traditional educational goals of rudimentary intellectual training and character formation, the circumstances and resources of each town resulted in different structures and organizations and thus in different school experiences for children. Each community had its successes, if judged by the values and goals expressed by its leaders and apparently shared by most of the community's residents. From a more critical viewpoint, in retrospect, each also had its failures. Judgments on the extent of these successes and failures must depend not only on the historical record but upon one's beliefs about American society in general.

Boxford people cared little for the world beyond Boxford, and they insulated themselves as well as they could from the influence of industrialization and state intervention. Lynn's leaders embraced industrial capitalism, and agonized over the disruptions of urban life while they marveled at the innovations made possible by the increasing scale of organization. They eagerly sought to build a school system that would make people competent and adjust them to the modern world as they interpreted it. Although we may today be nostalgic for the simplicity and intimacy of the rural community, we must acknowledge that Boxford's schools were physically scanty, their teachers inexperienced, and the educational program narrow. And though we must guard against viewing Lynn's capitalist class as a cold-hearted conspiracy, dominating and profiting from the school program, we may nonetheless regret that urban education was so uncritical, that it did so much to rationalize and so little to humanize the emerging structure, opportunities, and ethics of the nineteenth century.

Comparative studies run the risk of overlooking diversity of beliefs and circumstances within a single location. Yet our case studies of Boxford and Lynn do reveal impressive general community sentiment about education and other matters. Boxford's residents shared many attitudes; even the progressive school committees closed ranks with townspeople against various forms of innovation and state interference in education. Similarly, certain general beliefs about education, property, and urban life transcended class lines and other distinctions in Lynn, despite the tremendous range of material circumstance and the disparities of power within the city. The contrasting beliefs about education in the two communities did not come out of the blue. They evolved historically, as people with certain traditions, needs, and resources faced the demographic, economic, and cultural problems of their communities. Boxford residents weren't penurious just because fiscally conservative people like to live in the countryside; they were penurious because their resources were slim and getting slimmer. And Lynn's modern school system did not result merely from having a lot of children around; Lynn residents were able to keep up with their burgeoning school population and innovate with buildings and organization because their economic resources allowed them to do so.

In this chapter we have observed the great influence of population growth on the organization and control of schooling. In the next chapter we turn to financial resources as a factor in the educational development of nineteenth-century Massachusetts and its diverse communities.

7

Trends in educational funding and expenditures

Little effort has been made to analyze either the sources of educational funding or the nature of school expenditures in nineteenth-century Massachusetts. The financial aspects of educational development have been generally ignored.[1] Part of the explanation for the dearth of financial studies of education is that it is difficult to obtain the necessary data and, perhaps, that the subject impresses many as dry or unimportant. This situation is unfortunate, because financial considerations played a large role in decisions made about education at both the state and the local level. Using state and local records, we consider briefly in this chapter some aspects of school finance and how they influenced school policy.

Public and private school expenditures

One underlying factor that influences the financial strain of mass education in any society is the number of children relative to the number of adults. This statistic is a version of what demographers call a dependency ratio. The education of children requires considerable energy and resources. Whether the parents undertake this function or share it with other institutions, such as churches or schools, the extent of the burden of education depends to a large degree on the relative number of children who need formal or informal training. Societies with a high proportion of young children have to devote a larger percentage of their resources to educating youngsters than do those with relatively fewer children. The proportion of children in a given population is influenced by a variety of factors, such as the level of mortality, fertility, and the pattern of migration. Generally, the single most important factor in determining the proportion of children in a society is the rate of fertility. Areas with high birth rates usually have a much higher percentage of children than those with low birth rates. Thus the developing countries today, which have very high birth rates compared to the developed nations, have a larger proportion of their populations in the school-going ages. As a result, the problems of economic development in those countries are compounded by their need to devote a large percentage of their resources to educating their children.

Some nineteenth-century educators were aware of the implications of the dependency ratio for the development of schooling. James Carter, for example, argued in a speech before the Massachusetts House of Representatives that the burden of education was considerably heavier in the newly created states, which had a higher proportion of children, than in Massachusetts.

The proportion of children and youth varies in different sections of the country, and is always the greatest in the new states. The proportion under fifteen in Massachusetts, is only thirty-six percent, while in several of the Western and South Western States, Tennessee, Alabama and Missouri, it is above fifty percent. Where the necessities of education are the greatest, there the difficulties are the greatest, and the means the least.[2]

Massachusetts, then, was in a relatively advantageous situation. More important, the state's dependency ratio was declining over time. One measure of dependency is the number of persons ages birth to nineteen per thousand individuals ages twenty to fifty-nine. This ratio was 911 for Massachusetts in 1840; it dropped to 713 in 1880, owing to the decline in the birth rate and the influx of adult immigrants into the state. In other words, although there was a tremendous increase in the total number of young persons in the commonwealth during this forty-year period, there was an even greater increase in the number of persons ages twenty to fifty-nine who had to bear the educational costs either as parents or as taxpayers. The burden of education, from this demographic perspective, was lighter in 1880 than in 1840.

The cost of education is determined not only by the number of young children in society but also by the proportion of those who actually attend the schools. As we have detailed in Chapter 2, the proportion of persons under twenty years of age in school actually declined sharply from 63.7 percent in 1839–40 to 49.3 percent in 1879–80. Part of this decline can be explained by the change during this period in attitudes toward educating very young children. Whereas many three- and four-year-olds were in school in 1840, very few were attending school in 1880. The decline in the proportion of youngsters in the population, then, as well as the reduction in the percentage of persons under twenty enrolled in school, eased the burden of school education in nineteenth-century Massachusetts.

Two other trends, however, increased the cost of education – the increase in the regularity of attendance among students and the increase in the length of the public school year. As we documented in Chapter 2, average daily attendance as a percentage of total enrollment rose from 62.4 in 1839–40 to 76.4 in 1879–80. Thus average daily attendance as a proportion of all children under twenty remained relatively stable during the entire period (moving from 37.1 percent in 1839–40 to 37.9 percent in 1879–80). Furthermore, there was a significant increase in the average length of the public school year – from 150 days in 1840 to 192 days in 1880. As a result, the average number of days in public and private schools per person under twenty increased from 60.6 in 1839–40 to 71.6 in 1879–80. Massachusetts not only accommodated an increasing absolute number of young people going to school in the period 1840 to 1880, but also provided them with more days of education per person.

Despite the numerous problems associated with calculating the amount of money spent on education in nineteenth-century Massachusetts, we have constructed crude estimates for the period 1837 to 1880. Because Massachusetts experienced a high rate of inflation, particularly during the Civil War years, we adjusted all our estimates for changes in the cost of living (with 1860 equaling 100).[3] Some economists also calculate the opportunity costs of education, that is, the income foregone by students while they are in school, but we will confine our analysis to the actual costs incurred by the school system.

As anticipated, there was a sizable increase in the total amount of money spent on schooling in Massachusetts from 1837 to 1880 (see Figure 7.1). The $800,000 spent in the state for education in 1837 climbed to over $4.8 million by 1880. There was a steady rise in the total amount of money spent on education throughout these years except for the Civil War period, when educational expenditures failed to keep pace with the high rate of inflation.

Educational reformers frequently complained about the inadequacy of funding for public schools in Massachusetts. In part, they attributed this lack of support to the general public apathy toward all schools. But they also pointed to the large amount of money spent by wealthy individuals on the more expensive and exclusive private schools in the commonwealth. Thus, Horace Mann observed:

> Opposite to this class, who tolerate from apathy, a depression in the common schools, there is another class who affix so high a value upon the culture of their children, and understand so well the necessity of a skillful preparation of means for its bestowment, that they turn away from the common schools, in their depressed state, and seek, elsewhere, the help of a more enlarged and thorough education.[4]

Figure 7.1. Amount of money spent for Massachusetts schools, 1837–80, in dollars adjusted for cost of living (1860 = 100) (from Tables A7.1–A7.2)

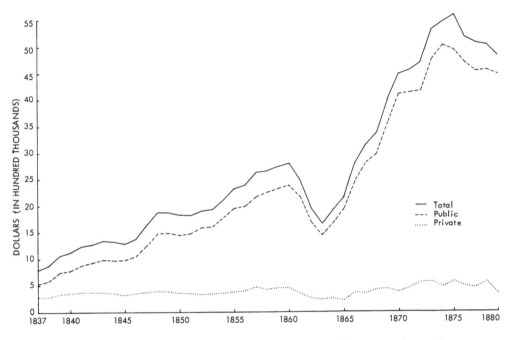

Yet despite the complaints by educational reformers about the amount of money spent on private schools, the Massachusetts public schools in 1837 already received a majority of the money devoted to education (63.5 percent). In Salem, which had a strong private school tradition, the mayor reported in 1843 that

> the expenditure for the Public Schools is the largest one for which Citizens are assessed, and . . . it will probably be increased until the result which seems inevitable should be reached, and all or by far the largest part of the children of the City shall be included within the Public Schools.[5]

Although the amount of money spent statewide for private education remained relatively constant, the funds expended for public education increased by over 750 percent. By 1880, as a result, public schools accounted for 92.9 percent of the money spent on schools in the commonwealth.

A large part of the rise in the overall school expenditures in Massachusetts between 1837 and 1880 can be explained by the growth in the

189

Figure 7.2. Cost per hundred days of school attended in Massachusetts, 1837–80, in dollars adjusted for cost of living (1860 = 100) (from Table A7.3)

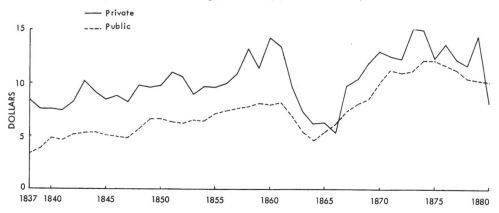

total number of students in the system as well as the increase in the length of the public school year. But there was also a significant increase in the cost of education per hundred days of school attended, beyond the increase caused by inflation (see Figure 7.2). In 1837 it cost $4.29 for each hundred days of school attended, whereas in 1879–80 the cost had risen to $9.88. In other words, the cost of educating children rose about 130 percent during this forty-year period, even after controlling for the increased number of students, the longer school year, and inflation.

It is also interesting to note that throughout this period, although private schooling cost more on the average than public schooling, the differential narrowed considerably. The cost of public education per hundred days of school attended increased dramatically during these years, whereas the equivalent cost of private education remained much more stable. If one were to assume some direct relationship between the cost of schooling and its quality, it would appear that the gap in the quality of education between private and public schools was diminishing.

As the overall costs of schooling rose, the ability of the state to finance either private or public education depended to a large extent upon the development of its economic resources. One way of looking at this issue is to calculate the extent of Massachusetts school expenditures per $1,000 of state valuation (see Figure 7.3). Although the state valuation is not necessarily an accurate index of the actual market value of property in Massachusetts, it is probably a reasonable indication of the relative value over time. Overall, there was a small rise in

Figure 7.3. Massachusetts school expenditures in dollars per $1,000 of state valuation, 1837–80 (from Table A7.4)

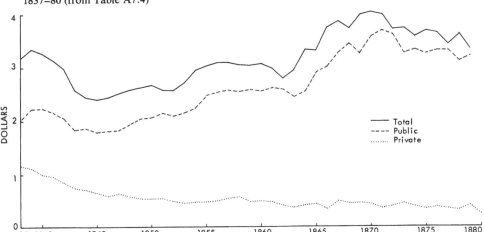

Massachusetts school expenditures per $1,000 of state valuation. Comparing the first five years (1837–42) with the last five years (1875–80), there was a modest 12 percent increase in that ratio, and the trend is irregular. During the 1840s school expenditures per $1,000 of state valuation declined significantly, and during the late 1860s they increased. Although there were no major secular trends in the total amount of Massachusetts school expenditures per $1,000 of state valuation from 1837 to 1880, there was a significant shift from private to public spending. While the extent of private school spending per $1,000 of state valuation declined sharply, that of public schools increased dramatically, from an average of $2.15 per $1,000 of state valuation in the period 1837–42 to an average of $3.22 per $1,000 of state valuation for the years 1875–80 – an increase of 49.8 percent. Thus, although the overall educational expenditures relative to assessed property wealth remained relatively constant during these years, the costs to the taxpayer rose steadily as parents increasingly relied upon public rather than private schools to educate their children. It is therefore appropriate to turn now from expenditure levels to the sources of educational funding.

Sources of school funding

For the private schools of nineteenth-century Massachusetts we can estimate expenditures only on the basis of tuition paid. No information

Figure 7.4. Distribution of income sources for Massachusetts public schools, 1837–80 (from Table A7.5)

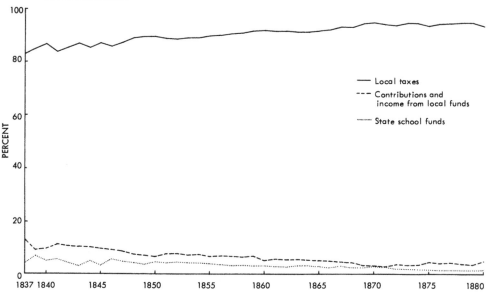

is available on the extent of income from endowments, but for most private schools it was probably negligible. It is possible to investigate in more detail the sources of public school funding because detailed income reports are available for public school expenditures other than construction and building maintenance.[6] Throughout the period, the major source of income for public schools was local taxes. In 1837 local taxes paid for 83.4 percent of school expenditures (excluding construction and maintenance of school buildings); by 1879–80 local taxes paid for 93.7 percent of school expenditures (see Figure 7.4). If we assume that all the funds for the construction and maintenance of public school buildings also came from local taxes rather than private contributions, then local taxes accounted for 86.5 percent of the public school expenditures in 1837 and for 94.5 percent of them in 1879–80. Much more than today, levels of educational expenditure depended upon local citizens' ability and willingness to pay school taxes.

There was a state component of educational funding, but its impact was more symbolic than fiscal. In 1834, Massachusetts established a state school fund, the income of which was to be used for the "aid and encouragement" of the public schools rather than as a substitute for local support. The legislature was reluctant to establish a large state

Figure 7.5. School expenditures as a percentage of overall town budgets, excluding state and county taxes, in eight Essex County communities and Boston, 1860 and 1880 (from Table A7.6)

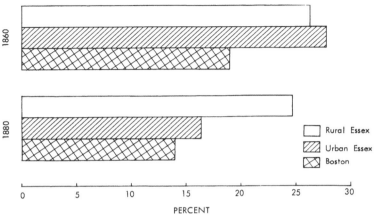

school fund because doing so might encourage local districts to cut back their school taxes. Although educational reformers wanted to increase the size of the state school fund in order to improve education and to exert more influence over local school districts, the legislature was unwilling to cooperate. As a result, the income from state school funds accounted for only 4.1 percent of public school expenditures in 1837 (not including construction and maintenance of buildings) and 1.6 percent in 1879–80. Even though the state board of education played an increasingly larger role in educational matters during these years, the financial involvement of the state in local districts diminished, reflecting the persistent belief that education was a local matter.

Because most of the burden of public school education fell on the local taxpayers, we wished to ascertain what proportions of local expenditures were devoted to education. We therefore examined the amount of the total town budgets (excluding state and county taxes) spent on education in Boston and in eight Essex County communities in 1860 and 1880 (see Figure 7.5).[7] In the five Essex County rural communities (Boxford, Hamilton, Lynnfield, Topsfield, and Wenham), public school expenditures in both 1860 and 1880 required about one-fourth of the overall town budget. In the three Essex County urban communities (Lawrence, Lynn, and Salem), school expenditures as a proportion of the municipal budget dropped from 27.9 percent in 1860 to 16.4 percent in 1880. Similarly, public school expenditures in Boston dropped from 19.0 percent of the overall budget in 1860 to 14.0 percent

Figure 7.6. Per capita school expenditures in budgets of eight Essex County communities and Boston, 1860 and 1880, in dollars adjusted for cost of living (1860 = 100) (from Table A7.7)

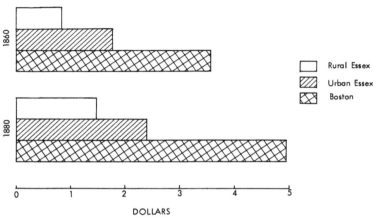

in 1880. Thus the rural communities tended to spend a higher proportion of their town budgets on education than did the urban areas – particularly in 1880. In all nine communities, school expenditures throughout this period were one of the single largest costs to local taxpayers. As a result, it is not surprising that local communities often disregarded the pleas of educational reformers for more financial support for their schools, because any increase in local school expenditures involved, relatively, a sizable increase in local taxes.

Although rural communities spent a higher proportion of their town budgets on education, the urban areas spent more per capita on public schools (see Figure 7.6). Whereas the rural Essex County towns spent $.84 per capita in 1860 and $1.47 per capita in 1880 on public schools, the three Essex County urban areas spent $1.76 and $2.40 per capita in those same years. Boston's per capita expenditures on public schools were even higher; the city devoted $3.56 in 1860 and $4.94 in 1880. Thus, although there was a decrease in the proportion of the total budget spent on public schools in both rural and urban communities between 1860 and 1880, there was a sizable per capita increase in educational expenditures during this period, even after adjusting for the rate of inflation.

We can examine the pattern of municipal expenditures in more detail by analyzing the Boston city budget from 1820 to 1880 (including state and county taxes). In order to obtain a comparative perspective on public school spending, we have also calculated city expenditures on

Figure 7.7. Public school, institutional, and police expenditures as percentages of the overall Boston city budget, including state and county taxes, 1820–80 (from Table A7.8)

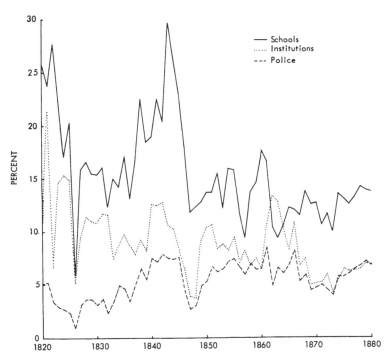

police and institutions, which included such items as the house of industry, the house of reformation, the house of correction, the lunatic hospital, and the overseers of the poor. From 1820 to 1880 the percentage of the city budget spent on public schools almost always exceeded the allotments for the police or institutions (see Figure 7.7). The differences among these items considerably narrowed over time as the percentage of spending on schools and institutions gradually declined while the proportion devoted to the police increased.

Expenditures on public schools were a large part of the Boston city budget at the beginning of the period (25.7 percent). During the late 1820s and 1830s the proportion of the budget devoted to public schools declined. The share of the municipal budget allocated for education rose sharply during the early 1840s and declined even more rapidly during the late 1840s. In the 1850s, 1860s, and 1870s, the proportion of the budget used for public schools in Boston remained relatively constant at about 10 to 15 percent.

Although the proportion of the Boston budget devoted to public schools and institutions declined while that for the police slightly increased, the per capita expenditures for all three areas increased dramatically from 1820 to 1880 (see Figure 7.8). Police expenditures rose from $.20 per capita in 1820 to $2.21 per capita in 1880, and municipal spending on institutions increased from $.43 per capita in 1820 to $2.21 per capita in 1880. The per capita allotments for Boston public schools grew from $1.03 in 1820 to $4.45 in 1880.

Education was benefiting, along with other public services, from a continually increasing governmental role. At the same time, education in the larger cities was becoming a smaller relative part of the total budget. These conditions, and the expansive economy, encouraged improvements in the quantity and quality of education and facilitated the many educational reforms of the mid-nineteenth century. However, the rural communities were hard pressed to follow the lead of the richer and larger towns. A writer in the *Common School Journal* congratulated rural Chelsea in 1839 for building a new schoolhouse, even though "the inhabitants have not the transferable capital nor the extra money of a commercial or a manufacturing community."[8] Towns that did not make such sacrifices were made keenly aware of their relative parsimony by the annual publication of local school expenditures by the board of education. Tables appended to the annual reports announced each town's rank within its county and in the whole state. That local school committees often commented upon these rankings demonstrates the effectiveness of the state board's tactics. Lawrence crowed in 1850 that to be 2nd in Essex County and 32nd in the state, as a brand-new city, showed that it was "unsurpassed" in commitment to common schooling. By the next year it was 1st in Essex and 5th in the state.[9] Meanwhile, at the other end of the rankings, the school committee in Wilbraham, ranked 228th of 316 towns in 1851, warned their fellow citizens that skimping on education was "false economy" that would lead to "poverty of the worst kind." In the same year the town of Palmer was lowest in the state in school expenditures, even though it was 58th in property value and 48th in population. This, the school committee said, was a "mortification."[10]

Some small towns despaired of trying to compete. Boxford, as we saw in Chapter 6, paid little heed to outside admonitions for educational improvements. In 1851 the report for Chester, in western Massachusetts, complained that teachers in the eastern part of the state commanded twice the wages Chester could afford, and in 1861 the Danvers committee declared that if teachers wanted to go to the cities

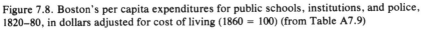

Figure 7.8. Boston's per capita expenditures for public schools, institutions, and police, 1820–80, in dollars adjusted for cost of living (1860 = 100) (from Table A7.9)

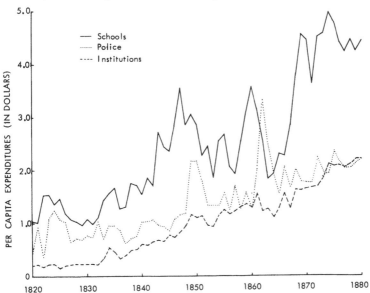

for higher pay, they should go. It "would be useless to attempt to retain those we employ if cities are determined to obtain their services."[11] It is not surprising, therefore, that much of the resistance to costly innovation and to an expanded state authority in education came from small towns and from western Massachusetts. However, even in small towns, particularly in the eastern part of the state, school committees often argued the position of the state board. As prominent citizens and school boosters, committee members associated educational development with the general prospects of their towns. "We live in an age of progress," said a Hamilton report. Towns could not ignore educational improvement "and still maintain their appropriate influence and respectability." The Lynnfield committee declared bluntly in 1851 that people would settle where there were good schools. In the town of Essex, school sessions were two months below the county average in 1860. The school committee lamented "the inadequate and comparatively small amount of schooling we are giving our children" and concluded that "we have not kept pace with the progressive spirit of the age."[12]

Considering the difficulties of financing education in the smaller and poorer towns, we decided to determine more precisely whether state action in nineteenth-century Massachusetts did anything to offset the rural disadvantage.

Trends in inequality in public school expenditures

One of the major educational policy issues today concerns the extent of inequality among communities in the amount of money spent for education. Children in wealthier districts receive a more costly education than children from poorer districts – a practice that critics claim reinforces the existing class structure in the United States. Various efforts have been made by both state and federal agencies to reduce the inequality in available school funds, but it is generally acknowledged that there is still a wide disparity in the amount of money available for education in different districts.[13] In 1969–70, for example, Boston spent $912 on each public school student, whereas the nearby wealthy suburb of Brookline spent $1,495. The disparity becomes even more striking when we consider smaller communities, like Dudley, which devoted only $573 to the education of each student.[14]

Despite the great concern about inequality in school funding today, no one has estimated whether there has been an increase or a decrease in inequality since the nineteenth century. A simple but useful index of inequality of expenditures among communities is the coefficient of variation: the standard deviation divided by the mean. The higher the coefficient of variation, the greater the inequality in expenditures among the towns. Using this index, we compared the degree of inequality in different years, and we learned that the extent of inequality of educational expenditures in nineteenth-century Massachusetts was considerably higher than that in recent years.

In 1969–70 the coefficient of variation among Massachusetts communities for the amount of expenditures per student in the public schools was .230 (the standard deviation was $213 and the mean was $927). It was .366 in 1840–1, the first year for which we could calculate the extent of inequality in public school funding for nineteenth-century Massachusetts communities (see Figure 7.9).[15] Although Horace Mann tried to reduce the inequality among communities in public school expenditures by persuading those at the bottom to increase their support of education, there was an increase in the extent of inequality during his years as the secretary of the Massachusetts Board of Education. In fact, it was not until the late 1860s that there was a significant reversal in the extent of inequality among Massachusetts communities in their financial support of public schools.

Figure 7.9. Trends in inequality among Massachusetts towns in public school expenditures per school-age child, 1841–80 (from Table A7.10)

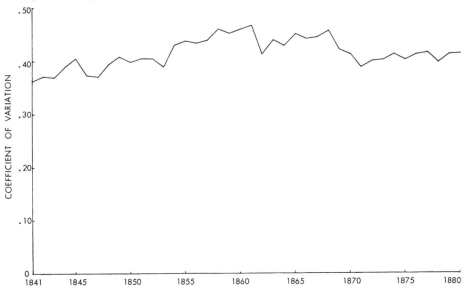

The most obvious factor that accounts for the reduction of inequality in public school funding in twentieth-century Massachusetts is state and federal aid to local schools. Whereas state aid to local education was never above 5 percent of the total annual public school expenditures in the commonwealth for the period 1837 to 1880 (and there were no federal funds available for local schools), in 1969–70 state funds accounted for 21.3 percent of the Massachusetts public school budget and federal funds accounted for another 4.0 percent. Indeed, even the meager state funds available for local education in the years 1834 to 1880 were not intended to redress inequality among communities. They were distributed mainly on the basis of the number of school-age children in each community and thus did little to alleviate inequality among the towns. The situation was quite different, however, in Massachusetts in 1969–70. The manner in which state and federal funds were then allocated significantly reduced the inequality in public school expenditures among the cities and towns. Whereas the coefficient of variation for only local appropriations per public school student was .298, the addition of state and federal funds produced a more equitable distribution of school funds (coefficient of variation equal to .229).

It may appear surprising that Massachusetts did not create a larger

Figure 7.10. Massachusetts public schoolteachers' monthly wages, including board, 1837–80, in dollars adjusted for cost of living (1860 = 100) (from Table A7.11)

school fund in the nineteenth century that might have been used to assist the less affluent communities. Certainly many educational leaders in nineteenth-century Massachusetts called for an expansion of the state school fund; but their pleas were usually ignored by the state legislature. It was often the rural representatives, whose communities might have benefited the most from an expansion of the state school fund, who opposed its enlargement.

Feminization of the teaching force

Teacher salaries were the largest item in school budgets in nineteenth-century Massachusetts. For example, salaries for instructors accounted for 59.9 percent of the total public school expenditures in Boston during the years 1840 to 1880. As a result, changes in the wages paid to teachers had a large impact on the overall costs of education in the commonwealth.

Public schoolteacher salaries increased significantly during the antebellum period (see Figure 7.10). Male teachers increased their real monthly wages by 118.6 percent between 1837 and 1859–60, and their female counterparts increased their real salaries by 93.0 percent during that same period.

The Civil War period was a time of hardship for teachers, as salaries failed to keep pace with the spiraling rate of inflation. Male teachers

200

Figure 7.11. Annual number of individuals who taught in Massachusetts public and private schools, 1834–80 (from Table A7.12)

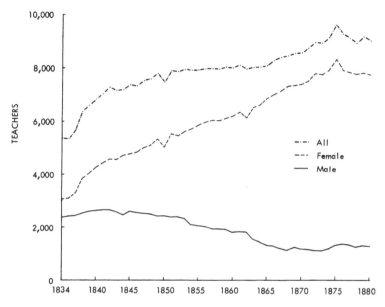

saw a 38.1 percent decrease in their real monthly salaries between 1859–60 and 1864–5; female teacher salaries dropped by 37.6 percent during the Civil War years. But the years after the Civil War witnessed a great increase in salaries, as teachers more than recouped their losses of the war period. Overall, male teachers increased their monthly salaries by 165.5 percent in the period 1837 to 1879–80, and female teachers improved their wages by an almost identical 168.7 percent.

The mid-nineteenth century also saw an increased demand for teachers in the commonwealth. Although there are no contemporary estimates of the total number of schoolteachers in Massachusetts's public and private schools, we have been able to construct our own estimates based on the local school returns (see Figure 7.11).[16] In 1834 there were an estimated 5,393 schoolteachers in public and private schools in Massachusetts. To keep up with the growing number of children in the schools during the period 1834 to 1880, the annual number of schoolteachers grew to 9,091 – an increase of 68.6 percent. But a disproportionate share of the increase in the number of schoolteachers was among female instructors. Whereas the annual number of male teachers decreased by 44.3 percent from 1834 to 1880, the number of female teachers increased by 156.3 percent. This feminization of the teaching force was one of the most dramatic changes in nineteenth-century education. To a large extent, it was related to the differential wages paid to male and female teachers. Throughout the nineteenth-century, female teachers were always paid less in the public schools than their male counterparts. In the period 1837 to 1880, female public schoolteachers usually received about 40 percent of the wages paid to males. Despite the fluctuations and changes in the monthly wages for teachers during these years, the ratio of female to male wages remained quite constant.

Women initially were used only in teaching the younger children in the summer sessions. Drawing upon the conventional sex stereotyping of the nineteenth century, Horace Mann argued that women were better suited for teaching young children than older ones:

All those differences of organization and temperament which individualize the sexes point to the female as the guide and guardian of young children. She holds her commission from nature. In the well developed female character there is always a preponderance of affection over intellect. However powerful and brilliant her reflective faculties may be, they are considered a deformity in her character unless overbalanced and tempered by womanly affections. The dispositions of young children of both sexes correspond with this ordination of Providence.[17]

There was widespread resistance to hiring female schoolteachers for instructing the older students in the winter schools. Many citizens as well as some educators felt that female schoolteachers would not be able to handle the older boys, who tended to be rowdy and difficult to discipline. Furthermore, it was argued that most women were not capable of teaching the more advanced intellectual subjects that were presented in the winter schools.[18]

Nonetheless, the rapidly rising cost of public school education encouraged many local districts to use female teachers in the winter sessions as well as in the summer sessions. Further encouragement came from reports of successful female teachers in other communities, publicized in the board of education annual reports. The grading of schools, an increasingly popular innovation after 1850, also facilitated the feminization of the teaching force by allowing one or more female teachers to work under the supervision of a male head teacher. As a result, the percentage of female schoolteachers rapidly increased from 56.3 in 1834 to 85.6 in 1879–80. Public schoolteaching became almost exclusively a female occupation in Massachusetts in the decades after the Civil War.[19] The growing feminization of the Massachusetts teaching force did reduce the rising costs of public education. Whereas monthly wages for both male and female public schoolteachers rose by about 165 percent from 1837 to 1880, the average monthly expenditures for public schoolteachers rose only 105 percent because of the increased proportion of lower-paid female teachers.

The substitution of females for males in the teaching force did not halt the spiraling costs of education in Massachusetts, but it did slow them down substantially. In its urban version this innovation led to a new sexually discriminatory hierarchy and the invention of the school principal. The Salem committee applauded "the system of placing a large number of scholars under the care of male principals with female assistants – the most economical as well as the most effective mode of instruction – and of securing the advantages of a division of labor."[20] Even in the country, however, school committees like that of Boxford eventually discovered that women teachers could and did manage winter schools by themselves. In little Newbury the school committee reported in 1851 that school sessions had increased to ten months a year because of the savings realized by hiring females. Then, in a rare passage, they admitted the injustice:

There seems but one drawback to this gain, which is this: that the economy rests upon the advantage taken by us of the low rate of female wages. The range of employments opened by society to well-educated women is so much narrower than that open to men, that the same order of merit can be obtained much more cheaply by employing a woman. The female teacher passes the same examination with the male teacher, and passes it ordinarily quite as well . . . Yet we have usually within the last year paid a woman about one half what we should under the circumstances, have paid a man.[21]

This brief fit of conscience, however, passed without any effect on differential wages in Newbury. Hiring female teachers was by mid-century a widespread economy tactic.

Another consequence of the feminization of the teaching force was that it provided new employment opportunities for women. On the one hand, women clearly were the victims of wage discrimination. On the other hand, teaching offered single women in nineteenth-century Massachusetts one of their major sources of employment outside the home. Of course, the percentage of women who taught school at any single point was not very large. We can calculate the percentage of white women ages fifteen to sixty who were teaching during each year from 1834 to 1880 (see Figure 7.12). Less than 2 percent of those women were teachers at any given time. Furthermore, there was a gradual decline in the percentage of women ages fifteen to sixty who were teachers.

Figure 7.12. Individuals who taught as percentages of the Massachusetts white population ages 15–59, 1834–80 (from Table 7.13)

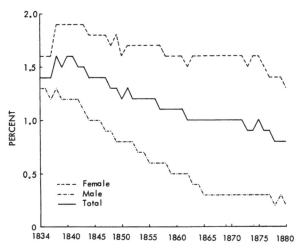

But this snapshot perspective of the participation of females in schoolteaching does not adequately portray the importance of teaching for women in nineteenth-century Massachusetts. Although only a very small percentage of women taught school at any given point, a much larger percentage taught at some time in their lives. Thus we should consider the role of teaching in the lives of the women from a life-course perspective.[22]

Compiling the number of Massachusetts women who ever taught during their lifetime is a rather involved task. Essentially, we proceeded by estimating the number of females who annually entered the profession, and then estimating from that figure the percentage of women who worked as teachers at some time in their careers. The number of yearly female entries into teaching was itself a composite of three factors: the new teachers replacing other teachers who left their duties, the new teachers filling newly created positions in expanding school systems, and the overall change in the sex ratio caused by these additions. Let us then consider each factor.

The crucial problem in verifying teacher replacement or turnover in the nineteenth century is the limited data available. Horace Mann's statewide tallies of the teaching experience of public school instructors in 1845–6 provide the only empirical information available for Massachusetts.[23] In the absence of more complete records, we have reluc-

Figure 7.13. Percentage of the Massachusetts white population ages 15–29 who have ever been teachers, 1834–80 (from Table A7.14)

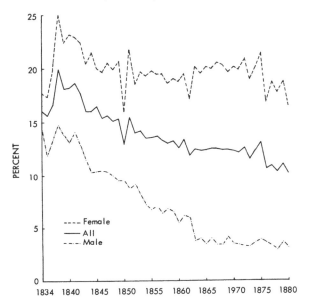

tantly applied his finding to the whole period. The average amount of teaching experience for all teachers, including beginners, was 2.1 years. For determining turnover, however, the critical figure is 2.6 years – the mean duration of tenure for those who had already begun to teach. The 1845–6 turnover rate for Massachusetts teachers was, therefore, the reciprocal of 2.6, or 38.5 percent. Unfortunately, we do not have comparable data for private schoolteachers; nonetheless, a combined replacement rate of 38.5 percent for all schools in the state during the nineteenth century is probably a reasonable estimate.

Once we estimated a turnover rate, it was easy to determine the number of new teachers required annually to replace those who retired. Next we calculated the number of new teachers necessary to staff the expansion of Massachusetts schools during these years (taking into account the fact that the number of female teachers was steadily increasing while the number of male teachers was actually declining). Having then established the total number of new male and female teachers entering both the public and private schools every year, we estimated the percentage of white men and women in the state who ever taught (Figure 7.13). The results of our calculations are quite startling: Approximately one out of every five white women in Massachusetts was a schoolteacher at some time in her life. Moreover, because almost all the teachers were native-born, probably one out of every four Massachusetts females born in the United States taught school at some time.

The social history of teaching has yet to be written, but our data suggest that teaching was a very common feature in the life course of nineteenth-century women.[24] With all its discriminatory attitudes and salary, and with all the classroom frustrations facing teachers of either sex, teaching nonetheless provided many young women with an interlude between parental and marital households, with remunerative work, and with responsibility.

Conclusion

Financial considerations played an important role in determining the constraints on educational development in Massachusetts. Although reformers focused on improving the quality of education, they also had to provide facilities for the great increase in the total number of students. This task was made even more difficult as the cost of educating each child rose and as the burden of education increasingly shifted to the local taxpayers, owing to the relative decline of private schools and the relative decrease in state aid to local school districts. Considering the increased costs involved, Massachusetts citizens were quite responsive to the pleas for improved public education in the commonwealth. One of the reasons for the ability of the state to absorb the additional costs of educating its children was the continued expansion of the Massachusetts economy, which increased the tax base. There was only a slight increase in the overall Massachusetts school expenditures per thousand dollars of state valuation from 1837 to 1880. Yet this advantage differed greatly from one community to another. Rural communities like Boxford, with declining population and declining agricultural productivity, were especially hard pressed to meet increased educational costs and continual demands for innovation. Many such towns responded by digging deeper into their pockets, because local pride, intercommunity competition, and commitment to education were strong. Others responded by resisting state involvement in local education, by tolerating poor facilities, and by begrudgingly hiring female teachers, sometimes as an explicit means of affording other needed reforms. It is no wonder, then, that towns not in the economic vanguard in nineteenth-century Massachusetts were also not the most enthusiastic supporters of the Board of Education and often found themselves near the bottom of the secretary's annual expenditure lists. For most communities, however, the generally expansive economy and the annual exhortations of the state board of education were sufficient to encourage an impressive expansion of local school expenditure.

8

The politics of educational reform in mid-nineteenth-century Massachusetts

Educational reform and state intervention in schooling appealed more to some communities and some individuals than others. Previous chapters have explored support and opposition through town records, census information, and case studies. Another way to get at conflict in the process of educational development is to examine the politics of education during the formative years when state intervention was still controversial.

Historians of American education have long been interested in the question of who supported educational reform in the 1830s and 1840s, and they have put forth a wide variety of answers. Some have seen the educational revivals of the thirties and forties as the result of dedicated humanitarian leaders, such as James Carter, Horace Mann, and Henry Barnard, who aroused an otherwise apathetic public to the value of common school education.[1] Others have argued that the educational reforms of the period resulted from the demands of workers who wanted educational opportunities for their children.[2] Some recent scholarship on antebellum education has stressed the role of capitalists in developing an extensive public school system in order to insure stability in the emerging industrial order.[3] There is, then, little agreement among historians about the relative importance of various groups in supporting educational reform in Massachusetts. Part of the disagreement has arisen because historians with different theories have used different types of evidence. Supporters of the great-crusader interpretation relied on the writings of elite reformers, common-man advocates looked to the platforms of worker organizations, and recent supporters of economic interpretations have analyzed the characteristics of towns that adopted educational reforms. In this chapter we hope to shed some light on the question by analyzing a rich and hitherto untapped source of information on this subject: the legislative roll-call vote, specifically, the vote to abolish the board of education in the Massachusetts House of Representatives in March 1840. Some historians have studied this legislative threat to the board of education by analyzing the majority and minority reports of the Committee on Education of the House, but no one has previously analyzed the actual vote on the bill.[4] A roll-call analysis of the vote will provide us with detailed information on the opponents and supporters of Mann's educational reforms among the 519 members of the Massachusetts House.

Massachusetts politics and the state board of education

During the 1820s and 1830s the Massachusetts legislature was frequently approached by individuals and groups who sought state assistance in improving the quality of education within the state. For example, James Carter petitioned the legislature in 1827 for aid in creating a seminary for training teachers, but the bill lost by a single vote in the Senate. In 1834 the legislature established a permanent school fund, the income of which was to be used in assisting local school systems. In 1836, George Emerson of the American Institute of Instruction again urged the legislature to provide assistance for the training of school teachers, but no action was taken.[5]

Prior to 1837 proposals to assist education in Massachusetts were directed toward specific projects, not toward creating a state agency to handle educational matters. In his annual message to the legislators in 1837, however, Governor Edward Everett urged that body to create a "board of commissioners of schools." His proposal was endorsed by the Committee on Education, which introduced a bill to create a board of education. After considerable initial opposition, the bill was enacted into law on April 20, 1837.[6]

The new law provided that the governor and the council should appoint eight members to the board of education (the governor and lieutenant governor were members ex officio). The power of the board was very limited; it was instructed only to collect information on education and to submit annual reports to the legislature. Horace Mann, a prominent Whig politician who was already active in various reform efforts, was selected as the first secretary of the board and remained at that post for the next twelve years.

Mann saw in education a means for improving future generations. As he accepted the job of secretary of the board of education, he noted in his private journal:

Henceforth, so long as I hold this office, I devote myself to the supremest welfare of mankind upon earth . . . I have faith in the improvability of the race – in their accelerating improvability. This effort may do, apparently, but little. But a mere beginning in a good cause is never little.[7]

Education and social change in nineteenth-century Massachusetts

The board of education had been suggested by a Whig governor and enacted by a Whig-controlled legislature. Furthermore, most of the leaders in the effort to establish the board were Unitarians. Nonetheless, the board members were selected to represent the various political, religious, and geographic factions within the state. Several years after the event, Mann defended the board by stressing the various considerations that were used in the selection of members.

I may speak with confidence here, for I had personal knowledge of the facts. All the great parties, into which the State was divided, were to be regarded. Religious views were among the most important. Political considerations could not be overlooked. Indications of public sentiment, in regard to men, whom the people had invested with office for a long course of years, were also worthy of attention. Even local residence, though among the weakest motives, must not be wholly forgotten.[8]

The deliberate effort to protect the board of education from outside criticism by including prominent members of various political and religious groups is one of the main reasons why the board was able to survive efforts to discredit it. When some Trinitarians denounced it for advocating Unitarian ideas and practices, the presence on the board of such Trinitarians as Rev. Emerson David and Rev. Thomas Robbins was effective in deflecting much of this criticism. Similarly, the fact that Robert Rantoul, Jr., one of the leading Democrats in eastern Massachusetts, was a board member made it easier for Mann to defend himself against the charges that the board of education was simply a means of furthering Whig interests. Nevertheless, although the board represented members of different religious and political orientations, it was dominated by Whigs and Unitarians. Of its first ten members, nine were Whigs and seven were Unitarians.[9]

After the board of education was established, Horace Mann plunged into the effort to improve the public schools throughout the commonwealth. He crisscrossed the state, examining the conditions in the local schools and trying in his lectures to arouse the public to the benefits of improved education. He also devoted long hours to gathering statistical information from the schools and to preparing condensed returns for the now-classic expositions on education in his annual reports to the board.

Despite Mann's continued efforts to avoid any controversies as board secretary, some of his proposals, such as the recommendation of particular books for school libraries, provoked strong opposition. Much of the opposition came from Trinitarians like Frederick Packard, who accused Mann of using the proposed list of library books as a

210

means of spreading Unitarian doctrines. Mann was able to counter these accusations by rallying support for the board among leading Trinitarians within the state. Even though Packard took his case to the newspapers, Mann succeeded in isolating him from his potential followers. Yet the appeals of Packard to the fears of the orthodox community were not forgotten. As the political situation in Massachusetts shifted against the Whigs, the board of education found itself under attack within the legislature in 1840. Potential support for the board's detractors lay with those who feared its Unitarian orientation.[10]

During the late 1830s the Whigs had continued to dominate Massachusetts politics. Governor Edward Everett, one of the founders of the board of education, was easily reelected in 1837 despite the growing strength of the Democrats within the state. But a bill that was passed by the legislature in April 1838 and reluctantly signed by Governor Everett proved to be his undoing. Proponents of temperance reform in Massachusetts campaigned vigorously in the mid-1830s to prohibit the sale of spirituous liquors. Although they failed to outlaw the sale of liquor, they were able to obtain a law that prohibited the sale of liquor in quantities of less than fifteen gallons – a measure designed to prevent the sale of drinks in saloons. The Whigs were split on the issue of the fifteen-gallon law, but the Democrats accused those who supported the law of discriminating against ordinary citizens: The wealthy could afford to buy as much liquor as they wanted. By remaining silent on the issue during the campaign of 1838, Governor Everett survived the furor and defeated the perennial Democratic candidate, Marcus Morton, by a vote of 51,642 to 41,795. However, largely as a result of the unpopularity of the fifteen-gallon law, Morton finally defeated Everett in 1839, by a single vote out of the more than 102,000 cast.[11]

Control of the governor's office changed parties, but the legislature remained under control of the Whigs. Of the 519 members elected to the Massachusetts House of Representatives of 1840, we have been able to identify the party affiliation of 493 (95.0 percent).[12] Of these, 55.2 percent were Whigs. There was a high turnover of members in the Massachusetts House during these years: 41.6 percent of the Whigs and 51.4 percent of the Democrats in the House had no previous legislative experience. Furthermore, only about a third of the Whigs and a fifth of the Democrats had two or more years of previous legislative experience.

The Whigs as a group were slightly older than the Democrats. For example, 37.8 percent of the Whigs were over fifty years old, compared to 31.8 percent of the Democrats. More than one-third of the legislators from both parties were in their forties.

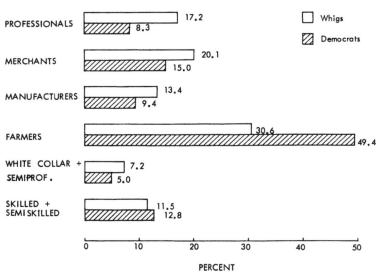

Figure 8.1. Occupational distribution of Massachusetts legislators, 1840 (from Massa-chusetts State Library, State House, Boston, Massachusetts, Legislative File)

Although there were no major differences between the Whigs and Democrats in previous legislative experience or age distribution, there were significant differences between them in occupations (see Figure 8.1). Although 49.4 percent of the Democrats were farmers, only 30.6 percent of the Whigs were. On the other hand, 50.7 percent of the Whigs but only 32.7 percent of the Democrats were professionals, merchants, or manufacturers.[13]

Geographically, the Democrats and the Whigs drew their strength in about the same proportions from the three regions of the state – central Massachusetts (Essex, Middlesex, and Suffolk counties), western Massachusetts (Berkshire, Franklin, Hampden, Hampshire, and Worcester counties), and southern Massachusetts (Barnstable, Bristol, Dukes, Nantucket, Norfolk, and Plymouth counties).[14] Among the Whig members, 36.0 percent were from central Massachusetts, 35.3 percent from western Massachusetts, and 28.7 percent from southern Massachusetts. Similarly, among the Democratic members, 33.0 percent were from central Massachusetts, 37.1 percent were from western Massachusetts, and 29.9 percent were from southern Massachusetts.

Although the Whigs and Democrats represented the three regions of the state in about equal proportions, they came from towns of very different population size. Generally, the Whigs came from larger towns

212

Figure 8.2. Distribution of Massachusetts legislators according to town population, 1840 (from Massachusetts State Library, Legislative File; U.S. census of 1840)

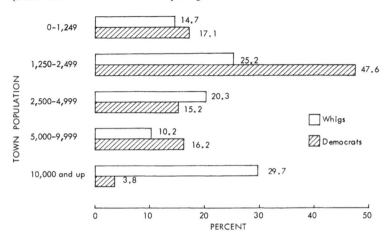

than the Democrats (see Figure 8.2). Thus, whereas 63.7 percent of the Democrats came from towns of less than twenty-five hundred people, only 39.9 percent of the Whigs represented such communities. Conversely, whereas 39.9 percent of the Whigs were from towns with more than five thousand inhabitants, the comparable figure for Democrats was 20.0 percent.

Finally, Democrats were much more likely than their Whig counterparts to represent constituents in the less-developed agricultural regions (see Figure 8.3). Thus, whereas 38.8 percent of the Democrats came from towns with low commerce and low manufacturing, only 22.3 percent of the Whigs represented such areas. Whig representatives were especially characteristic of towns heavily engaged in commerce.[15]

The attempt to abolish the board of education in the Massachusetts House in 1840

The board of education was not a campaign issue during the 1839 election. There was almost no mention of Horace Mann or the Board during the heated campaign.[16] An attack on the board by Orestes A. Brownson, one of the radical leaders of the Democrats, was a significant exception. In a review of the second annual report of the board of education, Brownson accused the board of trying to Prussianize the Massachusetts schools through increased centralization. Furthermore,

Figure 8.3. Distribution of Massachusetts legislators according to the economic development of their towns, 1840 (from Massachusetts State Library, Legislative File; U.S. census of 1840)

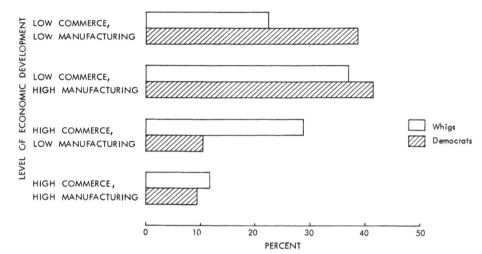

he saw the board as an agency for spreading Whig ideas throughout the commonwealth, and he advocated leaving control of school matters within the local districts.[17]

Mann worried about Brownson's partisan attack on the board, but it was an isolated episode. Many other prominent Democratic leaders, such as Robert Rantoul, Jr., and George Bancroft, supported the state board of education. In fact, when the Democrats held their state convention at Boston on October 2, 1839, and the committee on resolutions, chaired by Orestes A. Brownson, drew up the platform, they made no statements, positive or negative, about the board of education.[18] Although the campaign did not really discuss the board, the election of Marcus Morton as governor of the state caused considerable anxiety among its supporters. Mann noted in his journal at the start of the new year:

> I enter upon another year not without some gloom and apprehension, for *political madmen* are raising voice and arm against the Board; but I enter with a determination, that, I trust, will prove a match for *secondary* causes. If the First Cause has doomed our overthrow, I give it up; but, if anything short of that, I hold on.[19]

Morton had not committed himself on the issue of the board of education during the campaign. Finally, in his address to the legislature, he outlined his position on education. He made no specific references to the board but directed his remarks generally against the position of Mann and his supporters; he deemphasized the value of seminaries for teachers, one of Mann's major efforts, and emphasized the importance of keeping control of schools within the towns:

In the town and district meetings, those little pure democracies, where our citizens first learn the rudiments and the practical operation of free institutions, may safely and rightly be placed the direction and the government of these available seminaries. In my opinion, the main efforts and the most unceasing vigilance of the government should be directed to the encouragement of the primary schools. These are the fountains whence should flow the knowledge that should enlighten, and the virtue that should preserve, our free institutions. Let them ever be kept free and pure.[20]

Governor Morton's remarks on the virtues of district control of schools were quite incidental. The major portion of his legislative message was directed against private banks, special legislation for corporations, state aid for railroads, and the high cost of state government. Morton's general policy of retrenchment in state expenditures, however, posed a real threat to the board of education.

Morton's suggestions for the reduction in salaries of state officials and the abolition of some state offices were referred to a special committee of the House on January 31, 1840. The committee was composed of five members – three Whigs and two Democrats. With the Whigs in control of the committee, one might have anticipated that the effort to reduce salaries and abolish offices would have been defeated along partisan lines. But Cyrus Alden, a Whig from Sherburne, sided with the two Democrats to produce a majority report advocating a major retrenchment in expenditures for state officials. The committee recommended reductions in the salaries of most state officials, including the governor, and the elimination of many commissions, such as the board of bank commissioners.[21]

The majority report attacked the board of education as an unnecessary expense and a danger to political and religious freedoms within the commonwealth. "District schools, in a republican government," they argued, "need no police regulations, no systems of state censorship, no checks of moral, religious, or political conservatism, to preserve either the morals, the religion, or the politics of the state. 'Let them ever be kept free and pure.' " Having quoted Morton's annual message directly, they expanded upon his defense of local control:

Instead of consolidating the education interest of the Commonwealth in one grand central head, and that head the government, let us rather hold on to the good old principles of our ancestors, and diffuse and scatter this interest far and wide, divided and subdivided, not only into towns and districts, but even into families and individuals. The moment this interest is surrendered to the government, and all responsibility is thrown upon civil power, farewell to the usefulness of common schools, the just pride, honor and ornament of New England; farewell to religious liberty, for there would be but one church; farewell to political freedom, for nothing but the name of a republic would survive such a catastrophe.[22]

The committee recommended that the salary of the secretary of the board of education be eliminated. They wanted to abolish the board of education entirely, but they were unwilling to take that step without first investigating the effects such a move would have on existing school laws in the commonwealth. Therefore, the committee suggested that the standing Committee on Education be instructed to consider the expediency of abolishing the board of education and transferring its essential functions to the governor, council, and secretary of the commonwealth.[23]

Mann reacted angrily to the efforts to abolish the board in the name of economy. In a letter to his close friend, George Combe, he attributed the attack to party politics.

First came the Governor's Address, which committed that high treason to truth which consists in perverting great principles to selfish ends. Then the cry of expense has been raised; and, were an Englishman to hear it, he would think the Board of Education was trying to outvie the British national debt. But it will end in alienating a portion of the public mind from the cause which it will cost us another year's labor to reclaim.

What an enemy to the human race is a party-man! To get ashore himself is his only object: he cares not who else sinks.[24]

Mann's assumption that the effort behind the bill to reduce salaries and eliminate certain state officials was partisan is borne out by the vote on that bill. The bill lost narrowly in the House, by a vote of 222 to 232.[25] The voting was along party lines: 95.2 percent of the Democrats voted in favor of it and 92.7 percent of the Whigs voted against it. Despite the strong attacks on the board by the majority report of the committee, the final bill on reducing salaries did not include its abolition; instead, the board's fate was entrusted to the Committee on Education. But the vote on reducing salaries clearly indicated the dangers that lay ahead. If the Democrats, in their effort to abolish the board of education, were able to maintain the party unity of their effort to reduce salaries, the addition of a few Whigs who were disgruntled with Horace Mann would be sufficient to carry the proposal.

216

On March 3, 1840, the House directed its Committee on Education to "consider the expediency of abolishing the Board of Education, and the Normal Schools."[26] The Committee on Education, like the other committees in the legislature, was nominally controlled by the Whigs. Of its seven members, four were Whigs and three were Democrats. But on the issue of the board of education, the committee did not split along party lines. Two of the Whigs, Allen W. Dodge of Hamilton and Frederic Emerson of Boston, joined two of the Democrats in producing a majority report that called for the abolition of the board and the normal schools. On the other hand, Abel G. Duncan, a Democrat from Hanover, voted against the bill to abolish the board, even though he did not sign the minority report of the committee, which defended Horace Mann and the board.

The majority report from the Committee on Education, like that of the special Committee on the Reduction of Salaries, attacked the board of education as an unnecessary expense and dangerous precedent. The report emphasized the general fears among Democrats in Jacksonian America that any governmental intervention posed a potential danger to the liberties of the people.[27] Thus, even though the board of education had the power only to recommend legislation, the writers of the report worried that it might "be soon converted into a power of regulation."

And even if it were not, the vantage ground such a board occupies, must obviously give it, for all practical purposes, an equivalent power . . . If, then, the board has any actual power, it is a dangerous power, trenching directly upon the rights and duties of the Legislature; if it has no power, why continue its existence, at an annual expense to the Commonwealth.[28]

The majority report goes on to suggest that many of the board's activities, such as gathering data on schools and disseminating information on new teaching methods, could be done by the existing teacher associations within the commonwealth. Instead of improving the existing system of education, the report charged, the board was trying to remodel it after the centralized French and Prussian systems.

The establishment of a Board of Education, seems to be the commencement of a system of centralization and of monopoly of power in a few hands, contrary, in every respect, to the true spirit of our democratical institutions, and which, unless speedily checked, may lead to unlooked for and dangerous results.[29]

The report also appealed to the fears of orthodox Calvinists, who felt that the board was advocating Unitarian doctrines in the selection of books for school libraries. Rather than trusting the board to suggest appropriate books for a school library, the report urged that local school committees should make those selections. Finally, the report dismissed the newly created normal schools as an unnecessary expense. The members argued that the existing academies and high schools were "fully adequate . . . to furnish a competent supply of teachers."[30] Nor did they believe that teachers needed to become more professional.

Considering that our District Schools are kept, on an average, for only three or four months in the year, it is obviously impossible, and perhaps, it is not desirable, that the business of keeping these schools should become a distinct and separate profession, which the establishment of Normal Schools seems to anticipate.[31]

The minority report of the Committee on Education, produced by John A. Shaw of Bridgewater and Thomas A. Greene of New Bedford, in close consultation with Mann, defended the board of education and the normal schools. They scoffed at fears of potential harm from the board; rather, they argued, the actual operations of the board were clearly beneficial to the commonwealth:

The majority of our committee do not specify a single instance, so far as we can recollect, in which the Board of Education have attempted to control, or in any way to interfere with the rights of towns or school districts. They seem to be in great fear of *imaginary* evils, but are not able to produce a single fact to justify their apprehensions. It is the alleged tendencies of the Board, to which they object. There is a possibility, they think, of its doing wrong, of its usurping powers which would endanger freedom of thought.

If every institution is to be abolished, which it is possible to pervert to some evil purpose, we beg leave to ask, what one would be left? In all human affairs, the possibility to do wrong, goes with the power to do right. Take away the power of doing wrong, and the power of doing right will be destroyed at the same time.[32]

The minority report then pointed out the value of the board of education in assisting the associations of schoolteachers, promoting the construction of new and better schoolhouses, and developing facilities for training teachers. The report closed with a plea for additional time in which to demonstrate the value of this new experiment in education.

The controversy over the board of education and the normal schools does not appear to have become a major issue among the general public. Several petitions supporting the board and the normal schools were submitted, but they represented only a very small fraction of the communities in the state.[33] Most newspapers did not devote much attention to the effort to abolish the board. A few, such as the Whig-oriented *Boston Daily Advertiser,* strongly endorsed the efforts of Horace Mann and the board and predicted defeat of the bill.[34] Although Whig newspapers blamed the Democrats for the continued efforts to abolish the board of education, they were forced to acknowledge that the leadership in the fight against the board came from two of the Whigs on the Committee on Education. One Whig complained in a newspaper that the attempt to abolish the board "is a loco foco measure; the loco foco party go for it, as a party . . . and now they are chuckling and laughing in their sleeves, to think they have succeeded in throwing the odium of the measure upon their cats' paws, the two Whig members of the majority of the Committee."[35]

The debate in the House on the bill to abolish the board of education and the normal schools was held on March 18, 1840.[36] Allen W. Dodge, one of the Whigs on the Committee on Education and an orthodox minister, supported the bill from the floor. Dodge's antagonism toward the board resulted from his conviction that it was an agency for spreading Unitarian ideas; but his attacks on it reiterated the broader charges that were contained in the majority report of the committee.[37] Similarly, although Frederick Emerson's personal opposition to the board stemmed in part from his disappointment in not being named to it and from Mann's rejection of his textbook, his public denunciations of the board were less self-centered.

Several members took to the floor to defend Mann and the board of education during these debates. The defense was led by John Shaw, one of the coauthors of the minority report of the Committee on Education. Shaw not only defended the board from its critics, but he also accused the majority members of the Committee on Education of condemning the board and the normal schools without due deliberation.[38] The vote on the bill to abolish the board of education and the normal schools was decisive: The bill failed by a vote of 182 to 245. This vote saving the board and the normal schools provides us with detailed information on the supporters and the opponents of a state-regulated public school system among the members of the Massachusetts House in 1840.

A roll-call analysis of the bill to abolish the board of education and the normal schools

Description of variables

To analyze the roll-call vote we assembled information on the members of the Massachusetts House of Representatives in 1840 from a variety of sources. In order to compare the vote to abolish the board of education with other votes during that session, we computerized all of the twenty-four roll-call votes.[39] We then coded information on the personal characteristics of all members of the House: their occupations, ages, numbers of years in the legislature, and places of birth. We also coded the party affiliation for the 95 percent of the members whose party we could determine. Unfortunately, it was not possible to ascertain religious affiliations.

In addition to collecting data on the personal characteristics of the legislators and on the pattern of voting in the House, we also assembled an extensive file on the characteristics of the towns the legislators represented. As indexes of urban development, we used the total population of a town in 1840 as well as the number of acres of farmland per capita (a crude measure of population density).[40] The overall wealth level of each town was approximated by its average per capita valuation. We calculated the per capita valuation of manufactured products and of commercial ventures as well as the percentage of workers engaged in manufacturing and commerce as indexes of the economic development of the legislators' communities.[41] We used the percentage of votes received by each party in the gubernatorial races for 1839, 1840, and 1841 and in the presidential contest for 1840 to indicate the relative party strength within the towns.[42] The religious orientation of the towns was approximated by information on the number and types of churches within those communities.[43] We also collected data indicating whether the Bible was used in the local school systems between 1837 and 1841 and whether any ministers served as members of the local school committees during 1839–41.[44] Finally, in an effort to measure educational activity within the towns, we estimated the percentage of persons under twenty years of age enrolled in public schools, the percentage of persons under twenty in public or private schools, the average number of days the public schools were kept open, the average amount of money spent per public school student, the public school expenditures per person in the town, and the average number of days spent in school annually per person under twenty.[45]

Overall, we assembled over one hundred variables for each of the 519 members of the Massachusetts House in 1840. Many of the variables, of course, were measures of similar characteristics. Because the statistical procedures we employed assumed relative independence among the variables, the number of variables used in our final analysis was reduced, after much experimentation, to eight.

In order to analyze the relative association of these various legislator and constituent characteristics on House members' votes on the board of education bill we used multiple classification analysis (MCA), a statistical technique described in Chapter 4.[46] Two tables support the analysis that follows. Table 8.1 presents the class mean, the adjusted mean, the net deviation, and the number of cases for each class or category of each of the predictor variables, as well as the grand mean and the total number of cases for that particular MCA. Table 8.2 contains the eta² and beta coefficient for each of the predictor variables, as well as the overall adjusted R^2.

Results

The dependent variable in the analysis is the vote for or against the bill to abolish the board of education and the normal schools by the 427 members of the House who recorded their votes on this issue. Our final list of independent variables included each legislator's occupation, his age, his number of years in the legislature before 1840, his party affiliation, a commercial/manufacturing index of his town, a population/wealth index of his town, whether there was a Unitarian church in his town, and the geographic location of his district.

We expected that the occupation of the legislator might be an important determinant of his vote on the bill. Some scholars have recently argued that the major support for educational reform came from manufacturers, who saw in education a means of socializing children into accepting the discipline necessary in the new industrial order. According to this view, manufacturers were joined by other capitalists, such as the merchants, who shared the same fears of social disorganization.[47] Older accounts, on the other hand, have focused on the opposition to the board of education among the rural segments of the population, and our own work in local sources partially supports this view. Therefore, we anticipated that farmers would tend to be opposed to the board.

The vote on the bill to abolish the board of education seems to fit both of these hypotheses. The only group that strongly opposed the board were the farmers – 59.5 percent of them voted to abolish it. The professionals and the manufacturers were particularly supportive of Mann and the board: Three-quarters of them refused to abolish the board. These patterns hold even after we control for the effects of the other variables in the MCA analysis (see the adjusted means and net deviations in Table 8.1).

The occupational profile on this vote is nonetheless complex. Nearly one-quarter of the manufacturers opposed the board of education,

Table 8.1. Vote in the Massachusetts House of Representatives in 1840 to abolish the state board of education: class means, adjusted means, and net deviations (in percentages)

	Class mean	Ad-justed mean	Net devia-tion	Number of cases
Occupation of legislator				
Professional	23.5	37.2	-5.4	51
Merchant	37.8	45.0	+2.4	74
Manufacturer	26.1	32.7	-9.9	46
Farmer	59.5	47.4	+4.8	158
White collar & semiprof.	36.0	45.7	+3.1	25
Skilled and unskilled	36.0	39.6	-3.0	50
Not ascertained	39.1	37.5	-5.1	23
Age of legislator				
25-34	35.3	40.1	-2.5	51
35-39	36.2	35.0	-7.6	69
40-49	43.5	40.1	-2.5	138
50-59	44.1	47.8	+5.2	93
60 & up	55.3	56.2	+13.6	47
Not ascertained	41.4	38.7	-3.9	29
Number of years in legislature before 1840				
None	45.2	43.3	+.7	197
One year	47.8	46.5	+3.9	113
Two years	35.0	39.8	-2.8	40
Three or more years	30.9	36.5	-6.1	68
Not ascertained	44.4	37.3	-5.3	9
Party affiliation				
Whig from noncompetitive district	15.6	17.2	-25.4	147
Whig from competitive district	21.9	22.9	-19.7	64
Democrat from competitive district	54.7	54.6	+12.0	64
Democrat from noncompetitive district	73.9	72.8	+30.2	119
Party affiliation or competitivenes not ascertained	66.7	62.1	+19.5	33
Commercial/manufacturing index of town				
Low commerce, low manufacturing	70.2	57.4	+14.8	124
Low commerce, high manufacturing	38.5	40.2	-2.4	161
High commerce, low manufacturing	20.2	40.8	-1.8	84
High commerce, high manufacturing	11.9	19.4	-23.2	42
Not ascertained	68.8	23.2	-19.4	16

Table 8.1 (cont.)

	Class mean	Ad-justed mean	Net devia-tion	Number of cases
Population/wealth index of town				
Population 0-2,499, low valuation	53.6	42.1	-.5	110
Population 0-2,499, high valuation	59.4	37.9	-4.7	106
Population 2,500-9,999, low valuation	34.5	41.6	-1.0	55
Population 2,500-9,999, high valuation	30.1	44.1	+1.5	73
Population 10,000 & up high valuation	11.9	44.1	+1.5	67
Not ascertained	68.8	68.7	+26.1	16
Unitarian church in town				
Yes	32.0	43.2	+.6	225
No	54.5	42.0	-.6	202
Geographic location within state				
Central	33.3	40.8	-1.8	150
Western	61.8	55.1	+12.5	152
Southern	30.4	29.6	-13.0	125
Total	42.6			427

whereas 40 percent of the farmers supported it. There was considerable variation within each of the occupational categories in reactions to the board – even after controlling for the effects of the other factors. As a result, the occupation of the legislator by itself can account for only 6.5 percent of the variation in the vote (see the eta^2 in Table 8.2) and is only moderately important as a predictor, compared to such other factors as party affiliation (see the betas in Table 8.2). Furthermore, it is instructive to remember that the professionals, merchants, and manufacturers together provided only 48.6 percent of the votes against abolishing the board of education. In short, although the occupation of the legislator did affect his vote, it was only one factor among several others in predicting his response to Horace Mann and the board of education.

We included the age of the legislator in 1840 as another independent variable. We suspected that the younger members would be more apt to support the board and the normal schools than the older ones be-

Education and social change in nineteenth-century Massachusetts

Table 8.2. Vote in the Massachusetts House of Representatives in 1840 to abolish the state board of education : eta^2, beta, and R^2 values

	Eta^2	Beta
Occupation of legislator	.0648	.1046
Age of legislator	.0012	.1273
Number of years in legislature		
before 1840	.0060	.0687
Party affiliation	.2609	.4897
Commercial/manufacturing index		
of town	.1736	.2336
Population/wealth index of town	.1163	.1146
Unitarian church in town	.0492	.0118
Geographic location within state	.0797	.2085

$R^2 = .3788$

Note: Eta^2 and R^2 values have been adjusted for degrees of freedom.

cause they had been brought up in the commonwealth at a time when there were increasing efforts made to have the state foster and regulate educational reforms. The older members, on the other hand, were the product of late eighteenth- and early nineteenth-century educational arrangements, which minimized the role of the state in schooling. Nonetheless, we did not expect that the age of the legislator would be a very powerful predictor of his position. The results of the MCA analysis indeed uphold the notion that younger legislators were some-what stronger supporters of the board of education. The results also indicate strong hostility toward the board among those legislators over sixty years of age – even after controlling for the effects of other fac-tors. Yet in general, as we suspected, the age of the legislator was not a strong predictor of the way in which he voted on this bill – either by itself or when taking into consideration the other variables.

We hypothesized that new members of the House might have been more hostile to the board of education than the legislative veterans, because the latter might have been among those who initially created it and would have been more exposed to Mann's skillful lobbying ef-forts in the previous legislative sessions. The MCA analysis again gen-erally supports such an interpretation, except that those legislators who had one year of previous experience were actually more hostile to the board than those who were newly elected. In any case, the number of years of legislative experience before 1840 was not, when compared to other factors, a very important predictor of voting behavior on this bill.

Raymond Culver deemphasized the importance of party in this controversy – largely because the fight against the board was led by two Whig members of the Committee on Education.[48] However, many contemporaries commented on the partisan nature of the attacks on the board of education, and we anticipated that the party affiliation of the legislator would be a major factor. We wanted to go beyond party affiliation to test whether legislators from closely contested areas voted differently than those from noncompetitive districts; so we subdivided party affiliation by whether the legislator came from a competitive or a noncompetitive district, according to his party's performance in the previous gubernatorial election.[49] The results of the MCA analysis indicate that party affiliation was the single best predictor of the vote on the board of education. By itself, the party affiliation of a legislator accounted for 26.1 percent of the variation in the vote. When we controlled for other factors, party affiliation was by far the most important predictor. Whig legislators from noncompetitive districts were more supportive of the board of education than were those from competitive areas. The reverse was true for Democrats: Democrats from noncompetitive districts were more hostile to the board than were those from competitive districts. In other words, Whigs tended to support the board, whereas Democrats opposed it; however, a legislator from a shaky district, whether Whig or Democrat, was more likely to shift his vote toward the other party's position than was his counterpart from a safe district.

Although legislators who were themselves manufacturers or professionals voted in favor of the board more reliably than did those who were merchants, we wished also to assess the support for the board that was associated with the predominant economic activity of a legislator's constituents. To provide a measure of the economic character of the legislator's district we subdivided the towns into four categories: those with low commercial activity and low manufacturing, those with low commerce and high manufacturing, those with high manufacturing and low commerce, and those with high commerce and high manufacturing.[50] Horace Mann frequently complained of the hostility to his educational efforts in the rural and agricultural communities of the commonwealth. Therefore, we hypothesized that representatives from the less-developed areas (low commerce, low manufacturing) would be more hostile to the board of education than representatives from the highly developed communities (high commerce, high manufacturing), and this hypothesis proved correct. The extent of either commercial or manufacturing development of a town was an important predictor of the way its representative voted on the bill to abolish the board of education and the normal schools. Whereas 70.2 percent of the representatives from towns with few workers engaged in either commerce or manufacturing voted to abolish the board, only 11.9 percent of those from the highly developed communities opposed it. Even after controlling for the other factors, the economic development of the town was still the second most important predictor of the way in which a legislator voted on this issue.

The recent emphasis on the role of manufacturing interests in supporting the board of education should be qualified in light of this analysis. It was not the extent of manufacturing per se that predicted the vote on the board, but the overall economic development of the legislator's community. The board's strongest support came from areas with large percentages of workers engaged in commerce and in manufacturing. In addition, legislators from areas with a high proportion of workers in commerce but not in manufacturing supported the board to a greater extent than did those who represented communities with a low percentage of workers in commerce but a high percentage in manufacturing (however, after controlling for other factors, the representatives from these two types of towns supported the board in about equal proportions).[51]

Another perspective on the importance of the representative's town is provided by our combined index of the population size and per capita wealth of the community. Considering our results from the multiple regression analysis of town-level educational activities in 1860 (Chapter 5), we did not expect population size per se to be a strong predictor of voting on the board of education issue, once other variables were entered into the equation. The results indicate that representatives from the smaller communities were more likely than those from the larger towns to oppose the board and the normal schools. After controlling for the effects of the other variables, however, we found that fewer representatives from the smaller towns than from the cities of ten thousand or more inhabitants were opposed to the board. In other words, representatives from the small communities were in fact more opposed to the board, but not, it appears, because of the sizes of their towns; rather, small communities were less-developed economically and tended to send more farmers and Democrats to the legislature than did other areas.

The per capita wealth of the representatives' communities did not

The politics of educational reform

have a consistent effect on the voting pattern on this bill. In towns of fewer than 2,500 inhabitants, more representatives from low per capita valuation areas than from high per capita valuation communities tended to oppose the board of education, after we controlled for the effects of the other variables. However, the reverse was true for towns with populations between 2,400 and 9,999 inhabitants. Assessed community wealth was thus not a good predictor of legislative behavior on the issue of state regulation of schooling.

We wanted to include some measures of the religious orientation of the legislator and his constituents, but it was impossible to find data on the religion of the legislators. Instead, we had to settle for information on the different types of churches within their towns. We used the presence or absence of Unitarian churches in the towns as one of our independent variables because the religious debate associated with the board of education pitted Unitarians against orthodox Congregationalists and other traditional Calvinists. We hypothesized that representatives from communities with Unitarian congregations would be more likely to support the educational reforms of Horace Mann, because the board was dominated by Unitarians and because it espoused policies that were allegedly Unitarian.

As expected, representatives from communities with Unitarian churches were more likely than others to vote against the bill to abolish the board of education and the normal schools. However, that difference disappeared almost entirely when we controlled for the effects of the other variables. Although our analysis does not suggest a strong religious determinant of the pattern of voting on the bill, this does not necessarily mean that religion was not an important factor in this controversy, as our measures of religion are so crude. Especially lacking is information on the religion of the representatives. Nonetheless, although the religious question certainly motivated some leaders of the antiboard movement, such as Allen Dodge, our evidence suggests that Horace Mann had successfully defused the religious issue within the legislature. Party affiliation rather than religious affiliation seems to have been the key to the vote.

Finally, we examined the geographic pattern of voting on the bill. The state was subdivided into three regions that reflect socioeconomic differences – central Massachusetts (which in our scheme includes easternmost Essex County), western Massachusetts, and southern Massachusetts. The MCA analysis showed large regional variations. Whereas 61.8 percent of representatives from western Massachusetts opposed the board of education, only 30.4 percent of the legislators from southern Massachusetts voted against it. This general pattern remained the same even after we controlled for the other variables. The geographic location of the legislator became the third best predictor of the vote on the bill. The greatest antagonism to the efforts of the board of education came from western Massachusetts, where educational reforms were not as highly valued and state intervention was most strenuously resisted. Thus the strongest opposition to the board came from Berkshire, Franklin, and Hampden counties.[52] Southern Massachusetts, on the other hand, was an area that strongly supported Mann's efforts. The support for the normal schools was particularly strong in southern Massachusetts – especially in Plymouth County, where one of the three normal schools was located.[53] Central Massachusetts was split in its support of the board of education. Whereas 59.3 percent of the representatives from Middlesex County opposed it, only 26.4 percent of those from Essex County and 9.3 percent of those from Suffolk County favored abolition of the board of education and the normal schools.

Altogether, of the eight independent variables used in this MCA analysis, the strongest predictor of the vote on the bill to abolish the board of education and the normal schools was the party affiliation of the legislator. The degree of commercial and manufacturing development of the representative's town and its geographic location within the state were the two next best predictors. The presence of a Unitarian Church in a town and the number of years a representative had been in the legislature before 1840 were the two weakest predictors. Overall, our eight independent variables are able to account statistically for 37.9 percent of the variation on the vote.

We ran several other MCAs using the basic list of eight independent variables, as well as some additional variables. For example, because Mann had often been accused of trying to secularize the schools, we wanted to know whether there was more hostility to the board among representatives from towns whose schools had a measurable association with religion. To get at this question we ran two new MCAs. In the first one, we added the variable of whether one or more of the school committee members were clergymen. In the second, we added a measure of whether the Bible was used as a school text in 1840. Our assumption was that towns whose schools used Bibles as textbooks or included clergymen on their school boards were more inclined to stress the importance of religion in their schools.[54] We had hoped that coding these additional variables would help us document the much-vaunted religious element in the politics of education in early Massachusetts, and we expected some correlation between the religious tone of local schools and hostility to the board. We did not find such a correlation, however. Looking at either the unadjusted or the adjusted class means, representatives from towns whose schools used Bibles or whose school committees included members of the clergy were less hostile to the board of education than legislators from communities whose schools did not use Bibles or did not have ministers on their school boards. Again, the MCA analysis suggests that Mann and his supporters had surmounted the religious question. The results reinforce our previous finding that hostility to the board of education in the legislature was more associated with political than with religious considerations.[55]

We ran several MCAs using the basic list of eight independent variables and adding various measures of the educational efforts within the representatives' towns. We included variables on the per capita public school expenditures, the average number of days in public school per person under twenty years of age, and the average length of the public school year. Not surprisingly, the results generally indicated that representatives from the towns that spent less money and/or provided fewer educational opportunities for their children were more likely than representatives of the other towns to have voted to abolish the board of education and the normal schools. These measures of educational efforts at the local level were only moderately important as predictors of the vote.[56]

Finally, although party was the best predictor of a legislator's position on this vote, about one-third of the Democrats supported the board (thus saving it), and nearly a fifth of the Whigs abandoned their party and voted for abolition.[57] We therefore ran separate MCA analyses for the Whigs and Democrats to see whether removing party affiliation from the equation would further illumine the factors that led members of either party to deviate from the party position. Despite some minor differences in the relative strengths of the independent variables (e.g., age was a stronger predictor among Democrats than among Whigs; town size and wealth were stronger among Whigs than among Democrats), the segregated analyses confirmed what one would predict from the combined analysis. Whig farmers were more likely to bolt than Whig merchants and manufacturers, and the converse was true for Democrats. Being in a competitive district increased the chances that a legislator would deviate; older legislators, especially Democrats, were more hostile than others to the board. The regional variable behaved as predicted, displaying the same western hostility in both parties, when controlling for other variables. As before, the strongest predictors of voting behavior, aside from party, were the variables that measured the characteristics of the towns' development.

Education and social change in nineteenth-century Massachusetts

It is impossible for us to determine by our statistical measures whether the Whigs and the Democrats who deviated from the party position on this bill did so because they were worried about pleasing their constituents or because they lived in a different setting and hence shared a philosophy different from their colleagues'. Nonetheless, on the basis of our readings of literary materials as well as our effort to control for possible constituent pressure by the inclusion of the variable on the competitiveness of the district, it seems to us that Whigs from agricultural areas, especially those from western Massachusetts, did not subscribe to the general notions of the Whig Party in Massachusetts on the desirability or need of a state board of education. Conversely, Democrats from the larger and more economically developed towns, especially from central and southern Massachusetts, were less likely to share the traditional Democratic fears of excessive state power and unnecessary state expenditures on the issue of the board of education and the normal schools.

Conclusion

Our analysis of the attempt to abolish the board of education and the normal schools in the Massachusetts House in 1840 demonstrates that there were substantive differences between the Whigs and the Democrats on some educational issues. Of course, both the Whigs and the Democrats agreed on the value and the importance of a common school education; there was a consensus among almost all groups in Massachusetts that education should be provided in every community. But there was considerable disagreement on the proper content of education as well as on the role of the state in its development and control.

Most Democrats did not share the Whig enthusiasm for spending state money to create and maintain teacher seminaries – partly because many Democrats did not see the need for a corps of professionally trained teachers and partly because they felt that the task could be adequately handled by the existing private academies. An even more fundamental disagreement between Whigs and Democrats was over the proper role of state government in education. The Whigs argued that positive government intervention was a necessary and useful means of improving the quality of public schools throughout the commonwealth. The Democrats, on the other hand, felt that any increased state interference in local educational matters created the potential, if not the reality, of a centralized state school system that would dictate how children were to be educated. Furthermore, many Democrats felt that the board of education and the normal schools were unnecessary state expenses at a time when the state needed to retrench its expenditures.

Horace Mann and the Whigs never fully appreciated the depth of the fears of the Democrats that the creation of a state agency to do good might eventually result in a serious danger to freedom within the Republic. From Mann's perspective and personal experience, the board of education was not a threat to the liberties of the citizens but a vital and necessary force in educating children to preserve the Republic. He saw the minor cost of the board and the normal schools as a small price to pay for properly training future generations of voters. In short, most of the differences between Whigs and Democrats on the issue of education in Massachusetts were not over the value of public schools but over the best means of improving them and protecting the liberties of the people.

Although there were real differences between Whig and Democratic spokesmen on these issues, the legislators did not always accept the party position on this question. Both the Whig and the Democrat leaders appealed to their followers along party lines, but nearly a fifth of the Whigs and a third of the Democrats disregarded these pleas – even though on other vital issues, such as the reduction in state salaries and the laws involving corporations, they united solidly behind their parties.[58] There are several reasons for the unwillingness of some representatives to vote with the party on the issue of the board of education and the normal schools. First, Horace Mann had been quite successful in convincing many of the potential opponents of the board among the Democrats and orthodox Congregationalists that it was really a nonpartisan and nonsectarian agency dedicated to the promotion of better schools. This task was made much easier by the strong support given the board by such prominent Democrats as Robert Rantoul, Jr., and such eminent Trinitarians as Thomas Robbins. Second, the board of education and the normal schools were successful in developing strong constituent support – especially in the areas where the normal schools were located. Although there was no popular outcry to save the board and the normal schools during these legislative battles, there was sufficient constituent support for them in some areas that local representatives were anxious not to oppose these institutions. Third, although each party took a definite position on the board of education and the normal schools, these issues did not become important statewide campaign issues. Therefore, it was fairly easy for representatives to defect from the party's position on the bill without feeling that they had publicly betrayed the party principles. Thus, although party affiliation was the single best predictor of voting behavior on the bill, it was not so strong that legislators automatically voted along party lines. They often allowed personal and constituent preferences to overcome party preferences on this issue.

Some historians have emphasized the role of religion in this controversy. We do not deny the importance of religion as one factor, but our results do not support the idea that it is an important explanation of the division within the legislature on the bill. Religious opposition motivated some of the leaders in the fight against the board, but we doubt if the pattern of voting on the bill followed religious rather than political lines. Horace Mann and the board of education were successful in defending themselves against the charges of being advocates of Unitarianism in the schools.

Other historians have emphasized the role of manufacturers and other capitalists in creating and maintaining the board of education. Our analysis certainly confirms that representatives who were manufacturers were more likely to support the board than were some other groups. But it is also important to remember that nearly half of the Democratic manufacturers still opposed the board. Also, rather than finding that areas with a high degree of manufacturing were distinctly supportive of the board, we discovered support for it from all economically developed towns in the state – those with a high degree of either commercial or manufacturing development, or both.

Multiple classification analysis has allowed us to compare the importance of party affiliation with the personal and constituent characteristics of the House members and to demonstrate that the influence of party loyalty, though paramount, was substantially modified by the socioeconomic characteristics of the legislators and their towns. A central state board of education not only made more sense to one party than to the other, it also made more sense in some settings than in others.

9

Conclusion: the triumph of a state school system

Although substantial opposition to the board of education illustrates the kind of political, economic, regional, and cultural conflicts that accompanied the creation of a state school system in nineteenth-century Massachusetts, the victory of the board's supporters was symbolic of the major trends in education already emerging by 1840. The episode was also prophetic of the direction public education took in the succeeding decades. In this book we have attempted to present and analyze the most important of those trends. We have emphasized quantitative information that reflects mass behavior, rather than the ideas and viewpoints of educational reformers and other socially prominent people, although we have tried to relate the two types of evidence when it seemed appropriate. The resulting evidence does not support a picture of an evolving, benevolent, democratic school system opposed only by religious dissidents, bumpkins, and aristocrats, a picture that predominated in early times. On the other hand, we disagree at several points with some recent historians who have focused – too narrowly, we believe – on human exploitation in our economic system as the chief generator of public school development. Educational participation as well as reform attitudes were indeed often related to the economic status of an individual, a town, or a region, but education itself is so complex that it cannot be treated as a single variable and then pegged to a single historical development, out of which all other concerns flowed. There are, then, good reasons why there is a literature on capitalism and education, another group of works emphasizing urbanization and education, and still others focusing on the relationship of schooling to immigration, discrimination, religion, and nationalism. All these relationships are important, depending on what questions we ask about education and public policy.

Throughout our research, in compiling early attendance rates, in conducting our community case studies, and in reading early school reports, we found Massachusetts to be a state with a solid, early tradition of decentralized schooling. This tradition formed the basis of the apparent expansion of annual school enrollments in the late eighteenth and early nineteenth centuries, when expanding horizons, republican politics, and changing notions about women increased the demand for common schooling, while the spread of the district system increased the supply. Beginning in the 1830s, Massachusetts communities witnessed the development of a system of state-regulated, relatively expensive, nominally nonsectarian schooling, regarded widely as urban, eastern, Whig, and appropriate to an expansive capitalist economy, a a republican government, and a diverse population. The two key features of this reform of education were the intensification of schooling for Massachusetts children and a long-term trend toward the centralization of control at both state and local levels. The organization and content of the emerging public education system was appropriate for the economic and cultural goals of the predominant groups in the society. Increasing amounts of public schooling were more feasible for middle-class families than for working-class families, more appealing to native-born families than to immigrants, more fair to Protestants than to Catholics, more compatible with Whig political philosophy than with Democratic, and more likely in communities with high commercial or industrial development than in agricultural areas. This does not mean, of course, that there were no advocates of public education among workers, immigrants, Catholics, Democrats, or farmers. Public education served and built upon traditional purposes of schooling – literacy, good citizenship, and character building – and these found few opponents. Resistance to various aspects of public schooling arose sometimes from necessity, as with teenage laborers, sometimes from tradition, as with Democratic localists, and sometimes from cultural alienation, as with Catholics. In all these cases, objection to state intervention could be raised to the level of principle.

Still, the general trend – across communities and across social groups – was toward a greater role for schooling in children's lives and toward ever more similar school experiences, in content and amount, for different children. Those who defended nonintervention, local control, lower expenditures, and a limited role for schooling in society generally lost. Convergence and standardization could proceed just so far, of course. Rural schools did not become exactly like urban schools, nor were children of different groups treated alike within schools. Yet the brunt of nineteenth-century state policy in Massachusetts education greatly strengthened the role of schooling in society and made more similar the amount and type of education that children received.

Our quantitative sources tell us that this was so, and our literary sources tell us that reformers, social elites, and school officials – with considerable popular support – thought it was a desirable and proper policy. Our statistics and our literary sources testify that those who advocated state intervention, increased schooling, and standardized education prevailed, sometimes over persistent opposition, but with confidence, self-congratulation, and widespread support. More and more places became like Lynn, fewer and fewer like Boxford. Our studies do not tell us whether these trends in state educational policy have been effective or desirable, or whether they should be further fostered in the last quarter of the twentieth century. What history can legitimately contribute to policy is perspective on what happend in the past and why. History can remind us that there were costs as well as positive achievements in the development of state school systems, and that the reasons for the particular kinds of state intervention we have detailed here were historically specific. Although they were firmly rooted in social structure and in American mainstream culture, they are neither God-given nor immutable.

Statistical tables

Table A2.1. Total enrollment and average daily attendance, Massachusetts public schools, 1840–80

Year	Number of children 0–19 1	Public school enrollment all ages				Public school average daily attendance			
		Summer Number 2	% 0–19 3	Winter Number 4	% 0–19 5	Summer Number 6	% 0–19 7	Winter Number 8	% 0–19 9
1839–40	325,019	124,354	38.3	149,222	45.9	92,698	28.5	111,844	34.4
1840–1	336,219	131,761	39.2	155,041	46.1	96,892	28.8	116,308	34.6
1841–2	344,650	133,448	38.7	159,056	46.2	96,525	28.0	117,542	34.1
1842–3	345,948	138,169	39.6	161,020	46.1	98,316	28.2	119,989	34.4
1843–4	365,403	147,405	40.3	169,191	46.3	104,553	28.6	122,327	33.5
1844–5	374,604	149,189	39.8	169,977	45.4	106,941	28.5	125,259	33.4
1845–6	383,805	153,459	40.0	174,270	45.4	110,108	28.7	128,084	33.4
1846–7	393,006	160,952	41.0	178,776	45.5	121,439	30.9	139,655	35.5
1847–8	402,207	165,132	41.1	185,000	46.0	123,046	30.6	143,878	35.8
1848–9	411,407	173,659	42.2	191,712	46.6	126,502	30.7	142,967	34.8
1849–50	420,607	176,344	41.9	194,403	46.2	128,815	30.6	149,609	35.6
1850–1	431,676	179,497	41.6	199,429	46.2	132,422	30.7	152,564	35.3
1851–2	442,745	185,752	42.0	199,183	45.0	136,309	30.8	152,645	34.5
1852–3	453,814	187,022	41.2	202,081	44.5	140,482	30.9	155,716	34.3
1853–4	464,883	186,628	40.1	199,447	42.9	141,226	30.4	154,277	33.2
1854–5	475,951	189,997	39.9	202,709	42.6	143,973	30.2	157,657	33.1
1855–6	483,770	198,746	41.1	209,036	43.2	151,621	31.3	162,580	33.6
1856–7	491,589	195,881	39.8	203,031	41.3	150,375	30.6	158,579	32.3
1857–8	499,488	199,792	40.0	218,198	43.7	154,642	31.0	175,526	35.1
1858–9	507,228	204,925	40.4	211,388	41.7	160,108	31.6	166,520	32.8

Year								
1859-60	515,048	207,939	40.3	217,334	42.2	162,785	31.6	174,582	33.9
1860-1	516,277	212,786	41.2	220,010	42.6	166,714	32.3	175,035	33.9
1861-2	517,506	223,218	43.1	227,319	43.9	175,424	33.9	182,360	35.2
1862-3	518,736	225,921	43.6	227,252	43.8	180,062	34.7	182,041	35.1
1863-4	519,966	223,957	43.1	226,400	43.5	177,364	34.1	181,669	34.9
1864-5	521,196	223,297	42.8	229,514	44.0	175,225	33.6	183,462	35.2
1865-6	534,405	230,894	43.2	231,685	43.4	182,912	34.2	187,358	35.1
1866-7	547,614	235,241	43.0	237,364	43.3	189,149	34.5	190,954	34.9
1867-8	560,823	242,760	43.3	243,425	43.2	195,216	34.8	199,228	35.5
1868-9	574,032	240,846	42.0	247,381	43.1	192,029	33.5	200,962	35.0
1869-70	587,240	242,422	41.3	247,080	42.1	195,958	33.4	203,468	34.6
1870-1	600,171							
1871-2	613,102							
1872-3	626,033							
1873-4	638,964							
1874-5	651,894							
1875-6	657,500							
1876-7	663,106							
1877-8	668,712							
1878-9	674,318							
1879-80	679,924							

Notes: Summer and winter combined after 1870. See Table A2.2, columns 13-18.

See Appendixes B and C for discussion of the calculation of values in Tables A2.1 through A2.5.

Table A2.2. Length of Massachusetts public school sessions and
estimated annual attendance and enrollment, 1840-80

| | Length of public school | | State aver. length | Attendance |
Year	Number of public schools	Aggregate days school was held	State aver. length	Aver daily attendance (est.)
	10	11	12	13
1839-40	3,072	462,180	150	102,271
1840-1	3,103	489,143	158	106,600
1841-2	3,198	511,128	160	107,036
1842-3	3,173	503,052	159	109,153
1843-4	3,336	543,747	163	113,440
1844-5	3,382	562,023	166	116,100
1845-6	3,475	577,422	166	119,096
1846-7	3,538	594,245	168	130,547
1847-8	3,653	612,365	167	133,462
1848-9	3,749	630,965	168	134,735
1849-50	3,878	626,857	162	139,212
1850-1	3,987	653,168	164	142,493
1851-2	4,056	673,450	166	144,477
1852-3	4,113	682,932	166	148,099
1853-4	4,163	697,282	167	147,752
1854-5	4,215	706,574	168	150,815
1855-6	4,300	723,781	168	157,101
1856-7	4,360	736,503	169	154,477
1857-8	4,421	748,696	169	165,084
1858-9	4,444	649,603	172	163,314
1859-60	4,497	772,933	172	168,683
1860-1	4,561	784,932	172	170,874
1861-2	4,605	802,437	174	178,892
1862-3	4,626	797,271	172	181,052
1863-4	4,675	808,129	173	179,516
1864-5	4,749	814,789	172	179,344
1865-6	4,759	817,690	172	185,135
1866-7	4,848	849,147	175	190,052
1867-8	4,937	871,843	177	197,222
1868-9	4,959	870,001	179	196,495
1869-70	4,963	892,801	180	199,713
1870-1	5,076	920,346	181	201,750
1871-2	5,193	955,891	184	205,252
1872-3	5,305	982,860	185	202,882
1873-4	5,425	1,012,509	187	210,248
1874-5	5,551	1,067,511	192	216,861
1875-6	5,542	1,067,166	193	218,903
1876-7	5,556	1,048,020	189	222,704
1877-8	5,730	1,100,990	192	228,447
1878-9	5,558	1,060,249	191	234,249
1379-80	5,570	1,068,654	192	233,127

Aggregate days of public sch. attended (est.) 14	Aver. days public sch. per ch. 0-19 15	% of ch. 0-19 attend-ing daily 16	Enrollment	
			Total annual enrollment (est.) 17	% of ch. 0-19 en-rolled (est.) 18
15,340,650	47.2	31.5	180,310	55.5
16,842,800	50.1	31.7	187,981	55.9
17,125,760	49.7	31.1	192,418	55.8
17,355,327	49.7	31.3	195,562	56.0
18,490,720	50.6	31.0	206,042	56.4
19,272,600	51.4	31.0	207,274	55.3
19,769,936	51.5	31.0	212,635	55.4
21,931,896	55.8	33.2	219,014	55.7
22,288,154	55.4	33.2	226,283	56.3
22,635,480	55.0	32.7	235,127	57.2
22,552,344	53.6	33.1	238,488	56.7
23,368,852	54.1	33.0	244,303	56.6
23,983,182	54.2	32.6	223,926	50.6
24,584,434	54.2	32.6	248,837	54.8
24,674,584	53.1	31.8	246,104	52.9
25,336,920	53.2	31.7	250,208	52.6
26,392,884	54.6	32.5	258,722	53.5
26,106,613	53.1	31.4	252,001	51.3
27,899,196	55.9	33.1	268,146	53.7
28,090,008	55.4	32.2	262,619	51.8
29,013,476	56.3	32.8	269,319	52.3
29,390,328	56.9	33.1	273,206	52.9
31,127,208	60.1	34.6	283,123	54.7
31,140,858	60.0	34.9	283,732	54.7
31,056,354	59.7	34.5	282,389	54.3
30,847,082	59.2	34.4	285,338	54.7
31,843,220	59.6	34.6	289,409	54.2
33,259,100	60.7	34.7	296,174	54.1
34,908,294	62.2	35.2	304,115	54.2
35,172,605	61.3	34.2	307,592	53.6
35,948,340	61.2	34.0	307,685	52.4
36,516,750	60.8	33.6	273,661	45.6
37,766,368	61.6	33.5	276,602	45.1
37,533,170	59.9	32.4	283,872	45.3
39,316,376	61.5	32.9	297,025	46.5
41,637,312	63.9	33.3	302,118	46.3
42,248,279	64.3	33.3	305,776	46.5
42,091,055	63.5	33.6	307,832	46.4
43,861,824	65.6	34.2	310,181	46.4
44,741,559	66.4	34.7	311,528	46.2
44,760,384	65.8	34.3	306,777	45.1

Table A2.3. Attendance at Massachusetts incorporated academies, 1840–80

Year	Number of acad- emies 19	Average enroll- ment 20	Aver. daily attend- ance (est.) 21	Total annual enroll- ment (est.) 22	Length in days, aver. 23	Total days attended (est.) 24
1839–40	78	3,701	3,331	4,441	213	709,503
1840–1	80	3,825	3,443	4,590	213	733,359
1841–2	75	3,805	3,425	4,566	219	749,966
1842–3	71	3,379	3,041	4,055	211	641,651
1843–4	72	3,760	3,384	4,512	216	730,944
1844–5	66	3,939	3,545	4,727	222	786,990
1845–6	67	3,726	3,353	4,471	228	764,484
1846–7	67	4,220	3,798	5,064	242	919,116
1847–8	67	3,862	3,476	4,634	232	806,432
1848–9	64	3,864	3,478	4,637	207	719,946
1849–50	67	3,717	3,345	4,460	220	735,900
1850–1	69	4,154	3,739	4,985	220	822,580
1851–2	71	4,220	3,798	5,064	220	835,560
1852–3	64	4,062	3,656	4,874	220	804,320
1853–4	66	4,142	3,728	4,970	220	820,160
1854–5	71	4,716	4,244	5,659	220	933,680
1855–6	70	4,708	4,237	5,650	220	932,140
1856–7	69	4,346	3,911	5,215	220	860,420
1857–8	70	4,338	3,904	5,206	220	858,880
1858–9	63	3,932	3,539	4,718	220	778,580

1859–60	65	3,561	3,205	4,273	220	705,100
1860–1	63	3,925	3,533	4,710	220	777,260
1861–2	57	5,119	4,607	6,143	220	1,013,540
1862–3	56	5,822	5,240	6,986	220	1,152,800
1863–4	59	6,131	5,518	7,357	220	1,348,820
1864–5	59	6,590	5,931	7,908	220	1,449,800
1865–6	52	7,364	6,628	8,837	220	1,620,080
1866–7	55	7,696	6,926	9,235	220	1,693,120
1867–8	48	6,572	5,915	7,886	220	1,445,840
1868–9	45+	7,048	6,343	8,458	220	1,550,560
1869–70	47	3,957	5,361	7,148	220	1,310,540
1870–1	46	6,345	5,711	7,614	220	1,395,900
1871–2	46+	8,065	7,259	9,678	220	1,774,300
1872–3	46+	7,573	6,816	9,088	220	1,666,060
1873–4	43+	8,863	7,977	10,636	220	1,949,860
1874–5	44+	7,594	6,835	9,113	220	1,670,680
1875–6	46+	10,176	9,158	12,211	220	2,238,720
1876–7	40+	8,739	7,865	10,487	220	1,922,580
1877–8	41+	8,454	7,609	10,145	220	1,859,880
1878–9	39+	8,662	7,796	10,344	220	1,905,640
1879–80	73+	10,398	9,358	12,478	220	2,287,560

Table A2.4. Attendance at Massachusetts unincorporated academies, private schools, and schools kept to prolong the common schools, 1840-80

Year	Number of schools 25	Average enroll- ment 26	Aver. daily attend- ance (est.) 27	Total annual enroll- ment (est.) 28	Length in days, aver. 29	Total days attended (est.) 30
1839–40	1,308	28,635	25,772	34,362	140	3,608,080
1840–1	1,388	31,794	28,615	38,153	135	3,863,025
1841–2	1,281	28,422	25,580	34,106	144	3,683,520
1842–3	1,268	26,611	23,950	31,933	123	2,945,850
1843–4	1,238	25,850	23,265	31,020	141	3,280,365
1844–5	1,167	26,762	24,086	32,142	137	3,299,782
1845–6	1,091	24,318	21,886	29,182	128	2,801,408
1846–7	1,150	26,785	24,107	32,142	137	3,302,659
1847–8	1,096	27,216	24,494	32,659	122	2,988,268
1848–9	1,047	27,583	24,805	33,100	134	3,326,550
1849–50	845	19,534	17,581	23,441	164	3,203,576
1850–1	785	16,658	14,992	19,990	164	2,458,688
1851–2	749	16,131	14,518	19,358	164	2,380,952
1852–3	763	18,362	16,526	22,034	164	2,710,264
1853–4	674	17,322	15,590	20,786	164	2,556,760
1854–5	646	17,571	15,814	21,085	164	2,593,496
1855–6	701	18,909	17,018	22,691	164	2,790,952
1856–7	674	18,935	17,642	22,722	164	2,794,888
1857–8	672	18,044	16,290	21,653	164	2,663,360
1858–9	691	18,903	17,013	22,684	164	2,790,132

1859–60	640	15,933	14,340	19,120	164	2,351,760
1860–1	638	16,401	14,761	19,681	164	2,420,804
1861–2	611	16,175	14,558	19,410	164	2,387,512
1862–3	614	15,573	14,016	18,688	164	2,298,624
1863–4	611	16,124	14,512	19,349	164	2,379,968
1864–5	682	17,934	16,141	21,521	164	2,647,124
1865–6	596	16,387	14,748	19,664	164	2,418,672
1866–7	553	14,417	12,975	17,300	164	2,127,900
1867–8	550	13,957	12,561	16,748	164	2,060,004
1868–9	481	13,888	12,049	16,066	164	1,976,036
1869–70	466	13,916	12,524	16,699	164	2,053,936
1870–1	428	12,443	11,199	14,932	164	1,836,636
1871–2	463	13,687	12,318	16,424	164	2,020,152
1872–3	402	14,428	12,985	17,314	164	2,129,540
1873–4	402	13,144	11,830	15,773	164	1,940,120
1874–5	369	16,650	14,985	19,980	164	2,457,540
1875–6	341	14,513	13,062	17,416	164	2,142,168
1876–7	385	15,228	13,705	18,274	164	2,247,620
1877–8	399	15,540	13,986	18,648	164	2,293,704
1878–9	378	15,168	13,651	18,202	164	2,238,764
1879–80	350	—	—	15,891	164	—

Table A2.5. Annual enrollment and attendance, all Massachusetts schools, 1840–80

Year	Annual enrollment (est.) 31	% of children 0–19 enrolled 32	Enrollment, less dual attenders (est.) 33	% of ch. 0–19 enrolled, controlled for col. 33 34	Total days attended (est.) 35	Aver. days of school attended per ch. 0–19 36	% of ch. 0–19 attending school daily 37
1839–40	219,113	67.4	207,087	63.7	19,682,089	60.6	37.1
1840–1	230,724	68.6	217,370	64.7	21,455,791	63.8	37.7
1841–2	231,090	67.1	219,152	63.6	21,450,931	62.2	36.4
1842–3	231,550	66.4	220,373	63.2	20,942,828	60.0	36.1
1843–4	241,574	66.1	230,718	63.1	22,502,029	61.6	36.1
1844–5	244,143	65.2	232,903	62.2	23,359,372	62.4	36.1
1845–6	246,288	64.2	236,075	61.5	23,991,711	62.5	35.6
1846–7	256,220	65.2	244,970	62.3	26,153,671	66.5	38.2
1847–8	263,576	65.5	252,145	62.7	26,082,854	65.2	38.0
1848–9	272,864	66.3	261,279	63.5	26,681,976	65.2	37.5
1849–50	266,389	63.3	264,463	62.9	26,491,820	63.0	38.1
1850–1	269,278	62.4	269,278	62.4	26,650,120	61.7	37.3
1851–2	248,348	56.1	248,348	56.1	27,199,694	61.4	36.8
1852–3	275,745	60.8	275,745	60.8	28,099,018	61.9	37.1
1853–4	271,860	58.5	271,860	58.5	28,051,504	60.3	35.9
1854–5	276,952	58.2	276,952	58.2	28,864,096	60.6	35.9
1855–6	287,063	59.3	287,063	59.3	30,115,979	62.2	36.9
1856–7	279,938	56.9	279,938	56.9	29,761,921	60.5	35.7
1857–8	295,005	59.1	295,005	59.1	31,421,436	62.9	37.1
1858–9	290,021	57.2	290,021	57.2	31,658,720	62.4	36.2

Year						
1859–60	292,712	56.8	292,712	56.8	32,070,336	62.3	36.2
1860–1	293,710	56.9	293,710	56.9	32,588,392	63.1	36.6
1861–2	308,676	59.7	308,676	59.7	34,528,260	66.7	38.3
1862–3	309,406	59.7	309,406	59.7	36,592,282	70.5	38.6
1863–4	309,095	59.5	309,095	59.5	34,785,142	67.2	38.4
1864–5	314,767	60.4	314,767	60.4	34,944,006	67.1	38.6
1865–6	317,910	59.5	317,910	59.5	35,881,972	67.1	38.6
1866–7	322,709	58.9	322,709	58.9	37,080,120	67.7	38.3
1867–8	328,749	58.6	328,749	58.6	38,414,138	68.5	38.5
1868–9	332,116	57.9	332,116	57.9	38,699,201	67.4	37.4
1869–70	331,532	56.5	331,532	56.5	39,312,816	67.0	37.0
1870–1	296,207	49.4	296,207	49.4	39,749,286	66.2	36.4
1871–2	302,704	49.4	302,704	49.4	41,560,820	67.8	36.7
1872–3	309,774	49.5	309,774	49.5	41,328,770	66.0	35.6
1873–4	323,434	50.6	323,434	50.6	43,206,356	67.6	36.0
1874–5	331,211	50.8	331,211	50.8	45,765,532	70.2	36.6
1875–6	335,403	51.0	335,403	51.0	46,629,167	70.9	36.7
1876–7	336,593	50.8	336,593	50.8	46,261,255	69.7	36.5
1877–8	338,974	50.7	338,974	50.7	48,015,408	71.8	37.4
1878–9	340,124	50.4	340,124	50.4	48,885,963	71.2	37.9
1879–80	335,146	49.3	335,146	49.3	--	--	--

Table A3.1. Massachusetts school attendance of young children, 1840–1900

	Number of children in public school		% of children in public school	
Year	Under 4	Under 5	Under 4	Under 5
1839–40	7,835		10.5	
1840–1	7,823		10.2	
1841–2	7,224		9.2	
1842–3	7,337		9.2	
1843–4	7,083		8.7	
1844–5	6,997		8.4	
1845–6	6,018		7.1	
1846–7	4,782		5.5	
1847–8	3,656		4.2	
1848–9	3,326		3.7	
1849–50		17,782		15.6
1850–1		17,757		15.1
1851–2		18,260		15.0
1852–3		17,514		14.0
1853–4		16,093		12.5
1854–5		15,601		11.7
1855–6		14,969		11.0
1856–7		13,608		9.7
1857–8		12,370		8.6
1858–9		10,903		7.4
1859–60		10,428		6.9
1860–1		10,104		6.8
1861–2		8,764		6.1
1862–3		7,055		5.0
1863–4		5,730		4.2
1864–5		5,201		3.9
1865–6		4,783		3.5
1866–7		3,899		2.7
1867–8		3,450		2.3
1868–9		3,169		2.1
1869–70		2,894		1.9
1870–1		2,714		1.7
1871–2		2,825		1.7
1872–3		2,516		1.5
1873–4		2,552		1.5
1874–5		2,383		1.4
1875–6		2,084		1.2
1876–7		2,058		1.2
1877–8		1,945		1.1
1878–9		1,934		1.1
1879–80		1,833		1.0
1880–1		1,685		.9
1881–2		1,646		.9
1882–3		1,616		.9
1883–4		1,517		.8

Table A3.1 (cont.)

Year	Number of children in public school Under 4	Under 5	% of children in public school Under 4	Under 5
1884-5		1,465		.8
1885-6		1,433		.8
1886-7		1,375		.7
1887-8		1,178		.6
1888-9		1,130		.6
1889-90		2,578		1.3
1890-1		3,129		1.5
1891-2		2,912		1.3
1892-3		3,183		1.4
1893-4		3,742		1.6
1894-5		4,469		1.9
1895-6		5,630		2.3
1896-7		6,868		2.7
1897-8		7,702		2.9
1898-9		8,954		3.3
1899-1900		9,895		3.5

Source: Calculated from U.S. censuses of 1840, 1850, 1860, 1870,
 1880, 1890, and 1900 and Massachusetts censuses of 1855, 1865,
 1875, 1885, and 1895; and from Massachusetts Board of Education,
 Annual Reports for 1839-40 through 1899-1900.

Table A3.2. Percentage, by town size, of young children enrolled
in Massachusetts public schools, 1840, 1860, and 1875

Town size	1840 (ages 0-3) Mean	Standard deviation	1860 (ages 0-4) Mean	Standard deviation	1875 (ages 0-4) Mean	Standard deviation
0-1,249	17.2	15.1	12.1	5.6	6.2	4.1
1,250-2,499	15.0	11.8	8.9	4.6	3.6	2.6
2,500-4,999	11.9	11.5	7.1	4.0	2.4	1.8
5,000-9,999	5.5	6.1	4.6	2.7	1.0	1.1
10,000 & up	5.9	7.9	5.9	7.1	.5	.6
Boston	0	--	6.9	0	0	--
All towns	14.7	13.1	8.9	5.4	3.8	3.5

Source: Calculated from U.S. censuses of 1840 and 1860 and
 Massachusetts census of 1875; and from Massachusetts Board of
 Education, Annual Reports for 1840, 1860, and 1875.

Table A4.1. Average length (in days) of Massachusetts public school sessions, 1840-80

	5 rural communities	3 urban communities	Essex County	Massachusetts
1839-40	151	269	171	150
1844-5	146	260	197	166
1849-50	156	247	187	162
1854-5	153	221	206	168
1859-60	147	238	202	172
1864-5	143	234	198	172
1869-70	175	214	191	180
1874-5	184	225	208	192
1879-80	190	224	208	192

Source: Massachusetts Board of Education, Annual Reports for 1839-40 through 1879-80.

Table A4.2. Percentage of persons under 20 years of age enrolled in Massachusetts schools, 1840-80

	5 rural communities	3 urban communities	Essex County	Massachusetts
1839-40	74.8	56.1	58.5	63.7
1844-5	72.7	60.5	62.3	62.2
1849-50	74.8	52.9	60.2	62.9
1854-5	61.3	49.1	55.6	58.2
1859-60	65.2	50.9	56.2	56.8
1864-5	71.3	53.0	57.7	60.4
1869-70	70.4	53.3	56.2	56.5
1874-5	52.8	42.5	47.2	50.8
1879-80	49.8	47.1	49.7	49.3

Source: Calculated from Massachusetts Board of Education, Annual Reports for 1839-40 through 1879-80. For details on our estimation procedures, see Appendixes B and C.

250

Table A4.3. Annual number of days in Massachusetts schools per person under 20 years of age, 1840-80

	5 rural communities	3 urban communities	Essex County	Massachusetts
1839-40	61.7	92.8	63.7	60.6
1844-5	62.0	95.0	72.0	62.4
1849-50	73.0	83.9	70.6	63.0
1854-5	56.1	73.2	71.2	60.6
1859-60	62.3	77.7	70.3	62.3
1864-5	64.5	76.4	73.2	66.4
1869-70	70.1	70.5	68.8	65.7
1874-5	64.7	67.8	70.0	68.7
1879-80	60.1	74.8	75.1	72.2[a]

[a] 1878-9.

Source: Calculated from Massachusetts Board of Education, Annual Reports for 1839-40 through 1879-80. For details on our estimation procedures, see Appendixes B and C.

Table A4.4. Percentage of children ages birth to 19 attending school in eight Essex County towns, 1860

Age	Rural Male N	%	Rural Female N	%	Urban Male N	%	Urban Female N	%	Total Male N	%	Total Female N	%
0	45	0	49	0	129	0	143	0	174	0	192	0
1	48	0	49	0	113	0	113	0	161	0	162	0
2	56	0	49	0	142	0	138	0	198	0	187	0
3	54	9.3	59	3.4	119	.8	105	0	173	3.5	164	1.2
4	48	25.0	51	23.5	157	7.6	106	14.2	205	11.7	157	17.2
5	50	72.0	56	60.7	127	64.6	110	70.0	177	66.7	166	66.9
6	57	86.0	53	92.5	97	83.5	110	84.5	154	84.4	163	87.1
7	49	87.8	44	100.0	92	93.5	106	95.3	141	91.5	150	96.7
8	52	92.3	54	94.4	107	94.4	104	96.2	159	93.7	158	95.6
9	53	96.2	43	95.3	73	91.8	100	94.0	126	93.7	143	94.4
10	40	97.5	40	100.0	84	95.2	106	89.6	124	96.0	146	92.5
11	42	95.2	45	97.8	65	93.8	79	93.7	112	94.4	124	95.2
12	42	90.5	52	92.3	90	87.8	101	90.1	132	88.6	153	90.8
13	54	92.6	46	84.8	62	79.0	83	78.3	116	85.3	129	80.6
14	62	80.6	63	82.5	79	59.5	93	75.3	141	68.8	156	78.2
15	57	71.9	50	80.0	78	38.5	92	48.9	135	52.6	142	59.9
16	44	52.3	43	67.4	84	22.6	93	14.0	128	32.8	136	30.9
17	54	42.6	41	34.1	85	8.2	84	6.0	139	21.6	125	15.2
18	54	29.6	41	14.6	83	3.6	123	2.4	137	13.9	164	5.5
19	55	12.7	52	11.5	83	2.4	107	.9	138	6.5	159	4.4

N = total children in age group
% = percentage of this total who were in school

Table **A4.5.** Percentage of children ages birth to 19 attending school in eight Essex County towns, 1880

Age	Rural Male N	%	Rural Female N	%	Urban Male N	%	Urban Female N	%	Total Male N	%	Total Female N	%
0	35	0	34	0	106	0	92	0	141	0	126	0
1	33	0	33	0	65	0	88	0	98	0	121	0
2	39	0	38	0	110	0	97	0	149	0	135	0
3	33	3.0	34	0	101	3.0	95	0	134	3.0	129	0
4	28	10.7	40	20.0	115	2.6	102	2.9	143	4.2	142	7.7
5	32	43.8	39	71.1	90	23.3	96	34.4	122	28.7	135	45.2
6	36	86.1	35	71.4	101	58.4	98	76.5	137	65.7	133	75.2
7	45	75.0	35	88.6	97	76.3	107	82.2	142	76.1	142	83.8
8	33	78.8	38	84.2	84	83.3	89	80.9	117	82.1	127	81.9
9	31	90.3	30	93.3	73	89.0	96	88.5	104	89.4	126	89.7
10	44	90.9	35	94.3	94	89.4	74	91.9	138	89.9	109	92.7
11	35	94.3	24	91.7	87	93.1	82	82.9	122	93.4	106	84.9
12	35	94.3	32	96.9	100	87.0	97	84.5	135	88.9	129	87.6
13	37	100.0	25	100.0	89	80.9	80	78.8	126	86.5	105	83.8
14	41	78.0	33	81.8	97	61.9	95	53.7	138	66.7	128	60.9
15	27	77.8	25	80.0	93	40.9	98	35.7	120	49.2	123	44.7
16	32	43.8	27	59.3	94	21.3	107	26.2	126	27.0	134	32.8
17	30	23.3	32	58.1	89	11.3	76	18.4	119	14.3	118	28.0
18	34	11.8	33	18.2	91	7.7	115	11.3	125	8.8	148	12.8
19	47	6.4	36	13.9	103	4.9	107	6.5	150	5.3	143	8.4

Table A4.6. Comparison of the percentages of children attending school in eight Essex County towns, 1860, in the various samples

Age	Original sample N	Original sample %	MCA sample N	MCA sample %	Non-MCA sample N	Non-MCA sample %
Males						
4	205	11.7	188	12.2	17	5.9
5	177	66.7	159	66.0	18	72.2
6	154	84.4	140	85.7	14	71.4
7	141	91.5	126	91.3	15	93.3
8	159	93.7	142	95.8	17	76.5
13	116	85.3	98	88.8	18	66.7
14	141	68.8	116	69.0	25	68.0
15	135	52.6	104	52.9	31	51.6
16	128	32.8	96	34.3	32	28.1
17	139	21.6	113	23.9	26	11.5
18	137	13.9	83	14.5	54	13.0
19	138	6.5	89	7.9	49	4.1
Females						
4	157	17.2	139	15.8	18	27.8
5	166	66.9	153	66.7	13	69.2
6	163	87.1	150	89.3	13	61.5
7	150	96.7	136	96.3	14	100.0
8	158	95.6	140	95.0	18	100.0
13	129	80.6	110	85.4	19	52.6
14	156	78.2	128	82.0	28	60.7
15	142	59.9	113	68.2	29	27.6
16	136	30.9	100	39.0	36	8.3
17	125	15.2	88	17.1	37	10.8
18	164	5.5	93	8.6	71	1.4
19	159	4.4	82	6.1	77	2.6

Table A4.7. Comparison of the percentages of children attending school in eight Essex County towns, 1880, in the various samples

	Original sample		MCA sample		Non-MCA sample	
Age	N	%	N	%	N	%
Males						
4	143	4.2	126	4.8	17	0
5	122	28.7	113	29.2	9	22.2
6	137	65.7	126	65.9	11	63.6
7	142	76.1	135	74.8	7	100.0
8	117	82.1	106	83.0	11	72.7
13	126	86.5	106	89.6	20	70.0
14	138	66.7	121	67.8	17	58.8
15	120	49.2	106	51.9	14	28.6
16	126	27.0	108	27.8	18	22.2
17	119	14.3	99	16.1	20	5.0
18	125	8.8	99	11.1	26	0
19	150	5.3	111	7.2	39	0
Females						
4	142	7.7	131	6.9	11	18.2
5	135	45.2	121	47.1	14	28.6
6	133	75.2	120	72.5	13	100.0
7	142	83.8	131	83.2	11	90.9
8	127	81.9	112	83.9	15	66.7
13	105	83.8	92	84.3	12	83.3
14	128	60.9	115	63.5	13	38.5
15	123	44.7	106	48.1	17	23.5
16	134	32.8	115	35.7	19	15.8
17	118	28.0	85	31.8	33	18.2
18	148	12.8	119	16.0	29	0
19	143	8.4	98	11.2	45	2.2

Table A4.8.   School and remunerative work patterns of females ages
13-19 in eight Essex County towns, 1860 and 1880 (percentage of
each age group)

Age	N	School, no job	No school, no job	School & job	Job, no school
1860					
13	110	83.6	13.6	1.8	.9
14	128	78.9	16.4	3.1	1.6
15	113	66.4	15.9	1.8	15.9
16	100	35.0	34.0	4.0	27.0
17	88	14.8	46.6	2.3	36.4
18	93	8.6	41.9	0	49.5
19	82	3.7	43.9	2.4	50.0
13-19	714	45.8	28.6	2.2	23.4
1880					
13	92	80.4	6.5	4.3	8.7
14	115	60.0	13.9	3.5	22.6
15	106	45.3	18.9	2.8	33.0
16	115	34.8	24.3	.9	40.0
17	85	31.8	21.2	0	47.1
18	119	16.0	34.5	0	49.6
19	98	10.2	31.6	1.0	57.1
13-19	730	39.3	21.9	1.8	37.0

Table A4.9. School and remunerative work patterns of males ages 13-19 in eight Essex County towns, 1860 and 1880 (percentage of each age group)

Age	N	School, no job	No school, no job	School & job	Job, no school
1860					
13	98	88.8	11.2	0	0
14	116	65.5	25.0	3.4	6.0
15	104	46.2	23.1	6.7	24.0
16	96	25.0	16.7	9.4	49.0
17	113	9.7	10.6	14.2	65.5
18	83	6.0	20.5	8.4	65.0
19	89	3.4	12.4	4.5	79.8
13-19	699	36.3	17.2	6.7	39.8
1880					
13	106	81.1	5.7	8.5	4.7
14	121	58.7	5.8	9.1	26.4
15	106	43.4	4.7	8.5	43.4
16	108	25.9	9.3	1.9	63.0
17	99	13.1	13.1	3.0	70.7
18	99	7.1	5.1	4.0	83.8
19	111	6.3	10.8	.9	82.0
13-19	750	34.4	7.7	5.2	52.7

Table A5.1. The urbanization of Massachusetts, 1800-1900

Year	Total population	% in towns 2,500 and up	% in towns 10,000 and up
1800	422,845	32.0	5.9
1810	472,040	37.4	9.8
1820	523,287	38.8	10.7
1830	610,408	44.5	12.3
1840	737,699	55.6	22.2
1850	994,514	69.9	32.5
1860	1,231,066	77.7	39.0
1870	1,457,351	81.2	49.3
1880	1,783,085	84.9	59.2
1890	2,238,943	89.5	65.9
1900	2,805,346	91.5	73.1

Source: Calculated from the U.S. censuses of 1800-1900.

Table A5.2. Number of Massachusetts towns and aggregate population in the subgroups, 1840, 1860, and 1875

Town size	1840		1860		1875	
	N	Population	N	Population	N	Population
0-1,249	103	90,648	95	79,079	116	92,272
1,250-2,499	128	221,931	105	184,947	96	176,984
2,500-4,999	43	143,088	70	232,116	75	270,941
5,000-9,999	14	97,495	30	202,507	29	201,719
10,000 & up	5	70,434	15	301,619	24	565,905
Boston	1	93,383	1	177,388	1	341,919
All towns	294	716,979	316	1,177,656	341	1,649,741

Source: Calculated from U.S. censuses of 1840 and 1860 and Massachusetts census of 1875.

Table A5.3. Percentage, by town size, of children ages birth to 19 enrolled in Massachusetts public schools, 1840, 1860, and 1875

Town size	1840		1860		1875	
	Mean[a]	Standard deviation	Mean[a]	Standard deviation	Mean[a]	Standard deviation
0-1,249	62.4	16.9	57.7	10.7	54.7	8.6
1,250-2,499	58.6	13.0	52.5	9.0	52.6	7.6
2,500-4,999	52.0	7.3	49.0	6.9	49.7	6.5
5,000-9,999	42.9	10.7	45.0	5.2	46.7	5.2
10,000 & up	36.8	7.7	45.8	6.5	45.3	7.5
Boston	32.4	--	38.8	--	42.5	--
All towns	57.8	14.9	52.2	9.7	51.6	8.1

[a]Average of the town rates.

Source: Calculated from U.S. censuses of 1840 and 1860 and Massachusetts census of 1875; and from Massachusetts Board of Education, Annual Reports for 1840, 1860, and 1875.

Table A5.4. Percentage, by town size, of children ages birth to 19 attending Massachusetts public schools (average daily attendance), 1840, 1860, and 1875

Town size	1840		1860		1875	
	Mean[a]	Standard deviation	Mean[a]	Standard deviation	Mean[a]	Standard deviation
0-1,249	37.5	11.0	38.4	7.9	38.0	6.2
1,250-2,499	35.8	8.7	35.9	6.7	37.6	6.1
2,500-4,999	30.9	5.1	33.6	5.2	36.5	5.7
5,000-9,999	26.7	6.3	31.7	4.8	35.5	4.2
10,000 & up	26.6	6.2	30.9	3.6	31.3	6.7
Boston	24.3	--	31.5	--	31.9	--
All towns	35.0	9.6	35.5	7.0	36.9	6.2

[a]Average of the town averages.

Source: Calculated from U.S. censuses of 1840 and 1860 and Massachusetts census of 1875; and from Massachusetts Board of Education, Annual Reports for 1840, 1860, and 1875.

Table A5.5. Percentage, by town size, of young children enrolled in Massachusetts public schools, 1840, 1860, and 1875

Town size	1840 (ages 0-3)		1860 (ages 0-4)		1875 (ages 0-4)	
	Mean[a]	Standard deviation	Mean[a]	Standard deviation	Mean[a]	Standard deviation
0-1,249	17.2	15.1	12.1	5.6	6.2	4.1
1,250-2,499	15.0	11.8	8.9	4.6	3.6	2.6
2,500-4,999	11.9	11.5	7.1	4.0	2.4	1.8
5,000-9,999	5.5	6.1	4.6	2.7	1.0	1.1
10,000 & up	5.9	7.9	5.9	7.1	.5	.6
Boston	0	--	6.9	--	0	--
All towns	14.7	13.1	8.9	5.4	3.8	3.5

[a]Average of the town rates.

Source: Calculated from U.S. censuses of 1840 and 1860 and Massachusetts census of 1875; and from Massachusetts Board of Education, Annual Reports for 1840, 1860, and 1875.

Table A5.6. Percentage, by town size, of older children enrolled in Massachusetts public schools, 1840, 1860, and 1875

Town size	1840 (ages 16-19)		1860 (ages 15-19)		1875 (ages 15-19)	
	Mean[a]	Standard deviation	Mean[a]	Standard deviation	Mean[a]	Standard deviation
0-1,249	33.8	23.3	37.7	17.1	31.4	15.6
1,250-2,499	31.4	33.7	31.2	15.6	25.2	12.8
2,500-4,999	17.7	15.9	21.7	11.5	18.8	8.1
5,000-9,999	10.9	11.7	15.7	6.6	13.6	6.3
10,000 & up	5.5	4.2	14.2	9.7	14.2	5.9
Boston	.4	--	7.7	--	12.7	--
All towns	28.7	28.0	28.7	16.5	24.1	13.8

[a]Average of the town rates.

Source: Calculated from U.S. censuses of 1840 and 1860 and Massachusetts census of 1875; and from Massachusetts Board of Education, Annual Reports for 1840, 1860, and 1875.

Table A5.7. Percentage, by town size, of children ages birth to
19 enrolled in Massachusetts public and private schools, 1840,
1860, and 1875

Town size	1840 Mean[a]	1840 Standard deviation	1860 Mean[a]	1860 Standard deviation	1875 Mean[a]	1875 Standard deviation
0-1,249	71.2	21.4	64.0	18.0	56.7	10.7
1,250-2,499	71.2	17.8	60.0	12.5	57.4	18.4
2,500-4,999	65.4	11.2	53.2	8.1	53.2	7.9
5,000-9,999	55.2	11.4	48.7	8.1	49.1	6.7
10,000 & up	62.7	33.2	50.0	5.9	49.7	4.6
Boston	43.5	--	42.2	--	46.6	--
All towns	69.4	19.0	58.1	14.2	55.0	12.7

[a]Average of the town rates.

Source: Calculated from U.S. censuses of 1840 and 1860 and
Massachusetts census of 1875; and from Massachusetts Board of
Education, Annual Reports for 1840, 1860, and 1875.

Table A5.8. Average length (in days) of Massachusetts public
school sessions, by town size, 1840, 1860, and 1875

Town size	1840 Mean[a]	1840 Standard deviation	1860 Mean[a]	1860 Standard deviation	1875 Mean[a]	1875 Standard deviation
0-1,249	136.0	33.7	137.4	35.2	154.3	22.5
1,250-2,499	138.1	40.0	146.7	28.4	176.3	22.9
2,500-4,999	160.0	45.5	172.2	33.7	187.7	19.9
5,000-9,999	197.0	51.1	200.0	36.1	204.7	18.7
10,000 & up	246.2	21.5	230.7	36.8	214.8	9.5
Boston	264.0	--	228.6	--	201.9	--
All towns	145.8	44.3	158.8	41.5	176.5	28.5

[a]Average of the town averages.

Source: Calculated from Massachusetts Board of Education,
Annual Reports for 1840, 1860, and 1875.

Table A5.9. Average number of public school days attended per child ages birth to 19, by town size, in Massachusetts, 1840, 1860, and 1875

Town size	1840		1860		1875	
	Mean[a]	Standard deviation	Mean[a]	Standard deviation	Mean[a]	Standard deviation
0-1,249	50.9	18.9	51.9	13.3	58.2	10.1
1,250-2,499	49.5	16.4	52.1	11.9	66.1	12.8
2,500-4,999	49.3	15.1	57.7	14.3	68.6	13.0
5,000-9,999	50.5	10.0	63.9	16.3	73.0	12.3
10,000 & up	65.5	16.4	71.0	14.8	67.3	14.7
Boston	64.2	--	71.9	--	64.4	--
All towns	50.3	17.0	55.3	14.4	64.6	13.1

[a]Average of the town averages.

Source: Calculated from U.S. census of 1840 and 1860 and Massachusetts census of 1875; and from Massachusetts Board of Education, Annual Reports for 1840, 1860 and 1875.

Table A5.10. Average number of public and private school days attended per child ages birth to 19, by town size, in Massachusetts, 1840, 1860, and 1875

Town size	1840		1860		1875	
	Mean[a]	Standard deviation	Mean[a]	Standard deviation	Mean[a]	Standard deviation
0-1,249	56.3	21.3	59.8	20.0	61.3	14.2
1,250-2,499	61.1	21.6	62.2	15.0	74.4	35.4
2,500-4,999	61.3	16.3	63.4	15.3	74.4	16.1
5,000-9,999	70.0	14.5	68.7	16.9	76.6	13.7
10,000 & up	82.2	19.2	76.4	14.8	73.5	10.7
Boston	85.2	--	76.2	--	70.7	--
All towns	60.3	20.9	63.1	17.3	70.1	23.3

[a]Average of the town averages.

Source: Calculated from U.S. censuses of 1840 and 1860 and Massachusetts census of 1875; and from Massachusetts Board of Education, Annual Reports for 1840, 1860, and 1875.

Table A5.11. Average monthly male teacher wage rates (in dollars), including board, in Massachusetts public schools, 1840, 1860, and 1875

Town size	1840		1860		1875	
	Mean[a]	Standard deviation	Mean[a]	Standard deviation	Mean[a]	Standard deviation
0-1,249	22.60	7.50	24.60	12.81	33.07	25.73
1,250-2,499	25.90	6.49	33.92	12.78	61.04	40.27
2,500-4,999	28.91	4.87	46.96	16.01	91.65	39.14
5,000-9,999	40.14	13.62	67.37	21.27	122.25	43.89
10,000 & up	48.00	10.56	88.07	19.09	158.31	36.55
Boston	105.00	--	155.00	--	226.38	--
All towns	26.51	9.81	40.13	23.19	70.79	52.14

[a]Average of the town averages.

Source: Calculated from Massachusetts Board of Education, Annual Reports for 1840, 1860, and 1875.

Table A5.12. Average monthly female teacher wage rates (in dollars), including board, in Massachusetts public schools, 1840, 1860, and 1875

Town size	1840		1860		1875	
	Mean[a]	Standard deviation	Mean[a]	Standard deviation	Mean[a]	Standard deviation
0-1,249	11.01	3.32	16.67	3.43	29.30	5.91
1,250-2,499	11.70	2.89	18.27	2.79	33.66	5.51
2,500-4,999	13.05	2.24	20.49	2.87	38.05	6.70
5,000-9,999	13.43	2.56	23.23	4.19	43.72	8.19
10,000 & up	16.20	3.25	25.07	4.45	51.42	10.61
Boston	21.00	--	39.00	--	85.11	--
All towns	11.85	3.15	19.14	4.19	35.40	9.50

[a]Average of the town averages.

Source: Calculated from Massachusetts Board of Education, Annual Reports for 1840, 1860, and 1875.

Table A5.13. Percentage, by town size, of female public school-teachers in Massachusetts, 1840, 1860, and 1875

	1840		1860		1875	
Town size	Mean[a]	Standard deviation	Mean[a]	Standard deviation	Mean[a]	Standard deviation
0-1,249	61.8	15.1	78.0	14.9	83.3	13.6
1,250-2,499	59.6	10.6	79.6	11.5	84.7	10.5
2,500-4,999	59.8	14.7	77.9	10.3	85.0	8.3
5,000-9,999	64.7	9.2	79.5	8.3	88.7	6.7
10,000 & up	68.8	5.0	87.4	3.0	90.8	3.1
Boston	76.7	--	88.7	--	84.3	--
All towns	60.8	13.0	79.2	12.1	85.1	10.9

[a]Average of the town rates.

Source: Calculated from Massachusetts Board of Education, Annual Reports for 1840, 1860, and 1875.

Table A5.14. Female teacher wages as a percentage of male teacher wages by town size, in Massachusetts public schools, 1860 and 1875

	1860		1875	
Town size	Mean[a]	Standard deviation	Mean[a]	Standard deviation
0-1,249	59.1	12.2	74.2	18.6
1,240-2,499	53.8	11.4	60.7	24.0
2,500-4,999	47.0	12.6	46.8	18.4
5,000-9,999	36.8	9.1	37.7	15.4
10,000 & up	29.0	4.3	32.9	3.9
Boston	25.2	--	37.6	--
All towns	50.6	14.2	56.9	23.9

[a]Average of the town rates.

Source: Calculated from Massachusetts Board of Education, Annual Reports for 1860 and 1875.

Table A5.15. Average number of pupils per teacher, by town size, in Massachusetts public schools, 1840, 1860, and 1875

Town size	1840		1860		1875	
	Mean[a]	Standard deviation	Mean[a]	Standard deviation	Mean[a]	Standard deviation
0-1,249	27.3	6.8	21.5	6.4	12.2	4.4
1,250-2,499	31.4	8.3	26.4	5.4	18.3	5.7
2,500-4,999	32.8	8.9	32.4	6.0	23.7	5.8
5,000-9,999	38.0	9.0	36.8	5.9	28.6	5.7
10,000 & up	43.8	5.5	40.1	6.1	31.4	4.7
Boston	46.9	--	46.8	--	32.1	--
All towns	30.8	8.6	28.0	8.3	19.3	8.2

[a]Average of the town averages.

Source: Calculated from Massachusetts Board of Education, Annual Reports for 1840, 1860, and 1875.

Table A5.16. Average number of pupils per Massachusetts public school, by town size, 1840, 1860, and 1875

Town size	1840		1860		1875	
	Mean[a]	Standard deviation	Mean[a]	Standard deviation	Mean[a]	Standard deviation
0-1,249	26.3	7.4	20.6	6.7	18.7	5.7
1,250-2,499	31.9	11.3	26.5	6.1	26.7	6.5
2,500-4,999	34.1	9.4	34.4	8.7	33.3	6.3
5,000-9,999	42.7	15.2	43.3	10.0	41.0	6.4
10,000 & up	63.7	14.7	59.7	14.1	53.7	40.2
Boston	83.7	--	89.3	--	87.2	--
All towns	31.6	12.1	29.9	12.9	28.7	16.0

[a]Average of the town averages.

Source: Calculated from Massachusetts Board of Education, Annual Reports for 1840, 1860, and 1875.

Table A5.17. Massachusetts public school expenditures (in dollars) per student, by town size, 1840, 1860, and 1875

Town size	1840		1860		1875	
	Mean[a]	Standard deviation	Mean[a]	Standard deviation	Mean[a]	Standard deviation
0-1,249	3.09	5.65	4.78	2.83	8.92	3.87
1,250-2,499	2.48	.89	4.43	1.14	10.93	4.91
2,500-4,999	2.81	.91	5.17	1.62	11.94	5.19
5,000-9,999	4.06	1.35	6.86	3.05	13.91	5.55
10,000 & up	5.35	1.12	7.21	1.77	14.80	3.80
Boston	8.19	--	11.12	--	24.80	--
All towns	2.88	3.45	5.68	2.29	11.04	5.04

[a]Average of the town averages.

Source: Calculated from Massachusetts Board of Education, Annual Reports for 1840, 1860, and 1875.

Table A5.18. Massachusetts public school expenditures (in dollars) per capita, by town size, 1840, 1860, and 1875

Town size	1840		1860		1875	
	Mean[a]	Standard deviation	Mean[a]	Standard deviation	Mean[a]	Standard deviation
0-1,249	.84	1.29	1.12	.59	1.80	.60
1,250-2,499	.65	.18	.94	.22	2.15	.90
2,500-4,999	.65	.18	1.07	.36	2.31	.88
5,000-9,999	.75	.19	1.31	.56	2.61	1.03
10,000 & up	.81	.13	1.36	.29	2.67	.78
Boston	1.04	--	1.75	--	4.02	--
All towns	.73	.80	1.08	.44	2.15	.87

[a]Average of the town averages.

Source: Calculated from U.S. censuses of 1840 and 1860 and Massachusetts census of 1875; and from Massachusetts Board of Education, Annual Reports for 1840, 1860, and 1875.

Table A5.19. Massachusetts public school expenditure as a
percentage of assessed valuation, by town size, 1860 and 1875

	1860		1875	
Town size	Mean[a]	Standard deviation	Mean[a]	Standard deviation
0-1,249	.21	.29	.33	.13
1,250-2,499	.18	.05	.30	.08
2,500-4,999	.20	.05	.35	.08
5,000-9,999	.21	.05	.31	.08
10,000 & up	.21	.05	.31	.76
Boston	.10	--	.17	--
All towns	.20	.16	.32	.10

[a]Average of the town rates.

Source: Calculated from Massachusetts Board of Education,
Annual Reports for 1860 and 1875.

Table A5.20. Variables used in the 1860 regression analysis

Description of variables

Dependent variables
Y_1 % of persons under 20 enrolled in public or private school

Y_2 Average length of the public school year (days)

Y_3 Average number of days of public and private schooling per person under 20

Independent variables
X_1 Total population

X_2 Number of acres of farmland per 1,000 persons

X_3 % of the population ages 15 & up who are merchants

X_4 % of the population ages 15 & up who are engaged in manufacturing

X_5 Assessed valuation per capita ($)

X_6 Pauper expenses per capital ($)

X_7 % of the population foreign-born

X_8 Number of church seats per capita

X_9 Number of Catholic church seats per capita

Table A5.21. 1860 regression analysis: means and standard deviations

	Mean	Standard deviation
% of persons under 20 enrolled in public or private school	58.22	14.09
Average length of the public school year (days)	158.76	41.60
Average number of days of public and private schooling per person under 20	63.25	17.36
Total population	3,747.32	10,768.48
Number of acres of farmland per 1,000 persons	7.85	12.70
% of the population ages 15 & up who are merchants	1.05	.88
% of the population ages 15 & up who are engaged in manufacturing	18.47	19.37
Assessed valuation per capita ($)	498.04	206.08
Pauper expenses per capita ($)	.47	.28
% of the population foreign-born	12.84	9.23
Number of church seats per capita	.75	.31
Number of Catholic church seats per capita	.03	.11

Table A5.22. 1860 regression analysis: correlation matrix

	Y_1	Y_2	Y_3	X_1	X_2	X_3	X_4	X_5	X_6	X_7	X_8	X_9
Y_1	1.00	.54	-.39	-.16	.27	-.19	-.31	-.08	.32	-.56	.26	-.21
Y_2	-.39	1.00	.50	.31	-.42	.65	.15	.48	-.05	.45	-.17	.24
Y_3	.54	.50	1.00	.13	-.21	.42	-.10	.39	.25	-.10	.08	0
X_1	-.16	.31	.13	1.00	-.16	.35	.11	.41	-.04	.33	-.10	.17
X_2	.27	-.42	-.21	-.16	1.00	-.38	-.34	-.13	0	-.32	.17	-.16
X_3	-.19	.65	.42	.35	-.38	1.00	.06	.53	-.09	.31	-.12	.17
X_4	-.31	.15	-.10	.11	-.34	.06	1.00	-.12	-.10	.35	-.19	.24
X_5	-.08	.48	.39	.41	-.13	.53	-.12	1.00	.03	.28	-.06	.15
X_6	.32	-.05	.25	-.04	0	-.09	-.10	.03	1.00	-.32	.12	-.13
X_7	-.56	.45	-.10	.33	-.32	.31	.35	.28	-.32	1.00	-.25	.42
X_8	.26	-.17	.08	-.10	.17	-.12	-.19	-.06	.12	-.25	1.00	.21
X_9	-.21	.24	0	.17	-.16	.17	.24	.15	-.13	.42	.21	1.00

Table A5.23. Results of the regression analysis predicting the percentage of persons under 20 years of age enrolled in Massachusetts public or private schools, 1860 (Y_1)

	Regression coefficient	Beta
Total population	0	.007
Number of acres of farmland per 1,000 persons	.0840	.076
% of the population ages 15 & up who are merchants	-.5217	-.033
% of the population ages 15 & up who are engaged in manufacturing	-.0550	-.076
Assessed valuation per capita ($)	.0047	.068
Pauper expenses per capita ($)	7.6225	.150
% of the population foreign-born	-.6935	-.454
Number of church seats per capita	4.3017	.096
Number of Catholic church seats per capita	1.0142	.008

Constant = 58.807
R^2 = .350

Table A5.24. Results of the regression analysis predicting the average length (in days) of the Massachusetts public school year, 1860 (Y_2)

	Regression coefficient	Beta
Total population	-.0001	-.016
Number of acres of farmland per 1,000 persons	-.4925	-.150
% of the population ages 15 & up who are merchants	20.4619	.435
% of the population ages 15 & up who are engaged in manufacturing	.0100	.005
Assessed valuation per capita ($)	.0337	.167
Pauper expenses per capita ($)	10.1067	.067
% of the population foreign-born	.9571	.212
Number of church seats per capita	5.9359	-.045
Number of Catholic church seats per capita	19.1583	.049

Constant = 111.25
R^2 = .521

Table A5.25. Results of the regression analysis predicting the average number of Massachusetts public and private school days per person under 20 years of age, 1860 (Y_3)

	Regression coefficient	Beta
Total population	0	-.027
Number of acres of farmland per 1,000 persons	-.1978	-.145
% of the population ages 15 & up who are merchants	6.4262	.328
% of the population ages 15 & up who are engaged in manufacturing	-.0069	-.008
Assessed valuation per capita ($)	.0233	.277
Pauper expenses per capita ($)	11.4140	.182
% of the population foreign-born	-.4378	-.233
Number of church seats per capita	4.3755	.079
Number of Catholic church seats per capita	-1.9653	-.012

Constant = 43.727
R^2 = .328

Table A7.1. Amount of money spent for Massachusetts public
schools, 1837-80, in dollars adjusted for cost of living
(1860 = 100)

Year	Income for schools reported in state school returns	Estimated cost of new school construction and maintenance	Total
1837	422,048	95,805[a]	517,853
1838-9	484,811	110,052[a]	594,863
1839-40	605,389	137,423[a]	742,812
1840-1	636,083	144,391[a]	780,474
1841-2	718,897	163,190[a]	882,087
1842-3	752,020	170,709[a]	922,729
1843-4	802,800	182,236[a]	985,036
1844-5	796,160	180,728	976,888
1845-6	799,180	183,012[a]	982,192
1846-7	852,895	196,166[a]	1,049,061
1847-8	1,026,164	238,070	1,264,234
1848-9	1,189,490	309,267[a]	1,498,757
1849-50	1,162,245	334,727[a]	1,496,972
1850-1	1,121,005	353,117[a]	1,474,122
1851-2	1,108,854	380,337[a]	1,489,191
1852-3	1,165,846	432,529	1,598,375
1853-4	1,129,947	472,318[a]	1,602,265
1854-5	1,218,986	565,610	1,784,596
1855-6	1,321,547	619,806[a]	1,941,353
1856-7	1,350,821	640,289[a]	1,991,110
1857-8	1,464,975	701,723[a]	2,166,698
1858-9	1,515,347	733,428[a]	2,248,775
1859-60	1,553,756	759,787[a]	2,313,543
1860-1	1,593,754	787,314[a]	2,381,068
1861-2	1,445,960	721,534[a]	2,167,494
1862-3	1,128,168	568,597[a]	1,696,765
1863-4	954,763	485,974[a]	1,440,737
1864-5	1,110,479	570,786[a]	1,681,265
1865-6	1,294,588	671,891[a]	1,966,479
1866-7	1,607,751	842,462[a]	2,450,213
1867-8	1,841,995	970,731	2,812,726
1868-9	2,110,447	882,167	2,992,614
1869-70	2,342,411	1,255,532	3,597,943
1870-1	2,573,503	1,533,808	4,107,311
1871-2	2,832,148	1,282,963	4,115,111
1872-3	3,092,022	1,063,656	4,155,678
1873-4	3,487,350	1,276,370	4,763,720
1874-5	3,780,698	1,247,630	5,028,328
1875-6	3,927,852	1,013,386	4,941,238
1876-7	3,891,925	809,520	4,701,445
1877-8	3,985,708	554,013	4,539,721
1878-9	4,010,861	553,499	4,564,360
1879-80	3,940,480	555,608	4,496,088

[a]No information is available in the state school reports. Therefore, the estimates were made by calculating the ratio of school
construction and maintenance costs to reported school income and
interpolating those ratios for years with no data available on
the school construction and maintenance costs.

Source: Massachusetts Board of Education, Annual Reports for
1837-80.

Table A7.2. Tuition paid for Massachusetts incorporated and unincorporated academies, private schools, and schools kept to prolong common schools, 1837-80, in dollars adjusted for cost of living (1860 = 100)

Year	Incorporated academies	Unincorporated academies, private schools, and schools kept to prolong common schools	Total
1837	n.a.	n.a.	298,205
1838-9	49,645	248,130	297,775
1839-40	62,454	262,080	324,534
1840-1	61,454	281,655	343,109
1841-2	61,056	299,737	360,793
1842-3	66,382	300,708	367,090
1843-4	68,524	298,486	367,010
1844-5	61,764	285,263	347,027
1845-6	60,306	251,709	312,015
1846-7	67,708	278,378	346,086
1847-8	73,865	296,202	370,067
1848-9	79,095	308,692	387,787
1849-50	69,210	314,748	383,958
1850-1	71,317	289,470	360,787
1851-2	88,796	249,427	338,223
1852-3	79,874	235,523	315,397
1853-4	84,477	241,871	326,348
1854-5	79,323	260,856	340,179
1855-6	82,121	289,814	371,935
1856-7	72,924	323,542	396,466
1857-8	85,254	377,898	463,152
1858-9	74,223	333,940	408,163
1859-60	71,294	358,689	429,983
1860-1	83,544	346,072	429,616
1861-2	60,293	272,088	332,381
1862-3	52,858	199,478	252,336
1863-4	43,519	180,385	223,904
1864-5	67,129	181,180	248,309
1865-6	71,147	135,597	206,744
1866-7	91,415	265,092	356,507
1867-8	80,693	266,175	346,868
1868-9	75,399	328,005	403,404
1869-70	79,338	340,199	419,537
1870-1	85,286	301,061	386,347
1871-2	129,767	313,471	443,238
1872-3	195,739	354,312	550,051
1873-4	181,511	371,624	553,135
1874-5	131,070	355,234	486,304
1875-6	189,124	376,398	565,522
1876-7	111,603	372,545	484,148
1877-8	166,968	292,846	459,814
1878-9	280,578	285,673	566,251
1879-80	215,928	126,020	341,948

Source: Massachusetts Board of Education, <u>Annual Reports</u> for 1837-80.

Table A7.3. Cost per hundred days of school attended in
Massachusetts, 1837-80, in dollars adjusted for cost of living
(1860 = 100)

Year	Public	Private	Total
1837	3.34	8.38	4.29
1838-9	3.82	7.52	4.57
1839-40	4.84	7.52	5.43
1840-1	4.63	7.46	5.24
1841-2	5.15	8.14	5.76
1842-3	5.32	10.23	6.16
1843-4	5.33	9.15	6.01
1844-5	5.07	8.49	5.67
1845-6	4.97	8.75	5.39
1846-7	4.78	8.20	5.33
1847-8	5.67	9.75	6.27
1848-9	6.62	9.58	7.07
1849-50	6.64	9.75	7.10
1850-1	6.31	11.00	6.89
1851-2	6.21	10.52	6.72
1852-3	6.50	8.97	6.81
1853-4	6.49	9.66	6.88
1854-5	7.04	9.64	7.36
1855-6	7.36	9.99	7.68
1856-7	7.63	10.85	8.02
1857-8	7.77	13.15	8.37
1858-59	8.01	11.44	8.39
1859-60	7.97	14.07	8.55
1860-1	8.10	13.43	8.62
1861-2	6.96	9.77	7.24
1862-3	5.45	7.31	5.63
1863-4	4.64	6.23	4.80
1864-5	5.45	6.28	5.54
1865-6	6.18	5.33	6.08
1866-67	7.37	9.76	7.60
1867-8	8.06	10.32	8.26
1868-9	8.51	11.97	8.81
1869-70	10.00	12.98	10.25
1870-1	11.24	12.49	11.34
1871-2	10.89	12.25	11.01
1872-3	11.07	15.16	11.43
1873-4	12.11	14.97	12.36
1874-5	12.07	12.28	12.09
1875-6	11.69	13.60	11.86
1876-7	11.16	12.17	11.25
1877-8	10.35	11.59	10.45
1878-9	10.20	14.32	10.53
1879-80	10.04	8.08	9.88

Source: Calculated from Massachusetts Board of Education, Annual
  Reports for 1837-80.

274

Table A7.4. Massachusetts school expenditures in dollars per
$1,000 of state valuation, 1837-80

Year	Public	Private	Total
1837	2.02	1.16	3.19
1838-9	2.23	1.11	3.34
1839-40	2.27	1.00	3.27
1840-1	2.17	.96	3.13
1841-2	2.06	.84	2.90
1842-3	1.84	.74	2.58
1843-4	1.88	.70	2.58
1844-5	1.80	.64	2.44
1845-6	1.82	.58	2.40
1846-7	1.83	.61	2.44
1847-8	1.94	.57	2.51
1848-9	2.05	.53	2.59
1849-50	2.07	.53	2.61
1850-1	2.15	.53	2.68
1851-2	2.10	.48	2.58
1852-3	2.16	.43	2.58
1853-4	2.25	.46	2.71
1854-5	2.48	.47	2.95
1855-6	2.54	.49	3.03
1856-7	2.58	.52	3.10
1857-8	2.56	.55	3.10
1858-9	2.59	.47	3.06
1859-60	2.57	.48	3.05
1860-1	2.61	.47	3.08
1861-2	2.59	.40	2.99
1862-3	2.44	.36	2.80
1863-4	2.56	.40	2.96
1864-5	2.91	.43	3.34
1865-6	3.01	.32	3.32
1866-7	3.28	.48	3.75
1867-8	3.45	.43	3.88
1868-9	3.29	.44	3.73
1869-70	3.58	.42	4.00
1870-1	3.70	.35	4.05
1871-2	3.61	.39	4.00
1872-3	3.28	.43	3.71
1873-4	3.35	.39	3.74
1874-5	3.27	.32	3.59
1875-6	3.32	.38	3.70
1876-7	3.32	.34	3.66
1877-8	3.12	.32	3.43
1878-9	3.22	.40	3.62
1879-80	3.12	.24	3.35

Source: Calculated from Massachusetts Board of Education, Annual
Reports for 1837-80.

Table A7.5. Income sources for Massachusetts public schools, 1837–80, in dollars adjusted for cost of living (1860 = 100)

Year	Taxes for wages of teachers, board, and fuel	Board and fuel contributed	Income from local funds for education	Optional funds spent for education	Share of state school fund	Total
1837	351,931	43,910	8,701	--	17,506	422,048
1838–9	410,834	29,297	11,830	--	32,850	484,811
1839–40	518,718	40,510	16,598	--	29,563	605,389
1840–1	533,712	41,025	16,637	10,358	34,351	636,083
1841–2	614,346	46,874	15,956	12,332	29,389	718,897
1842–3	654,603	46,005	19,585	8,494	23,333	752,020
1843–4	685,588	47,439	20,551	12,158	37,064	802,800
1844–5	694,646	43,781	20,172	11,045	26,516	796,160
1845–6	686,407	43,772	17,434	9,429	42,138	799,180
1846–7	744,798	40,137	19,703	9,324	38,933	852,895
1847–8	909,570	43,246	26,077	5,865	41,406	1,026,164
1848–9	1,064,842	45,232	27,672	7,029	44,715	1,189,490
1849–50	1,041,767	41,812	22,854	10,499	45,313	1,162,245
1850–1	995,477	43,100	26,495	10,866	45,067	1,121,005
1851–2	978,727	42,772	27,804	12,168	47,383	1,108,854
1852–3	1,036,162	42,229	28,590	11,481	47,384	1,165,846
1853–4	1,003,438	37,684	31,789	10,592	46,444	1,129,947
1854–5	1,093,661	36,323	33,135	9,126	46,741	1,218,986
1855–6	1,190,150	37,774	39,259	8,474	45,890	1,321,547
1856–7	1,222,311	36,251	42,385	7,184	42,690	1,350,821
1857–8	1,327,527	35,681	46,463	7,515	47,789	1,464,975
1858–9	1,390,382	29,309	41,043	7,852	46,761	1,515,347

Table A7.5 (cont.)

Year	Taxes for wages of teachers, board, and fuel	Board and fuel contributed	Income from local funds for education	Optional funds spent for education	Share of state school fund	Total
1859–60	1,428,476	29,658	42,020	7,217	46,385	1,553,756
1860–1	1,461,335	30,664	49,410	6,992	45,353	1,593,754
1861–2	1,327,877	26,681	44,477	7,072	39,853	1,445,960
1862–3	1,031,665	18,867	37,726	4,627	35,283	1,128,168
1863–4	872,906	15,488	31,539	2,989	31,841	954,763
1864–5	1,018,642	17,938	36,157	3,043	34,699	1,110,479
1865–6	1,193,519	21,038	39,729	2,792	37,510	1,294,588
1866–7	1,500,322	20,618	44,082	2,830	39,899	1,607,751
1867–8	1,711,542	21,292	48,355	3,022	57,784	1,841,995
1868–9	1,988,917	19,519	51,004	2,955	48,052	2,110,447
1869–70	2,216,350	13,473	56,394	3,767	52,427	2,342,411
1870–1	2,423,952	9,289	56,154	4,622	79,486	2,573,503
1871–2	2,662,730	10,922	64,927	28,861	64,708	2,832,148
1872–3	2,924,100	10,177	70,195	22,636	64,914	3,092,022
1873–4	3,297,063	8,653	76,713	36,679	68,242	3,487,350
1874–5	3,543,515	25,030	97,793	42,317	72,043	3,780,698
1875–6	3,698,234	7,069	104,833	47,674	70,042	3,927,852
1876–7	3,670,911	4,474	101,668	50,194	64,678	3,891,925
1877–8	3,776,135	7,216	84,102	54,805	63,450	3,985,708
1878–9	3,799,862	4,947	80,456	59,162	66,434	4,010,861
1879–80	3,693,238	––	95,643	88,045	63,554	3,940,480

Source: Calculated from Massachusetts Board of Education, Annual Reports for 1837–80.

Table A7.6. School expenditures as a percentage of overall town budgets, excluding state and county taxes, in eight Essex County communities and Boston, 1860 and 1880

	1860	1880
Rural Essex (Boxford, Hamilton, Lynnfield, Topsfield, & Wenham)	26.3	24.7
Urban Essex (Lawrence, Lynn, & Salem)	27.9	16.4
Boston	19.0	14.0

Source: Calculated from annual budgets for the towns of Boxford, Hamilton, Lynnfield, Topsfield, Wenham, Lawrence, Lynn, and Salem; and from Charles Phillips Huse, The Financial History of Boston from May 1, 1822, to January 31, 1909 (Cambridge, Mass.: Harvard University Press, 1916).

Table A7.7. Per capita school expenditures in budgets of eight Essex County communities and Boston, 1860 and 1880, in dollars adjusted for cost of living (1860 = 100)

	1860	1880
Rural Essex (Boxford, Hamilton, Lynnfield, Topsfield, & Wenham)	.84	1.47
Urban Essex (Lawrence, Lynn, & Salem)	1.76	2.40
Boston	3.56	4.94

Source: Calculated from annual budgets for the towns of Boxford, Hamilton, Lynnfield, Topsfield, Wenham, Lawrence, Lynn, and Salem; Huse, The Financial History of Boston; and from U.S. censuses of 1860 and 1880.

Table A7.8. Public school, institutional, and police expenditures as percentages of the overall Boston city budget, including state and county taxes, 1820-80

Year	Public schools	Institutions	Police
1820	25.7	10.8	5.0
1821	23.8	21.3	5.2
1822	27.7	6.7	3.4
1823	20.9	14.7	2.9
1824	17.2	15.3	2.7
1825	20.3	14.9	2.3
1826	5.9	5.1	1.0
1827	15.9	9.5	3.1
1828	16.6	11.4	3.6
1829	15.5	11.0	3.6
1830	15.3	10.8	3.1
1831	16.1	11.7	3.6
1832	12.3	11.6	2.3
1833	14.9	7.4	3.4
1834	14.2	8.7	4.8
1835	17.1	9.7	4.6
1836	13.1	8.7	3.3
1837	16.7	7.8	5.0
1838	22.5	9.1	6.4
1839	18.5	8.1	5.4
1840	18.9	12.5	7.4
1841	22.5	12.4	7.1
1842	20.3	12.7	7.8
1843	29.5	10.6	7.4
1844	26.5	10.2	7.3
1845	23.1	8.2	7.5
1846	17.2	6.5	4.4
1847	11.8	3.8	2.7
1848	9.0	3.7	3.0
1849	12.7	9.1	4.8
1850	13.6	10.4	5.2
1851	13.6	10.6	6.6
1852	15.5	8.3	6.1
1853	12.2	8.7	6.3
1854	15.9	8.2	7.1
1855	15.8	9.3	7.3
1856	11.6	7.0	6.6
1857	9.3	8.1	5.8
1858	13.6	6.8	6.9
1859	14.5	7.4	6.3
1860	17.7	6.4	6.5
1861	16.7	10.7	8.3
1862	10.3	13.2	4.8
1863	9.3	12.7	6.5
1864	10.5	10.4	6.0
1865	12.2	8.2	6.8
1866	12.0	10.8	8.1
1867	11.5	6.8	5.2
1868	13.7	7.3	5.8

Table A7.8 (cont.)

Year	Public schools	Institutions	Police
1869	12.5	4.9	4.4
1870	12.6	5.0	4.6
1871	10.6	5.1	4.9
1872	11.7	5.9	4.4
1873	10.0	4.2	3.9
1874	13.5	5.3	5.7
1875	13.0	6.4	5.7
1876	12.5	6.2	6.0
1877	13.2	6.3	6.4
1878	14.2	6.4	6.7
1879	13.8	6.9	7.1
1880	13.7	6.8	6.8

Source: Calculated from Huse, The Financial History of Boston.

Table A7.9. Boston's per capita expenditures for public schools, institutions, and police, 1820-80, in dollars adjusted for cost of living (1860 = 100)

Year	Public schools	Institutions	Police
1820	1.03	.43	.20
1821	1.01	.91	.22
1822	1.52	.37	.18
1823	1.53	1.08	.22
1824	1.37	1.22	.22
1825	1.47	1.08	.17
1826	1.18	1.01	.20
1827	1.08	.64	.21
1828	1.02	.70	.22
1829	.97	.69	.22
1830	1.08	.77	.22
1831	.99	.72	.22
1832	1.10	1.03	.21
1833	1.42	.70	.33
1834	1.55	.95	.53
1835	1.66	.95	.45
1836	1.29	.86	.33
1837	1.30	.61	.39
1838	1.73	.70	.49
1839	1.71	.74	.50
1840	1.53	1.01	.60
1841	1.85	1.02	.59
1842	1.70	1.06	.65
1843	2.71	.97	.68
1844	2.44	.93	.66
1845	2.37	.84	.77
1846	2.83	1.07	.72
1847	3.55	1.15	.81
1848	2.86	1.18	.96
1849	3.05	2.19	1.15
1850	2.87	2.19	1.10
1851	2.29	1.79	1.12
1852	2.46	1.32	.96
1853	1.85	1.32	.95
1854	2.56	1.32	1.14
1855	2.68	1.57	1.23
1856	2.06	1.24	1.18
1857	1.93	1.70	1.21
1858	2.55	1.27	1.30
1859	3.10	1.57	1.35
1860	3.56	1.29	1.30
1861	3.15	2.01	1.55
1862	2.58	3.31	1.21
1863	1.82	2.49	1.27
1864	1.93	1.93	1.11
1865	2.31	1.56	1.29
1866	2.29	2.07	1.56

Table A7.9 (cont.)

Year	Public schools	Institutions	Police
1867	2.84	1.68	1.29
1868	3.80	2.03	1.62
1869	4.56	1.79	1.61
1870	4.46	1.77	1.64
1871	3.63	1.76	1.68
1872	4.51	2.26	1.70
1873	4.59	1.92	1.81
1874	4.98	1.95	2.12
1875	4.79	2.37	2.09
1876	4.41	2.18	2.10
1877	4.25	2.03	2.07
1878	4.47	2.04	2.13
1879	4.27	2.15	2.21
1880	4.45	2.21	2.21

Source: Calculated from Huse, The Financial History of Boston; and from U.S. censuses of 1830–80.

Table A7.10. Trends in inequality among Massachusetts towns in public school expenditures per school-age child, 1841–80

Year	Mean expenditure per child	Standard deviation	Coefficient of variation
1840–1	2.24	.82	.3661
1841–2	2.31	.86	.3723
1842–3	2.36	.88	.3729
1843–4	2.35	.92	.3915
1844–5	2.39	.97	.4059
1845–6	2.46	.93	.3780
1846–7	2.52	.94	.3730
1847–8	2.62	1.03	.3931
1848–9	2.75	1.12	.4073
1849–50	3.31	1.32	.3988
1850–1	3.40	1.38	.4059
1851–2	3.56	1.44	.4045
1852–3	3.70	1.45	.3919
1853–4	3.92	1.69	.4311
1854–5	4.09	1.80	.4401
1855–6	4.27	1.87	.4379
1856–7	4.56	2.02	.4430
1857–8	4.71	2.18	.4628
1858–9	4.77	2.17	.4549
1859–60	4.79	2.22	.4635
1860–1	4.94	2.32	.4696
1861–2	4.90	2.09	.4265
1862–3	4.51	2.00	.4434
1863–4	4.64	2.00	.4310
1864–5	5.18	2.34	.4517
1865–6	5.75	2.56	.4452
1866–7	6.42	2.88	.4486
1867–8	7.00	3.24	.4629
1868–9	7.53	3.24	.4303
1869–70	10.86	4.53	.4171
1870–1	8.72	3.45	.3956
1871–2	9.34	3.78	.4047
1872–3	9.97	4.06	.4072
1873–4	10.59	4.43	.4183
1874–5	10.91	4.43	.4060
1875–6	10.86	4.53	.4171
1876–7	10.59	4.45	.4202
1877–8	10.46	4.19	.4006
1878–9	10.00	4.14	.4140
1879–80	9.64	4.02	.4170

Source: Calculated from Massachusetts Board of Education, Annual Reports for 1841–80.

Table A7.11. Massachusetts public school teachers' monthly wages including board, 1837-80, in dollars adjusted for cost of living (1860 = 100)

Year	Males	Females	Female salary as % of male salary
1837	23.13	10.35	44.7
1838-9	29.27	11.30	38.6
1839-40	35.96	13.86	40.0
1840-1	36.74	13.92	38.7
1841-2	38.36	15.21	39.7
1842-3	41.17	16.44	39.9
1843-4	39.73	15.90	40.0
1844-5	38.69	15.76	40.7
1845-6	35.69	14.78	41.4
1846-7	36.47	15.28	41.9
1847-8	39.82	17.02	42.8
1848-9	43.62	18.19	41.7
1849-50	42.04	17.39	41.3
1850-1	39.45	16.58	42.0
1851-2	40.10	16.52	41.2
1852-3	39.78	16.57	41.6
1853-4	37.39	15.72	42.1
1854-5	39.89	16.63	41.7
1855-6	42.21	18.16	43.0
1856-7	44.41	18.26	41.1
1857-8	50.37	19.83	39.3
1858-9	48.90	19.02	38.9
1859-60	50.56	19.98	39.5
1860-1	47.24	19.75	41.8
1861-2	40.16	17.12	42.6
1862-3	32.28	13.60	42.1
1863-4	26.58	11.01	41.4
1864-5	31.30	12.47	39.8
1865-6	35.65	14.59	40.9
1866-7	42.62	16.84	39.5
1867-8	47.36	18.08	38.2
1868-9	49.01	19.60	39.9
1869-70	54.92	21.93	39.9
1870-1	56.62	23.46	41.4
1871-2	63.03	23.99	38.1
1872-3	70.41	25.67	36.5
1873-4	73.12	26.62	36.4
1874-5	71.85	28.74	40.0
1875-6	71.24	29.62	41.6
1876-7	69.68	29.07	41.7
1877-8	68.14	29.77	43.7
1878-9	62.44	31.02	49.7
1879-80	61.40	27.81	45.3

Source: Calculated from Massachusetts Board of Education, Annual Reports for 1837-80.

Table A7.12. Number of individuals who taught in Massachusetts public and private schools, 1834-80

Year	Male	Female	Total
1834	2,358	3,035	5,393
1835	2,405	3,077	5,482
1836	2,411	3,306	5,717
1837	2,536	3,842	6,378
1838-9	2,584	4,043	6,627
1839-40	2,586	4,256	6,842
1840-1	2,694	4,440	7,134
1841-2	2,692	4,591	7,283
1842-3	2,609	4,584	7,193
1843-4	2,486	4,739	7,225
1844-5	2,634	4,767	7,401
1845-6	2,571	4,825	7,396
1846-7	2,539	5,006	7,545
1847-8	2,509	5,125	7,634
1848-9	2,466	5,340	7,806
1849-50	2,469	5,031	7,500
1850-1	2,399	5,516	7,915
1851-2	2,406	5,491	7,897
1852-3	2,317	5,649	7,966
1853-4	2,166	5,738	7,904
1854-5	2,045	5,877	7,922
1855-6	2,013	5,981	7,994
1856-7	1,928	6,072	8,000
1857-8	1,930	6,066	7,996
1858-9	1,902	6,159	8,061
1859-60	1,782	6,229	8,011
1860-1	1,796	6,382	8,178
1861-2	1,788	6,192	7,980
1862-3	1,542	6,516	8,058
1863-4	1,421	6,660	8,081
1864-5	1,297	6,870	8,167
1865-6	1,283	7,015	8,298
1866-7	1,214	7,208	8,422
1867-8	1,171	7,327	8,498
1868-9	1,249	7,344	8,593
1869-70	1,222	7,444	8,666
1870-1	1,204	7,551	8,755
1871-2	1,186	7,812	8,998
1872-3	1,177	7,766	8,943
1873-4	1,223	7,980	9,203
1874-5	1,309	8,364	9,673
1875-6	1,338	7,946	9,284
1876-7	1,313	7,872	9,185
1877-8	1,257	7,729	8,986
1878-9	1,347	7,858	9,205
1879-80	1,313	7,778	9,091

Source: Calculated from Massachusetts Board of Education, Annual Reports for 1834-80; and from U.S. censuses of 1830-80.

Table A7.13. Individuals who taught as percentages of the
Massachusetts white population ages 15-59, 1834-80

Year	Male	Female	Total
1834	1.3	1.6	1.4
1835	1.3	1.6	1.4
1836	1.2	1.6	1.4
1837	1.3	1.9	1.6
1838-9	1.2	1.9	1.5
1839-40	1.2	1.9	1.6
1840-1	1.2	1.9	1.6
1841-2	1.2	1.9	1.5
1842-3	1.1	1.9	1.5
1843-4	1.0	1.8	1.4
1844-5	1.0	1.8	1.4
1845-6	1.0	1.8	1.4
1846-7	.9	1.8	1.4
1847-8	.9	1.7	1.3
1848-9	.8	1.8	1.3
1849-50	.8	1.6	1.2
1850-1	.8	1.7	1.3
1851-2	.8	1.7	1.2
1852-3	.7	1.7	1.2
1853-4	.7	1.7	1.2
1854-5	.6	1.7	1.2
1855-6	.6	1.7	1.2
1856-7	.6	1.7	1.1
1857-8	.6	1.6	1.1
1858-9	.5	1.6	1.1
1859-60	.5	1.6	1.1
1860-1	.5	1.6	1.1
1861-2	.5	1.5	1.0
1862-3	.4	1.6	1.0
1863-4	.4	1.6	1.0
1864-5	.3	1.6	1.0
1865-6	.3	1.6	1.0
1866-7	.3	1.6	1.0
1867-8	.3	1.6	1.0
1868-9	.3	1.6	1.0
1869-70	.3	1.6	1.0
1870-1	.3	1.6	1.0
1871-2	.3	1.6	1.0
1872-3	.3	1.5	.9
1873-4	.3	1.6	.9
1874-5	.3	1.6	1.0
1875-6	.3	1.5	.9
1876-7	.3	1.4	.9
1877-8	.2	1.4	.8
1878-9	.3	1.4	.8
1879-80	.2	1.3	.8

Source: Calculated from Massachusetts Board of Education, Annual
    Report for 1834-80; and from U.S. censuses of 1830-80.

Table A7.14. Percentage of the Massachusetts white population
ages 15-29 who have ever been teachers, 1834-80

Year	Male	Female	Total
1834	14.3	17.7	16.0
1835	11.9	17.3	15.7
1836	13.4	19.9	16.7
1837	14.8	25.0	19.9
1838-9	13.8	22.4	18.1
1839-40	13.2	23.2	18.2
1840-1	14.1	22.9	18.6
1841-2	12.9	22.4	17.7
1842-3	11.5	20.4	16.0
1843-4	10.3	21.4	16.0
1844-5	12.6	20.0	16.4
1845-6	10.5	19.7	15.3
1846-7	10.3	20.5	15.6
1847-8	10.0	19.9	15.1
1848-9	9.5	20.6	15.3
1849-50	9.5	16.0	12.9
1850-1	8.7	21.8	15.5
1851-2	9.1	18.5	14.0
1852-3	8.1	19.7	14.2
1853-4	7.1	19.3	13.5
1854-5	6.7	19.7	13.6
1855-6	7.0	19.5	13.7
1856-7	6.4	19.4	13.3
1857-8	6.8	18.6	13.1
1858-9	6.5	19.0	13.2
1859-60	5.5	18.8	12.6
1860-1	6.2	19.5	13.3
1861-2	5.9	17.1	11.9
1862-3	3.8	20.1	12.5
1863-4	4.0	19.5	12.3
1864-5	3.5	20.1	12.4
1865-6	4.0	20.0	12.5
1866-7	3.4	20.5	12.5
1867-8	3.4	20.3	12.4
1868-9	4.2	19.7	12.4
1869-70	3.5	20.1	12.3
1870-1	3.4	19.9	12.2
1871-2	3.3	20.8	12.6
1872-3	3.3	19.0	11.6
1873-4	3.6	20.1	12.4
1874-5	3.9	21.3	13.1
1875-6	3.6	16.9	10.7
1876-7	3.3	17.7	10.9
1877-8	2.9	16.8	10.3
1878-9	3.7	17.7	11.1
1879-80	3.1	16.5	10.2

Source: Calculated from Massachusetts Board of Education, Annual
Reports for 1834-80; and from U.S. censuses of 1830-80.

Definition of the variables contained in Tables A2.1 through A2.5, Appendix A

Note: A discussion of the following definitions is found in Appendix C.

The abbreviation R equals values that are taken directly from the published statistical abstracts of the *Annual Reports* of the secretary of the Massachusetts Board of Education.

Table A2.1

Col. 1. Number of children 0–19.
Source: Reported figures are from the U.S. censuses of 1840, 1850, 1860, 1870, and 1880, and from the Massachusetts censuses of 1855, 1865, and 1875. Interim years are extrapolated on the assumption of constant arithmetic annual increases between censuses. Figures are for all races. (See discussion, Appendix C, Section 1.)

Col. 2. Number of children enrolled in public schools, all ages, summer term.
Source: R.

Col. 3. Percentage of children birth to 19 enrolled in public schools, summer term.
Definition: Col. 2/Col. 1.

Col. 4. Number of children enrolled in public schools, all ages, winter term.
Source: R.

Col. 5. Percentage of children birth to 19 enrolled in public schools, winter term.
Definition: Col. 4/Col. 1.

Col. 6. Average daily number of children attending public schools, summer term.
Source: R

Col. 7. Average percentage of children birth to 19 attending public schools daily, summer term.
Definition: Col. 6/Col. 1.

Col. 8. Average daily number of children attending public schools, winter term.
Source: R.

Col. 9. Average percentage of children birth to 19 attending public schools daily, winter term.
Definition: Col. 8/Col. 1.

Definition of the variables, Tables A2.1 through A2.5

Table A2.2

Col. 10. Number of public schools.
Source: R.

Col. 11. Aggregate days of school, county data.
Source: Total of county aggregates given in the reports, converted to a 22-day school month (number of months × 22, plus number of days × .785) (See discussion, Appendix C, Section 2.)

Col. 12. State average length of public school session.
Definition: Col. 11/Col. 10, to the nearest whole day.

Col. 13. Estimated average daily attendance all year, public schools.
Definition: for 1840–69, (Col. 6 + Col. 8) / 2; for 1870–80, R.

Col. 14. Estimated total days of public school attended.
Definition: Col. 12 × Col. 13.

Col. 15. Average number of days of public school attended by all children birth to 19.
Definition: Col. 14/Col. 1.

Col. 16. Average percentage of children birth to 19 attending public school daily.
Definition: Col. 13/Col. 1.

Col. 17. Estimated total annual enrollment, all ages, public schools.
Definition: 1840–69, Col. 4 + (.25 × Col. 2); 1870–80, R. (See discussion, Appendix C, Section 3.)

Col. 18. Estimated percentage of all children birth to 19 enrolled in public school.
Definition: Col. 17/Col. 1.

Table A2.3

Col. 19. Number of incorporated academies.
Source: R

Col. 20. Average enrollment in incorporated academies.
Source: R (the "average number of scholars in incorporated academies"), corrected for charitable institutions in Boston, 1860–80. (See discussion, Appendix C, Section 4.)

Col. 21. Estimated average daily attendance, incorporated academies.
Definition: Col. 20 × .9, to the nearest whole number. (See discussion, Appendix C, Section 5.)

Col. 22. Estimated total annual enrollment, incorporated academies.
Definition: Col. 20 × 1.2, to the nearest whole number. (See discussion, Appendix C, Section 5.)

Col. 23. Average length of incorporated academy session, in days.
Source: 1840–49, R; 1850–80, not reported. Estimate = 220 days, the average for years 1840–49.

Col. 24. Estimated total days of incorporated academy attended.
Definition: Col. 21 × Col. 23.

Appendix B

Table A2.4

Col. 25. Number of unincorporated private schools.
Source: R.

Col. 26. Average number of scholars enrolled in unincorporated private schools.
Source: R (the "average number of scholars in unincorporated academies, private schools, etc.").

Col. 27. Estimated average daily attendance, unincorporated private schools.
Definition: Col. 26 × .9, to the nearest whole number. (See discussion, Appendix C, Section 5.)

Col. 28. Estimated total annual enrollment, unincorporated private schools.
Definition: Col. 26 × 1.2, to the nearest whole number. (See discussion, Appendix C, Section 5.)

Col. 29. Average length of unincorporated schools, in days.
Source: 1840–49, R; 1850–80, constant of 164, estimate. (See discussion, Appendix C, Section 6.)

Col. 30. Estimated total days of unincorporated private schools attended.
Definition: Col. 27 × Col. 29.

Table A2.5

Col. 31. Estimated total annual enrollment at all schools.
Definition: Col. 17 + Col. 22 + Col. 28.

Col. 32. Estimated percentage of all children birth to 19 enrolled at school, public and private.
Definition: Col. 31/Col. 1.

Col. 33. Estimated total annual enrollment, less extended common schools.
Definition: For 1840–49, Col. 31 is adjusted by subtracting the estimated number of students attending both private and public schools (dual-attenders), shown in Table C.4, Col. 3. For 1850–80, the figures are the same as for Col. 31.

Col. 34. Percentage of children birth to 19 enrolled at schools, public and private, controlling for extended common schools.
Definition: Col. 33/Col. 1.

Col. 35. Estimated total days of school attended, public and private.
Definition: Col. 14 + Col. 24 + Col. 30.

Col. 36. Estimated average number of days of public or private school attended by all children birth to 19.
Definition: Col. 35/Col. 1

Col. 37. Average percentage of children birth to 19 attending school daily, public and private.

Definition of the variables, Tables A2.1 through A2.5

Definition: For 1840–49:

$$\frac{\text{Col. } 13 + \text{Col. } 21 + [(\text{Col. } 26 - \text{Table C.4, Col. } 3) \times .9]}{\text{Col. } 1}$$

For 1850–79:

$$\frac{\text{Col. } 13 + \text{Col. } 21 + \text{Col. } 27}{\text{Col. } 1}$$

Discussion of adjustments, estimates, and extrapolations made in calculating Tables A2.1 through A2.5, Appendix A

1. The discrepancy between population census figures and school committee returns of school-age children

Problem: Local school committees in Massachusetts were required by law to determine annually the number of school-age children (four to sixteen until 1850, five to fifteen thereafter). All the attendance ratios calculated by Horace Mann and his successors were based on these figures for school-age children. However, no funds were provided to the committees for these annual censuses, and it is apparent that some towns performed this duty casually at best. In 1850, for example, the town of Dracut admitted that it had simply reported the number of school attenders. The Lawrence school committee complained of inaccurate answers from householders, commenting that "in the minds of many of the less informed part of our peculiar community, the census-taker is associated with taxation."[1] The only available check on these suspect figures are the population censuses taken by the federal government and, in mid-decade, by the state. The discrepancy between the annual school committee census figures and the periodic population figures is often substantial, sometimes as great as 10 to 15 percent. Moreover, there is a rural–urban bias in the discrepancy. The school figures for smaller towns more closely approximate the census figures than do those for large towns, which more consistently underestimate their school-age populations and thereby overestimate school enrollment. For example, Table C.1 gives the rates of attendance and enrollment for three urban and five rural towns in Essex County for 1860, using as a denominator first the census figure for children five to fifteen (that is, those above five and not yet fifteen) and then the school census figures for children five to fifteen. Contrary to the usual nineteenth-century practice, committees were told to interpret this directive to include children who were fifteen years old.[2] This makes the upward bias in the enrollment figures even more suspect: additional school-age children in the denominator of the ratio should have depressed the rates of attendance relative to the rates based on census figures. The committees, clearly, found fewer children to count than did the federal census marshals. The tendency for the rural school committees (except Topsfield) to approximate more closely the census figures is evident in Table C.1.

Table C.1. Attendance figures for eight Essex County towns, 1860, comparing U.S. census population figures and town population figures

Town	Population 1860	Average daily attendance, all ages		Total annual enrollment, children 5-15	
		% of children 5-14 (U.S. census)	% of children 5-15 (town committee)	% of children 5-14 (U.S. census)	% of children 5-15 (town committee)
Salem	20,934	60.0	74.2	103.3	111.5
Lawrence	16,114	52.6	61.5	83.4	97.4
Lynn	15,713	79.3	89.7	102.7	116.2
Topsfield	1,250	43.3	59.7	60.4	83.5
Wenham	1,073	76.4	73.0	96.8	92.6
Boxford	1,034	78.0	72.4	98.7	91.6
Hamilton	896	73.8	71.8	100.7	98.0
Lynnfield	883	80.0	85.8	100.6	108.1

Appendix C

Solution: The population censuses are not perfect; like the school censuses, they missed some people. But because federal and state censuses were more strictly regulated, with detailed instructions to appointed and paid marshals, we believe that they are more reliable, and we have used them for the denominator of our attendance ratios throughout, extrapolating arithmetically for interim years. Also, school committee figures were collected only for the arbitrarily defined school-age range (five to fifteen after 1850), even though children under five and over fifteen continued to attend school. Thus a population base of all ages from birth to nineteen is the most appropriate.

2. Converting length of school session, reported in months and days, into days when school was held

Problem: Vinovskis, in his "Trends in Massachusetts Education," used a twenty-eight-day month to calculate the number of days that schools were held, noting that this exaggerated somewhat because there was no deduction for Sundays and holidays. Apparently, Horace Mann used the same figure.[3] However, by the time of Barnas Sears, Mann's successor, the printed school return form explicitly stated that "a month is four school weeks; a half month is ten, eleven, or twelve days, according to the length of the school week, as fixed by custom in the several towns. In most towns a school-month is twenty-two days." Later instructions reduced the school month further, to twenty days.[4]

Solution: We have used the twenty-two-day school month throughout our period, a compromise aimed at estimating as closely as possible the actual average number of days of schooling attended by children in this period. We have therefore multiplied the number of whole months reported by school committees by twenty-two days. Because the part-months, reported in days, often exceeded twenty-two, we assume that towns were reporting the time that had elapsed while schools were open, not the number of days school was held. Thus we have converted the reported additional days into school days according to the ratio 22/28, or .785. For example, a town that reported the average length of public school as four months, fourteen days, was interpreted as meaning ninety-nine days, calculated as follows:

$$4 \text{ months} \times 22 \quad = 88 \text{ school days}$$
$$+ \ 14 \text{ days} \times .785 \quad = \underline{11} \text{ school days}$$
$$99 \text{ school days}$$

Problem: A second substantial problem arises from the manner in which state officials calculated the state average length of public school sessions. Mann and other early data gatherers, though industrious, often took the easy way out when compiling state averages. In this case they took the average length of public school for each county, totaled them, and divided by the number of counties, thus giving equal weight to the most populous and least populous counties. In other words, the reported state average length of public

294

Table C.2. State average length of Massachusetts public school sessions, 1841-2, calculated with weighted and nonweighted county averages

County	Reported aver. length of public schools Months	Days	Converted to days (22-day school month)	Weighted by number of schools Number of public schools	Aggregate days public schools held
Suffolk	11	26	262	124	32,488
Essex	9	1	199	282	56,118
Middlesex	7	27	175	412	72,100
Worcester	5	23	128	554	70,912
Hampshire	6	20	148	208	30,784
Hampden	7	21	171	208	35,568
Franklin	5	25	130	247	32,110
Berkshire	7	3	156	259	40,404
Norfolk	8	9	183	194	35,502
Bristol	6	5	136	280	38,080
Plymouth	7	9	161	250	40,250
Barnstable	6	18	146	151	22,046
Dukes	4	8	94	17	1,598
Nantucket	12	0	264	12	3,168
State total			2,353	3,198	511,128

	Average of county averages	Weighted average
State average (nearest whole day)	2353/14 = 168	511,128/3198 = 160

school session is an average of the county averages. Obviously, this distorts the effective length of school experienced by the schoolchildren in the state. In particular, the Massachusetts state average was artificially inflated in the 1840s by the fact that tiny Nantucket County, with fewer than twenty public schools, reported every year that the county's schools had been held a full twelve months.

Solution: The most accurate state average would weight every school by the number of students attending it. This data, however, is not available. Town by town data is available, but weighting by town would require about three hundred calculations for each year. We have instead recalculated the state average length of public school, weighting each county by the number of public schools in it. This procedure proved manageable and avoided the gross distortions by averaging the county averages equally. The method employed for each year is shown in Table C.2. As Table C.3 demonstrates, the differences

Table C.3. State average length of Massachusetts public school
sessions, 1840-80, comparing weighted and nonweighted averages

Year	Reported (aver. of county averages)	Recalculated (weighted by no. of schools)
1839–40	162	150
1840–1	167	158
1841–2	168	160
1842–3	167	159
1843–4	171	163
1844–5	174	166
1845–6	174	166
1846–7	174	168
1847–8	171	167
1848–9	173	168
1849–50	161	162
1850–1	165	164
1851–2	166	166
1852–3	165	166
1853–4	167	167
1854–5	167	168
1855–6	167	168
1856–7	164	169
1857–8	166	169
1858–9	167	173
1859–60	168	172
1860–1	176	172
1861–2	177	174
1862–3	176	172
1863–4	169	173
1864–5	167	172
1865–6	169	172
1866–7	--	175
1867–8	178	177
1868–9	179	179
1869–70	181	180
1870–1	188	181
1871–2	182	184
1872–3	182	185
1873–4	182	187
1874–5	185	192
1875–6	189	192
1876–7	188	189
1877–8	189	192
1878–9	188	191
1879–80	189	192

between our recalculated averages are substantial, particularly in the early part of our period. For the mid-1860s and 1870s, when the public school sessions had become longer and more uniform, the discrepancy between the two methods of calculation is less. Nonetheless, we have consistently used our weighted county averages.

3. Determining annual enrollments from figures for winter and summer terms

Problem: Until 1870, Massachusetts collected separate figures on winter and summer terms, without asking the total number of different children who attended during the year. Enrollment in the summer term was consistently lower than in the winter, due to the seasonal nature of agricultural work. It is a commonplace of mid-nineteenth-century local reports to insist upon male teachers for the winter session in order to cope with the discipline problems of older boys, who attended only in the winter. However, it is not clear that all the children who attended the summer session also attended during the winter; thus interpreting the winter enrollment to be the total annual enrollment might be inaccurate. It would also not wholly reflect the children who moved in and out of the community during the entire year.

Solution: We have estimated the total number of children taught all year as equal to the winter enrollment plus 25 percent of the summer enrollment. This is essentially a guess about attendance practices and mobility rates. The scant evidence available is erratic. Boxford reported in 1880 that winter enrollment was 115, spring enrollment 109, and fall term 103, whereas the whole number of different pupils taught was 135 – that is, the winter enrollment plus 24 percent of the spring enrollment. In Lynn, in 1847–48 the total annual enrollment equaled the winter enrollment plus 5 percent of the summer enrollment, but in 1854–55 it equaled the winter enrollment plus 32 percent of summer.[5] Our estimate is a compromise among the values yielded from these rare examples in which towns included both types of figures.

The statewide gap between summer and winter enrollments narrowed as the state urbanized. By 1870, therefore, our estimate is probably somewhat high, which is demonstrated by the drop from 52.4 percent enrolled in 1869–70, to 45.6 percent enrolled in 1870–71 when actual annual enrollment rates were reported. Thus our Figure 2.1, a graph of declining total enrollment, dips artificially in 1870 due to the change in reporting categories. The long-range decrease is real but more gradual.

4. Erratic reporting of incorporated academies by Boston

In the 1860s and 1870s Boston sometimes included its Roman Catholic educational institutions among its incorporated academies and sometimes did not. For the missing years we made estimates and revised the enrollment figures upward, which raised the state totals correspondingly. The increased enrollments are real students, but because some of them probably represent a category shift, or possibly children not previously reported, the rise in incorporated academy students during these decades should be interpreted with some caution.

5. Average enrollment figures for private schools

Problem: The printed school returns instructed local officials to report the whole number of pupils in public schools during the year; but for private schools, both incorporated and unincorporated, the forms requested the "average number of scholars attending each," and the detailed instructions said to "give an aggregate of the average numbers for the year in all the Academies and Private Schools, according to the best information obtained." Indeed, the forms from 1850 on label the column for unincorporated schools an "estimated" average.[6] The language of these forms suggests average, not total, enrollment, and common sense supports this interpretation. Private schools submitted no returns; it seems unlikely that the public school committee would know the number of different scholars attending all year, or even the average daily attendance. More likely they estimated the number of scholars normally belonging to a given private school.

What, then, is the relationship between average enrollment and total annual enrollment, on the one hand, or average enrollment and average daily attendance, on the other?

Solution: We infer from all the available evidence that throughout our period the reported figures for private schools are average enrollment, while those for public schools are for total cumulative enrollment, that is, the total number enrolled during the period reported. We estimate that average daily attendance at private schools is 90 percent of average enrollment and that total enrollment is 120 percent of average enrollment.

These ratios are consistent with figures for public schooling in 1880 and 1885, when all three statistics are known. The ratio of average daily attendance to average enrollment is 89 percent in 1880 and 90 percent in 1885. Total enrollment is 120 percent of average enrollment in 1880 and 125 percent in 1885. These two estimates combine to result in a ratio of average daily attendance to total annual enrollment of 75 percent. This relationship is known for public schools throughout our period. The grand mean of public school daily attendance to annual enrollment for the period 1840–80 is 75.9 percent. Although one might argue that the ratio of daily attendance to average enrollment should be higher for schools where tuition was paid (and presumably motivation was thereby greater) and especially at boarding schools (though they were a small portion of the whole number), we know of no way to attach a value to this speculation. Our approach is thus a middling solution, supported by the available data.

6. Counting students who enrolled in both public and private schools

Problem: Many children who were counted as private school students were public school students whose parents were extending their brief public school education at private schools. This was particularly true before 1850, when even the schools expressly labeled as "kept to prolong the common schools" were counted as private. Whether they are designated "public" or "private" is in itself not very important, for in terms of financial support they were a hybrid. However, their status as public or private affects total enrollment estimates: in the private column their students were double counted, and in the public column, after 1850, they were not. In Horace Mann's years, then, more students were being double counted than after his successor, Sears, directed that "when such schools are prolonged by private subscriptions and open as before to all of the children of the district, they are still to be reckoned as Public Schools." Thus, in his Third Report, Mann estimated that there were about twelve thousand students who were "wholly dependent" upon private schooling, even though (according to our estimates) there were over thirty thousand students enrolled at private schools that year. Mann repeated the twelve thousand estimate in later reports, and it may have been close to the truth.[7] But it was stated in a casual way – there were "say, 12,000" students enrolled only in private schools – and we wished to investigate the matter further. Despite the relatively small private sector in schooling by the 1840s, the replacement of parental and private teacher initiative by state initiative in the nineteenth century is an important subject. Moreover, for our statistical series, we needed some means to estimate the length of session of unincorporated private schools after 1850 when actual figures were no longer collected. If the short-term "prolonging" schools were shifted to the public category, the average length of session in the unincorporated private category must have risen, because the remaining schools were longer term.

Solution: No data is available on dual public–private attendance, so we cannot explore the enrollment question directly. But data is available on the numbers of students enrolled in unincorporated private schools held for different lengths. In 1848–49, the last year that the "prolonging" schools were counted as private, the manuscript school returns of 151 towns give information about the average enrollments and length of session for individual unincorporated private schools.[8] We divided the schools into those that met less than three months and those that met three or more months, and we designated these "short-term" and "long-term" private schools. These categories are not synonymous with dual-attenders or private-only-attenders. Some students in the long-term schools may have also attended public school, and, conversely, some who went only a month or two to private school may have had no other schooling, public or private. However, it seems reasonable to assume (and is supported by scattered evidence in the manuscript returns) that the "schools kept to prolong the common schools," all of whose students were double counted, were all in the short-term group; and it is this group we wished to control for, because it is this group that must have accounted for the sharp decline in unincorporated private schools in 1850, when the reporting instructions changed.

Our detailed survey of the 1848–49 returns yielded the following breakdown. Of the 9,470 students in the private schools of the 151 towns providing figures

Appendix C

Table C.4. Calculation of estimated long-term and short-term students, 1848-9 and 1849-50

	Average enrollment, all unincorporated	Long-term students	Short-term students
1848-9	27,583	17,929 (65%)	9,654 (35%)
1849-50	19,534 (decrease of 8,049)	17,929 (92%) (assumed constant)	1,605 (8%) (decrease of 8,049)

for individual schools, 3,297 (or 35 percent) were in schools held less than three months, while 6,173 (or 65 percent) were in schools whose sessions were three months or longer. Using these percentages as estimates for the whole decade, we calculated the breakdown between short-term and long-term private schools prior to Sears's category shift, and we subtracted the short termers (as equivalent to doubly enrolled public–private students) in our adjusted total enrollment estimate (See Appendix A, Table A2.5, Column 33). This is in accord with Horace Mann's reference in 1838 to "those small and short private schools which are kept in the districts between the winter and summer terms, and which comprise, probably, more than one-half of the scholars attending the whole number" of private schools and academies.[9]

In order to estimate the average length of private schools after 1850 (when the prolonging schools were eliminated and the average length no longer reported), we calculated hypothetical 1850 figures based on the following assumptions: we attributed the entire abrupt drop (8,049 students) to the short-term schools, which had previously included the schools kept to prolong the common schools, and we left the enrollment in long-term schools constant from 1849 to 1850. This resulted in estimated figures given in Table C.4. By 1850, if our assumption is correct, the short-term schools enrolled only 8 percent of the total in the category, whereas the long-term schools enrolled 92 percent. To estimate the new average length of session for the whole category after the removal of the prolonged common schools, we assumed that the short-term average length remained at 44 days (an estimate based on the manuscript returns) and that the long-term average length was equal to the average of the previous eleven years, or 175 days. Combining these estimates with the estimated proportion of short-term (8 percent) and long-term (92 percent) enrollments in 1850 yielded an estimated length of session of 164 days for the whole category (see Table C.5). We have used that as our constant estimate after 1850. After 1850 we ceased adjusting for dual enrollment because state policy, with apparent success, was bent on eliminating schools kept by subscription to prolong the common schools, and, by our rough estimates, short-term schools were already less than 10 percent by 1850.

Table C.5. Estimated division of Massachusetts unincoporated private schools into short-term and long-term schools, 1840-50

	Short-term schools				Long-term schools			
Year	Average enrollment less than 3 months	Average attendance short-term	Total enrollment short-term	Average length short-term (days)	Average enrollment 3 months or more	Average attendance long-term	Total enrollment long-term	Average length long-term (days)
	1	2	3	4	5	6	7	8
1839-40	10,022	9,020	12,026	44	18,613	16,752	22,336	192
1840-1	11,128	10,015	13,354	44	20,666	12,599	22,319	184
1841-2	9,948	8,953	11,938	44	18,474	16,627	19,952	198
1842-3	9,314	8,383	11,177	44	17,297	15,567	18,680	166
1843-4	9,047	8,142	10,856	44	16,803	15,123	18,148	193
1844-5	9,367	8,430	11,240	44	17,395	15,656	18,787	187
1845-6	8,511	7,660	10,213	44	15,807	14,226	17,071	173
1846-7	9,375	8,438	11,250	44	17,410	15,669	18,803	187
1847-8	9,526	8,573	11,431	44	17,690	15,921	19,105	164
1848-9	9,654	8,689	11,585	44	17,929	16,136	19,363	182
1849-50	1,605	1,445	1,926	44	17,929	16,136	19,363	173

7. A final note

For those who have made their way through this arcane discussion, we hope that this appendix, in addition to documenting the revised time series presented in Chapter 2, has served as an object lesson in the complexities of nineteenth-century school statistics, which are, unfortunately, often not what they seem to be on the surface. We hope that our effort, far from discouraging those interested in the quantitative dimensions of nineteenth-century education, will prompt similar efforts to construct adjusted time series for other states and other periods.

NOTES

PREFACE

1 The classic example of this point of view is Ellwood P. Cubberley, *Public Education in the United States*, rev. edn. (Boston: Houghton Mifflin, 1934).
2 Some of the key works on the nineteenth century are Michael B. Katz, *The Irony of Early School Reform: Educational Innovation in Mid-Nineteenth Century Massachusetts* (Cambridge, Mass.: Harvard University Press, 1968); Stanley K. Schultz, *The Culture Factory: Boston Public Schooling, 1789–1860* (New York: Oxford University Press, 1973); Carl F. Kaestle, *The Evolution of an Urban School System: New York City, 1750–1850* (Cambridge, Mass.: Harvard University Press, 1973); Samuel Bowles and Herbert Gintis, *Schooling in Capitalist America* (New York: Basic Books, 1976); David B. Tyack, *The One Best System: A History of American Urban Education* (Cambridge, Mass.: Harvard University Press, 1974); and Alexander J. Field, "Educational Reform and Manufacturing Development in Mid-Nineteenth Century Massachusetts" (Ph.D., diss., University of California, Berkeley, 1974).

1. MASSACHUSETTS AS A CASE STUDY

1 See the discussions of education and manufacturing in Chapters 2 and 5.
2 See Alex Inkeles and David H. Smith, *Becoming Modern: Individual Change in Six Developing Countries* (Cambridge, Mass.: Harvard University Press, 1974). For an attempt to apply the modernization concept to American history while eschewing the equation of modernity and progress, see Richard D. Brown, *Modernization: The Transformation of American Life, 1600–1865* (New York: Hill & Wang, 1976).

2. TRENDS IN SCHOOL ATTENDANCE

1 Gordon C. Lee, ed., *Crusade against Ignorance: Thomas Jefferson on Education* (New York: Teachers College Press, 1961), pp. 81–92; Frederick Rudolph, ed., *Essays on Education in the Early Republic* (Cambridge, Mass.: Harvard University Press, 1965), pp. 1–25 and passim.
2 Harlan Updegraff, *Origins of the Moving School in Massachusetts* (New York: Teachers College Bureau of Publications, 1908); Robert F. Seybolt, *Source Studies in American Colonial Education: The Private School*, University of Illinois Bulletin XXIII (Urbana, 1925); Kaestle, *Evolution of an*

Urban School System, chap. 1; Lawrence A. Cremin, *American Education: The Colonial Experience, 1607–1783* (New York: Harper & Row, 1970), chaps. 16 and 17.

3 Massachusetts Board of Education, *Ninth Annual Report of the Board of Education, Together with the Ninth Annual Report of the Secretary of the Board* (Boston, 1846), p. 61. Hereinafter, citations to these reports will be abbreviated according to the pattern MBE, *Ninth Annual Report, 1845* – dated one year prior to the publication date because the report includes the statistical information for the school year 1844–5.

4 Cubberley, *Public Education in the United States*, p. 76

5 Elsie G. Hobson, *Educational Legislation and Administration in the State of New York, 1777–1850* (Chicago: University of Chicago, 1918), pp. 8–9.

6 George H. Martin, *The Evolution of the Massachusetts Public School System* (New York: D. Appleton and Co., 1894), pp. 83–94; John W. Dickinson, "Educational History of Massachusetts," in William T. Davis, ed., *The New England States: Their Constitutional, Judicial, Educational, Commercial, Professional, and Industrial History* (Boston, 1897), IV, 1853; Bernard J. McKearney, "A Study to Determine the Factors Responsible for Connecticut's Loss of Leadership in the Common School Movement between 1820 and 1850" (Ph.D. diss., University of Connecticut, 1966), p. 133; Samuel S. Randall, *History of the Common School System of the State of New York* (New York, 1871), chap. 1; Edward A. Fitzpatrick, *The Educational Views and Influence of DeWitt Clinton* (New York: Teachers College Bureau of Publications, 1911), p. 43; Alice Felt Tyler, *Freedom's Ferment: Phases of American Social History from the Colonial Period to the Outbreak of the Civil War* (Minneapolis: University of Minnesota Press, 1944), p. 235.

7 Albert Fishlow, "The American Common School Revival: Fact or Fancy?" in H. Rosovsky, ed., *Industrialization in Two Systems* (New York: Wiley, 1966), Table 2, p. 49.

8 Maris A. Vinovskis, "Trends in Massachusetts Education, 1826–1860," *History of Education Quarterly* 12 (Winter 1972), 501–29.

9 Fishlow, "Common School Revival," p. 42.

10 Ibid., p. 46.

11 The thesis that state intervention in American schooling was not in the interests of common people is best exemplified by Katz, *Irony of Early School Reform*, and Field, "Educational Reform and Manufacturing Development." E. G. West advances the thesis that state intervention was undesirable and unnecessary in England in his *Education and the Industrial Revolution* (New York: Barnes and Noble, 1975).

12 Fishlow, "Common School Revival," p. 42.

13 West, *Education and the Industrial Revolution*, p. 256.

14 Fishlow, "Common School Revival," p. 47.

15 For calling our attention to these returns we are indebted to James M. Banner, Jr. Fishlow's reference to 1798 figures cites only the U.S. Commissioner of Education, *Report for 1895–96* (Washington, D.C., 1896), I,

221, which states the combined enrollment in the sixteen counties that filed reports, but not the school-age population of the towns involved. We assume, lacking any statement to the contrary, that Fishlow's reference to this figure as an enrollment level is impressionistic.

16 J. Stephen Hopkins, "Schenectady: A Case Study in the Development of Education in New York State from 1780 to 1854" (Honors thesis, Union College, 1965), p. 85.

17 Samuel S. Randall, *The Common School System of the State of New York* (Troy, N.Y., 1851), p. 91.

18 See, for example, MBE, *Fourth Annual Report,* 1840, pp. 35–7.

19 Kaestle, *Evolution of an Urban School System,* p. 51.

20 Enrollment and population figures for 1826 are from Massachusetts, Secretary of the Commonwealth, School Returns for 1826, MS, Massachusetts State Library, Annex, Vault (this repository, located in the Massachusetts State House, Boston, will hereinafter be abbreviated MSL, Annex); for 1840, from *Sixth Census of the United States* (Washington, D.C. 1841), pp. 46–7; for 1850, from *Seventh Census of the United States* (Washington, D.C., 1853).

21 Fishlow, "Common School Revival," p. 48.

22 See Cremin, *American Education: The Colonial Experience,* chap. 15; Edmund Morgan, "The American Revolution as an Intellectual Movement," in Arthur M. Schlesinger, Jr., and Morton White, eds., *Paths of American Thought* (Boston: Houghton Mifflin, 1963), pp. 11–33; and Gordon Wood, *The Creation of the American Republic, 1776–1787* (Chapel Hill: University of North Carolina Press, 1969), chaps. 2 and 3.

23 On literacy in about 1790, see Kenneth Lockridge, *Literacy in Colonial New England: An Enquiry into the Social Context of Literacy in the Early Modern West* (New York, W. W. Norton, 1974), pp. 38–42; for 1840 see Richard M. Bernard and Maris A. Vinovskis, "Beyond Catharine Beecher: Female Education in the Antebellum Period," *Signs* 3 (Summer 1978), 856–69. For the expansion of female education, see Kathryn Kish Sklar, "Public Expenditures for Schooling Girls in Massachusetts Towns, 1750–1800," paper presented at the annual meeting of the History of Education Society, Cambridge, Massachusetts, October 1976; and Thomas Woody, *A History of Women's Education in the United States,* 2 vols. (New York: Science Press, 1929), I, chap. 4.

24 We are indebted to Prof. David Fischer of Brandeis University for sharing with us preliminary results of his research.

25 William Bentley, *The Diary of William Bentley, D.D., Pastor of the East Church, Salem, Mass.,* 4 vols. (Salem: Essex Institute, 1905–14), I, 188, entry for July 28, 1790. In fact, Bentley was not quite up to date. After 1789, girls could attend Boston's grammar schools, although for shorter hours and a shorter school year. See Schultz, *Culture Factory,* p. 15. See also Bentley's entry for July 1, 1794, where he comments after a school inspection, "We saw at no school any girls." Bentley, *Diary,* II, 96. Woody cites a Lynn man who wrote, "In all my school days, which ended in 1801,

I never saw but three females in public schools, and they were there only in the afternoon to learn to write." Woody, *Women's Education,* I, 146.

26 *Salem Register,* May 21, 1827.

27 Updegraff, *Moving School,* p. 172; Norwood M. Cole, "The Origin and Development of Town School Education in Colonial Massachusetts, 1635–1775" (Ed.D. diss., University of Washington, 1957), pp. 457–80, 514.

28 Richard G. Durnin, "New England's Eighteenth-Century Academies: Their Origin and Development to 1850" (Ed.D. diss., University of Pennsylvania, 1968), app. H; MBE, *Sixth Annual Report,* 1841, p. 231; Woody, *Women's Education,* I, chap. 8.

29 MBE, *Tenth Annual Report,* 1846, p. 91.

30 Lawrence School Committee, *Annual Report,* 1854; Chicopee School Committee, *Annual Report,* 1861. Annual school reports from all the towns of Massachusetts are located in MSL, Annex. Some are in manuscript and some printed; the titles vary slightly. Because we consulted several hundred, and because they are all available in a single archive, we have standardized the citations to the form given here.

31 For an earlier attempt to interpret the Massachusetts statistics, Vinovskis, "Trends in Massachusetts Education," 501–29, of which the present section is an extension and revision.

32 Both Vinovskis, in "Trends in Massachusetts Education," and Field, in "Educational Reform and Manufacturing Development," treat the statistics as equivalent.

33 See, for example, Waltham School Committee, School Return, 1849–50, MS, MSL, Annex.

34 For another problem with the denominator – which estimate of school-age population to use – see Appendix C, Section 1.

35 MS School Returns for Newbury, Dracut, and South Hadley, 1849–50, MSL, Annex.

36 MBE, *Thirteenth Annual Report,* 1849, p. 33.

37 For a critique of the historiography of English education based on previous writers' equation of officially approved schools with all schools, see West, *Education and the Industrial Revolution,* pt. 1.

38 MBE, *First Annual Report,* 1837, pp. 48,57.

39 For this process in the private schools of New York City, see Kaestle, *Evolution of an Urban School System,* pp. 91–3. Research is needed on the social origins of New England academy students.

40 Salem, Massachusetts, Mayor, *Annual Report . . . 1842–43* (Salem, 1843), p. 7.

41 See Chapter 4.

42 Cited in Tyack, *The One Best System,* p. 177.

43 By "an ideological dimension," as we argue in Chapter 6 for the case of Lynn, we mean conscious working-class resistance to values promoted in the public schools and perceived as middle class; there is little or no direct evidence for this sort of opposition in America. Opposition to schools dominated by the middle class was more common in early industrial

England. See Brian Simon, *Studies in the History of Education, 1780–1870* (London: Lawrence & Wishart, 1960), chaps. 4 and 5.

44 See Forest Ensign, *Compulsory School Attendance and Child Labor* (Iowa City, Iowa: Athens Press, 1921).

45 Fishlow, "Common School Revival," pp. 42, 65.

46 See, for example, Douglass C. North, *The Economic Growth of the United States, 1790–1860* (Englewood Cliffs, N.J.: Prentice-Hall, 1961), pp. 8–9, 155; and Nathan Rosenberg, *Technology and American Economic Growth* (New York: Harper & Row, 1972), pp. 35–6, 84.

47 The best summary is by Richard Easterlin, in Lance E. Davis et al., *American Economic Growth: An Economists' History of the United States* (New York: Harper & Row, 1972) pp. 152–5. Easterlin ignores the subject of work discipline and social control, which is the central theme of Field, "Educational Reform and Manufacturing Development."

48 See North, *Economic Growth*, chap. 7; and Robert B. Zevin, *The Growth of Manufacturing in Early Nineteenth Century New England* (New York: Arno Press, 1975).

49 Field, "Educational Reform and Manufacturing Development," chap. 8.

50 Rosenberg, *Technology*, chap. 3.

51 See Maris A. Vinovskis, "Horace Mann on the Economic Productivity of Education," *New England Quarterly* 43 (December 1970), 550–71.

52 See Chapter 5; and Carl F. Kaestle, "Social Change, Discipline, and the Common School in Early Nineteenth-Century America," *Journal of Interdisciplinary History* 9 (Summer 1978), 1–17.

53 Bowles and Gintis, *Schooling in Capitalist America*, chap. 6; Field, "Educational Reform and Manufacturing Development," chap. 2. Earlier statements of the same connection in English history include Edward P. Thompson, "Time, Work Discipline and Industrial Capitalism," *Past and Present* 38 (1967), 56–97; and Sidney Pollard, "Factory Discipline in the Industrial Revolution," *Economic History Review* 16 (1963), 254–71.

54 In addition to Kaestle, "Social Change, Discipline, and the Common School," see Barbara Finkelstein, "In Fear of Childhood: Relationships between Parents and Teachers in Popular Primary Schools in the Nineteenth Century," *History of Childhood Quarterly* 3 (Winter 1976), 321–35; and Anne S. MacLeod, *A Moral Tale: Children's Fiction and American Culture, 1820–1860* (Hamden, Conn.: Archon Press, 1975).

55 Inkeles and Smith, *Becoming Modern*, chap. 11. Increased productivity through on-the-job learning may have involved skills as well as discipline, of course, despite the general reduction in skill requirements. See Paul A. David, "The 'Horndal Effect' in Lowell, 1834–56: A Short-Run Learning Curve for Integrated Cotton Textile Mills," *Explorations in Economic History* 10 (Winter 1973), 131–50; and Kenneth J. Arrow, "The Economic Implications of Learning by Doing," *Review of Economic Studies* 29 (June 1962), 155–73.

56 The case for manufacturers' intense involvement is made in Field, "Educational Reform and Manufacturing Development," pp. 253–60; but see

our Chapter 8. Our research in the writings and papers of prominent Massachusetts manufacturers does not support the notion that public schooling was one of their prime concerns.

57 Easterlin, in Davis et al., *American Economic Growth*, p. 155. On educational expansion in the later nineteenth century, see John K. Folger and Charles B. Nam, *Education of the American Population* (Washington D.C.: Bureau of the Census, 1967); Albert Fishlow, "Levels of Nineteenth-Century American Investment in Education," *Journal of Economic History* 26 (December 1966), 418–36; and Lewis C. Solmon, "Estimates of the Costs of Schooling in 1880 and 1890," *Explorations in Economic History*, 2nd ser. 7, no. 4, supplement (1970), 531–81.

3. FROM APRON STRINGS TO ABCs

1 On Puritan education, see Cremin, *American Education: The Colonial Experience;* Bernard Bailyn, *Education in the Forming of American Society* (Chapel Hill: University of North Carolina Press, 1960); James Axtell, *The School upon a Hill: Education and Society in Colonial New England* (New Haven: Yale University Press, 1974); and Edmund S. Morgan, *The Puritan Family: Religion and Domestic Relations in Seventeenth-Century New England*, rev. edn. (New York: Harper & Row 1966).

2 Cremin, *American Education: The Colonial Experience*, p. 181.

3 Geraldine Joanne Murphy, "Massachusetts Bay Colony: The Role of Government in Education" (Ph.D. diss., Radcliffe College, 1960).

4 Lockridge, *Literacy in Colonial New England*.

5 Quoted in Robert H. Bremner et al., eds., *Children and Youth in America: A Documentary History* (Cambridge, Mass.: Harvard University Press, I, 1970) 41.

6 For useful essays on this issue, see Egil Johansson, ed., *Literacy and Society in a Historical Perspective: A Conference Report* (Umea, Sweden: Umea University, 1973).

7 Lockridge, *Literacy in Colonial New England*, p. 7.

8 The law is given in Bremner et al., eds., *Children and Youth in America*, I, 40.

9 Cotton Mather, *Corderius Americanus* . . . (Boston, 1708), quoted in Wilson Smith, ed., *Theories of Education in Early America, 1655–1819* (Indianapolis: Bobbs-Merrill, 1973), p. 27.

10 John Demos, "The American Family in Past Time," *American Scholar* 43 (Summer 1974), 428.

11 For some examples of the precocity of children in colonial America, see Alice Morse Earle, *Child Life in Colonial Days* (New York: Macmillan, 1922), pp. 176–95.

12 John Locke, *Some Thoughts concerning Education*, abridged and edited by F. W. Garforth (Woodbury, N.Y.: Barron's, 1964), p. 186. On Locke's influence in America, see Cremin, *American Education: The Colonial Experience*, pp. 361–5, 419–23. On the problems of using child-rearing

guides as indicators of behavior, see Jay Mechling, "Advice to Historians on Advice to Mothers," *Journal of Social History* 9 (Fall 1975), 44–63. In the case of Locke, however, specific references to his work are found in some of the colonial diaries and letters that discuss child rearing. For example, Mrs. Pinckney writes to a friend:

Shall I give you the trouble my dear Madam to buy my son a new toy (a description of which I inclose) to teach him according to Mr. Locke's method (which I have carefully studied) to play himself into learning. Mr. Pinckney (his father) himself has been contriving a sett of toys to teach him letters by the time he can speak. You perceive we begin betimes for he is not yet four months old.

Quoted in Earle, *Child Life in Colonial Days*, p. 182. Some middle- and upper-class parents, it seems, did read and follow Locke's suggestions.

13 Oscar Handlin and Mary F. Handlin, eds., *The Popular Sources of Political Authority: Documents on the Massachusetts Constitution of 1780* (Cambridge, Mass.: Harvard University Press, 1966), p. 467. Yet religion remained a very important factor in encouraging education in antebellum Massachusetts. Many of the early school reformers were motivated as much by religious and moral considerations as by social and economic factors.

14 See Charles E. Bidwell, "The Moral Significance of the Common School: A Sociological Study of Local Patterns of School Control and Moral Education in Massachusetts and New York, 1837–1840," *History of Education Quarterly* 6 (Fall 1966), 50–91; and Raymond B. Culver, *Horace Mann and Religion in the Massachusetts Public Schools* (New Haven: Yale University Press, 1929).

15 See Peter G. Slater, "Views of Children and of Child Rearing during the Early National Period: A Study in the New England Intellect" (Ph.D. diss., University of California, Berkeley, 1970). See also Bernard Wishy, *The Child and the Republic* (Philadelphia: University of Pennsylvania Press, 1968); and Anne S. Kuhn, *The Mother's Role in Childhood Education: New England Concepts, 1830–1860* (New Haven: Yale University Press, 1947).

16 Joseph M. Wightman, *Annals of the Boston Primary School Committee From Its First Establishment in 1818 to Its Dissolution in 1855* (Boston, 1860), pp. 25–6. For a good discussion of this controversy, see Schultz, *Culture Factory*, pp. 30–44.

17 Wightman, *Annals of the Boston Primary School Committee*, p. 28.

18 Boston School Committee, *Report of the School Committee of the City of Boston on the State of the Schools, May 1826* (Boston, 1826).

19 Ibid. The estimate is based on the Boston School Committee's figure for the number of children under four years of age in private schools and on an estimate of the number of children under four years of age from the 1820 and 1830 federal censuses.

20 Our discussion of infant schools draws heavily on an earlier essay by Dean May and Maris A. Vinovskis, " 'A Ray of Millenial Light': Early Educa-

tion and Social Reform in the Infant School Movement in Massachusetts, 1826–1840,'' in Tamara K. Hareven, ed., *Family and Kin in American Urban Communities, 1800–1940* (New York: New Viewpoints, 1976), pp. 62–9. We have also greatly benefited from John W. Jenkins, ''Infant Schools and the Development of Public Primary Schools in Selected American Cities before the Civil War'' (Ph.D. diss., University of Wisconsin, 1978).

21 *Boston Recorder and Scriptural Transcript,* July 9, 1829.
22 Ibid.
23 *Ladies' Magazine* 2 (February 1829), 89–90.
24 On the teaching profession during the antebellum years, see Paul H. Mattingly, *The Classless Profession: American Schoolmen of the Nineteenth Century* (New York: New York University Press, 1975); and Richard Bernard and Maris A. Vinovskis, ''The Female School Teacher in Ante-Bellum Massachusetts,'' *Journal of Social History* 10 (Spring 1977), 332–45.
25 The analysis of the Concord school register is discussed in May and Vinovskis, '' 'A Ray of Millenial Light.' '' The Worcester school registers for the 1830s are located at the American Antiquarian Society, Worcester, Mass. We have analyzed the age distributions of children in the Worcester public schools during those years.
26 When Mann first inquired of school committees the number of children under four years of age in public school in 1840, some of the committees were unable to provide the information for that year because they had not collected it. Unfortunately, when Mann reported the number of children under four in his published report, he did not make the distinction between those towns that had no children under four going to school and those that simply had not been able to report the information. Therefore, calculating from Mann's annual report the percentage of children under four who were attending school in 1840 underestimates that figure. An examination of the manuscript local returns for 1840 indicates that the actual figure for children under four in public school in 1840 would be about 13 percent rather than the 10 percent derived from Mann's published annual report for that year. Most local school committees remedied their lack of information on this issue by 1841, so that Mann's reports of the number of children under four are very good estimates after 1840.
27 Quoted in David Salmon and Winifred Hindshaw, *Infant Schools: Their History and Theory* (London, 1904), p. 27.
28 See Kuhn, *The Mother's Role in Childhood Education;* and Wishy, *The Child and the Republic.*
29 On woman's work see Nancy F. Cott, *The Bonds of Womanhood: "Woman's Sphere" in New England, 1780–1835* (New Haven: Yale University Press, 1976), chap. 1. See ibid., chap. 2, for an interesting discussion of the functions of the domesticity ideal.
30 Quoted in Gerald Lee Gutek, *Pestalozzi and Education* (New York: Ran-

dom House, 1968), p. 86. See also Will S. Monroe, *History of the Pestaloz-zian Movement in the United States* (Syracuse, N.Y., 1907).

31 For example, see William Woodbridge, "Infant Education," *American Annals of Education* 1 (August 1830), 355–6.

32 "Suggestions to Parents," *American Journal of Education* 2 (March 1827), 166; "Sketches of Hofwyl," *American Annals of Education and Instruction for the Year 1831 and Part of 1830* 1 (March 1831), 89; Dr. J. V. C. Smith, "The Infantile Frame," *American Annals of Education and Instruction for the Year 1834* 4 (February 1834), 75.

33 Amariah Brigham, *Remarks on the Influence of Mental Cultivation and Mental Excitement upon Health*, 2nd edn. (Boston, 1833), pp. 15, 55.

34 "Mental Precocity," extracts from the *London Christian Observer*, in *American Annals of Education and Instruction for the Year 1833* 3 (June 1833), 269; Dr. Samuel B. Woodward to Horace Mann, December 7, 1840, in MBE, *Fourth Annual Report*, 1840, app.

35 May and Vinovskis, " 'A Ray of Millenial Light.' "

36 Lydia Sigourney, *Letters to Mothers* (Hartford, 1838), p. 147.

37 Heman Humphrey, *Domestic Education* (Amherst, 1840), pp. 11–12. For reactions against early education in the domestic literature, see Kuhn, *Mother's Role in Childhood Education*, pp. 98–119.

38 Humphrey, *Domestic Education*, pp. 71–3.

39 MBE, *Fourth Annual Report*, 1840, p. 370

40 Ibid., p. 322.

41 MBE, *Sixteenth Annual Report*, 1852, pp. 36–7.

42 MBE, *Third Annual Report*, 1839, p. 38.

43 Palmer School Committee, *Annual Report*, 1841, MSL, Annex.

44 The posited relationship between early education and insanity was a com-plicated one. Many of the physicians and superintendents who discussed that relationship saw early education as a predisposing factor rather than an immediate cause of insanity. Yet it is interesting to note that, of the 6,427 patients admitted at the Worcester State Hospital from 1833 to 1850, only 29 cases were listed as caused by excessive intellectual activity. These figures are some preliminary results of a large-scale study of patient records at four insane asylums in antebellum America by Barbara Rosenkrantz and Maris Vinovskis. Two excellent surveys of the beliefs of hospital superin-tendents and physicians on the causes of insanity in nineteenth-century America, are Norman Dain, *Concepts of Insanity in the United States, 1789–1865* (New Brunswick, N.J.: Rutgers University Press, 1964); and Gerald N. Grob, *Mental Institutions in America: Social Policy to 1875* (New York: Free Press, 1973).

45 MBE, *Twenty-second Annual Report*, 1858, pp. 93–4.

46 Ibid., pp. 57–8; abstract of Stoneham annual report in ibid., p. 116; Spring-field School Committee, *Annual Report*, 1861; Salem School Committee, *Annual Report*, 1880; MBE, *Thirty-seventh Annual Report*, 1874, pp. 66–7.

47 Lynn School Committee, *Annual Report*, 1880, p. 35.

48 For a more detailed analysis, which treats immigration level, industrial and commercial status, community wealth, and other factors as independent variables in determining a community's enrollment of young children, see Carl F. Kaestle and Maris A. Vinovskis, "From Apron Strings to ABC's: Parents, Children, and Schooling in Nineteenth-Century Massachusetts," in Sarane Boocock and John Demos, eds., *Turning Points: Historical and Sociological Essays on the Family* (Chicago: *American Journal of Sociology* 84, supplement, 1978–9), pp. 539–80, of which this chapter is an abridgment and a revision. For a discussion of the participation of women in the labor force in late nineteenth-century Massachusetts, see Karen Oppenheim Mason, Maris A. Vinovskis, and Tamara K. Hareven, "Women's Work and the Life Course in Essex County, Massachusetts, 1880," in Tamara K. Hareven, ed., *Transitions: The Family and the Life Course in Historical Perspective* (New York: Academic Press, 1978), pp. 187–216.
49 Carl F. Kaestle and Maris A. Vinovskis, "From Fireside to Factory: School Entry and School Leaving in Nineteenth-Century Massachusetts," in Hareven, ed., *Family Transitions and the Life Course in Historical Perspective*, pp. 135–86.
50 On the European background of kindergartens, see Salmon and Hindshaw, *Infant Schools*, pp. 92–125; Ilse Forest, *Preschool Education: A Historical and Critical Study* (New York: Macmillan, 1927).
51 On early kindergartens in America, see Ruth M. Baylor, *Elizabeth Palmer Peabody: Kindergarten Pioneer* (Philadelphia: University of Pennsylvania Press, 1965), pp. 23–40.
52 On the role of Elizabeth Peabody, see Baylor, *Elizabeth Palmer Peabody*; Mary J. Garland, "Elizabeth P. Peabody, 1804–94," in *Pioneers of the Kindergarten in America* (New York, 1924), pp. 19–25; Lucy Wheelock, "Miss Peabody as I Knew Her," in ibid., pp. 26–38.
53 Elizabeth P. Peabody, *Guide to the Kindergarten and Intermediate Class* (New York, 1877), p. 71.
54 For a detailed discussion of kindergartens in Massachusetts, see Marvin Lazerson, *Origins of the Urban School: Public Education in Massachusetts, 1870–1915* (Cambridge, Mass.: Harvard University Press, 1971), pp. 36–73. See also Robert Tank, "A Comparative Study of Educational Reform during the Progressive Era: The Establishment and Growth of Kindergartens in the Public Schools of Massachusetts and Michigan, 1888–1915" (Seminar paper, University of Michigan, April 1976). We are indebted to Robert Tank for sharing with us his materials on the kindergarten movement.

4. THE PROSPECTS OF YOUTH

1 See John Modell, Frank Furstenberg, and Theodore Hershberg, "Social Change and Transitions to Adulthood in Historical Perspective," *Journal of Family History* 1 (Autumn 1976), 7–33.

2 Kaestle and Vinovskis, "From Fireside to Factory."
3 Previous studies of nineteenth-century school attendance at the individual level include Selwyn K. Troen, "Popular Education in Nineteenth-Century St. Louis," *History of Education Quarterly* 13 (Spring 1973), 23–41; Michael B. Katz, "Who Went to School?" ibid., 12 (Fall 1972), 432–54; and Frank Denton and Peter George, "Socio-Economic Influences on School Attendance: A Study of a Canadian County in 1871," ibid., 14 (Summer 1974), 223–32. The latter article prompted a debate, found in Michael B. Katz, "Reply," ibid., 233–4; Frank Denton and Peter George, "Socio-Economic influences on School Attendance: A Response to Professor Katz," ibid. 14 (Fall 1974), 367–9; and Daniel H. Calhoun, "Letter to the Editor," ibid. 14 (Winter 1974), 545–6. See also Lee Soltow and Edward Stevens, "Economic Aspects of School Participation in the United States," *Journal of Interdisciplinary History* 8 (Autumn 1977), 221–44; and Ian E. Davey, "Educational Reform and the Working Class: School Attendance in Hamilton, Ontario, 1851–1891" (Ph.D. diss., University of Toronto, 1975).
4 Because the various studies to be made of this population all deal with family history, we omitted persons in institutions and in boarding houses (defined as households with thirteen or more unrelated members).
5 See Marie L. Ahearn, "The Rhetoric of Work and Vocation in Some Popular Northern Writings before 1860" (Ph.D. diss., Brown University, 1965); and Rex Burns, *Success in America: The Yeoman Dream and the Industrial Revolution* (Amherst: University of Massachusetts Press, 1976).
6 Burns, *Yeoman Dream,* chap. 3; Stephan Thernstrom, *Poverty and Progress: Social Mobility in a Nineteenth Century City* (Cambridge, Mass.: Harvard University Press, 1964), pp. 155–7.
7 On labor in the life of male teenagers see Joseph F. Kett, *Rites of Passage: Adolescence in America, 1790 to the Present* (New York: Basic Books, 1976), pp. 144–6. On the lack of emphasis on formal schooling for success, see Irwin G. Wyllie, *The Self-Made Man in America: The Myth of Rags to Riches* (New Brunswick, N.J.: Rutgers University Press, 1954). On the nonvocational character of secondary education up to 1880, see Edward A. Krug, *The Shaping of the American High School, 1880–1920* (Madison: University of Wisconsin Press, 1964), pp. 169–71; Tyack, *The One Best System,* pp. 73–6; and Bernard E. McClellan, "Education for an Industrial Society: Changing Concepts of the Role of Public Schooling, 1865–1900" (Ph.D. diss., Northwestern University, 1972), chap. 1.
8 Massachusetts Laws, 1836, chap. 245; 1838, chap. 107; 1842, chap. 60; 1850, chap. 294; 1852, chap. 240.
9 Ensign, *Compulsory School Attendance and Child Labor;* John W. Perrin, *The History of Compulsory Education in New England* (Meadville, Pennsylvania, 1876). For contemporary documents on this issue, see especially Henry K. Oliver, *Report of Henry K. Oliver, Deputy State Constable, Especially Appointed to Enforce the Laws Regulating the Employment of Children . . .* (Boston, 1869).

10 Massachusetts Laws, 1867, chap. 285; 1873, chap. 262; 1873, chap. 279; 1874, chap. 233; 1876, chap. 52; 1876, chap. 257.

11 Massachusetts Bureau of the Statistics of Labor, *Annual Report, 1870* (Massachusetts General Court, Senate Document No. 120, Boston, 1870), pp. 135–40.

12 Quoted in Perrin, *The History of Compulsory Education in New England,* p. 58.

13 George E. McNeill, *Factory Children: Report on the Schooling and Hours of Labor of Children Employed in the Manufacturing and Mechanical Establishments of Massachusetts* (Boston, 1875), p. 4. This report is Massachusetts Senate Document No. 50 for 1875.

14 Wenham School Committee, *Annual Report,* 1880.

15 Lawrence School Committee, *Annual Report,* 1880, p. 39; Massachusetts Bureau of the Statistics of Labor, *Annual Report,* 1883.

16 Lynn School Committee, *Annual Report,* 1880, p. 29.

17 See Kett, *Rites of Passage,* p. 144 and passim, on the relatively short period of dependency in the second half of the nineteenth century. The census schedules for 1860 and 1880 did not ask identical questions on the occupations of individuals. In 1860 the census asked: "Profession, occupation, or trade of each person, male or female, over 15 years of age." In 1880 the census asked of each person ten years of age and more: "Profession, occupation, or trade of each person, male or female; in addition the number of months this person has been unemployed during the census year."

Some of the census enumerators in 1860 did record the ages of working children between the ages of ten and fifteen, whereas others did not do so. Therefore, one should be very cautious about trying to compare the rates of labor force participation for children ages ten to fifteen between 1860 and 1880.

Instructions for these censuses can be found in C. D. Wright and W. C. Hunt, *History and Growth of the United States Census* (Washington, D.C., 1900). For useful discussions about the meaning of questions relating to labor force participation in this period, see Solomon Fabricant, "The Changing Industrial Distribution of Gainful Workers: Comments on the Decennial Statistics, 1820–1940," *Studies in Income and Wealth* 11 (1949), 3–45; and P. K. Whelpton, "Occupational Groups in the United States, 1820–1920," *Journal of the American Statistical Association* 21 no. 155 (1926), 335–43.

18 *The Census of Massachusetts: 1885* (Boston, 1888), vol. II.

19 MBE, *Forty-fourth Annual Report,* 1880; Salem School Committee, *Annual Report,* 1880, p. 95.

20 We also eliminated the few children whose fathers' occupations were not given. Constructing an occupational category based on so few cases would have created statistical problems.

21 We provide a brief explanation of multiple regression analysis in Chapter 5. For an excellent introduction to multiple classification analysis, see

Frank M. Andrews, J. N. Morgan, John A. Sonquist, and Laura Klem, *Multiple Classification Analysis*, 2nd edn. (Ann Arbor, Mich.: Institute for Social Research, 1973). Demographers and sociologists have long used MCA. For example, see Otis Dudley Duncan, "Residential Areas and Differential Fertility," *Eugenics Quarterly* 11 (1964–5), 82–9; and, more recently, James A. Sweet, *Women in the Labor Force* (New York: Academic Press, 1973). Stepwise MCA may be used when a group of predictors is logically prior to others; see, for example, Allan Schnaiberg, "The Modernizing Impact of Urbanization: A Causal Analysis," *Economic Development and Cultural Change* 20 (October 1971), 80–104.

22 For a detailed discussion of the interaction problem, see John A. Sonquist, *Multivariate Model Building: The Validation of a Research Strategy* (Ann Arbor: Survey Research Center, University of Michigan, 1970).

23 The categories employed for each occupation are based on Stuart Blumin's classification, and we are indebted to Professor Blumin for making it available to us. See Stuart M. Blumin, "Rip Van Winkle's Grandchildren: Family and Household in the Hudson Valley, 1800–1860," *Journal of Urban History* 1 (May 1975), 293–315. We have aggregated the professionals and semiprofessionals because the latter category alone was too small. Similarly, we have combined skilled workers, a small category, with the lower-level white-collar workers. The number of families in these groups was not sufficient for separate treatment in an analysis like ours. Also, the attendance patterns of these two small groups were not as different as one might have suspected.

The entire issue of categorizing nineteenth-century occupations by using census data is very complex. For a good introduction to these issues, see Michael B. Katz. *The People of Hamilton, Canada West: Family and Class in a Mid-Nineteenth-Century City* (Cambridge, Mass.: Harvard University Press, 1976), chaps. 3 and 4. See also Stuart Blumin, "The Historical Study of Vertical Mobility," *Historical Methods Newsletter* 1 (September 1968), 1–13; Clyde Griffen, "Occupational Mobility in Nineteenth-Century America: Problems and Possibilities," *Journal of Social History* 5 (Spring 1972), 310–30; Michael B. Katz, "Occupational Classification in History," *Journal of Interdisciplinary History* 3 (Summer 1972), 63–8; Theodore Hershberg et al., "Occupation and Ethnicity in Five Nineteenth-Century Cities: A Collaborative Inquiry," *Historical Methods Newsletter* 7 (June 1974), 174–216.

24 Michael B. Katz, "The Origins of Public Education: A Reassessment," *History of Education Quarterly* 16 (Winter 1976), 397–9. See also Katz's *Irony of Early School Reform*, pp. 91–3.

25 Our effort to develop a work/consumption ratio for the nineteenth-century family was influenced by the use of such variables in contemporary sociological studies. For example, see Sweet, *Women in the Labor Force;* and James N. Morgan, *Five Thousand American Families: Patterns and Economic Progress* (Ann Arbor: University of Michigan, 1974), vols. I and II. For the numerator of the family work/consumption ratio we calculated

the number of equivalent male adult workers in the family. Relying on very crude estimates based on various studies of wage earners for the late nineteenth century, we used the following weights:

Age	Male	Female
10	.1	.1
11	.2	.2
12	.3	.3
13	.4	.4
14	.5	.5
15	.6	.6
16	.7	.6
17	.8	.6
18	.9	.6
19–99	1.0	.6

The weights used in the denominator of our work/consumption index were derived after examining the consumption figures presented by Peter Lindert in his *Scarcity and Fertility in America* (Princeton: Princeton University Press, 1978). Lindert assembled information on consumption patterns from a variety of late nineteenth- and early twentieth-century surveys of family expenditures. The weights used were .55 for children ages birth to four, .65 for children ages five to nine, .75 for children ages ten to fourteen, and 1.0 for everyone fifteen and above.

Admittedly, our weights for both workers and consumers are very crude. Though some of these weights may be improved when more detailed studies of nineteenth-century family budgets become available to us, any weighting scheme that provides a set of weights distinguished only by sex and age for occupations and consumption patterns must of necessity be very crude. However, we feel that these weights are reasonable and useful approximations that do provide additional data on a family's economic situation, beyond the occupation of the head and/or the total number of members in that family.

The definition of our work/consumption index is identical to that used in Mason, Vinovskis, and Hareven, "Women's Work." However, because the particular computer program that we were using (OSIRIS) truncated the results of computer ratios to integers, it was necessary to multiply our work/consumption index by one hundred in order to have our results accurate to at least two decimal places. Furthermore, because the OSIRIS MCA program does not allow interval independent variables, it was necessary for us to categorize our work/consumption index. As a result, though the work/consumption index in this book is identical to the one utilized in the Mason, Vinovskis, and Hareven essay, it appears to be slightly different.

26 Second- and third-generation status was determined by the subject's father if present, mother if not. Our analysis contrasts with those of recent scholars who have viewed ethnicity as subordinate to, or as an aspect of,

economic circumstances. Katz, in "Who Went to School," p. 444, states, "It was the poverty that accompanied laboring status and not Catholicism or Irish birth that did most to keep children out of school." Troen, in "Popular Education in St. Louis," p. 33, concludes that "class became the most important parameter." Soltow and Stevens, in "Economic Aspects of School Participation," p. 241, conclude that wealth was the most important determinant, and that ethnicity "should not be overemphasized."
27 Andrews, *Multiple Classification Analysis,* p. 48.

5. FROM ONE ROOM TO ONE SYSTEM

1 William Torrey Harris, "Elementary Education," in Nicholas M. Butler, ed., *Education in the United States* (Albany, N.Y., 1900), pp. 46–7. Representative documents among the mountains of literature on rural schools include Horace Mann, MBE, *Tenth Annual Report,* 1846, pp. 129–32; Barnas Sears, MBE, *Thirteenth Annual Report,* 1849, pp. 56–7; Ellwood Cubberley, *Rural Life and Education* (Cambridge, Mass.: Riverside Press, 1914); National Education Association, *Report of the Committee of Twelve on Rural Schools* (Chicago, 1897). Attempts by historians to analyze the rural school "problem" are few; see David B. Tyack, "The Tribe and the Common School: Community Control in Rural Education," *American Quarterly* 14 (March 1972), 3–19; Ann Keppel, "The Myth of Agrarianism in Rural Educational Reform, 1890–1914," *History of Education Quarterly* 2 (1962), 100–12. A survey of the historical and the contemporary problem, from a rural point of view, is now available in Jonathan B. Sher, ed., *Education in Rural America: A Reassessment of Conventional Wisdom* (Boulder, Colo.: Westview Press, 1977).
2 For the antebellum period, see Katz, *Irony of Early School Reform;* Kaestle, *Evolution of an Urban School System;* Schultz, *Culture Factory;* Michael B. Katz, *Class, Bureaucracy, and Schools: The Illusion of Educational Change in America,* 2nd edn. (New York: Praeger, 1975); Bowles and Gintis, *Schooling in Capitalist America,* chap. 6; and Field, "Educational Reform and Manufacturing Development." For more optimistic assessments, see Selwyn K. Troen, *The Public and the Schools: Shaping the St. Louis System, 1838–1920* (Columbia: University of Missouri Press, 1975); and Diane Ravitch, *The Great School Wars: New York City, 1805–1973* (New York: Basic Books, 1974).
3 Katz, *Irony of Early School Reform,* p. 218.
4 Schultz, *Culture Factory,* p. ix.
5 Kaestle, *Evolution of an Urban System,* p. 190.
6 Tyack, *The One Best System,* pp. 5–6. See his caveats that follow this definition. He does not see urbanization as an abrupt or strictly linear process.
7 Ibid., p. 6.
8 See Howard Becker, *Through Social Values to Social Interpretation* (Durham, N.C.: Duke University Press, 1950); Philip H. Hauser, "Observations

on the Urban–Folk and Urban–Rural Dichotomies as Forms of Western Ethnocentrism,'' in Philip H. Hauser and Leo F. Schnore, eds., *The Study of Urbanization* (New York: Wiley, 1965), pp. 503–17; R. E. Pahl, ''The Rural–Urban Continuum,'' *Sociologia Ruralis* 6 (1966), 299–329; Joseph R. Gusfield, ''Tradition and Modernity: Misplaced Polarities in the Study of Social Change,'' *American Journal of Sociology* 72 (January 1967), 351–62.

Helpful discussions of scholarship on urbanization are found in Leonard Reissman, *The Urban Process: Cities in Industrial Societies* (New York: Free Press of Glencoe, 1964); and in Charles Tilly, ed., *An Urban World* (Boston: Little, Brown, 1974). Seminal essays by members of the Chicago School are reprinted in Richard Sennett, ed., *Classic Essays on the Culture of Cities* (New York: Appleton-Century-Crofts, 1969).

9 On Wirth, see Hauser, ''Ethnocentrism,'' p. 506; Pitirim Sorokin and Carle C. Zimmerman, *Principles of Rural–Urban Sociology* (New York: Holt, Rinehart and Winston 1959), p. 14; Otis D. Duncan, ''Community Size and the Rural–Urban Continuum,'' in Otis D. Duncan and Albert J. Reiss, eds., *Cities and Society*, (Glencoe, Ill.: Free Press, 1957), p. 35; and Pahl, ''Rural–Urban Continuum,'' p. 299.

10 Hauser, ''Ethnocentrism,'' pp. 508–9, citing Otis D. Duncan and Albert J. Reiss, *Social Characteristics of Urban and Rural Communities, 1950* (New York: John Wiley, 1956).

11 Duncan, ''Community Size,'' p. 40.

12 Richard Dewey, ''The Rural–Urban Continuum: Real but Relatively Unimportant,'' *American Journal of Sociology* 66 (July 1960), 65.

13 Hope Tisdale [Eldridge], ''The Process of Urbanization,'' *Social Forces* 20 (March 1942), 312.

14 Dewey, ''Rural–Urban Continuun,'' pp. 63–5.

15 Philip M. Hauser, ''Urbanization: An Overview,'' in Hauser and Schnore, eds., *The Study of Urbanization*, pp. 19, 25.

16 G. Lenski, *The Religious Factor*, (New York: Doubleday Anchor, 1963), p. 328; Bert F. Hoselitz, ''A Survey of the Literature on Urbanization in India,'' in Roy Turner, ed., *India's Urban Future* (Berkeley, 1962); Herbert J. Gans, ''Urbanism and Suburbanism as Ways of Life,'' in Arnold M. Rose, ed., *Human Behavior and Social Processes* (Boston: Houghton Mifflin, 1962).

17 Claude S. Fischer, ''On Urban Alienation and Anomie: Powerlessness and Social Isolation,'' *American Sociological Review* 38 (June 1973), 311–26; Albert J. Reiss, Jr., ''Rural–Urban and Status Differences in Interpersonal Contacts,'' *American Journal of Sociology* 65 (1959), 182–95.

18 Oscar Lewis, ''Further Observations on the Folk–Urban Continuum, and Urbanization with Special Reference to Mexico City,'' in Hauser and Schnore, eds., *The Study of Urbanization*, p. 495.

19 Gideon Sjoberg, ''The Rural–Urban Dimension in Preindustrial, Transitional, and Industrial Societies,'' in Robert E. L. Faris, ed., *Handbook of Modern Sociology* (Chicago, 1964), pp. 127–59.

20 Glenn V. Fuguitt, "The City and Countryside," *Rural Sociology* 28 (September 1963), 246–61.
21 For example, see Daniel Lerner, *The Passing of Traditional Society: Modernizing the Middle East* (Glencoe, Ill.: Free Press, 1958); and, more recently, Allan Schnaiberg, "The Modernizing Impact of Urbanization."
22 Duncan, "Community Size," p. 37.
23 "Urbanization" here refers to the increase in urban population as a proportion of the total population. On the complexities of other definitions, see Jeffrey G. Williamson, "Antebellum Urbanization in the American Northeast," *Journal of Economic History* 25 (December 1965), 595–6; and Eric E. Lampard, "The Evolving System of Cities in the United States: Urbanization and Economic Development," in Harvey S. Perloff and Lowdon Wingo, Jr., eds., *Issues in Urban Economics* (Baltimore: Johns Hopkins Press, 1968), pp. 110–11.
24 George R. Taylor, "American Urban Growth Preceding the Railway Age," *Journal of Economic History* 27 (September 1967), 308–39. See also Richard D. Brown, "The Emergence of Urban Society in Rural Massachusetts, 1760–1820," *Journal of American History* 61 (June 1974), 29–51.
25 Williamson, "Antebellum Urbanization," p. 599. See also Jeffrey G. Williamson and Joseph A. Swanson, "The Growth of Cities in the American Northeast, 1820–1870," *Explorations in Entrepreneurial History* 4, supplement (Fall 1966), 3–101.
26 Williamson, "Antebellum Urbanization," p. 607.
27 Lampard, "Evolving System of Cities," p. 118.
28 See, for example, Schultz, *Culture Factory*, on the antebellum crisis in Boston; Raymond A. Mohl, *Poverty in New York, 1783–1825* (New York: Oxford University Press, 1971), for New York's strains in the 1820s; Roger Lane, *Policing the City: Boston, 1822–1885* (Cambridge, Mass.: Harvard University Press, 1967), chap. 1, for Boston in the 1820s; and Michael H. Frisch, *Town into City: Springfield, Massachusetts, and the Meaning of Community, 1840–1880* (Cambridge, Mass.: Harvard University Press, 1972), on Springfield's crisis of the 1870s.
29 On life expectancy in antebellum Massachusetts, see Maris A. Vinovskis, "The 1789 Life Table of Edward Wigglesworth," *Journal of Economic History* 31 (September 1971), 570–90; and Maris A. Vinovskis, "Mortality Rates and Trends in Massachusetts before 1860," ibid., 32 (March 1972), 184–213.
30 On the Five Points, see Carroll Smith Rosenberg, *Religion and the Rise of the American City: The New York City Mission, 1812–1870* (Ithaca, N.Y.: Cornell University Press, 1971), pp. 34–6. On conditions of health in Boston, see John B. Blake, *Public Health in the Town of Boston, 1630–1822* (Cambridge, Mass.: Harvard University Press, 1959); and Barbara Gutmann Rosenkrantz, *Public Health and the State: Changing Views in Massachusetts, 1842–1936* (Cambridge, Mass.: Harvard University Press, 1972).
31 The classic work is Oscar Handlin, *Boston's Immigrants: A Study in*

Acculturation, rev. edn. (Cambridge, Mass.: Harvard University Press, 1959). See also Robert Ernst, *Immigrant Life in New York City, 1825–1863* (New York: King's Crown Press, 1949); Donald B. Cole, *Immigrant City: Lawrence, Massachusetts, 1845–1921* (Chapel Hill: University of North Carolina Press, 1963).

32 Constance McLaughlin Green, *Holyoke, Massachusetts: A Case Study of the Industrial Revolution in America* (New Haven: Yale University Press, 1939).

33 David Ward, *Cities and Immigrants: A Geography of Change in Nineteenth Century America* (New York: Oxford University Press, 1971), p. 106. See also David Ward, "The Internal Spatial Structure of Immigrant Residential Districts in the Late Nineteenth Century," *Geographical Analysis* 1 (October 1969): 337–53; and Virginia Yans McLaughlin, "Patterns of Work and Family Organization: Buffalo's Italians," *Journal of Interdisciplinary History* 2 (Autumn 1971), 299–314.

34 On the increasing productivity, see Robert Gallman, "The Pace and Pattern of American Economic Growth," in Davis et al., *American Economic Growth*, pp. 15–60. On wealth inequality, see Peter Lindert and Jeffrey Williamson, "Three Centuries of American Inequality" (Working paper, University of Wisconsin, Economic History Program, 1976).

35 Lane, *Policing the City*, pp. 221–2; Howard M. Gitelman, *Workingmen of Waltham: Mobility in American Urban Industrial Development, 1850–1890* (Baltimore: Johns Hopkins Press, 1974), pp. 158–9.

36 For example, see David J. Rothman, *The Discovery of the Asylum: Social Order and Disorder in the New Republic* (Boston: Little, Brown, 1971); Donald G. Mathews, "The Second Great Awakening as an Organizing Process, 1780–1830: An Hypothesis," *American Quarterly* 21 (Spring 1969), 23–43; Rosenberg, *Religion and the Rise of the City*, pp. 7–9; and John L. Thomas, "Romantic Reform in America, 1815–1865," *American Quarterly* 17 (Winter 1965), 656–81.

37 Percy W. Bidwell, "The Agricultural Revolution in New England," *American Historical Review* 26 (July 1921), 683–702. Also see Clarence H. Danhof, *Changes in Agriculture: The Northern United States, 1820–1870* (Cambridge, Mass.: Harvard University Press, 1969).

38 Cited in Bidwell, "Agricultural Revolution," p. 694.

39 An editor estimated in 1834 that only about one in fifty farmers in New York State had the opportunity to read any journal. See Donald B. Marti, "Agrarian Thought and Agricultural Progress: The Endeavor for Agricultural Improvement in New England and New York, 1815–1840" (Ph.D. diss., University of Wisconsin, 1966), p. 264. A more ample estimate – that one out of eight rural adults in New England and New York was reading a journal in 1840 – is found in Sidney L. Jackson, *America's Struggle for Free Schools: Social Tension and Education in New England and New York, 1827–1842* (New York: Columbia University, 1941), p. 113.

40 Jackson, *America's Struggle for Free Schools*, p. 113.

41 James T. Batal, "Robert Frost Tells of his High School Days in Lawrence," *Lawrence Telegram,* March 28, 1925, p. 14. See also Barbara M. Solomon, "The Growth of the Population in Essex County, 1850–1860," *Essex County Historical Collections* 95 (April 1959), 85.

42 See the research on rural–urban differences in intelligence in Sweden as described by Leo Schnore in "The Rural–Urban Variable: An Urbanite's Perspective," *Rural Sociology* 31 (June 1966), 140–1; also see Schnaiberg, "The Modernizing Impact of Urbanization," for lower educational levels among rural females in Turkey.

43 For introductions to multiple regression analysis, see N. R. Draper and H. Smith, *Applied Regression Analysis* (New York: John Wiley, 1966); William L. Hays, *Statistics* (New York: Holt, Rinehart and Winston, 1963), pp. 490–577; Fred N. Kerlinger and Elazar J. Pedhazur, *Multiple Regression in Behavioral Research* (New York: Holt, Rinehart and Winston, 1973); and Hubert M. Blalock, Jr., *Social Statistics,* 2nd edn. (New York: McGraw-Hill, 1972), pp. 429–70. On correlations among the independent variables, see J. Johnston, *Econometric Methods,* 2nd edn. (New York: McGraw-Hill, 1972), pp. 159–68; and Hubert M. Blalock, Jr., "Correlated Independent Variables: The Problem of Multicollinearity," *Social Forces* 62 (1963), 233–8.

44 The estimate for the number of acres of farmland is based on the Massachusetts state valuation for 1860. The total number of acres of land in each town is also calculated from that valuation. Oliver Warner, *Journal and Documents of the Valuation Committee of the Year 1860* (Boston, 1861).

45 The number of merchants in these towns was printed in the summary of the 1860 federal census for Massachusetts. Oliver Warner, *Abstract of the Census of Massachusetts, from the Eighth U.S. Census* (Boston, 1863), pp. 345–55. Because information on the number of people engaged in manufacturing was not available in the printed sources, it was necessary for us to go to the manuscript federal census of manufacturing for 1860, which is located in the Massachusetts Archives, State House, Boston. These schedules provided the number of males and females employed in manufacturing establishments producing goods valued at five hundred dollars or more per annum.

46 For one such transition in nineteenth-century Massachusetts, see Thomas A. McMullin, "Industrialization and Social Change in a Nineteenth-Century Port City: New Bedford, Massachusetts, 1865–1900" (Ph.D. diss., University of Wisconsin, 1976). Michael B. Katz's important recent work, *The People of Hamilton, Canada West,* catches that city at the point of transition.

47 Available from the state valuation of 1860. Warner, *Journal and Documents of the Valuation Committee.*

48 The data for pauper expenditures are derived from Massachusetts, Secretary of the Commonwealth, *Abstracts of the Returns Relating to the Poor, and to Indigent Children . . . in Massachusetts, 1860* (Boston, 1861).

49 Data on the number of church seats in each town were obtained from the 1860 manuscript federal census for Massachusetts, which is located in the Massachusetts Archives.

50 A very helpful statistical reviewer questioned the large standard deviations on some variables in an earlier report of this regression analysis, which prompted us to recheck our procedures for eliminating mistaken values. We discovered some miscoded values for a few towns on pauper expenses and on percentage of immigrants. The new regression analysis, with these errors eliminated, did not change our general interpretation, although it did yield stronger associations of our educational variables with pauper expenses and level of foreign-born people in the towns, as we had hypothesized at the outset.

51 See also Lewis C. Solmon, "Opportunity Costs and Models of Schooling in the Nineteenth Century," *Southern Economic Journal* 37 (July 1970), 66–83.

52 On overcrowded schools, see, for example, Schultz, *Culture Factory*, p. 288.

53 An interesting perspective on the role of religion in pan-Protestant, Victorian culture in America is found in Daniel Walker Howe, "American Victorianism as a Culture," *American Quarterly* 27 (December 1975), 507–32. See also David B. Tyack, "Onward Christian Soldiers: Religion in the American Common School," in Paul Nash, ed., *History and Education* (New York: Random House, 1970), 212–55; and David B. Tyack, "The Spread of Public Schooling in Victorian America: In Search of a Reinterpretation," *History of Education* 7 (October 1978), 173–82. For Horace Mann's battles and orthodox Congregationalists, see Culver, *Horace Mann and Religion in the Massachusetts Public Schools*.

54 If work discipline is the salient motive, one would expect the association to be stronger for manufacturing towns than for commercial towns, and indeed, Field's study, based on multiple regression analysis of data from the Massachusetts censuses of 1855 and 1865, yields such an association (as our 1860 regressions do not); see Field, "Educational Reform and Manufacturing Development," app. B. The discrepancy is explained by the fact that we used as our industrial variable the percentage of the work force engaged in manufacturing, which Field admits does not have a significant association with length of public school session; Field used average size of manufacturing establishment – a better measure, he argues, of the onset of large-scale factory production and the alleged attendant work-discipline problems. This argument has some merit, but the empirical discrepancies between his sample years and ours do not end there. Using our 1875 data, which have a wealth of information regarding manufacturing activity, we investigated several alternative measures of industrialization and their relationship to educational variables. These included average size of manufacturing establishment, percentage of women in the work force, and even a measure of each town's combined water and steam power. None of these variables displayed stronger associations with educational variables

(including length of session) than the proportion of workers in manufacturing; so we reverted to that basic variable, not only because it is widely used by others as a measure of increasing industrialization, but also because, with our data, it displays associations with educational practice as strong as or stronger than those of other variables. The problem requires further study.

6. EDUCATION IN TWO NINETEENTH-CENTURY COMMUNITIES

1 See Paul G. Faler, "Workingmen, Mechanics and Social Change: Lynn, Massachusetts, 1800–1860" (Ph.D. diss., University of Wisconsin, 1971); and Alan C. Dawley, "The Artisan Response to the Factory System: Lynn, Massachusetts, in the Nineteenth Century" (Ph.D. diss., Harvard University, 1971). The Dawley study has been published in revised form as *Class and Community: Lynn, Massachusetts in the Industrial Revolution* (Cambridge, Mass.: Harvard University Press, 1977). The most important secondary source on Boxford is Mary J. Foley, "A Study of the Economic History of Three Marginal Farm Towns in Massachusetts" (Ph.D. diss., Massachusetts State College, 1933).
2 George Herbert Palmer, *The Life of Alice Freeman Palmer* (Boston: Houghton Mifflin, 1908), p. 278.
3 Foley, "Three Marginal Farm Towns," pp. 6, 37A, 37B, 38, 39, 39B.
4 Foley, "Three Marginal Farm Towns," pp. 28A, 32.
5 Foley, "Three Marginal Farm Towns," pp. 39, 72–3, 76; Diary of member of Sawyer family, 1856–60, "Freeman Sawyer" file, MS, Boxford Historical Society, Boxford; Boxford School Committee, *Annual Reports;* Arthur G. Sias, "The Industries of Boxford, and Boxford's Most Unforgettable Characters," address to Reading Antiquarian Society, Reading, Mass., July 29, 1844, MS, Boxford Historical Society, p. 7.
6 Foley, "Three Marginal Farm Towns," pp. 10–11, 73–8; Lawrence G. Dodge and Alice Cole Dodge, *Puritan Paths from Naumkeag to Piscataqua* (Newburyport: Newburyport Press, 1963), p. 32; Sias, "Industries of Boxford," pp. 4–12; Sidney Perley, *History of Boxford* (Boxford, 1880), p. 339.
7 "Boxford Lets Things Burn," Boston *Globe*, January 31, 1896; MBE, *Annual Reports,* 1841–80.
8 Foley, "Three Marginal Farm Towns," pp. 11–12, 45–59; U.S. Department of Commerce, Bureau of the Census, *Statistics of the United States, 6th Census, 1840* (Washington, D.C., 1842) p. 54; Winthrop P. Haynes, "Address Delivered at First Parish Church Boxford," August 2, 1842, MS, Boxford Historical Society.
9 William B. Fowle and Asa Fitz, *An Elementary Geography for Massachusetts Children* (Boston, 1845), p. 94.
10 "Boxford Lets Things Burn."
11 George Herbert Palmer, "A Non Decadent Country Town," *The Congre-*

gationalist, n.d., clipping in "Celebrations" file, Boxford Historical Society.

12 Reverend Page, in "Discourse Delivered at Boxford, Massachusetts, May 10, 1863, by Reverend William S. Coggin, on the 25th Anniversary of His Settlement, Together with the Proceedings and Addresses at a Social Gathering on the Following Day" (August, 1864), p. 50, MS, Boxford Historical Society.

13 Boxford Town Meeting Minutes, 1893, MS, Boxford Town Hall.

14 Boxford Town Meeting Minutes, 1791–1839; Minutes of Meetings of School Districts Two, Three, and Four, 1798–1839, MS Boxford Town Hall, and of School District Seven, 1839–62, Boxford Historical Society; Martin, *Massachusetts Public School System*, p. 92; Perley, *History of Boxford*, p. 307.

15 Perley, *History of Boxford*, p. 286; Third Congregational Society in Boxford, *Facts and Observations Respecting the Doings of the First Church in Boxford* (Andover, Mass., 1825); Winifred C. Parkhurst, *History of the First Congregational Church, Boxford, Massachusetts* (Topsfield: Perkins Press, 1952), p. 53; Boxford School Committee, *Annual Report*, 1845, p. 13; Diary of Timothy Fuller, 1798–1801, typescript excerpts in Boxford Historical Society.

16 MBE, *Annual Reports*, 1837–40; "A History of the Lands in the North Part of Boxford," typescript, Boxford Historical Society, pp. 46–7; Sidney Perley, *Dwellings on Boxford* (Salem: Essex Institute, 1893), pp. 105, 257; 1829 catalog of and typewritten notes on Boxford Academy, Boxford Historical Society; Marcia Brockelman, "State Has Taken Command of Reading and Writin' Many Times in Boxford," Lawrence *Eagle-Tribune*, August 1, 1970; "Reopening of the Barker Free Academy," brochure, West Boxford Public Library, 1922; Boxford School Committee, *Annual Report*, 1845, pp. 17–18; D. Hamilton Hurd, *History of Essex County, Massachusetts* (Philadelphia, 1888), p. 964.

17 Barbara Perley, taped interview, West Boxford Public Library, 1975; Boxford School Committee, *Annual Reports*, 1841, p. 7; 1860–1869; 1879, pp. 5–6; 1885, p. 8; 1886, p. 7.

18 Boxford School Committee, *Annual Report*, 1854, p. 7.

19 Ibid., 1866, p. 7.

20 Ibid., 1861, p. 9.

21 Ibid., 1855, pp. 7–8.

22 Ibid., 1866, p. 7.

23 Ibid., 1873, p. 4.

24 Ibid., 1857, p. 9.

25 Ibid., 1841, p. 8.

26 Ibid., 1852, p. 6; Fuller, Diary.

27 MBE, *Annual Reports*, 1837–80.

28 Boxford School Committee, *Annual Report*, 1874, p. 8.

29 Ibid., 1870, pp. 6–7.

30 Ibid., 1852, p. 5.

31 Ibid., 1873, p. 8.
32 Boxford Town Meeting Minutes, 1864, 1880.
33 Boxford School Committee, *Annual Report,* 1857, p. 10.
34 Ibid., 1880, p. 4; 1888, p. 4.
35 Ibid., 1841, p. 9; 1842, pp. 3–4; 1843, p. 7; Essex County Teachers Association, *Report on Schoolhouses* (Newburyport: Hiram Tozer, 1833).
36 Boxford School Committee, *Annual Report,* 1883, pp. 3–5; Minutes of School District Seven, 1843.
37 Town Meeting Minutes, November 7, 1796.
38 Boxford School Committee, *Annual Reports,* 1841, p. 3; 1843, p. 6; 1844, pp. 1–2; 1845, pp. 15–16; 1853, p. 10; 1863, p. 10.
39 Ibid., 1841, p. 38; 1873, p. 3; 1879, p. 7.
40 Ibid., 1841, p. 8; 1851, p. 7; 1869, p. 7; 1878, pp. 4–5; Jacob Batchelder, Jr., to his parents, September 25, 1825, and William Kimball to Caroline A. Stiles, April 5, 1860, MSS, Boxford Historical Society; Eugine F. Clark, *A Son's Portrait of Dr. Francis E. Clark* (Boston: Williston Press, 1930), p. 42.
41 Boxford School Committee, *Annual Reports,* 1841–95.
42 Clark, *Francis Clark,* p. 42; Charles Bradley to Frank A. Manny, January 23, 1929, November 24, 1930, MSS, Boxford Historical Society; Frank A. Manny, "Findings: Old Boxford in Essex," *North Shore Breeze and Reminder,* May 23, 1930; "Transcendentalists in Boxford," typescript, Boxford Historical Society.
43 Minutes of School Districts Two, Four, and Seven, 1798–1869; Boxford School Committee, *Annual Reports,* 1841–81. Note that although low wages for female teachers accounted in part for the disproportionately small summer appropriations, a more important factor was the need to buy fuel in winter.
44 Boxford, School Committee, *Annual Reports,* 1847, p. 5; 1851, p. 7.
45 Ibid., 1851, pp. 1–4; 1854, pp. 1–3; 1857, p. 7; 1859, pp. 4–5; Minutes of School District Two.
46 Boxford School Committee, *Annual Report,* 1870, p. 4.
47 MBE, *Annual Reports,* 1840–80.
48 Boxford School Committee, *Annual Reports,* 1872, p. 7; 1875, p. 5; 1878, pp. 8–9.
49 Ibid., 1840–80.
50 Foley, "Three Marginal Farm Towns," p. 35E; "Boxford Lets Things Burn"; Elizabeth Pearl, taped interview, West Boxford Public Library, 1975.
51 Boxford School Committee, *Annual Reports,* 1844, pp. 4–7; 1845, p. 18; 1852, p. 2; 1856, pp. 7–8; 1872, p. 5; 1905, p. 45; Minutes of School District Two, 1864; Charles Bradley to Frank A. Manny, November 24, 1930, MS, Boxford Historical Society.
52 Boxford School Committee, *Annual Reports,* 1843, p. 5; 1870, pp. 6–9; 1868, p. 11; 1870, pp. 1–3; 1871, p. 4; Boxford Town Meeting Minutes, 1866–72.

53 Boxford School Committee, *Annual Report,* 1864, p. 6.
54 Ibid., 1843, p. 5; 1870, pp. 6–9; 1868, p. 11; 1870, pp. 1–3, 1871, p. 4; Boxford Town Meeting Minutes, 1866–72.
55 Boxford School Committee, *Annual Reports,* 1897, p. 10; 1898; pp. 9–10; 1899, p. 9; 1901, pp. 6, 9–11.
56 Ibid., 1901, pp. 9–10; 1903, pp. 50–1; 1905, p. 45.
57 Ibid., 1905, p. 46; 1906, p. 44.
58 Ibid., 1879, pp. 5–6; 1884, pp. 9–11; 1885, p. 8; 1886, p. 7; 1888, p. 4; 1889, p. 5; 1901, p. 12; "Boxford Lets Things Burn"; Martin, *Massachusetts Public School System,* p. 199.
59 "Boxford Lets Things Burn"; Boxford School Committee, *Annual Reports,* 1900, pp. 4–5; 1901, pp. 11–12.
60 Tyack, "The Tribe and the Common School," p. 4.
61 Boxford School Committee, *Annual Reports,* 1841, p. 10; 1855, p. 6; Fuller, Diary; Essex County Teachers Association, *Report on Schoolhouses,* p. 22; Minutes of School District Seven, 1839, 1843.
62 Faler, "Workingmen, Mechanics and Social Change," p. 60; see also Alonzo Lewis and James R. Newhall, *History of Lynn, Essex County, Massachusetts: Including Lynnfield, Saugus, Swampscot, and Nahant* (Boston, 1865), vol. I.
63 For a good chronological overview of the growth of Lynn in this period, see James R. Newhall, *History of Lynn, Essex County, Massachusetts: Including Lynnfield, Saugus, Swampscott, and Nahant* (Lynn, 1897), II, 35, 73, and 276–7. For the population figures, see the U.S. censuses for 1800 and 1830.
64 Newhall, *History of Lynn,* II, 277–8; Faler, "Workingmen, Mechanics and Social Change," passim; and the U.S. censuses for 1830 and 1850.
65 Most information for this paragraph is taken from Newhall, *History of Lynn,* II, 35, 39, 45, 55, 57, 67, 278–82, 331–42, and 352. Population figures are from the U.S. census for 1850 and 1900. The *Lynn Directory* (Lynn, 1854), pp. 160–9, constitutes the 1854 business directory; the *Lynn Directory* (Lynn, 1901), pp. 805–68, constitutes the business directory for that year.
66 See, for 1855 figures, *Statistical Information Relating to Certain Branches of Industry in Massachusetts, For the Year ending June 1, 1855* (Boston, 1856), p. 140; for 1865 figures, *Statistical Information Relating to Certain Branches of Industry in Massachusetts, for the Year ending May 1, 1865* (Boston, 1866), p. 159, and *Census of Massachusetts: 1875* (Boston, 1877), II, 879; for 1880 figures, *Census of Massachusetts: 1880* (Boston, 1883), p. 548; and for 1895 figures, *Census of the Commonwealth of Massachusetts: 1895* (Boston, 1900), V, 601.
67 See Faler, "Workingmen, Mechanics and Social Change"; and Dawley, *Class and Community.*
68 Dawley, *Class and Community,* chap. 9.
69 Dawley, "Artisan Response," pp. 47, 86.

70 Ibid., pp. 233, 238.
71 Ibid., pp. 303, 305.
72 Ibid., p. 196.
73 Ibid., pp. 209–12.
74 Quoted in ibid., p. 313.
75 Ibid., pp. 313–14.
76 Ibid., p. 317.
77 On the general question of character-forming institutions, see Rothman, *Discovery of the Asylum.*
78 Faler, ''Workingmen, Mechanics and Social Change,'' pp. 207–8.
79 Ibid., pp. 220, 221.
80 See Kaestle, *Evolution of an Urban School System;* and Schultz, *Culture Factory.*
81 *Lynn Awl,* March 8, 1845.
82 Katz, *Irony of Early School Reform,* pp. 1–2.
83 *Lynn Awl,* March 1, 1845.
84 Lynn, Massachusetts, Mayor, *Inaugural Addresses, 1850–1861* (bound volume, Lynn Public Library), January 3, 1859, p. 12.
85 Ibid.
86 Ibid., January 7, 1861, p. 6.
87 Lynn, Massachusetts, Mayor, *City Documents, 1876–1878* (bound volume, Lynn Public Library), January 1879, pp. 12–13.
88 Lynn, Massachusetts, Mayor, *City Documents, 1879–1881* (bound volume, Lynn Public Library), January 1880, pp. 15–16.
89 See *An Exposition of the Course Pursued by the School Committee of the City of Lynn in Relation to Samuel W. King . . .* (Lynn, 1857); and the *Lynn Reporter,* September 14 and 25, and October 2, 1878.
90 David N. Johnson, *Sketches of Lynn* (Lynn, 1880), p. 378.
91 Ibid., pp. 382–3.
92 Ibid., p. 387
93 Quoted in ibid., pp. 392–3.
94 Lynn School Committee, *Annual Reports,* 1822, p. 8; 1824, p. 99; 1837–8, p. 4; 1850–1, p. 1.
95 Ibid., 1827, pp. 189–90.
96 Ibid., 1847–8, p. 8.
97 Ibid., 1850–1, p. 2.
98 Ibid., 1860, pp. 7–9.
99 Ibid., 1865, p. 7.
100 Ibid., 1869, p. 29.
101 See ibid., 1850, p. 24; 1854, p. 11; 1860, pp. 5–6; 1861, p. 7; 1863, p. 11; and 1864, p. 7.
102 Ibid., 1849–50, p. 21.
103 Ibid., 1856, p. 7.
104 Ibid., 1865, pp. 14–15.
105 Ibid., p. 21.

106 Ibid., p. 22.
107 Ibid., 1870, p. 17. See also ibid., 1869, p. 32.
108 Ibid., 1865, p. 10.
109 Ibid., 1857, pp. 15–16.
110 Ibid., 1869, pp. 4–5.
111 Ibid., 1876, pp. 13–14.
112 Ibid., 1877, p. 5.
113 Ibid., 1879, p. 37.
114 Ibid., 1880, p. 17.

7. TRENDS IN EDUCATIONAL FUNDING AND EXPENDITURES

1 Exceptions include Solmon, "Estimates of the Costs of Schooling in 1880 and 1890"; Fishlow, "Nineteenth-Century American Investment in Education"; Stanley L. Engerman, "Human Capital, Education, and Economic Growth," in Robert W. Fogel and Stanley L. Engerman, eds., *The Reinterpretation of American Economic History* (New York: Harper & Row, 1971), pp. 241–56.
2 James G. Carter, *Speech of Mr. Carter, of Lancaster, Delivered in the House of Representatives of Massachusetts, February 1, 1837* (Boston, 1837), p. 11.
3 We used the Hoover Consumer Price Index for the years 1851 to 1880 and the Federal Reserve Bank of New York Cost-of-Living Index for the years 1820 to 1850. These series are reprinted in the U.S. Department of Commerce, *Historical Statistics of the United States: Colonial Times to 1970* (Washington, D.C.: Bureau of the Census, 1975), pt. 1, ser. E174 and E183.
4 Horace Mann, *First Annual Report of the Board of Education,* cited in Lawrence A. Cremin, ed., *The Republic and the School: Horace Mann on the Education of Free Men* (New York: Teachers College Press, 1957), p. 30.
5 Salem, Massachusetts, Mayor, *Annual Report . . . 1842–43* (Salem, 1843), p. 7.
6 Massachusetts towns were annually required to report financial information on both public and private schools. For the public schools, data were gathered on the average monthly wages paid to male and female schoolteachers, the amount of money raised by taxes for the support of public schools (including only the wages of teachers, board, and fuel), the amount of board and fuel contributed, the income from local funds, and the income of surplus revenue appropriated for public schools. For private schools, information was gathered only on the aggregate amount of tuition paid for incorporated and unincorporated academies.
7 The data on local school expenditures as well as on other town services for the eight Essex County communities in 1860 and 1880 were obtained from the annual published town budgets. The data on Boston were obtained

from Charles Phillips Huse, *The Financial History of Boston, From May 1, 1822, to January 31, 1909* (Cambridge, Mass.: Harvard University Press, 1916).

8 *Common School Journal* 1 (April 1839), 123.
9 Lawrence School Committee, *Annual Report,* 1849–50; ibid., 1850–1.
10 Wilbraham School Committee, *Annual Report,* 1850–1; Palmer School Committee, *Annual Report,* 1850–1.
11 Chester School Committee, *Annual Report,* 1850–1; Danvers School Committee, *Annual Report,* 1860–1.
12 Hamilton School Committee, *Annual Report,* 1850–1; Lynnfield School Committee, *Annual Report,* 1850–1; Essex School Committee, *Annual Report,* 1860–1.
13 On inequalities in school resources among communities, see John E. Coons, William H. Clune III, and Stephen D. Sugarman, *Private Wealth and Public Education* (Cambridge, Mass.: Harvard University Press, 1970).
14 The data on Massachusetts schools for 1969–70 are from Commonwealth of Massachusetts, *Annual Report of the Department of Education for the Year Ending June 30, 1970* (Boston: Massachusetts Department of Education, 1970), pt. 2.
15 In 1841 the annual Massachusetts school reports began to provide graduated tables for the amount of money appropriated by towns for each school-age child. We used these graduated tables to compute the extent of inequality in per child expenditures among the towns.
16 This section on the feminization of the teaching force relies on Bernard and Vinovskis, "The Female School Teacher in Ante-Bellum Massachusetts." We have extended the data on Massachusetts's female schoolteachers between 1860 and 1880 and have provided information on the financial implications of the feminization of the teaching force in Massachusetts.
17 Horace Mann, MBE, *Seventh Annual Report,* 1843, p. 28.
18 On the nineteenth-century stereotypes of women, see Barbara Welter, "The Cult of True Womanhood: 1820–1860," *American Quarterly* 18 (Summer 1966), 151–74; and Cott, *Bonds of Womanhood.*
19 See Keith E. Melder, "Woman's High Calling: The Teaching Profession in America, 1830–1860," *American Studies* 13 (Fall 1972), 19–32.
20 Salem School Committee, *Annual Report,* 1840–1; see also ibid., 1842–3.
21 Newbury School Committee, *Annual Report,* 1850–1.
22 Historians are beginning to use a life-course approach for analyzing the careers of women, rather than relying only on a cross-sectional perspective based on a single point. For a discussion of the strengths and weaknesses of a life-course approach, see Glen H. Elder, "Age Differentiation and the Life Course," *Annual Review of Sociology* 1 (1975), 165–90; and Maris A. Vinovskis, "From Household Size to the Life Course: Some Observations on Recent Trends in Family History," *American Behavioral Scientist* 21 (November/December 1977), 263–87.
23 MBE, *Ninth Annual Report,* 1846.

24 See Bernard and Vinovskis, "The Female School Teacher in Ante-Bellum Massachusetts."

8. THE POLITICS OF EDUCATIONAL REFORM

1 For example, see Martin, *Massachusetts Public School System;* and Ellwood P. Cubberley, *Changing Conceptions of Education* (Boston: Houghton Mifflin, 1909).

2 Frank Tracy Carlton, *Economic Influences upon Educational Progress in the United States, 1820–1850* (New York: Teachers College Press, 1965).

3 Bowles and Gintis, *Schooling in Capitalist America;* Field, "Educational Reform and Manufacturing Development."

4 The most detailed analysis of the legislative fight in 1840 is Culver, *Horace Mann and Religion in the Massachusetts Public Schools,* pp. 127–62. Culver stressed the seriousness of the threat to the board of education and attributed it to the efforts of the religious opponents of the board. In contrast, the most recent biography of Horace Mann argues that the threat to the board of education in the legislature was exaggerated by Mann and by historians who believed him. Jonathan Messerli, *Horace Mann: A Biography* (New York: Alfred Knopf, 1972), pp. 309–48. Messerli did not, however, fully investigate the political situation in the legislature and the state in 1840, and thus he underestimated the dangers to the board. For a study of the legislative challenge to the board of education in relation to Mann's ideas on the economic value of education, see Vinovskis, "Horace Mann on the Economic Productivity of Education."

5 Jonathan Messerli, "James G. Carter's Liabilities as a Common School Reformer," *History of Education Quarterly* 5 (March 1965), 14–25; Massachusetts Laws, 1834, chap. 169; Henry Barnard, *American Educational Biography, Memoirs of Teachers, Educators, and Promoters of Education, Science, and Literature* (New York, 1974), p. 339.

6 *Address of His Excellency Edward Everett to the Two Branches of the Legislature, on the Organization of the Government, for the Political Year Commencing January 4, 1837* (Massachusetts General Court, Senate Document No. 1, Boston, 1837), p. 17. The House first defeated the bill by a vote of 113 to 61, but James Carter succeeded in getting the measure reconsidered. Culver, *Horace Mann and Religion in the Massachusetts Public Schools,* p. 30.

7 Horace Mann, "Journal," June 30, 1837, MS, Horace Mann Papers, Massachusetts Historical Society, Boston.

8 *The Common School Controversy; Consisting of Three Letters of the Secretary of the Board of Education, of the State of Massachusetts, in reply to Charges Preferred against the Board, by the Editor of the Christian Witness and by Edward A. Newton, Esq., of Pittsfield, Once a Member of the Board; to Which Are Added Extracts from the Daily Press, in Regard to the Controversy* (Boston, 1844), p. 27.

9 For a discussion of the membership of the first board of education, see

Culver, *Horace Mann and Religion in the Massachusetts Public Schools,* pp. 31–2. Robert Rantoul's support of the board was very important because of his position within the Democratic Party. For a discussion of his career, see Robert DeGross Bulkley, Jr., "Robert Rantoul, Jr., 1805–1852: Politics and Reform in Antebellum Massachusetts" (Ph.D. diss., Princeton University, 1971).

10 For an analysis of Horace Mann's controversies with Frederick Packard, see Culver, *Horace Mann and Religion in the Massachusetts Public Schools,* pp. 55–110.

11 The best analysis of the political situation in Massachusetts in the late 1830s can be found in Arthur B. Darling, *Political Changes in Massachusetts, 1824–1848: A Study of Liberal Movements in Politics* (New Haven: Yale University Press, 1925); see also Robert J. Haws, "Massachusetts Whigs, 1833–1854" (Ph.D. diss., University of Nebraska, 1973). On the politics of temperance, see Joseph R. Gusfield, *Symbolic Crusade: Status Politics and the American Temperance Movement* (Urbana: University of Illinois Press, 1963), pp. 36–60.

12 Most of the party affiliations came from a list in the *Boston Daily Advertiser* of January 1, 1840. In addition, we used William Lincoln's list of Whigs and Democrats in the Massachusetts House in 1839 and his list of members of the Whig Convention in 1840. Lincoln's lists can be found in the Lincoln Papers at the American Antiquarian Society.

13 The information on tenure in the legislature and on the ages and occupations of the legislators were obtained from the Tillinghast Manuscript Catalogue of Massachusetts Legislators in the Massachusetts State Library. Every effort was made to code the occupation exactly as it was given in that file. In cases where more than one occupation was given for a legislator, we coded two occupations (if more than two were given, the two most important ones were selected, with the one that seemed most important listed first). We experimented with our analysis to see how the listing of more than one occupation would affect our results and found that it altered our findings very little.

The identification numbers assigned to these occupations come from the larger occupational dictionary based on Blumin's work that we used in Chapter 4. However, we recategorized the occupations into professionals, merchants, etc., after studying the data and comparing our scheme to other schemes for categorizing nineteenth-century occupations. The reader should be aware that the occupational designations in the sources are very broad and difficult to interpret: For example, does a "comb maker" manufacture combs, or merely work in a shop that produces them? Similarly, does a "miller" own a mill or merely work in one? We cannot be confident of the meaning or status of any particular occupation of a legislator; however, for purposes of the analysis in this chapter, we were more interested in the vertical occupational sectors of agriculture, commerce, manufacturing, and the professions than in the crude hierarchical rankings of assumed wealth or status that occupational designations yield.

14 These geographic subdivisions, which reflect socioeconomic differences within the state, were drawn from another study of the determinants of fertility differentials. For a more detailed discussion of these regions, see Maris A. Vinovskis, *Demographic Changes in America from the Revolution to the Civil War: An Analysis of the Socio-Economic Determinants of Fertility Differentials and Trends in Massachusetts from 1765 to 1860* (New York: Academic Press, 1979).

15 The data on the percentage of workers engaged in commerce or manufacturing in each town come from the U.S. census of 1840. On the basis of the distributions of our legislators, a town was defined as having low commerce if fewer than 20 percent of its workers engaged in commerce, and as having low manufacturing if fewer than 30 percent of its workers were employed in manufacturing.

16 One interesting index of the relative importance of various campaign issues in 1839 is a circular sent by the Whig State Central Committee to the chairmen of the Whig town committees. The seventh question on the circular asked: "Were the voters influenced by other considerations than those of a political character? If so, please state, in a general manner, whether they were local, or grew out of the legislation on temperance, the militia, railroads, or other causes." The replies from forty-six Worcester County towns have been preserved. The most commonly cited issue was the legislation on temperance. None of the returns even mentioned any issue relating to the board of education or to the normal schools. These manuscript replies are cataloged under Worcester County Statistical Materials, 1765–1840, at the American Antiquarian Society. We also examined a large number of Massachusetts newspapers for 1839 and 1840 but found very little mention of education in them. Similarly, we went through the personal papers of a variety of leading politicians, such as Edward Everett, George Bancroft, Marcus Morton, and John Davis, but found almost no discussion of the board of education or the normal schools.

17 Orestes Augustus Brownson's attack on the board of education is found in the October 1839 issue of his magazine, *Boston Quarterly Review*. On Brownson's role and ideas, see Arthur M. Schlesinger, Jr., *A Pilgrim's Progress: Orestes A. Brownson* (Boston: Little, Brown, 1939); and Leonard Gilhooley, *Contradiction and Dilemma: Orestes Brownson and the American Idea* (New York: Fordham University Press, 1972).

18 Culver, *Horace Mann and Religion in the Massachusetts Public Schools*, pp. 130–1.

19 Mann, "Journal," January 5, 1840.

20 *Address of His Excellency Marcus Morton to the Two Branches of the Legislature, on the Organization of the Government, for the Political Year Commencing January 1, 1840* (Massachusetts General Court, House Document No. 9, Boston, 1840), p. 30.

21 *Reports on the Reduction of Salaries and the Abolishing of Commissions* (Massachusetts General Court, House Document No. 22, Boston, 1840), pp. 1–48.

22 Ibid., pp. 21–2.
23 Ibid., pp. 22–3.
24 Mary Peabody Mann, *Life of Horace Mann* (Washington, D.C., 1937), pp. 123–4.
25 Roll-call vote number twenty in the *Journal of the House of Representatives for 1849*, located at the Massachusetts State Library.
26 The resolution was introduced by Cyrus Alden, the Whig member of the Committee on the Reduction of Salaries who sided with the Democrats on this issue.
27 See Rush Welter, *The Mind of America: 1820–1860* (New York: Columbia University Press, 1975), pp. 165–89.
28 *Report of the Committee on Education* (Massachusetts General Court, House Document No. 49, Boston, 1840), pp. 2–3.
29 Ibid., p. 6.
30 Ibid., p. 9.
31 Ibid., p. 10.
32 *Minority Report of the Committee on Education* (Massachusetts General Court, House Document No. 53, Boston, 1840), p. 2.
33 Petitions in support of the board of education and the normal schools were sent by the citizens of New Bedford, the citizens of Lexington, Elisha Bartlett and seventeen other signers, the officers of the Barre Normal School Association, and the Salem School Committee. These petitions are available in the Massachusetts House File for 1840, No. 817 at the Massachusetts Archives.
34 *Boston Daily Advertiser*, March 18, 1840.
35 *Boston Mercantile Journal*, March 12, 1840.
36 Though the full debate on the bill to abolish the board of education and the normal schools was held on March 18, 1840, there were numerous skirmishes on the issue in the preceding two weeks. The course of the bill can be followed in the *Journal of the House of Representatives for 1840*.
37 A summary of Dodge's speech can be found in the *Boston Daily Advertiser*.
38 The text of Shaw's speech can be found in the *Common School Journal* 2 (1840), 293 ff.
39 The roll-call votes are found in the *Journal of the House of Representatives for 1840*.
40 See Chapter 5.
41 The information on the occupational distribution of workers in the towns was obtained from the U.S. census of 1840. The data on the per capita valuation of manufacturing and commerce is based on the state valuation data for 1840.
42 The votes for Massachusetts elections were obtained from the manuscript returns of elections in the Massachusetts Archives.
43 Information on the number and type of churches in each town was obtained from the *Massachusetts Register and the United Calendar for 1840* (Boston, 1840), pp. 128–45. Unfortunately, it is impossible to distinguish Unitarian churches from Orthodox Congregational churches in this source.

Therefore, we used information from the Unitarian Yearbook on Unitarian churches in 1846.

44 Both information on the use of Bibles in schools and the names of the school committee members were gathered from MBE, *Annual Reports*.

45 The data on various indexes of educational effort were calculated from MBE, *Annual Reports*.

46 Political historians have used sophisticated techniques, such as Guttman scaling, factor analysis, and cluster analysis, to ascertain patterns of voting from series of roll-call votes. However, they have not used multiple classification analysis to relate the personal and constituent characteristics of the legislators to their patterns of voting. For an example of the use of multiple regression analysis to predict the outcome of legislative voting from the personal and constituent characteristics of state legislators, see Maris A. Vinovskis, R. Marshall Jones, and Thomas New, "Determinants of Legislative Voting Behavior on Population Policy: An Analysis of the Massachusetts House of Representatives in 1970 and 1971," in Elihu Bergman et al., eds., *Population Policymaking in the American States: Issues and Processes* (Lexington, Mass.: Lexington Books, 1974), pp. 239–55. For voting behavior on local issues in Jacksonian America, see Herbert Ershkowitz and William G. Shade, "Consensus or Conflict? Political Behavior in the State Legislatures during the Jacksonian Era," *Journal of American History* 58 (December 1971), 591–621; Peter Levine, "State Legislative Parties in the Jacksonian Era: New Jersey, 1829–1844," ibid. 62 (December 1975), 591–608.

47 Bowles and Gintis, *Schooling in Capitalist America;* Field, "Educational Reform and Manufacturing Development."

48 Culver, *Horace Mann and Religion in the Massachusetts Public Schools.*

49 We defined as noncompetitive those areas where the gubernatorial candidate of the legislator's own party received at least 55 percent of the vote.

50 A town was defined as having low commerce in 1840 if fewer than 20 percent of its workers engaged in commerce, and as having low manufacturing in that year if fewer than 30 percent of its workers engaged in manufacturing.

51 On the importance of separating manufacturing from commercial development as much as possible in analyzing nineteenth-century economic development, see Vinovskis, *Demographic Changes in America from the Revolution to the Civil War.*

52 On the opposition to Horace Mann and the board of education in western Massachusetts, see Richard D. Birdsall, *Berkshire County: A Cultural History* (New Haven: Yale University Press, 1959), pp. 103–51.

53 For a discussion of the creation of the normal schools and the political problems associated with their location, see Culver, *Horace Mann and Religion in the Massachusetts Public Schools,* pp. 111–26.

54 On the use of Bibles and the presence of clergymen as indexes of religious orientation in the schools, see Bidwell, "The Moral Significance of the Common School."

55 We also ran an MCA that used as a variable whether the schools in the town in question had used the Bible at any point between 1837 and 1841. The results of that analysis were nearly identical to the one in which we asked if the schools in the town were using the Bible in 1840.

56 One interesting sidelight is that we were able to test the strength of the relationship between the length of the public school year and the vote on the bill to abolish the board of education. Alexander Field has used the length of the public school year as the index of support for educational reform in Massachusetts. Field, "Educational Reform and Manufacturing Development." We found that although there was a positive relationship between the length of the public school year and the vote on this bill, the relationship between these two variables by themselves was not strong (adjusted eta^2 = .1156). The use of the length of the public school year as an index of support for the educational reforms of Horace Mann is questionable.

57 The Rice index of cohesion for Whigs on the vote was 62.2; for the Democrats it was only 34.4.

58 The Rice index of cohesion for Whigs on the bill to reduce the salaries of state officials was 83.2; for the Democrats it was 90.8.

APPENDIX C. CALCULATING TABLES A2.1 THROUGH A2.5

1 Dracut School Committee to the Secretary of the Board of Education, MS letter filed with School Return, 1849–50, MSL, Annex; Lawrence School Committee, *Annual Report*, 1854.

2 See, for example, the printed instructions to the School Return forms for 1875, MSL, Annex.

3 Vinovskis, "Trends in Massachusetts Education," n. 16.

4 The quotation is from the School Return form for 1850–1, MSL, Annex. For twenty-day school months, see instruction 15 for 1875–6.

5 Boxford School Committee, *Annual Report*, 1880; Lynn School Committee, *Annual Report*, 1848; ibid., 1855.

6 School Return forms, MSL, Annex. See, for example, forms for 1850–1 and 1859–60.

7 MBE, *Third Annual Report*, 1840. The estimate is repeated in the seventh, eleventh, and twelfth reports.

8 In 1848–9 there were 314 towns in Massachusetts; 242 towns reported that they had incorporated private schools, and of these, 151 reported enrollments and length of term for each school.

9 MBE, *First Annual Report*, 1837, p. 52.

BIBLIOGRAPHY

PRINCIPAL ARCHIVAL LOCATIONS

American Antiquarian Society, Worcester, Massachusetts
Boxford Historical Society, Boxford, Massachusetts
Essex Institute, Salem, Massachusetts
Lynn Historical Society, Lynn, Massachusetts
Massachusetts State Library (herein abbreviated MSL), State House, Boston,
    Massachusetts
    Annex, Vault
    Archives
    Tillinghurst Collection

PUBLISHED PRIMARY SOURCES

Periodicals

American Annals of Education
American Journal of Education
Common School Journal
Godey's Ladies Book

Newspapers

Boston Daily Advertiser
Boston Mercantile Journal
Lynn Awl
Salem Gazette
Salem Register

Other published primary sources

Bentley, William. *The Diary of William Bentley, D.D., Pastor of the East
    Church, Salem, Mass.* 4 vols. Salem: Essex Institute, 1905–14.
Bremner, Robert H., John Barnard, Tamara K. Hareven, and Robert M.
    Mennel, eds. *Children and Youth in America: A Documentary History.*
    Vol. I. Cambridge, Mass.: Harvard University Press, 1970.
Brigham, Amariah. *Remarks on the Influence of Mental Cultivation and Men-*

tal Excitement upon Health. 2nd edn. Boston, 1833.

Carter, James G. *The Schools of Massachusetts in 1824*. Boston: Old South Leaflets, n.d.

Essex County Teachers Association. *Report on Schoolhouses*. Newburyport: Hiram Tozer, 1833.

McNeill, George E. *Factory Children: Report on the Schooling and Hours of Labor of Children Employed in the Manufacturing and Mechanical Establishments of Massachusetts*. Massachusetts General Court, Senate Document No. 50. Boston, 1875.

Massachusetts Board of Education. *Annual Reports*. Boston, 1839–1900.

Massachusetts General Court. *Laws and Resolves Relating to Public Instruction*. Boston, 1853.

    House of Representatives. *Documents*. For example:

    Petition of a Convention of Delegates from Each of the Towns in Plymouth County and Part of Norfolk, on the Subject of Elementary Education. House Document No. 14. Boston, 1837.

    Reports on the Reduction of Salaries and the Abolishing of Commissions. House Document No. 22. Boston, 1840.

    Report of the Committee on Education. House Document No. 49. Boston, 1840.

    Senate. *Documents*. For example:

    Address of His Excellency Edward Everett to the Two Branches of the Legislature, on the Organization of the Government, for the Political Year Commencing January 4, 1837. Senate Document No. 1. Boston, 1837.

    House of Representatives.

    Journal of the House of Representatives.

Massachusetts. Secretary of the Commonwealth. *Abstracts of the Returns Relating to the Poor, and to Indigent Children . . . in Massachusetts, 1860* Boston, 1861.

Metropolitan Catholic Almanac and Laity's Directory. Baltimore: F. Lucas, 1848, 1855, 1859–61.

Northrup, Birdsey. *Defects Existing, and Improvements Needed in the Public Schools of Massachusetts*. Boston, 1862.

Oliver, Henry K. *Report of Henry K. Oliver, Deputy State Constable, Especially Appointed to Enforce the Laws Regulating the Employment of Children . . .* Boston, 1869.

Peirce, Cyrus. *The First State Normal School in America. The Journals of Cyrus Peirce and Mary Swift*. Cambridge, Mass.: Harvard Documents in the History of Education, 1926.

Randall, Samuel S. *The Common School System of the State of New York*. Troy, N.Y., 1851.

    History of the Common School System of the State of New York. New York, 1871.

Rudolph, Frederick, ed. *Essays on Education in the Early Republic*. Cambridge, Mass.: Harvard University Press, 1965.

Bibliography

Smith, Wilson, ed. *Theories of Education in Early America, 1655–1819.* Indianapolis: Bobbs-Merrill, 1973.

U.S. Department of Commerce. *Historical Statistics of the United States: Colonial Times to 1970.* Washington, D.C.: Bureau of the Census, 1975.

Walker, George H. *Atlas of Essex County.* Boston, 1884.

Wightman, Joseph M. *Annals of the Boston Primary School Committee: From Its First Establishment in 1818 to Its Dissolution in 1855.* Boston, 1860.

Wright, Carroll D. *History of Wages and Prices in Massachusetts, 1752–1883.* Boston, 1885.

PUBLISHED SECONDARY SOURCES

Arrington, Benjamin F., ed. *Municipal History of Essex County in Massachusetts.* New York: Lewis Historical Publishing Company, 1922.

Axtell, James. *The School upon a Hill: Education and Society in Colonial New England.* New Haven: Yale University Press, 1974.

Bailyn, Bernard. *Education in the Forming of American Society.* Chapel Hill: University of North Carolina Press, 1960.

Bernard, Richard M., and Maris A. Vinovskis. "The Female School Teacher in Ante-Bellum Massachusetts." *Journal of Social History* 10 (Spring 1977), 332–45.

"Beyond Catharine Beecher: Female Education in the Antebellum Period." *Signs* 3 (Summer 1978), 856–69.

Bidwell, Percy W. "The Agricultural Revolution in New England." *American Historical Review* 26 (July 1921), 683–702.

Bidwell, Charles E. "The Moral Significance of the Common School: A Sociological Study of Local Patterns of School Control and Moral Education in Massachusetts and New York, 1837–1840." *History of Education Quarterly* 6 (Fall 1966), 50–91.

Bowles, Samuel, and Herbert Gintis. *Schooling in Capitalist America.* New York: Basic Books, 1976.

Brown, Richard D. "The Emergence of Urban Society in Rural Massachusetts, 1760–1820." *Journal of American History* 61 (June 1974), 29–51.

Burns, James A., and Bernard J. Kohlbrenner. *A History of Catholic Education in the United States.* New York, 1937.

Burns, Rex. *Success in America: The Yeoman Dream and the Industrial Revolution.* Amherst: University of Massachusetts Press, 1976.

Butler, Vera. *Education as Revealed by New England Newspapers prior to 1850.* Philadelphia: Temple University, 1935.

Carlton, Frank Tracy. *Economic Influences upon Educational Progress in the United States, 1820–1850.* New York: Teachers College Press, 1965.

Cole, Donald B. *Immigrant City: Lawrence, Massachusetts, 1845–1921.* Chapel Hill: University of North Carolina Press, 1963.

Cott, Nancy F. *The Bonds of Womanhood: "Woman's Sphere" in New England, 1780–1835.* New Haven: Yale University Press, 1976.

Cremin, Lawrence A. *American Education: The Colonial Experience, 1607–*

1783. New York: Harper & Row, 1970.

Culver, Raymond B. *Horace Mann and Religion in the Massachusetts Public Schools.* New Haven: Yale University Press, 1929.

Danhof, Clarence H. *Changes in Agriculture: The Northern United States, 1820–1870.* Cambridge, Mass.: Harvard University Press, 1969.

Darling, Arthur B. *Political Changes in Massachusetts, 1824–1848: A Study of Liberal Movements in Politics.* New Haven: Yale University Press, 1925.

Davis, Lance E., et al. *American Economic Growth: An Economists' History of the United States.* New York: Harper & Row, 1972.

Dawley, Alan. *Class and Community: Lynn, Massachusetts in the Industrial Revolution.* Cambridge, Mass.: Harvard University Press, 1977.

Dow, George F. *History of Topsfield, Massachusetts.* Topsfield: Topsfield Historical Society, 1940.

Engerman, Stanley L. "Human Capital, Education, and Economic Growth," in Robert W. Fogel and Stanley L. Engerman, eds., *The Reinterpretation of American Economic History*, pp. 241–56. New York: Harper & Row, 1971.

Ensign, Forest. *Compulsory School Attendance and Child Labor.* Iowa City, Iowa: Athens Press, 1921.

Fishlow, Albert. "The American Common School Revival: Fact or Fancy?" in Henry Rosovsky, ed., *Industrialization in Two Systems*, pp. 40–67. New York, Wiley, 1966.

"Levels of Nineteenth-Century American Investment in Education." *Journal of Economic History* 26 (December 1966), 418–36.

Folger, John K., and Charles B. Nam. *Education of the American Population.* Washington, D.C.: Bureau of the Census, 1967.

Frisch, Michael H. *Town into City: Springfield, Massachusetts, and the Meaning of Community, 1840–1880.* Cambridge, Mass.: Harvard University Press, 1972.

Green, Constance McLaughlin. *Holyoke, Massachusetts: A Case Study of the Industrial Revolution in America.* New Haven: Yale University Press, 1939.

Grizzell, Emit Duncan. *Origin and Development of the High School in New England before 1865.* Philadelphia: MacMillan Company, 1922.

Handlin, Oscar. *Boston's Immigrants: A Study in Acculturation.* Rev. edn. Cambridge, Mass.: Harvard University Press, 1959.

Hareven, Tamara, and Maris A. Vinovskis, eds. *Demographic Processes and Family Organization in Nineteenth-Century Society.* Princeton: Princeton University Press, 1978.

Hobson, Elsie. *Educational Legislation and Administration in the State of New York, 1777–1850.* Chicago, University of Chicago: 1918.

Howe, Daniel Walker. "American Victorianism as a Culture." *American Quarterly* 27 (December 1975), 507–32.

Inglis, Alexander J. *The Rise of the High School in Massachusetts.* New York, 1911.

Bibliography

Jackson, Sidney L. *America's Struggle for Free Schools: Social Tension and Education in New England and New York, 1827–1842.* New York: Columbia University, 1941.

Kaestle, Carl F. *The Evolution of an Urban School System: New York City, 1750–1850.* Cambridge, Mass.: Harvard University Press, 1973.

"Social Change, Discipline, and the Common School in Early Nineteenth-Century America." *Journal of Interdisciplinary History* 9 (Summer 1978), 1–17.

Kaestle, Carl F., and Maris A. Vinovskis. "From Apron Strings to ABC's: Parents, Children, and Schooling in Nineteenth-Century Massachusetts," in Sarane Boocock and John Demos, eds., *Turning Points: Historical and Sociological Essays on the Family*, pp. 539–80. Chicago: *American Journal of Sociology* 84, supplement, 1978–9.

"From Fireside to Factory: School Entry and School Leaving in Nineteenth-Century Massachusetts," In Tamara K. Hareven, ed., *Transitions: The Family and the Life Course in Historical Perspective*, pp. 135–86. New York: Academic Press, 1978.

Katz, Michael B. *The Irony of Early School Reform: Educational Innovation in Mid-Nineteenth Century Massachusetts.* Cambridge, Mass.: Harvard University Press, 1968.

"Who Went to School?" *History of Education Quarterly* 12 (Fall 1972), 432–54.

Class, Bureaucracy, and Schools: The Illusion of Educational Change in America. 2nd edn. New York: Praeger, 1975.

"The Origins of Public Education: A Reassessment." *History of Education Quarterly* 16 (Winter 1976), 397–9.

The People of Hamilton, Canada West: Family and Class in a Mid-Nineteenth-Century City. Cambridge, Mass.: Harvard University Press, 1976.

Kett, Joseph F. *Rites of Passage: Adolescence in America, 1790 to the Present.* New York: Basic Books, 1976.

Kuhn, Anne S. *The Mother's Role in Childhood Education: New England Concepts, 1830–1860.* New Haven: Yale University Press, 1947.

Lazerson, Marvin. *Origins of the Urban School: Public Education in Massachusetts, 1870–1915.* Cambridge, Mass.: Harvard University Press, 1971.

Lockridge, Kenneth. *Literacy in Colonial New England: An Enquiry into the Social Context of Literacy in the Early Modern West.* New York: W. W. Norton, 1974.

Martin, George H. *The Evolution of the Massachusetts Public School System: An Historical Sketch.* New York: D. Appleton and Co., 1894.

Mason, Karen Oppenheim, Maris A. Vinovskis, and Tamara K. Hareven, "Women's Work and the Life Course in Essex County, Massachusetts, 1880," in Tamara K. Hareven, ed., *Transitions: The Family and the Life Course in Historical Perspective*, pp. 187–216. New York: Academic Press, 1978.

Mattingly, Paul H. *The Classless Profession: American Schoolmen of the*

Nineteenth Century. New York: New York University Press, 1975.

May, Dean, and Maris A. Vinovskis, " 'A Ray of Millennial Light': Early Education and Social Reform in the Infant School Movement in Massachusetts, 1826–1840," in Tamara K. Hareven, ed., *Family and Kin in American Urban Communities, 1800–1940*, pp. 62–9. New York: New Viewpoints, 1976.

Melder, Keith E. "Woman's High Calling: The Teaching Profession in America, 1830–1860." *American Studies* 13 (Fall 1972), 19–32.

Messerli, Jonathan. "James G. Carter's Liabilities as a Common School Reformer." *History of Education Quarterly* 5 (March 1965), 14–25.

Horace Mann: A Biography. New York: Alfred Knopf, 1972.

Newhall, James R. *History of Lynn, Essex County, Massachusetts*. Lynn, 1897.

North, Douglass C. *The Economic Growth of the United States, 1790–1860*. Englewood Cliffs, N.J.: Prentice-Hall, 1961.

Perley, Sidney. *History of Boxford*. Boxford, 1880.

Perrin, John W. *The History of Compulsory Education in New England*. Meadville, Pennsylvania, 1876.

Pollard, Sidney, "Factory Discipline in the Industrial Revolution." *Economic History Review* 16 (1963), 254–71.

Quinlan, Richard J. "Growth and Development of Catholic Education in the Archdiocese of Boston." *Catholic Historical Review* 22 (1936), 27–41.

Riley, Glenda. "Origins of the Argument for Improved Female Education." *History of Education Quarterly* 9 (Winter 1969), 455–70.

Rosenkrantz, Barbara Gutmann. *Public Health and the State: Changing Views in Massachusetts, 1842–1936*. Cambridge, Mass.: Harvard University Press, 1972.

Rothman, David J. *The Discovery of the Asylum: Social Order and Disorder in the New Republic*. Boston: Little Brown, 1971.

Schultz, Stanley K. *The Culture Factory: Boston Public Schooling, 1789–1860*. New York: Oxford University Press, 1973.

Solmon, Lewis C. "Estimates of the Costs of Schooling in 1880 and 1890." *Explorations in Economic History* 2nd ser. 7, No. 4, supplement (1970), 531–81.

"Opportunity Costs and Models of Schooling in the Nineteenth Century." *Southern Economic Journal* 37 (July 1970), 66–83.

Soltow, Lee, and Edward Stevens. "Economic Aspects of School Participation in the United States." *Journal of Interdisciplinary History* 8 (Autumn 1977), 221–44.

Sullivan, Mary Xaveria. *History of Catholic Secondary Education in the Archdiocese of Boston*. Washington, D.C.: Catholic University of America Press, 1946.

Suzzallo, Henry. *The Rise of Local School Supervision in Massachusetts (The School Committee, 1635–1827)*. New York: Teachers College, 1906.

Swift, Fletcher H. *A History of Public Permanent Common School Funds in the United States, 1795–1905*. New York, 1911.

Bibliography

Thernstrom, Stephan. *Poverty and Progress: Social Mobility in a Nineteenth Century City*. Cambridge, Mass.: Harvard University Press, 1964.

Thompson, Edward P. "Time, Work Discipline and Industrial Capitalism." *Past and Present* 38 (1967), 56–97.

Thompson, Eleanor Wolf. *Education for Ladies, 1830–1860: Ideas in Magazines for Women*. New York: King's Crown Press, 1947.

Troen, Selwyn K. "Popular Education in Nineteenth-Century St. Louis." *History of Education Quarterly* 13 (Spring 1973), 23–41.

Tyack, David B. "Onward Christian Soldiers: Religion in the American Common School," in Paul Nash, ed., *History and Education*, pp. 212–55. New York: Random House, 1970.

"The Tribe and the Common School: Community Control in Rural Education." *American Quarterly* 14 (March 1972), 3–19.

The One Best System: A History of American Urban Education. Cambridge, Mass.: Harvard University Press, 1974.

"The Spread of Public Schooling in Victorian America: In Search of a Reinterpretation." *History of Education* 7 (1978), 173–82.

Tyler, Alice Felt. *Freedom's Ferment: Phases of American Social History from the Colonial Period to the Outbreak of the Civil War*. Minneapolis: University of Minnesota Press, 1944.

Updegraff, Harlan. *Origins of the Moving School in Massachusetts*. New York: Teachers College Bureau of Publications, 1908.

Vinovskis, Maris A. "Horace Mann on the Economic Productivity of Education." *New England Quarterly* 43 (December 1970), 550–71.

"Trends in Massachusetts Education, 1826–1860." *History of Education Quarterly* 12 (Winter 1972), 501–29.

"From Household Size to the Life Course: Some Observations on Recent Trends in Family History." *American Behavioral Scientist* 21 (November/December 1977), 263–87.

Demographic Changes in America from the Revolution to the Civil War: An Analysis of the Socio-Economic Determinants of Fertility Differentials and Trends in Massachusetts from 1765 to 1860. New York: Academic Press, 1979.

Wellman, Thomas B. *History of the Town of Lynnfield, Massachusetts, 1635–1895*. Boston: Blanchard and Watts, 1895.

Welter, Barbara. "The Cult of True Womanhood: 1820–1860." *American Quarterly* 18 (Summer 1966), 151–74.

Welter, Rush. *The Mind of America: 1820–1860*. New York: Columbia University Press, 1975.

West, E. G. *Education and the Industrial Revolution*. New York: Barnes and Noble, 1975.

Whitten, Robert H. *Public Administration in Massachusetts: the Relation of Central to Local Authority*. New York: Columbia University, 1898.

Williamson, Jeffrey G. "Antebellum Urbanization in the American Northeast." *Journal of Economic History* 25 (December 1965), 592–608.

Williamson, Jeffrey G., and Joseph A. Swanson. "The Growth of Cities in the

American Northeast, 1820–1870." *Explorations in Entrepreneurial History* 4, supplement (1966), 3–101.

Wishy, Bernard. *The Child and the Republic*. Philadelphia: University of Pennsylvania Press, 1968.

Woody, Thomas. *A History of Women's Education in the United States*. 2 vols. New York: Science Press, 1929

Zevin, Robert B. *The Growth of Manufacturing in Early Nineteenth Century New England*. New York: Arno Press, 1975.

UNPUBLISHED SECONDARY SOURCES

Cole, Norwood M. "The Origin and Development of Town School Education in Colonial Massachusetts, 1635–1775." Ed.D. diss., University of Washington, 1957.

Cunningham, Homer. "The Effect of the Decline of the Puritan Oligarchy upon the Schools of Massachusetts, between 1664 and 1758." Ph.D. diss., New York University, 1954.

Dublin, Thomas L. "Women at Work: The Transformation of Work and Community in Lowell, Massachusetts, 1826–1860." Ph.D. diss., Columbia University, 1975.

Durnin, Richard G. "New England's Eighteenth-Century Academies: Their Origin and Development to 1850." Ed.D. diss., University of Pennsylvania, 1968.

Faler, Paul G. "Workingmen, Mechanics and Social Change: Lynn, Massachusetts, 1800–1860." Ph.D. diss., University of Wisconsin, 1971.

Field, Alexander J. "Educational Reform and Manufacturing Development in Mid-Nineteenth Century Massachusetts." Ph.D. diss., University of California, Berkeley, 1974.

Finkelstein, Barbara J. "Governing the Young: Teacher Behavior in American Primary Schools, 1820–1880: A Documentary History." Ed.D. diss., Columbia University, 1970.

Foley, Mary J. "A Study of the Economic History of Three Marginal Farm Towns in Massachusetts." Ph.D. diss., Massachusetts State College, 1933.

Gould, David A. "Policy and Pedagogues: School Reform and Teacher Professionalization in Massachusetts, 1840–1920." Ph.D. diss., Brandeis University, 1977.

Hopkins, J. Stephen. "Schenectady: A Case Study in the Development of Education in New York State from 1780 to 1854." Honors thesis, Union College, 1965.

Jenkins, John W. "Infant Schools and the Development of Public Primary Schools in Selected American Cities before the Civil War." Ph.D. diss., University of Wisconsin, 1978.

Kirk, Jeffrey Jr. "Family History: The Middle-Class American Family in the Urban Context, 1830–1870." Ph.D. diss., Stanford University, 1972.

Marti, Donald B. "Agrarian Thought and Agricultural Progress: The Endeavor

Bibliography

for Agricultural Improvement in New England and New York, 1815–1840." Ph.D. diss., University of Wisconsin, 1966.

Murphy, Geraldine Joanne. "Massachusetts Bay Colony: The Role of Government in Education." Ph.D. diss., Radcliffe College, 1960.

Sklar, Kathryn Kish. "Public Expenditures for Schooling Girls in Massachusetts Towns, 1750–1800." Paper presented at the annual meeting of the History of Education Society, Cambridge, Massachusetts, October 1976.

Slater, Peter G. "Views of Children and of Child Rearing during the Early National Period: A Study in the New England Intellect." Ph.D. diss., University of California, Berkeley, 1970.

INDEX

academies, 10, 17, 27, 31, 34, 218; *see
    also* private schools
Adams, Mary, 153
Ahearn, Marie L., 313n
Alcott, Bronson, 68
Alden, Cyrus, 215
American Annals of Education, 58–9
American Journal of Education, 58
Awl, 168, 172–3
Axtell, James, 308n

Bailyn, Bernard, 308n
Bancroft, George, 214
Banner, James M., 304n
Barnard, Henry, 10, 208
Baylor, Ruth M., 312n
Bentley, William, 26
Bernard, Richard M., 305n, 329-30n
Bible, 46, 48–50, 172, 228–9
Bidwell, Charles E., 309n, 334n
Blumin, Stuart, 315n, 331n
Book of Common Things (Hooker), 179
Boston Daily Advertiser, 219
Boston, Massachusetts, 108, 110, 115–16,
    127, 129, 139, 146, 164–6, 172, 297
  debate over primary schools, 51–3
  enrollment rates, 18–9, 21
  funding of schools, 17, 123, 200
  infant schools, 54, 61
  literacy rate, 47
  school expenditures, 193–8
  urban crisis, 113
  urban school system, 103
Boston Recorder, 53
Boutwell, George, 64–5
Bowles, Samuel, 3, 43, 303n, 307n, 317n,
    330n, 334n
Boxford, Massachusetts, 74, 80–1, 108,
    110, 140–64, 193, 196, 203, 206, 235

Breed, Hiram, 169, 173
Brigham, Amariah, 59, 62
Brownson, Orestes A., 213–14
Bruce, O. B., 183
Bushnell, Horace, 115

Calhoun, Daniel H., 313n
capitalists and education, 43–4, 75, 134–
    5, 172–4, 208, 221–3, 232–3, 308n
Carter, James, 187, 208–9
Catholics, 32, 80, 128–9, 131–2, 134, 136,
    138, 167, 234
Channing, William Ellery, 51
charity schools, 16–18
children
  child labor, 36, 75–80, 135
  child-rearing manuals, 56–7, 309n
  early intellectual activity, 49–50, 53,
    55, 58–60, 70, 311n
  infant damnation, 51, 69
  miniature adults, 49
*Christian Examiner and General
    Reviewer,* 59
Clark, F. Eugene, 154
Cole, Norwood M., 306n
Combe, George, 216
commercialization, 18
  and industrialization, 127–8
  and length of school year, 132
  and Massachusetts Board of Education,
    221–3, 225–6
  and per capita schooling, 135–6
  and school attendance, 20–2, 26, 130
  see also industrialization
Common School Journal, 196
compulsory attendance, 17, 37, 66, 73,
    75–7, 132; *see also* truants
consolidation of school districts, 109,
    160–1; *see also* district system

345

Cott, Nancy F., 310n, 329n
Cremin, Lawrence A., 304–5n, 308n, 328n
Cubberly, Ellwood, 10
Culver, Raymond, 225, 322n, 330–2n, 334n

dame schools, 17, 46, 48
Davey, Ian E., 313n
David, Emerson, 210
Davis, Edward S., 173
Dawley, Alan, 168–70, 323n, 326n
Demos, John, 49, 308n
Denton, Frank, 313n
deviants, 53, 114–15
Dewey, Richard, 106–7
discipline
  in school, 68, 104, 148–50, 155, 158–9, 163, 174, 179–80, 182, 202
  in workplace, 42–4, 75, 121, 134–5, 307n
district system, 10, 26, 100, 145, 153, 156, 159–60, 163, 172, 176, 180, 183, 215–18, 234; *see also* consolidation of school districts, school organization
Dodge, Allen W., 217, 219, 227
Duncan, Abel G., 217
Duncan, Otis D., 105, 110
Durkheim, Emile, 107, 111
Durnin, Richard G., 306n
Dwight, Edmund, 44

Easterlin, Richard, 45
educated citizenry, 9–10, 50, 167, 177
educational reform and politics, 208–32
Elder, Glen H., 329n
Eldridge, Hope Tisdale, 106–7
Emerson, Frederic, 217, 219
Emerson, George, 209
Essex County, Massachusetts
  family data file, 3, 73–4
  school enrollment, 36, 72–99
  school expenditures, 193–4
evening schools, 37, 79–80
Everett, Edward, 209, 211

Faler, Paul, 164, 171–2, 323n, 326–7n
Fellenberg, Emmanuel, 58
female seminaries, 17
female teachers, 26–7, 68, 90, 122–3, 147, 153–6, 163, 200–6; *see also* teachers

Field, Alexander, 3, 43, 134, 303–4n, 306–7n, 317n, 322n, 330n, 334–5n
Finkelstein, Barbara, 307n
Fischer, Claude S., 108
Fischer, David, 26, 305n
Fishlow, Albert, 11–17, 23, 41–2, 304–5n, 307–8n
Foley, Mary J., 141–2
Founding Fathers, 9, 25
Froebel, Friedrich, 68
Frost, Robert, 117
Fuller, Margaret, 154
Fuller, Timothy, 150, 154
Furstenberg, Frank, 312n

Gans, Herbert J., 108
George, Peter, 313n
Gintis, Herbert, 3, 43, 303n, 307n, 317n, 330n, 334n
Glenville, New York, 16, 22–3
Gould, Sarah, 158
grammar schools, 27, 47, 51, 80, 161, 174, 176, 180–3, 305n
Greene, Thomas A., 218
Griffen, Clyde, 315n
Gutek, Gerald Lee, 310n

Hamilton, Massachusetts, 74, 80–1, 193, 197
Hareven, Tamara, 3, 92, 312n, 316n
Harris, William Torrey, 101
Hauser, Philip H., 105, 107, 109, 111
Hershberg, Theodore, 312n, 315n
high schools, 30, 80, 146, 155, 162–3, 172–3, 176–9, 218
Hobson, Elsie, 10
Hoselitz, Bert F., 108
Howard, Phebe, 28
Humphrey, Herman, 60

immigrants, 36–7, 93–8, 103, 106, 112–14, 128, 131, 134, 136, 141, 234
impact of education
  character formation, 44, 172–3, 177, 181
  economic productivity, 41–5, 307n
  individual success, 74–5
  on women, 43
independent day school, 17
industrialization
  definition of, 322–3n

and education levels, 42
and length of school year, 133
and Lynn education, 164–84
and Massachusetts Board of Education, 225–6
and per capita schooling, 136
and school attendance, 130
see also commercialization
infant schools, 17, 53–60, 66–70

Jefferson, Thomas, 9
Jenkins, John W., 310n
Johansson, Egil, 308n
Journal of American Education, 53

Kaestle, Carl, 17–20, 103, 303n, 305–7n, 312–13n, 317n, 327n
Katz, Michael, 3, 90, 103, 173, 303–4n, 313n, 315n, 317n, 321n, 327n
Keppel, Ann, 317n
Kett, Joseph F., 313–14n
Kieffer, Donald, 23
kindergartens, 62, 68–9
Knights of St. Crispin, 169
Krug, Edward A., 313n
Kuhn, Anne S., 309–10n

Ladies' Magazine, 53–4, 59
Lancasterian schools, 17
Lane, Roger, 114
Lawrence, Massachusetts, 74, 103, 111, 113, 117, 292
  employment of youth, 78–80
  private schools, 80
  school attendance, 81
  school expenditures, 193, 196
  truants, 27, 76–7, 151
Lazerson, Marvin, 312n
length of school year, 23–5, 38–9, 132–5
  Essex County, 82
  by town size, 24–5, 82, 118–19
Lenski, G., 108
Lerner, Daniel, 105
Lewis, Henry, 159
Lewis, Oscar, 108–9
Lincoln, D. F., 65
Lindert, Peter, 316n
literacy, 25-6, 42, 47–8, 52, 87
Locke, John, 49, 70, 171
Lockridge, Kenneth, 47–8, 305n, 308n
London Christian Observer, 59

Lynn Directory, 165
Lynn Greenback Club, 170
Lynn, Massachusetts, 74, 114, 127, 235, 297
  education in, 164–84
  length of school day, 65
  school attendance, 81
  school expenditures, 193
  truancy, 76, 151
Lynnfield, Massachusetts, 74, 81, 193, 197

McCall, Samuel, 154
McClellan, Bernard E., 313n
McKearney, Bernard J., 304n
McMullin, Thomas A., 321n
McNeil, George, 76
Mann, Horace, 10–11, 23, 27, 31–4, 36, 44, 61, 68, 100–1, 123, 157, 188, 198, 202, 208–11, 213–25, 227–8, 231–2, 292–3, 299–300
Mason, Karen, 92, 312n, 316n
Massachusetts Board of Education, 60–2, 64–5, 101, 120, 157, 193, 197, 206–32
Massachusetts State School Fund, 192–3, 199–200, 209
Mather, Cotton, 49
Mattingly, Paul H., 310n
May, Dean, 309–11n
Mechling, Jay, 309n
Melder, Keith E., 329n
Messerli, Jonathan, 330
Modell, John, 312n
Morgan, Edmund S., 308n
Morrell, J. G., 161
Morton, Marcus, 211, 214–15
moving schools, 26, 144–5, 176
multiple classification analysis, definition of, 82–5, 94
multiple regression analysis, definition of, 125–6
Murphy, Geraldine, 47, 308n

New York City, 17–18, 25, 103, 113, 172
New York State, 11–22, 15–18
normal schools, 155, 215, 218–19, 228

Oliver, Henry, 76
The One Best System (Tyack), 104, 108, 138
Owen, Robert, 55–6

Index

Packard, Frederick, 210–11
Pahl, R. E., 105
Palmer, George Herbert, 140
parents and education
  father's role, 49
  mother's role, 25, 43, 56, 65–6, 91
  responsibility of parents, 46–7, 50–3,
    56–7, 60, 62–3, 65–6, 69, 145, 151–2,
    158–9
Park, Calvin E., 145
parochial schools, 32, 80, 129, 132
pauper support, 128
  and length of school year, 134
  and per capita schooling, 136
  and school attendance, 130–1
Peabody, Elizabeth, 68–9
Peabody, Jacob, 146
Pearl, Harriet, 153
per capita schooling, 119–20, 135–6
Pestalozzi, Johann Heinrich, 58, 68,
  70
private schools, 15–18, 21–2, 33–5, 80
  in Boxford, 145–6
  definition of, 31–2
  and early education, 62
  and infant schools, 52–4
  and school expenditures, 186–91
  shift to public schools, 11, 15, 21–2,
    33–4, 52–3, 69
Progressives, 101
Puritans, 10, 46–50, 69, 171

Randall, Samuel S., 14–15, 22
Rantoul, Robert, Jr., 210, 214, 231
Ravitch, Diane, 317n
reading, 146–7, 172
  colonial America, 47–9, 69
  early nineteenth-century, 51, 90
  infant schools, 54–5
  kindergartens, 68–9
Redfield, Robert, 105, 108
Reiss, Albert J., 108
religion and education, 121, 128–9, 137–8,
  309n
  Boxford, 145, 149
  colonial America, 46–51, 69–70
  length of school year, 134
  Lynn, 173
  Massachusetts Board of Education,
    210–11, 217–19, 227–9, 232

per capita schooling, 136
school attendance, 132
*Remarks on the Influence of Mental
  Excitement upon Health* (Brigham),
  59
Reynolds, Eveline, 145
Robbins, Thomas, 210, 231
Rosenkrantz, Barbara, 311n
rural education, 10
  Boxford, 140–64
  concept of, 105–11
  enrollment, 20–2
  Essex County, 80–2, 86–7
  funding, 16
  infant schools, 53
  length of school year, 24, 39
  rise in education, 25–6
  rural crisis, 115–16
  rural–urban differences, 82–3, 100–38,
    234–5
Rush, Benjamin, 9, 56
Russell, William, 53, 58

Salem, Massachusetts, 74, 111, 127, 146,
  164
  age of entering school, 65
  enrollment rates, 18–19, 21, 25, 81
  female teachers, 203
  petty schools, 46
  private schools, 26, 80
  school expenditures, 17, 35, 189, 193
  truancy, 76
Sanderson, George P., 169–70, 173
Schnore, Leo F., 109, 111
school attendance, 9–40, 129–32
  concern about, 27–8
  definition of, 13–14, 28–33, 72–3, 292–
    302, 310n
  and early education, 61–3
  in England, 12
  in Essex County, 73, 81, 86–99
  and idea of "decline," 10–11
  and infant schools, 55
  and town size, 20–2, 66–8, 81, 117–18,
    129–30
school expenditures
  Boston, 194–7
  Boxford, 156–7
  Essex County, 193–4
  inequalities, 198–200

Massachusetts, 191–3
per pupil, 123–4
and town size, 122–3
school laws
Connecticut, 10
Massachusetts, 10, 26, 47, 49, 51, 75–6,
145, 192, 209
New York, 10, 17
school organization, 37, 47, 80–2
and decline of early education, 64–5, 70
and fear of centralization, 215–18
in Lynn, 175–84
and productivity, 43
and urban schools, 102–4
schoolbooks, 152–3, 159, 219
schoolhouses, 26, 142, 145, 152, 158, 163,
175, 180, 196, 218
Schultz, Stanley, 103, 303n, 305n, 309n,
317n, 319n, 322n
Sears, Barnas, 31–2, 60, 63–4, 294, 300
Shattuck Report, 113
Shaw, John A., 218–19
Sigourney, Lydia, 59–60
Sjoberg, Gideon, 109
Sklar, Kathryn, 26, 305n
Slater, Peter G., 309n
Smith, J. V. C., 58
social class and education, 17–18, 33–4,
53–4, 87–98, 103, 167–74, 208
Solomon, Lewis C., 308n, 322n
Soltow, Lee, 313n, 317n
Stevens, Edward, 313n, 317n
Stone, Melville, 161
subscription schools, 16, 31, 34
Sunday schools, 17, 53–4

Tank, Robert, 312n
Taylor, George R., 111
teacher salaries, 117, 196–7
in Boxford, 154–5
male–female differences, 120–2
in Massachusetts, 200–1
by town size, 121–2
teachers
in Boxford, 145, 148–50, 153–6

and early education, 64–5
and infant schools, 54–5
in Massachusetts, 200–6
pupils per teacher, 122
training of, 100, 218
see also female teachers
Thernstrom, Stephan, 74, 313n
Tönnies, Frederick, 105
Topsfield, Massachusetts, 74, 81, 193
Troen, Selwyn K., 313n, 317n
truants
in Boxford, 151–2
concern about, 37
in Lawrence, 27
laws and enforcement, 75–7
in Lynn, 174–5
Tyack, David, 104, 108, 138, 163, 303n,
306n, 317n, 322n, 326n

Updegraff, Harlan, 26
urbanization, 111–15
concept of, 105–11, 126–7
crisis in education, 101–4
length of school year, 39, 133
per capita schooling, 135
school attendance, 129–30
see also rural education

Vinovskis, Maris, 3, 11, 43, 92, 294, 304–
7n, 309–13n, 316n, 319n, 329–30n,
332n, 334–5n

Ward, David, 114
Weber, Max, 105
Welter, Barbara, 329n
Welter, Rush, 333n
Wenham, Massachusetts, 74, 81, 193
West, E. G., 12
Wilderspin, Samuel, 55
Wirth, Louis, 105–7
Wishy, Bernard, 309n
women and education, 25–7, 43, 47–8,
305–6n; see also female teachers
Woodbridge, William, 58
Woodward, Samuel, 59
Wyllie, Irwin G., 313n

For EU product safety concerns, contact us at Calle de José Abascal, 56–1°, 28003 Madrid, Spain or eugpsr@cambridge.org.

www.ingramcontent.com/pod-product-compliance
Ingram Content Group UK Ltd.
Pitfield, Milton Keynes, MK11 3LW, UK
UKHW042144130625

459647UK00011B/1171